Marine and Coastal Protected Areas

Marine and Coastal Protected Areas

A Guide for Planners and Managers

Third Edition

Rodney V. Salm and **John R. Clark**
with
Erkki Siirila

International Union for Conservation of Nature and Natural Resources
Gland, Switzerland

Made possible through the support
of the US Agency for International Development

This publication has been made possible in part by funding from the US Agency for International Development, the John D. and Catherine T. MacArthur Foundation, and the Edith and Curtis Munson Foundation.

Published by: IUCN, Gland, Switzerland and Cambridge, UK

 Citation: R.V. Salm, John Clark, and Erkki Siirila (2000). *Marine and Coastal Protected Areas: A guide for planners and managers.* IUCN. Washington DC. xxi + 371pp.

ISBN: 2-8317-0540-1

Layout and printing by Editions MultiMondes
Printed in Canada

Available from:
IUCN Publications Services Unit
219c Huntingdon Road, Cambridge CB3 0DL, UK
Tel: +44 1223 277894, fax +44 1223 277175
E-mail: info@books.iucn.org
www.iucn.org/bookstore/index.html

And from:
IUCN Marine Programme
1630 Connecticut Ave NW
Washington DC 20009-1053 USA
Tel: ++01 202 387 4826, fax 4823
E-mail oceans@iucnus.org

  The text of this book is printed on recycled and acid free paper.

Foreword

I've always taken comfort in the ocean. It embodies constancy in a world of uncertainty and change. Like many drawn to the ocean, however, I've come to realize that what we thought to be immutable does change, and is fragile. We've observed ocean ecosystems under assault, from over-development of the coastal zone, overfishing, over-enthusiastic coastal tourism, and from our naïve belief that the ocean would absorb anything we could throw into it.

Almost twenty years ago at the Third World Parks Congress in Bali, Indonesia, Rodney Salm and others assembled a seminal group of experts on the management of the coastal ocean to discuss what was then a relatively new concept; marine protected areas. The first edition *of Coastal and Marine Protected Areas: guidelines for planners and managers,* was the product of that meeting. This book presented a banquet of ideas for those concerned with conservation of the marine environment. Thanks to its cover, it came to be known as the "Orange Book". In the course of the intervening years, the Orange Book has remained surprisingly fresh and current, and in demand, even long after it has gone out of print.

As a Peace Corps volunteer in West Africa in the mid 1980s, I advised the government of Sierra Leone on protected area development. The Orange Book was my companion and guide, even in terrestrial contexts, because it captured the social context for protected area planning and management better than anything else available to me. Only time will tell if the engagement with communities based in part on lessons from the book will pay off in conservation terms, but those of us who have been on the front lines of conservation know that there is no better hope.

Partly because of the desire to capture some of the experiences since the last edition, and partly to take the strain off of IUCN's photocopiers, Rod Salm and John Clark have graciously agreed to undertake a major revision of the Orange Book, with the help of many friends. To be sure, this is not a new book. It does not seek to provide a comprehensive overview of the latest theories on the application of the reserve concept to the conservation of biological diversity. Its emphasis and true value is in capturing the practical aspects of establishing and managing marine protected areas – including successes and failures.

Mindful of the particular needs of managers in tropical developing countries, the emphasis is given to tropical marine ecosystems such as coral reefs and mangroves, and the case studies are drawn from those environments. It is with those environments, and the people that live within them and depend upon them, in mind that we dedicate our renewed efforts to protect the resiliency of the marine environment through protection of its fragile and highly productive areas. And bearing in mind that in the end, it is not the environment, but we ourselves, that we manage, I commend this book to you. May it serve you well, and strengthen you in your capacity and resolve to protect the ocean and the life within it.

John Waugh
IUCN Marine Programme

Preface

Approaches to planning and managing marine protected areas (MPAs) have evolved considerably since the first edition of this book was published in 1984. The original version arose from the Workshop on Managing Coastal and Marine Protected Areas, held in October 1982 during the World Congress on National Parks in Bali, Indonesia. A second edition was printed in 1989, with minor revisions. This second edition was exhausted several years ago, but demand for the book remained high. However, as so much has changed over the past 15 years, and so many new lessons have been learned, there is evident need for a major update. This Third Edition answers that demand.

Even today, some 15 years later, the feedback we have received is that the book is a practical tool with an applied, "hands-on," viewpoint. This was the book's original intention and remains the main goal of this revision. It is still intended as a guide for people who find themselves with mandates to plan individual or national systems of marine protected areas (MPAs), or both, and need a philosophical context for marine protected areas along with some basic principles and approaches to establish them. Wherever possible, case studies are used to illustrate points or processes by "real world" examples. We would like to think that practitioners today will find this version as useful as our counterparts and colleagues did the original "Orange Book" during the past many years.

The book derives from many sources, including the 1982 Bali Workshop papers and summary reports of session chairs and rapporteurs. The participants of the workshop remain contributors to this version of the book. It is heartening to find how relevant these original outputs are today. But the field of conservation science and theory have evolved enormously over the past two decades, which has been a period of catch-up for marine protected areas with those on land. We have reached the point where one book can only introduce the huge body of thought and publications on theory, science and policy surrounding MPAs and the vast quantity of new practical experience (largely embodied in the gray literature). In revising this book, we have accessed some of the least accessible techniques and practices, many of which remain unpublished.

One new trend is important—the emphasis on community participation mechanisms. Also, there have been major advances in the last two decades on the challenge of sustainability of MPAs through innovative financing mechanisms, partnerships with the private sector and NGOs, and collaborative management between government and coastal communities. These advances have brought along with them new approaches for MPA establishment and management that are more participatory, involving communities through interaction and collaboration rather than prescription.

While it has become popular to write about participatory and collaborative management, we are still testing and refining different approaches. We may need ten more years in most cases before we can separate reality from easy optimism and say that one or another approach is a real success. This applies especially to the emerging field of collaborative management—partnership between government and communities, NGOs and/or the private sector (especially those concerned with tourism).

In the search for published material to use in the first edition of this book, it soon became apparent that relevant publications on planning and managing marine and coastal protected areas were scarce. There are more today. In the early 1980's, the MPA creation and management field was new and evolving with few tested practical tools and little to publish. As a result, the book drew heavily on personal experience and displayed a strong bias toward personal styles of approach. These days we are blessed with a wider variety of published materials and tools, but there still exists a deficit of tested, proven, practical results, particularly in collaborative management. So again, the personal experiences of the authors tend to influence the book.

This is a book for practitioners in tropical countries. It is meant to complement modern texts covering policy aspects of MPA selection and design by providing approaches and tools for everyday application at field sites. Until the modern theories are tried, tested, refined, proven, and generally absorbed into everyday practice, there will always be the need for approaches that get results on the ground. Given the urgency to act now and safeguard what we have before it is lost, we need to lock up what we can in conservation and to strive over the longer term for perfection. Practitioners who see their reefs being blasted apart, their mangroves being cut, their beaches and dunes eroding, their coastal wetlands being clogged with silt, or their MPA boundaries being ignored or encroached upon often make the same remark: "We need to do something now to safeguard what we have, based on the best available information." That "something" often means "We need to engage the stakeholders (communities, private sector, tourism industry, government) and work with them to achieve compliance with our programme and its objectives, and we need to do it fast." It is to this audience that we are attempting to cater: to give the practitioner in a tropical country some very basic approaches and tools to take those immediate first steps.

Rodney V. Salm and John R. Clark

Acknowledgements

T his book largely remains the inspiration of the Workshop on Managing Coastal and Marine Protected Areas, held in October 1982 during the World Congress on National Parks in Bali, Indonesia, whose participants provided the material from which the original book was fashioned. This book has undergone considerable revision to include supplemental material and updated concepts, case studies, and approaches. However, the original contributions still provide the framework on which this book is built, and we would like to acknowledge those contributions.

It is our pleasure to acknowledge the help of Ivor Jackson, co-convenor of the workshop, and the contributions of all the leaders and rapporteurs of the workshop break-out sessions.

In the original version, certain workshop papers served as virtually the sole source for an entire subsection, like the papers by de Klemm and Navid (law), Gardner (institutional arrangements), Odum (estuaries), and Wace (islands). Summary reports of the workshop break-out groups that were of particular value include those by Carr and Jin-Eong (estuaries), Foster and Kenchington (planning), Kelleher and Lausche (law), Kelleher and Van't Hof (management), Kenchington and Alcala (coral reefs), and Ogilvie and Wace (islands).

Charlotte de Fontaubert contributed the section on Legislative and Institutional Support. Lucy Emerton, IUCN, Nairobi, contributed the section on Economic Innovations.

Sue Wells, Richard Kenchington and Lee Kimball did extensive reviews of certain sections.

Erkki Siirila organized and supplied many of the photographs for the revised edition.

The efforts of the numerous writers of the case histories in Part III are gratefully acknowledged. Each author is credited in his or her particular case history.

Readers Guide

T his book is addressed mainly to conservation of the natural resources of tropical coasts and seas. To facilitate its use as a sourcebook, the volume is arranged in three parts.

Part I introduces Marine Protected Areas (MPAs) as an important approach to managing coastal and marine resources, discussing in its six sections: roles of MPAs, site planning, community involvement, systematic selection of MPAs, strategies and tools for planning and managing MPAs, and the legal basis of MPAs.

Part II considers principles and mechanisms for planning and managing protected areas in four different environments: coral reefs, estuaries and lagoons, small islands, and beaches. Emphasis is on technical knowledge about particular habitats and how this knowledge is used to meet management objectives. We recognize that many MPAs are composed of two or more of these environments but the guidance for each can be combined in the MPA plan.

Part III presents case histories covering a wide variety of MPA experience around the world to help protected area planners and managers carry out their tasks. The emphasis in each case history is on lessons learned that are of wide application. E-mail addresses of the authors are given to assist the reader in following up on case details. A "Guide to the Cases" is presented to enhance the reader's search for relevant items.

In the selection of materials for this book we have given priority to the types of resource conservation problems faced by MPA planners and managers in subtropical and tropical countries where the need for assistance appears to be the greatest.

In Parts I and II most of the material is based on written sources for which the specific references are listed alphabetically with date of publication in Part IV, References. Case Histories are individually referenced.

Table of contents

Review of Highlights of Case Histories 245

Part IV References

Introduction

S ustainable use of coastal resources requires that some coastal areas be retained in their natural state or as near to natural as possible. Safeguarding critical habitats for fish production, preserving genetic resources, protecting scenic and coastal areas, and enjoying natural heritage all may require the protective management of natural areas.

With the sustainable use of resources foremost in mind, the policy of all nations should be to provide the necessary legal basis for managing important habitats and beneficial species. This book presents information helpful to tropical coastal countries in organizing national systems of marine and coastal protected areas and in planning and managing selected MPA sites.

Viewpoint

We recognize that all marine protected areas (MPAs) are not created with the same purpose in mind—each is motivated by a different vision. But two main categories of conservation enter into the management equation: 1) *material*, ensuring the sustainability of economic resources, which may be termed "conservation" and 2) *spiritual*, including the important, but less economically tangible, values of species protection, biodiversity conservation, and landscapes, which may be termed "environmental protection" (Clark, 1998).

Coastal and marine area protection is usually aimed at practical goals. Except for spiritual resources, the habitats, ecosystems, species, and communities that we are trying to conserve have present or potential commercial uses. These resources are exploitable, currently exploited, or overexploited. The value of marine conservation can often be readily demonstrated in terms of fish in the diet or cash income, and people can be actively involved in conservation to avoid conflicts between industry and conservation and to integrate conservation and development.

Building effective partnerships between the management authority and communities remains a major challenge. It is of the utmost importance that communities be motivated toward active involvement in all stages of MPA planning and operation. During the last two decades the number of communities effectively participating in MPA affairs through collaborative management (or co-management), approaches has increased greatly. But involving communities and building the requisite level of trust between them and the authorities takes time. However, this is time well invested, and this step should not be rushed.

This book recognizes that area protection is but one technique of marine conservation, which integrates many mechanisms and disciplines—international conventions, management authorities, species population protection, fisheries management, coastal zone management, and land use planning. Distinguishing "protected areas" from other resource management regimes is not always easy. Exclusive economic zones, for example, to which a nation has declared exclusive rights to manage and harvest resources adjacent to its coast, could conceivably be considered a form of protected area. Nevertheless, these programmes, which do not single out areas for their resource values, are excluded from discussion, though their value is recognized in establishing the broad conservation background needed to protect specific areas.

We believe that the principal goal of all MPAs is conservation of resources so they yield the greatest benefit to present generations without losing their potential to meet the needs and ambitions of future generations. This concept of conservation that includes elements of protection, use and management is the interpretation of sustainability applied throughout this book.

Balance

Sustainability does not mean that all MPAs must be sanctuaries. Where possible commercial uses could be permitted on a controlled and sustainable basis; for example, fishing, rotational mangrove tree felling, use of foliage for fodder, and use by tourists. But strict protection of MPA zones to safeguard nesting areas or to provide sanctuary for breeding fish to replenish neighboring fishing grounds is justifiable.

While careful design and implementation of management can ensure continued benefits from natural areas, some types of uses inevitably conflict. For example, it is impossible to remove timber from mangroves and study natural processes at the same site. But it should always be possible to preserve at least a representative ecosystem for appropriate research and monitoring, while achieving overall conservation of biodiversity, fishery replenishment and tourism. MPAs can be designed and managed for multiple uses; i.e., to address activities so that pursuing one benefit does not exclude the pursuit of others.

People will continue to need fishes from reefs, wood and fodder from mangroves, access to beaches and seas for recreation, land for seaside housing, and seas for waste disposal. Conservation aims to satisfy these immediate needs in a way that ensures maintenance of the resources in the long term. MPAs help channel development to avoid sacrificing one resource by harvesting another or by modifying habitats or polluting the sea. As temporary custodians of the world's resources we are privileged to use them. We are not justified in using them carelessly—we are obliged to maintain them and pass them on undepleted to later generations.

Premises

Of the major ecological premises underlying this book, the most important is recognizing the intrinsic linkage between marine, coastal, and terrestrial realms, which precludes the effective management of a marine area independent of managing adjacent land habitats. That coastal ecosystems include both land and water components and that they should be managed together is considered fundamental. In fact, much discussion here concerns protecting landforms that border the sea, such as beaches, dunes, barrier islands, and small oceanic and coral islands. Also emphasized are situations where coastal or marine protected areas would be degraded without attention to inland areas, such as the watersheds and coastal rivers that must be managed to maintain the water balances of protected estuaries (Figure 1). In short, the ecological linkage of land and sea is a major consideration in formulating strategies for marine protected areas. The implication of the linkage for management, or connectivity, is that conserving coastal and marine resources requires extending management to shorelands and even inland areas.

Another important premise is that ocean currents, wind drifts, and animal migrations link distant regions of the ocean. For example, wind transports industrial pollutants that may be observed elsewhere as acid rain. These agents also transport nutrients, food, seeds, larvae, organisms, and pollutants

FIGURE 1.

Photo by Erkki Siirila.

A river discharges runoff water, nutrients and sediments—all damaging to coral reefs—into the ocean near Cairns in Queensland, Australia. The ecological linkage of land and sea is a major consideration in the management of the Great Barrier Reef lying just offshore.

across oceans, transcending biogeographic provinces and political boundaries. Thus, the management of vast areas, via multinational treaties and transboundary reserves to protect shared resources, along with alliances for conservation are all necessary. This does not undermine the value of protecting specific small areas, which remain essential for safeguarding vital habitats like seabird colonies, but the management of these should be integrated with that of larger, multiple use areas and regional initiatives whenever possible.

In most countries the fringing sea is open to all who care to use it, as is generally true on the high seas beyond national jurisdictions (see Box 1). It follows that individual users are not often active in caretaking, which leads to difficulties in conserving seabed and open water resources. The general "free for all" exploitation of resources that has resulted has led to the economic extinction of certain fisheries. An exception is seen in certain Pacific island nations, for example, where inhabitants have evolved traditional methods of resource sharing and conservation. The solution, at the national level, is regulation of fishing activities, government allocation of fishery resources, and enforced protection of habitats by creating a management authority with a mandate broad enough to manage activities throughout the coastal zone (including both terrestrial and marine areas). Beyond the national level there is need for effective international custodial programmes for marine areas and their resources.

Box 1. The Doctrine of the Commons

In most countries coastal waters and their resources are considered "commons"; that is, they are not owned by any person or agency but are common property available equally to all citizens, with the government as "trustee"—this is an ages old public right, *jure communia*, going back to the Institutes of Justinian: '*Et quidem naturali jure communia sunt omnium haec: aer, aqua profluens, et mare per hoc litora maris*'. In English this means: 'By the law of nature these things are common to mankind—the air, running water, the sea and consequently the shores of the sea'.

Further, this influential doctrine states that: 'No one, therefore, is forbidden to approach the seashore, provided that he respects habitations, monuments, and buildings, which are not, like the sea, subject only to the law of nations'. And now "environment" must be added to the "he respects" list. A primary aim of coastal conservation is to provide for sustainable use of the resources of the Commons, a responsibility that should be shared by all people and all levels of government. As "Trustee", the government is empowered to make rules for the Commons that all must obey for the public good.

Source: Clark, 1998.

Distinctions

It is the special burden of marine conservationists that people cannot easily see what happens underwater. The sea remains inscrutable, mysterious to people. On land we see the effects of our activities and we are constantly reminded of the need for action, but we see only the surface of the sea. Not only are we less aware of our impact on submerged life, but it is also more difficult to investigate. Boat based and underwater research and monitoring are far more difficult and costly than their equivalents on land.

Another distinction of the sea is its limited endemism: marine species and subspecies are only rarely limited to certain small areas. There is great mixing of the ocean and its species and few sharply defined biogeographic provinces with unique species compositions.

Since very few species are confined to narrowly bounded habitats, the chance that any species would be extinguished by human activities is low. Saving species from extinction is thus not as strong or universal a motivation for marine protected areas as is conserving commercial resources (Figure 2).

The ecological systems of the sea can achieve great complexity, as in coral reefs, or high bioproductivity, as in "upwelling" areas where ocean waters rise to the surface. These systems differ from terrestrial systems in many ways. Three-dimensional phenomena are more marked and important in the ocean, where organisms are less tied to the solid bottom than are land organisms to the earth. Because of the fluid nature of the seas, whole biological communities exist as floating plankton-based entities distributed horizontally and vertically through broad ocean spaces. Currents transport organic nutrients to distant locations and carry planktonic eggs and larvae of organisms to distant habitats. In addition, many marine species migrate long distances. And, since marine organisms are in close chemical contact with their surrounding medium, they are jeopardized chemical contaminants.

FIGURE 2.

Photo by Gonzalo Ivan Arcila.

Birds include the most endangered of species occupying coastal areas.

Critical Areas and Ecosystems

Among the most ecologically critical and threatened resources are fringing coral reefs, tideflats, coastal wetlands and shallows, especially lagoons and estuaries and their grass beds and mangrove swamps. These areas provide food and shelter for waterfowl and for the fishes, crustaceans, and molluscs utilized by an estimated two thirds of the world's fisheries including some of the world's most lucrative fisheries (e.g., shrimp). Sea grass meadows are vital because they act as "nurseries" (special habitats that nurture the young of marine and coastal species) and as nutrient suppliers for economically important fish stocks. Wetlands, floodplains, sea grass beds, and coral reefs are being degraded, or even destroyed the world over (Carpenter, 1983; IUCN/UNEP, 1988; Wells and Hanna, 1992; Wilkinson, 1992, 1998), with severe effects on the economies that depend on them. Coral reef ecosystems are of great significance to tropical countries, providing habitats for the seafood on which many rural communities in developing countries depend.

In addition, coastal wetlands and coral reefs are extremely important for protecting shorelines and coastal villages against storm waves and shore erosion (Figure 3). In Sri Lanka, the removal of corals to produce lime was so damaging that a local fishery collapsed—mangroves, small lagoons, and coconut groves disappeared because of increased shore erosion, and local wells were contaminated with salt before protection was implemented through a coastal zone management programme.

FIGURE 3.

Photo by John Clark.

A beach damaged by erosion. Beach erosion is often the result of sand and coral mining for construction materials.

Fisheries

As fisheries for finfish, crustaceans, and molluscs become more fully exploited, the effects of habitat destruction and pollution will become more evident, particularly on those species depending on coastal wetlands and shallows or on inland wetlands and floodplains for nutrients or for spawning grounds and nurseries.

Most of the world catch of marine species—87 million tonnes in 1996—comes from within 320 km of land. The continental shelf directly leads to high production because it concentrates activity into a thin water layer and provides a substrate (solid surface) for fixed plants and benthic animals. In addition, the topography of the shelf stimulates the upwelling of deeper waters carrying chemical nutrients to the surface.

In many parts of the world, seafood supplies most of the protein and much of the livelihood for large populations of people (Figure 4). In Africa artisanal fisheries provide the bulk of the fish eaten by local people, but these fisheries are widely considered to be fully exploited (Brainerd, 1994; Hatziolos *et al.*, 1994; Insull *et al.*, 1995; Tvedten & Hersoug, 1992), with some being exploited beyond the level of sustainability. But because fisheries are typically not managed for sustainability, their contribution to national diets and income is diminishing and is likely to continue diminishing.

FIGURE 4.

Fishermen at work; Inhaca Island, Mozambique.

Past and present overfishing has led many of the world's most valuable fisheries to be seriously depleted. Nor can it be assumed that depleted stocks will recover to reach their full potential. In fact, this is most unlikely for several reasons: juvenile fishes may continue to be caught by "industrial" fisheries and ground up for animal feed; other species may take the place of depleted species and not yield to their return; and habitats essential for spawning or as nurseries may be degraded or destroyed.

In addition to depleting fish, crustacean, and mollusc stocks, overfishing has nearly extinguished certain species of whales, sea cows, and sea turtles. Many aquatic animal groups are also under pressure because of incidental exploitation (bycatch); that is, they are captured along with "target" species, killed, and discarded. An example of this wasteful practice is the incidental capture and killing of sea turtles in fishing nets in several countries, which threatens the survival of several species.

Preserving Biodiversity

Preserving diversity is a matter of both ethics and economic survival. For example, genetic diversity (a component of biodiversity) is needed to sustain and improve agricultural, forestry, and fisheries production, to keep future options open, to guard against harmful environmental change, and to secure the raw material for much scientific and industrial innovation.

For practical economic reasons, preserving biodiversity is necessary both to secure food, fiber, and certain drugs and to advance scientific and industrial innovation. Such preservation is also necessary to ensure that the functioning of ecological processes is not impaired by loss of species. It is unlikely that other communities can readily replace the particular communities of plants, animals, and microorganisms that make up the ecosystems associated with so many essential processes. The genetic variety and compositions of such ecosystems may be crucial for their performance, and for their response to long-term events like climate change.

The huge coral mortality associated with the 1998 El Niño related coral bleaching event drives home the value of different physiological responses to stress by corals, responses that are presumably seated in their genetic differences. In the western Indian Ocean and West Pacific, for example, adjacent coral colonies responded differently to the elevated sea water temperatures: they bleached at different rates, some bleached and died, others bleached and recovered, and yet others barely bleached at all. But in some places more than 90 percent of the corals died.

Ethical issues of biodiversity relate particularly to species extinction. Human beings have become a major evolutionary force, lacking the knowledge to control the biosphere, but having the power to change it radically. We should be committed to our descendants and to other creatures to act prudently. We cannot predict what species may prove important, therefore, we should not cause the extinction of a species.

Just as many varieties of domesticated plants and animals are disappearing, so too are many species of wild plants and animals. An estimated 25,000 plant species (Lucas and Synge, 1978) and more than a thousand vertebrate species and subspecies (IUCN, 1975) were already threatened with extinction in the early to mid-1970s. The most serious threat was considered to be habitat destruction (Lucas and Synge, 1978; Allen and Prescott-Allen, 1978). This destruction took and continues to take many forms: (1) the replacement of entire habitats by settlements, harbors, and other human constructions, by cropland, grazing land, and plantations, and by mines and quarries; (2) the effects of dams (blocking spawning migrations, drowning habitats, and altering chemical or thermal conditions) (Figure 5) (3) drainage, channelization, and flood control; (4) pollution and solid waste disposal (from domestic, agricultural, industrial, and mining sources); overuse of groundwater aquifers (for domestic, agricultural, and industrial purposes); (5) removal of materials (such as vegetation, gravel, and stones) for timber, fuel, construction, and so on; (6) dredging and dumping; and (7) erosion and siltation. Since that time, conversion of coastal mangroves and related habitats into brine ponds for salt production and prawn farms has emerged as a major issue.

FIGURE 5.

Dams change river flows and usually have negative effects on coastal resources.

The Coastal Zone Approach

For marine conservation and area protection one should think of the ocean as including the bays, lowlands, tidelands, and floodplains along the shoreline and forming the inner edge of what is called the "Coastal Zone"—a combination of shallow sea and lowlying land. Here people increasingly congregate to live, work, and play (Figures 6 and 7). This crowding at the coast is common in many countries, as in the United States, where half or more of the population lives on the fraction of the total land that is coastal. These people place a tremendous burden on the coastal environment, needing living space, support services and industries, recreational areas, and dump sites for domestic and industrial wastes.

Enhanced economic development is typically perceived as the necessary first step in a nation's social development. Coastlines often receive much economic development in the form of tourism and urban, agricultural, and industrial development. Unfortunately, the price of short-term benefits from resulting land reclamation, drainage, or conversion to rice fields, fishponds, coconut plantations, or pasturage is resultant pollution and the depletion of natural resources. Certain damaging activities, such as dredging, landfill, coral mining, fishing with explosives, dumping at sea, and pollution, are direct and easy to recognize. Other effects are not so obvious, especially when they are far removed from the activity causing them (for example, hydro-electric dams across rivers, irrigation projects, and forest cutting in watersheds). Thus, even inland development programmes must be persuaded to consider the coastal environment.

FIGURE 6.

Pattay in Thailand offers many facilities for coastal recreation. Crowding of the beach is not uncommon.

Photo by Erkki Siirila.

It is difficult to protect an MPA sited near a highly developed coastline. Impacts on coastal ecosystems from land based activities are widespread: industrial and agricultural pollution, siltation from eroded uplands; filling to provide sites for industry, housing, recreation, airports, and farmland; dredging to create, deepen, and improve harbors; quarrying; and the excessive cutting of mangroves for fuel. In many parts of the world the construction of dams has blocked the passage of marine species migrating to inland spawning sites (Figure 7). The habitats of many other aquatic animals also are threatened; for example, roads, housing and other developments have encroached on turtle nesting beaches.

Reactive management alone is insufficient to safeguard the values of coastal and marine habitats and species under such pressures. Broad proactive programmes of management which seek to deal comprehensively with marine conservation are needed. Whereas the impact of carefully planned development can be minimal, poorly planned development projects may exact a heavy toll on naturally productive coastal habitats (Figure 8). Destructive activities must be contained and ecologically critical areas protected, difficult tasks for an MPA manager acting alone.

FIGURE 7.

Occupation of the shoreline of the Isla Comprida Estuary, Brazil.

The solution for MPA siting is to ensure that development impacts are controlled by a wider programme which is authorized to combat pollution and habitat damage in the Coastal Zone surrounding the MPA site. This can best be done by officially nesting the MPA into a Coastal Zone Management jurisdiction with powers to control development impacts (see Section I-5).

FIGURE 8.

Shrimp farms took over mangrove areas in Bali, Indonesia, causing loss of natural production.

PART I

Creating Marine Protected Areas

The Roles of
Protected Areas

M arine and coastal habitats may be protected individually or through national or regional systems of marine protected areas (MPAs). The success of either depends on the existence of appropriate legal frameworks, acceptance by coastal communities, an effective and well supported management system, and the delineation of areas so their boundaries are clear and they can be treated as self-contained units.

An MPA is formed by a part of the sea and (often) shorelands habitat designated by the owner or custodian as a conservation area. Each MPA has boundaries and a declaration of permitted and non-permitted uses within it. The owner or custodian (public or private) grants authority to a specific entity to manage the area within the MPA boundaries according to the purposes for which the MPA was created. A simple example is a small island designated by the Government (owner) for protection of nesting seabirds with no visitation permitted and which is managed by a Wildlife Department. A complex example would be a multiple use area created by the Government (custodian) wherein a variety of uses are permitted—line fishing, diving, boating, beach use—but no removal of corals or disturbance of sand dunes is permitted.

An MPA may be designated for any one or a combination of reasons (multiple use): (1) it is the best example of an important ecosystem or habitat type; (2) it is needed for sustainability of fisheries such as through "no-take" zones; (3) it has high species diversity; (4) it is a location of intense biological activity; (5) it is a "natural wonder"

FIGURE I-1.

Photo by Erkki Siirila.

A hawksbill turtle returning to the sea after having laid its eggs on Grand Anse Beach, a critical habitat considered for protection in St. Lucia.

FIGURE I-2.

Photo by Erkki Siirila.

Villagers have planted cacti to control beach erosion north of Tanga in Tanzania. The erosion is also reduced by protected coral reefs in front of the beach.

or a tourist attraction; (6) it provides a critical habitat for particular species or groups of species (Figure I-1); (7) it has special cultural values (such as historic, religious, or recreational sites); (9) it protects the coastline from storms (Figure I-2), and (10) it facilitates necessary research or determination of "natural" baseline conditions.

There is increasing need to justify protected areas in measurable and convincing terms to satisfy social, commercial, development, and planning interests. Solely ethical arguments (spiritual values) are convincing only in a few privileged nations, and then not always. For these reasons conservation agencies and protected area planners should have a well defined policy and a clear idea of the purpose of each protected site, stressing the practical (material) aspects.

1.1 Multiple Objective MPAs

MPAs should be designed to simultaneously accomplish as many conservation objectives as possible. Multiple-objective programmes may be prescribed for a particular designated MPA or applied to broader management schemes that incorporate one or more protected areas. Such programmes can include any of the following:

Limiting, as necessary, particular exploitative uses of coastal and marine waters and their resources or of linked areas that influence life in MPA waters (for example, preventing the mining of living coral reefs to maintain their value to fisheries and to protect the coast).

Protecting particular vital parts of coastal or ocean ecosystems (for example, critical habitats such as prime coral reefs or mangrove forests).

Restoring earlier conditions (for example, closing areas to enable the recuperation of damaged habitats or depleted stocks, or prohibiting activities that are physically damaging or polluting).

Enhancing certain economically important activities such as fishing or tourism.

Defining sustainable levels of use and appropriate management structures and implementing activities to monitor and control these.

Obtaining and transferring information (for example, through research, education, and interpretive programmes).

An example of a multiple-objective MPA is the Cousin Island Special Reserve, a sea and land bird sanctuary in the Seychelles which also protects turtles, coral reefs and vegetation (Part III, Case No. 6), and includes research and limited tourism among its objectives.

Impressive benefits have resulted from protecting other coral reefs; e.g., in the Netherlands Antilles (Bonaire Marine Park), where diving tourism has increased; in the Seychelles (Ste. Anne National Marine Park), where the park is used by both residents and tourists for picnicking, swimming, sailing, snorkeling, diving and glass bottom boat excursions; in Fiji (Tai Island), where subsistence catches have increased, tourist activity has expanded, and the holders of traditional fishing rights are involved in managing resorts and boats; and in Kenya (Malindi/Watamu, Mombasa, and Kisite/Mpunguti National Parks and Reserves), where resultant tourism generates revenues through gate, guide, and camping fees, rental of boats and equipment, and hotel expenses. It also has indirect benefits, creating jobs in hotels and for guides and boatmen.

Protecting lagoons and estuaries has also provided measurable benefits. An example is the Tortuguero National Park in Costa Rica which has conservation of turtles as a primary objective but also protects nearly 19,000 ha of tropical wet forest and palm swamp, a priceless remnant of the diminishing wilderness of the Caribbean lowlands. In another example, about 3,000 people depend on the fisheries in or at the mouth of Laguna de Tacarigua National Park in Venezuela, where the annual yield of fishery products is approximately 1,000 tons. In addition, the lagoon offers recreation, protects feeding grounds for flamingos and roosting and nesting sites for scarlet ibises and seabirds like frigate birds and boobies, and conserves endangered species like crocodile and tortoise (see Case History in Part III for details).

Enlightened programmes can accomplish conservation along with other activities. For example, restricting access to a military area in Queensland, Australia, has resulted in the protection of a large number of endangered dugong *(Dugong dugon)*, which is compatible with military activities. Similarly, military activities on Diego Garcia Island in the Chagos Archipelago provide for turtle protection. However, bombing practice by U.S. Navy pilots has disturbed the coral-based ecosystem of Vieques Island near Puerto Rico.

Properly designed protected areas can provide for a variety of uses and use controls in large scale integrated resource management programmes (Figure I-3). The management of Australia's Great Barrier Reef is an example of such integrated management. The government established a multiple-use management regime over this 300,000-km area, which is zoned to separate incompatible activities and to reserve sites for their most appropriate uses. Example zones are Marine National Park Zones, Scientific Research Zones, Preservation Zones, Replenishment Areas, and Seasonal Closure Areas (Part III, Case No. 10).

FIGURE I-3.

Photo by Erkki Siirila.

Biodiversity is important for tropical ecosystems and is attractive to tourists.

1.2 The Value of Biodiversity

It is popular to use tropical rainforests as the yardstick by which to compare biodiversity. However, as Ray and Grassle (1991) pointed out, "...marine systems are extraordinarily diverse in all aspects, from genetic to taxonomic to ecological." The ocean floor communities may be as diverse as any land area. Ray (1988) stated that tropical reefs have a variety of species equal to tropical forests, but overall, the seas have about twice the number of phyla as land. As the majority of marine phyla occur in the coastal zone, the marine portion of this zone could be considered the most biologically diverse area of the world (Ray, 1991) and, by extension, the most in need of protection.

Conserving the diversity of life is an objective of all MPAs, regardless of the specific intent for their creation. But it is necessary to recognize the difference between *biodiversity*, reflected by the number of species, and *genetic diversity* (a subset of biodiversity), reflected by the variation within species. The land has more species than the sea, and hence greater biodiversity. Marine organisms, however, tend to exhibit more genetic variability; thus they have great genetic diversity. Both types of diversity are important and of value to people.

The value of biodiversity has been at the heart of most publications concerning the need for its conservation. It is addressed generally in "Global Biodiversity Strategy" (Raven, 1992), "Caring for the Earth" (IUCN/UNEP/WWF, 1991), in "Economics and Biological Diversity" (McNeely, 1988), in detail in "Global Biodiversity" (WCMC, 1992), in a special issue of the journal *Ambio* (Vol. 21(3), 1992), and by Norse (1993) in his landmark book "Global Marine Biological Diversity".

Marine species are survivors of 3.5 billion years of change (Norse, 1993). So which are more or less important to conserve? If we asked a selection of people from different user groups we might expect them to answer as below:

Subsistence and artisanal fishermen: "prawns, crabs, lobsters, snappers, groupers, emperors, rabbitfishes, sardines."

Industrial fishermen: "kingfishes, tunas, prawns."

Sport fishermen: "sailfishes, marlins, tunas, kingfishes."

Sea farmers: "prawns, oysters, red algae (*Euchema*)."

Traders in aquarium species: "ornamental reef fishes, anemones and certain colourful reef invertebrates."

Biologists: "coelacanths, corals, mangroves, sharks, toxic animals."

Ecologists: "coral reef communities, mangrove forests, various keystone species."

Conservationists: "turtles, mother-of-pearl shells, dugongs, whales, coconut crabs."

Person on the beach: "dolphins and whales, coral reef fishes, birds, shade trees."

These constructed examples above show the importance of biodiversity in satisfying the requirements of different users. It also shows how we need to conserve a full range of species and, consequently, their supporting habitats (Figure I-4).

FIGURE I-4.

Biodiversity-based tourism is big business in the Caribbean.

The variety of species offers us opportunities for the discovery of new uses for them, as in medicine and mariculture (the farming of marine organisms). The genetic variation within a species offers opportunities to refine its uses, for example, by selective breeding for increased growth rate or resistance to diseases.

The application of marine taxa in biomedical research and pharmacology is a real value backed up by numerous examples. Many marine organisms have highly active biochemical compounds that have yielded extracts with direct antimicrobial, antileukemic, anticoagulant and cardio-active properties. The species producing these compounds may be important in the direct production of pharmaceuticals, such as anticancer drugs, or their compounds may provide models for the synthesis of new and effective drugs.

The value of wild genetic resources in the improvement of terrestrial food crops and livestock has been convincingly demonstrated, but examples of marine applications are largely lacking.

Given the expanding development of mariculture worldwide, especially for prawns, oysters, mussels, and salmon, wild genetic material will inevitably be increasingly drawn upon to improve farmed stock. Most stock for mariculture is obtained from the wild, such as seaweeds, turtle eggs and hatchlings, edible oyster and mussel spat, pearl oysters, juvenile prawns, and milkfish fry.

FIGURE I-5.

Photo by Erkki Siirila.

The underwater forests of giant kelp around Santa Catalina Island (California) provide feeding areas for a wide variety of marine organisms including the Garibaldi (in the foreground).

In situ protection of species (protecting them in their natural habitats) offers the best method for preserving genetic diversity. *In situ* protection requires habitat conservation, and this is best achieved by establishing MPAs (Figure I-5).

1.3 Preserving Biodiversity

For the purposes of this discussion, marine biodiversity is taken simply as the variety of life forms (species, communities, populations) in the seas and along the coasts of our ocean planet. However, underlying this simplistic definition is the understanding that these life forms in their various assemblages are the expressions of a variety of processes, and that these processes are integral components of biodiversity. Species and their environment are inextricably linked through complex interrelationships, and it is these synergistic feedbacks that sustain the structure and functioning of ecosystems (Perrings *et al.*, 1992).

Today, species of plants and animals are being plunged into extinction at unprecedented rates largely because their habitats are being destroyed (Norse, 1993). Coral reefs are being blasted by dynamite fishers, poisoned, broken up by nets, and smothered by silt washed down from eroding hinterlands, rendering them near lifeless mounds of coral rubble. Turtles and dugongs are gone from parts of their former range, and endemic plants, birds and mammals falter on the brink of extinction as the last remnants of coastal forests are cleared for fuelwood.

In the last decade, biodiversity has risen from a new and undefined term in our vocabulary to a global issue, and major works on the subject have been published in the last few years (see section above). Norse (1993) provides an extremely detailed account of biodiversity in the seas, including patterns of distribution, threats, and conservation needs, tools and priorities. The United Nations Convention on Biological Diversity has put biodiversity on the agenda of governments, donor agencies, and NGOs as a high priority.

We are committed to our descendants and to other creatures to act prudently. We cannot predict what species may become useful to us. We may learn that many apparently dispensable species can provide important products, like pharmaceuticals, or are vital parts of life support systems on which we depend. For practical economic reasons, preserving biodiversity is necessary both to secure food, fiber, and certain drugs and to advance scientific and industrial innovation. For reasons of both ethics and economic self-interest, therefore, we should not cause the extinction of a species.

Fishes are the most abundant group of vertebrates, both in terms of numbers of species (22,000 out of a total 43,000 vertebrates) and individuals (WCMC, 1992). More than 63% of fishes are marine, exhibiting great diversity in size (ranging from 1 cm long to 15 m), shape (long thin and snakelike, disc-shaped, globular or box-shaped), and habitat (from polar seas to the tropics, from under ice to thermal vents, from intertidal through all depths to the ocean floor), yet they remain the least known of the vertebrates.

In considering biodiversity from the perspective of species richness, the total number of species may not be as important a parameter as the composition of species (Figure I-6). Thus, species should be evaluated, not simply enumerated. Many inconsequential species may not be as valuable as fewer important ones.

For example, Matthes and Kapetsky (1988) have compiled comprehensive lists of algae, molluscs, crustaceans, echinoderms, and fishes of economic importance that are associated with mangroves. Totaling species over all the taxa they list yields the following totals: western Central Pacific 732, eastern Indian Ocean 640, western Indian Ocean 654. While mangroves might be low on a species diversity scale, they are of inestimable value as: nurseries for many species of direct commercial or subsistence value; species of no immediately apparent value to people; and as ecological support systems for the inshore marine environment (FAO, 1994; Saenger *et al.*, 1983)

FIGURE 1-6.

Photo by John Clark.

Diverse habitats encourage diverse species; Yanbu Reef, Red Sea.

Also, certain species, such as predatory or nonterritorial fishes, may have large area requirements, especially if they are poor at dispersing among separated habitats, and may be absent in smaller habitat areas. For example, in the Chagos Archipelago (West-Central Indian Ocean) specific corals were found only on reefs larger than a certain minimum size (Salm, 1995).

1.4 Preserving Genetic Diversity

Wild genetic resources are lost either through the extinction of a species or through the extinction of individual populations of that species (genetic impoverishment). The first process is final and irreversible. The second is a matter of degree and is to some extent reversible (FAO/UNEP, 1981). In the sea, where endemism (the restricted distribution of a species to a relatively small geographic area) is low compared to that on land, the problem is less one of species extinction than of genetic impoverishment. No significant or detectable increase in extinction rates of fish species has been observed in the ocean, but overfishing, pollution, and habitat destruction have extinguished populations (Norse, 1993). Organisms occupying diminishing habitats will likely never again reach their present levels of genetic diversity.

Human activities diminish genetic variation and encourage the extinction of species in a number of ways:

Pollution and other environmental changes that stress a population, causing differential mortality, extinction, or both.

Fishing pressure, which can favor some genotypes over others.

Artificial selection and domestication, which can result in conscious or unconscious inbreeding and genetic impoverishment.

Introduction of exotic species and diseases.

A dam in a river, for example, may create a habitat unsuitable for existing riverine species that depend on periodic flooding or moving water. It may also prevent the reproduction of anadromous species (those that move up rivers from the sea to spawn) and catadromous species (those that move down rivers to the sea to spawn). Such species will be lost or seriously depleted. Yet the lifespan of the genetic reservoir will be too short by many thousands of years for the evolution of new replacement lake species.

Broadly speaking, there are three ways to preserve marine genetic resources against such human-caused losses. One is establishing *gene banks*, that maintain genes for future use (more widely used for terrestrial genetic resources, such as through seed banks, botanical gardens, and zoos). A second means is preventing the overexploitation of species by *managing the harvest*, or by supplementing the harvest of wild stocks with cultivated products, or by prohibiting the harvest and trade of depleted and endangered species. A third means is *creating protected areas* for habitats, since a major threat to the survival of some populations of species is the destruction of critical elements of their habitat. Such coastal and marine protected areas function as *in situ* gene banks, preserving genetic material within an ecosystem rather than a special storehouse (Prescott-Allen and Prescott-Allen, 1984).

Coastal and marine protected areas can help maintain *in situ* gene banks in a number of ways. They protect rare, threatened, and endangered species and populations or species known or likely to be of value as genetic resources (e.g., the wild relatives of farmed species or other wild species useful to people). Local extinction and depletion of stocks have resulted in part from habitat destruction and in part from the high demand for such species, for example, whales, turtles, dugongs, and certain molluscs and corals (Figure I-7).

Preserving genetic diversity is important for maintaining the fitness of species, with all its social and economic implications, and is equally important for maintaining the native variety that helps to maintain the integrity of biological communities.

To feed and accommodate 1,000 or more species in the limited area of a coral reef, for example, there must be tremendous subdivision of niches (the functions of species in their community, habitat, or ecosystem). This subdivision requires the constituent species to be highly specialized. Also, the different species live close together on the reef, and constantly interact so there is great species interdependence (e.g., fish species living commensally with anemones or fish that feed by removing parasites from the gills of larger fishes). A result of this species interdependence is that eliminating one will likely lead to losses of others. The effects could be far-reaching through the coral reef community, particularly if the original biodiversity is not

FIGURE I-7.

Photo by John Clark.

Whales breed in several protected lagoons in Baja California, Mexico.

maintained. It is this diversity that enables recruitment of larvae best suited to the new conditions in decimated areas, and it is recruitment that begins community restoration.

Genetic material determines how much species can adapt to changes in their environment. In several organisms, including some fish species, individuals having the most genetic variation (and hence greater tolerance of environmental changes) have been shown to have better survival rates or higher relative growth rates (FAO/UNEP, 1981). New genetic variation arises in a population from either the spontaneous mutation of a gene or the immigration of genetically different individuals from a different population of the same species. For example, there are pale or smoky varieties of the tiger cowrie (*Cypraea tigris*) and dark ones. These varieties are the expressions of different genotypes, i.e., combinations of genes. Alternative forms of a particular gene (called alleles) cause variation among individual organisms, for example, in the background colour of shell. The number and relative abundance of alternative forms of a gene in a population is a measure of genetic variation (called heterozygosity). The total amount of genetic variation in all populations of a species is a measure of its genetic diversity. Finally, genetic diversity is a measure of a population's ability to adapt to environmental change or stress, and thus of its ability to survive (FAO/UNEP, 1981).

Genetic differences may explain the differential susceptibilities of corals of the same species to elevated seawater temperatures at various locations. While unable to save a population in one location, these differences could confer resilience to climate change in a species over all its range. Although the mechanism is not clear, an example of susceptibility to climate change is provided by the corals along the

Arabian Sea and Gulf of Oman coasts in the northwestern Indian Ocean. The corals *Euphyllia, Tubipora, Goniastrea,* and *Montastrea* are all found alive in a few restricted locations off the southern Oman coast, but have all died out in the north and central coasts where they occur only in Pleistocene beach deposits (Salm, 1993). A similar pattern is demonstrated by the molluscs *Cypraeacassis rufa, Lambis lambis*, and *Tridacna*. While the majority of corals and molluscs were able to survive the changes accompanying the transition from Pleistocene to present, the few mentioned above fell victim.

A species must adapt or die out when faced with environmental change. Did the corals and molluscs in northern Oman die out because the communities there were less diverse than further south, hence more susceptible to perturbations? Pimm (1984) suggested that species might be more resilient to environmental change if the food web is more diverse. However, there is no evidence to show that complex tropical reef systems are any more resilient than less diverse polar ones.

Genetic resources cannot be preserved in the wild without maintaining ecological processes and life support systems. Both ecological processes and genetic resources must be maintained, then, for the sustainable utilization of species and ecosystems.

1.5 Conserving Ecosystems and Maintaining Ecological Processes

MPAs can conserve entire ecosystems that are unique, particularly rich in species, representative of biogeographical units, or exceptionally productive of seafood. There may be unique ecosystems that have complements of species that are found nowhere else, having evolved to live in their specific environmental conditions. These ecosystems represent a high-risk natural investment of biodiversity and related genetic resources, all of which may be lost if such habitats are destroyed. Ecosystems rich in species—of high biodiversity—represent good investments since they yield a high number of options for the conservation effort expended.

Different ecosystems have, among their complement of species, genetic resources influenced by different ecological conditions. Some species are confined to specific biogeographical regions, while others have separate populations in different regions. Such separate populations may be genetically distinct, each having developed specific characters favoring survival in the different regions. As Prescott-Allen and Prescott-Allen (1984) observe, "Not all populations are equally useful; and useful populations are not distributed evenly throughout the range of the species they comprise. Consequently it is possible for valuable genotypes to be threatened with extinction even though the species is widespread and abundant."

The ecological systems of the sea may have great complexity—as in coral reefs—or very high bioproductivity—as in "upwelling" areas where nutrient-laden deep ocean waters rise to the surface. These examples differ from terrestrial systems in many ways. Three-dimensional phenomena are more marked and important in the ocean, where organisms are less tied to the solid bottom than are land organisms to the earth. But, more important because of the fluid nature of the seas, whole biological communities exist as floating plankton-based entities distributed horizontally and vertically through broad ocean spaces. Ocean currents are great mixers, transporting organic nutrients produced at one site to distant locations and carrying planktonic eggs and larvae of organisms to colonize distant habitats. In addition, many marine species migrate long distances, like tunas, turtles, whales, and eels, and yet other creatures, such as seabirds, depend on these. Since marine organisms are in closer chemical contact with their surrounding medium than land organisms, they are jeopardized more by pollution.

Conservation management of such large-scale ecosystems is a difficult challenge and for the most part we must focus our protected area efforts on concrete situations. For example, among the most ecologically critical and threatened areas are coastal wetlands and shallows, especially lagoons and estuaries and their mangrove swamps. Coral reef ecosystems are of more local, but nonetheless great, significance, providing habitats for the fish on which many rural communities in developing countries depend.

Wetlands, sea grass beds, and coral reefs are being degraded (Figure I-8), or even destroyed the world over (Carpenter, 1983; IUCN/UNEP, 1991; Wells and Hanna, 1992; Wilkinson, 1992, 1998), with severe effects on the economies that depend on them. In Sri Lanka, the removal of corals to produce lime was so extensive that a local fishery collapsed.

FIGURE I-8.

Photo by John Clark.

Reef fishes need healthy coral reef ecosystems to prosper.

MPAs help maintain ecosystem productivity; safeguarding essential ecological processes by controlling activities that disrupt them or that physically damage the environment. Some of these processes are physical, such as the movement of water, food, and organisms by gravity, waves, and currents. Others are chemical, such as concentration and exchange of gases and minerals, and biological, such as nutrient transfer from one trophic level to another. Some, such as nutrient cycling, are of all three types. It is these processes that maintain ecosystem integrity and productivity. Lake Ichkeul in Tunisia is an example of an MPA where ecosystem processes are maintained (see Box I-1).

Box I-1. Ecosystem Conservation: Lake Ichkeul in Tunisia

Lake Ichkeul in Tunisia is an example of a protected area where ecosystem processes are maintained. Lake Ichkeul was declared a National Park by the Tunisian government and also nominated as a World Heritage Site, a Wetland of International Importance (under the so-called Ramsar Convention) and a Biosphere Reserve (under the United Nations Man and the Biosphere Reserve Programme). In the early 1980s it was the only area in the world with three international categories. This reflected the richness of its biota, its ecological diversity, its regional importance, and the value of the processes that sustain it.

Lake Ichkeul is considered to have the most important wetlands (marshlands) in the Mediterranean region. Hundreds of thousands of migratory birds rely on its marshes as a seasonal habitat, making this a crucial site in the international conservation of these species, which are of high economic value at both the north and the south extremes of their migrations.

The water balance of Lake Ichkeul is determined by the alternation of summer evaporation (lowering the water level and causing an influx of salt water) and winter inundation (raising the water level and causing dilution of the lake). In winter, 250 to 400 million cu. m of freshwater flow into the lake from five main sources. The flooded marshes of the lake then give shelter to migratory birds flying over the Mediterranean to spend the winter in North Africa. Toward the end of spring, as the water drops below sea level, seawater flows into the lake. Between 10 and 30 million m^3 of saltwater flow into Ichkeul annually through the Tinja Canal to compensate for summer evaporation, and the lake's salinity increases tenfold. The ecosystem depends on these annual cycles. The marshes, birds, and fishes are all adapted to these processes in the site's complex hydrology.

Source: Baccar, 1982.

External impacts on coastal ecosystems are widespread: industrial and agricultural pollution, siltation from eroded uplands; filling to provide sites for industry, housing, recreation, airports, and farmland; dredging to create, deepen, and improve harbors; quarrying; and the excessive cutting of mangroves for fuel. As the commercially valuable fisheries for fish, crustaceans, and molluscs become more fully exploited, the effects of habitat destruction and pollution will become more evident, particularly on those species depending on coastal wetlands and shallows or on wetlands for nutrients or for spawning grounds and nurture areas (Figure I-9). Correction of these problems can be addressed by integrated systems, such as Coastal Zone Management (CZM), which are mainly intended to control shore based impacts.

A system of protected areas that includes examples of representative, unique, and critical habitats, as well as species-rich habitats, along with the processes that link them into the complex marine-coastal ecosystem, provides the maximum guarantee of biodiversity conservation and the continuity of native stock available to

FIGURE 1-9.

Photo by John Clark.

Mangrove stands provide shelter and nutrients for coastal species.

restore depleted areas. Also, this habitat mix can maintain a genetic pool of unexploited species that may prove especially valuable in the future; for example, in medicine and mariculture. It is this mix of species, habitats, supporting processes, and ecosystems that helps to *maintain the integrity of entire living systems* that, as Norse (1993) has indicated, is essential for the preservation of biodiversity.

1.6 Sustainable Use

A basic assumption of this book is that it is in every country's best interest to achieve a sustainable yield of its resources. Sustainable use requires control of harvest of individual species and marine communities together with conservation of the habitats and ecosystems on which they depend, so that their current and potential usefulness to people is not impaired. Resources should be managed so that the ability of a resource to renew itself is never jeopardized. Such management maintains biological potential and enhances the long-term economic potential of marine renewable natural resources.

Another fundamental fact to consider here is that many millions of people living along the coasts of the world have small cash incomes (less than $300 per year) and subsist on local resources. The lives and destinies of these people are linked to the sustainability of their resources. They will continue to turn to these resources with or without conservation (Figures I-10, 11). Some may manage for themselves using customary practices, but often they need help.

Intervention into ecosystems falls into three broad categories. First are uses that permanently alter ecosystems (e.g., urban, industrial, and agricultural developments). Second are extractive uses, which include

FIGURE I-10.

Photo by R. Salm.

Fishermen rely on the most accessible resources, with little knowledge that they can cause rapid depletion of stocks. Turtle carapaces make useful containers for salting fish, turtle meat, and eggs, but excessive exploitation can ruin the resource (Pukkulam Village, Sri Lanka).

harvest of edible resources (e.g., fishes) and of resources having other values, such as construction (e.g., mangrove poles, coral blocks, sand, lime, and other building materials), ornamental (e.g., corals, pearls, and shells), domestic (e.g., sponges), scientific (a wide range of species), industrial (e.g., giant clams and species yielding pharmaceuticals), and maricultural (e.g., oysters and mussels)—people harvest these for subsistence, commercial, research, and recreational purposes. The third category of use is non-extractive, including recreational activities (e.g., diving, boating, bird watching, and swimming), research, education, development of marine parks and reserves, and the use of coastal habitats as natural boat harbors (e.g., estuaries and atoll lagoons) and for coastal protection (e.g., dunes, barrier islands, mangroves, and coral reefs).

FIGURE I-11.

Photo by R. Salm.

In many developing countries fisherfolk are among the poorest people, despite long hours of hard and dangerous work to contribute to the nutrition of their communities. The critical habitats on which their livelihoods depend need protection.

1.7 Protecting Commercially Valuable Species

Of great economic importance is maintaining productivity for fisheries—an obvious example of an ecological process directly supporting people's economic well-being (Figure I-12). Naturally productive ecosystems, such as coral reefs and estuaries, provide free of cost what expensive mariculture can barely match—continued fish production. Continued fish production means a reliable source of food and continued livelihood for fishers and for others in the fishing industry, including boat builders, trap and net makers, packers, distributors, and retailers. Finally, continued livelihood means continued social, cultural, economic, and political stability.

In many parts of the world, seafood supplies most of the animal protein and much of the livelihood for large populations of people (Figure I-13). In Africa, where artisanal fisheries provide the bulk of the fish eaten by local people, these

FIGURE I-12.

Photo by John Clark.

Artisanal fishermen in Palau depend upon healthy reef ecosystems to provide their catches.

FIGURE I-13.

Photo by Erkki Siirila.

In Dominica these boys do their share by supplying seafood to the community of Portsmouth. They carry typical West Indian fish traps.

fisheries are widely considered to be fully exploited (Brainerd, 1994; Hatziolos *et al.*, 1994; Insull *et al.*, 1995; Tvedten & Hersoug, 1992), with some already being exploited beyond the level of sustainability with no margin for feeding increasing populations. Because demand is increasing with population growth and prosperity, fisheries are typically not managed for sustainability; their contribution to national diets and income is diminishing and is likely to continue diminishing. MPAs can help sustain such fisheries.

Past and present overfishing has caused many of the world's most valuable fisheries to be seriously depleted. Nor can it be assumed that depleted stocks will recover naturally to reach their full potential. In fact, this is most unlikely for several reasons: juvenile fishes will continue to be caught for the aquarium trade or as bycatch by "industrial" fisheries and ground up for animal feed; other species may invade the territories of depleted species and prevent their return and; habitats essential for spawning or as nurture areas may be degraded or destroyed and lose power to regenerate stocks. Also many lucrative and exploitative and destructive fisheries are being accelerated such as those that catch and transport large live fish and those that stun fish with cyanide.

In addition to depleting fish, crustacean, and mollusc stocks, overfishing has nearly extinguished some popular species, like whales, dolphins, and sea turtles. Some are the victims of incidental capture as bycatch along with "target" species and are killed and discarded. An example of this wasteful practice is the incidental capture and killing of sea turtles in fishing nets, which threatens the survival of several species.

Protecting critical habitats may be necessary to maintain high fisheries returns or even to prevent the "economic extinction" of commercially important species. Many commercially valuable species are not now threatened with biological extinction, but because they are heavily exploited they could nevertheless be "commercially threatened."

Invertebrates are often very important to subsistence and artisanal fishers. For example, the palolo worm, *Eunice viridis,* an important food resource in Fiji and Samoa, is reported to be declining. While the causes of the decline have not been scientifically determined, they may include a variety of factors, such as destruction of coral reefs, siltation, and pollution. Reserves to protect its main breeding areas have been established, for example, the Palolo Deep Reserve in Western Samoa.

The coconut crab, *Birgus latro,* is another invertebrate species that is an important food resource for many island peoples (Figure I-14). Although still abundant on islands like Aldabra, where exploitation is negligible, populations declined on many others, including the Chagos Archipelago and Guam (Sheppard, 1979; Amesbury, 1980).

Giant clams (family Tridacnidae) have been overexploited throughout much of their range. Mariculture may prove a major tool in conserving and managing these resources (Munro and Heslinga, 1982), but in the meantime MPAs are probably the only way of preserving the remaining stocks in some countries. In Australia, giant clam populations are protected by the Great Barrier Reef Marine Park. These reserves may play important roles with the development of mariculture operations. Programmes are well under way for the queen conch,

FIGURE I-14.

The rare coconut or robber crab *(Birgus latro)* is a tasty, easily caught creature in desperate need of protection (Aldabra Atoll Strict Nature Reserve and World Heritage Site).

giant clams, and commercial trochus *Trochus niloticus* (Berg, 1981; Munro and Heslinga, 1982; Heslinga and Hillman, 1980). One of the objectives of such programmes is restocking overexploited areas. The areas will have to be protected to establish the new populations.

In Indonesia and the Philippines some invertebrate populations are declining at alarming rates. In Indonesia, sites were sought for reserves specifically to protect certain species. For example, a marine reserve was delineated for an area off Irian Jaya, which is still rich in one species, *Tridacna gigas,* and another reserve was identified for the species *T. derasa* in the Flores Sea. In the Philippines, there is little protection for clams. One exception is the marine reserve along the west side of Sumilon Island, Cebu, which protects substantial numbers of the clam species *T. crocea, T. maxima, T. squamosa,* and *Hippopus hippopus* (Alcala, 1982).

1.8 Replenishing Depleted Stocks

Protected areas can contribute to the replenishment of threatened marine resources through creation of No-Fishing Zones (No-Take Zones, Sanctuaries). They can safeguard breeding sanctuaries from which individuals can disperse to stock exploited areas. Other MPA protections may be necessary to safeguard recognized nurture areas (nursery areas) for juvenile stages (Clark, 1996).

Coastal and marine protected areas can benefit the breeding stocks of valuable but vulnerable species, like such predatory fishes as snapper (lutjanids), jacks (carangids), groupers (serranids), and porgies (lethrinids). These are the first fishes to disappear from heavily fished areas, as in Indonesia where they may be rare or absent on many reefs. Protected areas can aid the replenishment of depleted stocks by preserving seed stock that can be transported to depleted areas. In addition, protecting key breeding stocks in certain protected areas can help replenish depleted habitats nearby through out migration.

In the Philippines, trials with closing a part of the coral reef around each of several small islands as fish stock replenishment zones have been successful. In the 1970s, 15 ha of a 50 ha reef area surrounding Sumilon Island was closed to fishing to serve as a sanctuary. In the other 35 ha, "ecologically sound" fishing methods were prescribed. The total catch went from 3,633 kg in 1976 to 6,948 kg in the first 10 months of 1979 (Alcala, 1979). Apparently the closed sanctuary served to enhance the regenerative and other capabilities of the stocks. But political difficulties ended the trial.

Then in 1984, a new project involving intensive community participation, was commenced at three Islands—Apo, Balicasag, and Pamilacan. About 20 percent of the reefs were closed at each with good results. The programmes continue to the present at each island. In a survey in 1997, fishermen of all three islands agreed that fishing was better because of the reserve and its sanctuary, which served as a *semilyahan* (breeding place). A site survey in 1992 showed increases over the six years since 1986 of 83, 32, and 7 percent respectively in food fishes, total fishes, and species richness. Coral reef cover has remained stable. Dive tourism increased significantly.

The professional staff who worked with the islanders helped them to understand the ecological processes involved, to organize effective marine management committees with core groups, to get supportive ordinances in place, to build community centers (funds provided by project), and explore opportunities for additional income. After this initial assistance, the programme has continued successfully as a community based operation and without significant outside intervention, according to White. (Part III, Case No. 4).

Another example is Looe Key Reef, a well developed bank reef in the lower Florida Keys (USA) which had seen heavy spearfishing for many years. As a result, its predator species were depleted, including snapper, grouper, hogfish, snook, and barracuda. Individuals of these species were also significantly smaller than those on reefs where there was less spearfishing. With predators scarce, prey species and non-target fish, such as parrotfish, damselfish, grunt, and sea urchins, had become more abundant. Following its designation in 1981 as a national marine sanctuary and the prohibition of spearfishing, a major increase in the number of key fish species on Looe Key Reef was seen in sanctuary-supported research (Clark *et al.*, 1989). Scientists suspect that part of the increase results from an influx of adults and young juveniles from other reefs and part from security of those already there. Furthermore, in many reefs under protection, larger, attractive fish appear to be less frightened of fish watchers and do not flee so quickly when approached (Figure I-15).

FIGURE I-15.

Large yellowtail snapper at Roatan Reef, Honduras.

1.9 Education and Research

Natural areas are used for both education and formal training, as well as research. Public education is usually organized around on-site interpretive programmes in the protected areas. Such programmes may take the form of guided or self-guided trails, for example: boardwalks through coastal wetlands (Figure I-16), underwater trails like those through the reefs at Buck Island National Monument in the U.S. Virgin Islands (Figure I-17), and underwater viewing chambers like those found at Green Island on the Great Barrier Reef (Australia) and in several marine parks in Japan. Off-site interpretive programmes involve publications, lectures, and film or slide shows provided at visitor centers, schools, and other institutions, or through television.

FIGURE I-16.

Boardwalks facilitate educational visits to coastal protected areas (Umhlanga Nature Reserve, South Africa).

FIGURE I-17.

Underwater signs inform visitors of the marine organisms in the Buck Island National Monument, U.S. Virgin Islands.

Field trips to marine protected areas and research stations by school and university students exemplify their use for formal training. Natural areas can serve as "outdoor laboratories," providing living examples of ecological principles taught in class (Figure I-18).

FIGURE I-18.

Photo by Erkki Siirila.

A group of U.S. and Mexican college students listen to a teacher during a boat trip in the Gulf of California. The students spent a semester studying marine mammals and visiting protected areas near La Paz, Mexico.

Marine protected areas offer opportunities for academic research (e.g., on specific behavioral or physiological subjects), applied research (on resource management needs and the biomedical applications of reef biocompounds), and monitoring of specific events (e.g., coral bleaching, crown-of-thorns outbreaks) or long term trends (such as the impact of silt linked to land fill and dredging on corals of the Ste. Anne Marine National Park in Seychelles), or the recovery of corals following control of blast fishing as in Komodo National Park, Indonesia. The particular advantage of protected areas for research is that they enable long-term continuing studies of the same group of organisms or of the same plot of habitat without the disturbance of inquisitive visitors, poachers, or vandals. The need to protect research areas is recognized by the exclusive research zones created at Australia's Great Barrier Reef and the USA's Florida Keys Sanctuary.

1.10 Protection from Natural Hazards

An important, and often underestimated, function of habitats along wave-swept shores is coastal protection against natural hazards. This protection is particularly important where fringing and barrier reefs and mangrove forests help protect low lying coastal plains, plantations, and villages from the ravages of tropical storms and tsunamis. It is important, too, along high energy coastlines characterized by sand dunes stabilized by specific sand-binding plants adapted to the harsh dune environment (Figure I-19).

FIGURE I-19.

Sand binding plants build strong dunes and should be protected.

Barrier islands and sand cays are dynamic habitats that protect coastal communities from storm waves—their shapes and positions are determined by prevailing winds, currents, and waves and the stabilizing influences of reefs and vegetation. Interference with the processes of island building and stabilization can lead to the loss of houses, hotels, and other buildings, along with the loss of valuable island and lagoon habitats. Designated MPAs can help safeguard such sensitive environments by controlling access, uses, and restricting construction to safe zones.

In Sri Lanka mangroves, small lagoons, and coconut groves disappeared because of increased shore erosion, caused by mining of coral reef systems for lime products (Figure I-20). The National Government responded by establishing a Coastal Zone Management programme to control the mining. In Bangladesh, a "green belt" of mangroves along the shoreline greatly reduced the damage caused by a major cyclone in 1991.

Nature too suffers from catastrophic hazardous events. In many areas such events are part of a natural cycle of destruction and recovery. Natural disasters (tropical storms, tornadoes, floods, or even a heavy downpour at low tide, elevated sea water temperatures and related coral bleaching, and crown-of-thorns starfish outbreaks) may devastate certain coastal habitats and their associated communities. Afterward, propagules (larvae and seeds) drifting in from nearby areas can replenish depleted communities and speed the recovery of these habitats. If thriving and intact communities are nearby, recruitment potential is high and recovery can be complete. Having sufficient protected areas helps ensure adequate recruitment.

FIGURE I-20.

Sri Lanka suffered severe erosion of its shoreline when protected coral reefs were degraded by mining for construction products.

1.11 Recreation and Tourism

SCUBA diving, snorkeling, swimming, fishing, beach walking, surfing, and sunbathing bring tourists to small island nations that have attractive shorelands (Figure I-21). For example, the natural beauty, coral sand beaches, reefs, and rich natural history of the Seychelles Islands and Mauritius are these countries' major attractions for European tourists. Each year millions of North Americans and Europeans visit Caribbean and Pacific islands, Mediterranean coasts, and Florida's beaches to relax in the sun at the water's edge, dive over wrecks and reefs, sail and waterski, fish, and feast on seafood. Bali's reef protected beaches draw hundreds of thousands of tourists.

Tourism is a major industry in these places, bringing to the countries scarce jobs, revenue, and foreign exchange. The creation of protected areas should thus be considered in national planning for tourism development in coastal countries. Marine parks not only arouse interest but also may help to maintain the quality of the recreational resources that attract tourists (Figure I-22).

FIGURE I-21.

FIGURE I-22.

The beaches of St.Lucia offer many forms of recreation to tourists, many of whom come from Europe, Canada and the United States.

A visitor observes the graceful elegance of a California sea lion in the protected sea lion colony of Los Islotes, Baja California, Mexico. Visitation to the colony is not allowed.

Where there is tourism in MPAs, it is useful to set aside special tourism zones for swimming, snorkeling, and other water sports. This will encourage tourists and minimize conflicts with other uses, such as fishing. Also it can separate conflicting tourism uses such as between speedboats and swimmers.

1.12 Social and Economic Benefits

There is a growing need to justify protected areas economically; that is, to show that an area's monetary benefits can exceed its monetary costs. This is a difficult task. It is always easier to describe the values of protected areas than to quantify them. For example, we can say that a particular coastal or marine protected area is a source of inspiration, spiritual enrichment, and recreation and enjoyment or that it serves as a nurturing place for commercial species, a sanctuary for endangered species, and a protector of migrating species. All these are the heritage of both a nation and the world regardless of economic costs and benefits.

A statement like that of Kalati Poai, Department of Agriculture and Forests, Apia, Western Samoa (Lucas, 1984), illustrates the cultural wealth of protected areas: "National Parks belong to the people. Every man, woman and child in the country has, as a heritage, these areas which are set aside forever to give pleasure to present and succeeding generations. Thus those who use the parks have responsibility to themselves and to others to treat this great heritage with care and respect. Reserves are very important in the country. There are many important things in our life that could become rare. If we do not preserve or protect some of our lands and seas, these will be lost".

However, it is very difficult to put monetary values on such inspirational, natural, and cultural heritage benefits, or on those of national pride and international obligation. Nevertheless, there is an increasing demand to counter mariculture proposals or development schemes that promise large financial returns with solid arguments based on valuations of the social and economic benefits of natural production and the costs of degraded systems. These arguments should include the benefits of marine protected areas and demonstrate that they can be self-financing, especially in the developing world.

In the above examples the reader will find that some of the values can be easily measured as "marketplace transactions"; that is, people pay specific amounts of money for specific benefits. In an economic analysis, the costs of providing the benefits are subtracted from what people have paid to obtain them (a cost-benefit analysis). Other economic benefits are more difficult to express in monetary terms, e.g., the additional food provided for a village by protecting and managing a lagoon. Economists can create simulated measures (e.g., "shadow prices" or "willingness to pay") to judge such benefits in monetary terms. But there are many types of benefits that cannot, and should not, be measured in conventional monetary terms. These include most ethically based values like protecting endangered species and conserving communities' "way of life."

A review of some recent methods of economic valuation, with specific references for marine biodiversity, coral reefs, and mangrove valuations, is given in Section I-5.10. A warning of the numerous pitfalls of such valuations, also given, should be taken seriously. A comprehensive economic valuation of protected area benefits should not be undertaken lightly, and should be done by competent specialists according to the most recent techniques.

Site Planning and Management

M arine protected areas (MPAs) require a specific planning process, which is best done prior to the management phase, whether they are discrete sites or sites within a larger management framework. The product of site planning is a Site Management Plan.

It is important to differentiate between planning and management. *Planning* provides the basis for decisions on how resources are to be allocated and protected, for example, through the analysis and selection processes (covered in the next section), and through the design or zoning and management programmes discussed below. *Management* addresses the strategies and operations needed to attain the objectives of the management plan.

Site planning should look at past progress, the current issues, and future needs to identify priority actions from the full range of possible management interventions.

2.1 The Site Management Plan

The Management Plan for a particular site is a working document that is updated periodically. Because its arrangement and complexity must be tailored to the needs of the site, generic models may be suggestive but not prescriptive. Each site needs its own customized plan.

There are many practical considerations in designing MPAs that are to be addressed during the planning phase: location of MPA facilities; types of boats and motors for surveillance and transport; boundary demarcations; zoning of activities to separate incompatible uses where necessary; recruiting and training of staff; the development schedule and budgets; analysis of visitor use compatibility and safety considerations; conflict resolution and cooperative arrangements with local communities and industries; and such ecological factors as the types of habitats to include, and the size of the protected area and its different zones. Also there should be consideration of external impacts on the site and procedures to minimize these effects.

FIGURE I-23.

But before these items can be addressed effectively, there is a need to define the process that will be used to determine exactly what needs to be managed (the issues), the prioritization of these, and how they will be tackled (the actions). This is the *issue-action analysis* process, described later in this section, that in this form, or another, is the basis of the management plan.

The general objectives of the Site Management Plan are to conserve habitats and ecological processes in order to preserve the value of the area for tourism, fisheries, research (Figure I-23), education, or other goals, and to protect certain species and biotic communities. All these objectives can be accomplished through an active and appropriate management programme leading to sustainable use of coastal and marine resources.

Photo by Erkki Siirila.

A diver counting reef fish in the Soufriere Marine Management Area, St.Lucia, to study the benefits of non-fishing zones.

2.2 Planning Approach

As the first step in the site planning sequence, a strategy document (or Preliminary Plan) interprets the policies that need to be implemented, states the programme goals, and lays out a basic strategy for achieving the programme. Planning a strategy involves all the preliminary investigation, data collection, issues analysis, dialogue, negotiation, and draft writing that is necessary to define the problems, to understand the options and to lay the foundation for the Management Plan. Once the strategy document is approved by policy makers, administrators, and stakeholders, the way is clear to create an acceptable management format.

The importance of the strategy planning function cannot be overemphasized— it is the key to all that follows in site management planning and implementation of the MPA programme. It helps to organize the programme, to identify the main issues and anticipate the questions that superiors, politicians, and supporters will ask, and to provide the data to answer these questions.

The initial Site Management Plan should not be considered as final, or cast in stone. On the contrary, new knowledge revealed through management experience and monitoring will reveal additional issues for resolution, actions and approaches that require improvement, and planning mistakes that will have inevitably occurred. Allowance for review and feedback on such matters as boundary delineation, user rights and activities, and even the basic objectives for the area, should be provided for in the Management Plan and used to modify management actions. It is exceedingly important, therefore, that adaptable mechanisms are provided to enable management flexibility, and that management plans include monitoring and feedback mechanisms such as periodic stakeholder meetings, and internal and external reviews.

The MPA site may not need a full management plan to *begin* operations, but it does need one for long term programme development. When circumstances—like shortages of funds, time, or personnel—delay outside participation in site planning for an MPA, managers should take action themselves to initiate plan formulation. In fact, an important general rule for management planning is that the MPA site manager should be identified during planning and should have a high level of participation in the site planning process.

FIGURE I-24.

Management goals outlined in the Strategy Plan should address the long-term ideal state and should be somewhat open ended, identifying desired conditions more than specific actions. Management objectives represent short term, measurable steps toward attaining these goals. For example, one goal for a coral reef protected area might be to protect and maintain the integrity and natural quality of the coral reef system. One objective for the MPA, then, might be to implement a specific programme to protect the coral reef habitat from damage. Such a programme might include developing a boater's guide to safe anchoring procedures, re-establishing corals destroyed by visitor related activities, placing moorings at diving sites to prevent anchor damage, and periodically closing heavily used sites to enable their recovery (Figure I-24).

Photo by Erkki Siirila.

Mooring buoys for visiting yachts and dive boats are an important coral conservation tool in marine protected areas (Soufriere, St.Lucia).

Box I-2. Typical Objectives Addressed in the Strategy Document or Preliminary Plan

- Maintain a high quality coastal environment. Coastal habitats are a major resource, providing commerce, food, recreation, and spiritual refreshment. Habitats near coastal settlements can easily become polluted, ugly, and unproductive if protection is not supplied.

- Protect species diversity. A quality marine environment is needed to sustain species and their habitats. MPAs can protect species.

- Protect environmentally sensitive areas. Certain ecosystems are of such outstanding biodiversity and ecological value that they should be set aside and protected from alteration by development.

- Conserve special habitats. Habitats of special importance include stands of mangrove trees, coral reefs, kelp beds, submerged meadows of sea grass, sandy beaches and dunes, and certain tideflat habitats. Wherever these occur on the coast they are presumed to be critical habitats, the loss of which would reduce productivity, species well-being, and ecological balance.

- Conserve critical ecological processes. Certain ecological processes are critical to the productivity of coastal ecosystems; e.g., light penetration through the water (which can be blocked by excessive turbidity), nutrient transfer and trophic balance (which can be disturbed by loss of natural organic materials such as happens when mangroves are clear-felled).

- Maintain water quality. Pollution from point sources and from land runoff as well as accidental spills of contaminants can foul coastal habitats and waters causing human health problems, ecological disruption and reduced productivity, as well as killing organisms or contaminating shellfish beds. The MPA programme should attempt to keep the area clean and productive.

- Combine natural hazards protection with nature conservation. The measures best suited to conserving habitats are often the same as those needed for barriers to storms and flooding; e.g., protection of natural features like coral reefs, sand dunes, and mangrove stands.

- Restore damaged ecosystems. Many otherwise productive coastal ecosystems have been damaged but are restorable by passive or active means. Restoration of coral reefs, mangrove stands and other wetlands, sea grass beds, sand dunes, etc. may be a prime objective.

- Replenish depleted fisheries. MPAs have been shown to be effective in replenishment of depleted fisheries because they safeguard breeding stocks of target fish species. In MPAs these fishes are able to grow large enough to breed and produce juveniles that then move out to settle in depleted areas.

- Involve and educate the community. MPAs can play an important role in creating public awareness of ecological values and needs for coastal and marine conservation.

Source: Modified from Clark, 1996.

2.3 Site Planning Procedure

The site planning process is based on clearly defined conservation *goals and objectives* as interpreted during strategy planning, as shown in Box I-2. To achieve these goals, information on the site is needed, particularly site surveys to determine characteristics of the resource, the uses of the resource, and threats to the resource. The design of the MPA—based on this inventory—can be done following the general guidelines presented in Box I-3 which identify many of the basic elements necessary for designing MPAs and preparing the Site Management Plan.

Box I-3. Site Planning Guidelines

1. The strategy document identifies steps to establish a protected area and forms the foundation for the Management Plan. It is the preliminary document by which approvals are gained and designation of an MPA site is formalized. The strategy document is thus an important part of the management process.

2. The Management Plan for the site is the operational guide for the MPA and identifies actions to resolve specific management issues. It is thus a guiding tool for management.

3. The principal goal of the Management Plan is generally to maintain the natural resource values (seascapes, species habitats, ecological processes) of an area, and to ensure that all uses are compatible with that aim.

4. The Management Plan should aim to conserve natural values, optimize economic uses, and integrate traditional uses. Through zoning, it should attempt to separate incompatible activities, ensuring that particular uses are permitted only in suitable areas and sustainable levels of use are specified.

5. The Management Plan derives directly from management issues and their related objectives and activities. It needs to encompass legal and administrative concerns and educational and social objectives along with ecological and physical ones.

6. The Management Plan should function to achieve interagency coordination and cooperation among stakeholders (management authority, concerned departments of government, neighboring communities and other user groups) and to facilitate communication between MPA administration and management.

7. Initiation of site management need not be delayed until a MPA plan is completed. In countries where lengthy bureaucratic procedures or other factors delay the completion of the plan, an interim management document (operational plan) can be formulated and implemented.

8. Management plans may be required to function as interpretive documents, being designed for the public as well as for management. Planning workshops should be conducted to garner interest from the nearby community as well as certain sectors of the public.

9. Planning should examine the effects that MPAs have on local people and find ways to avoid negative effects or compensate for these. Public consultation is important both to identify current uses and to avoid conflict with local traditions and to encourage participation in planning.

Table I-1. Model Outline for MPA Site Management Plan

Executive Summary

Introduction

    A. Purpose and scope of plan

    B   Legislative authority for the action

Management Content

    A. Regional setting: location and access

    B. Resources (facts pertinent to management; other data in an appendix or separate document)

        1. Physical: beaches, dunes, shoals, bars, reefs, currents, bathymetry, hydrology

        2. Biological: ecosystems (coral reefs, seagrass beds, mangroves, dunes, forests, Grasslands); critical habitats (nesting, feeding, spawning, roosting); species (endangered, commercial, showy)

        3. Cultural: archaeological, historical, religious.

    C. Existing uses (description, facilities, etc.)

        1. Recreational

        2. Commercial

        3. Research and education

        4. Traditional uses rights, and management practices

    D. Existing legal and management framework

    E. Existing and potential threats and implications for management (i.e., analysis of compatible or incompatible uses, solutions)

    F. The plan

        1. Goals and objectives

        2. Management tactics

            a. Advisory committees

            b. Interagency agreements (or agreements with private organizations, institutions or individuals)

            c. Boundaries

            d. Zoning plan

            e. Regulations

            f. Social, cultural, and resource studies plan

            g. Resource management plan

            h. Interpretive plan

        3. Administration

            a. Staffing

            b. Training

            c. Facilities and equipment

            d. Budget and business plan, finance sources

        4. Surveillance and enforcement

        5. Monitoring and evaluation of plan effectiveness

    G. Appendices

    H. References

The value of the written Site Management Plan for an MPA is that it specifies particular courses of action for interested persons, decision makers, and especially the Site Manager for whom it will serve as an operational guide for daily management actions. The plan establishes a philosophy of management to guide managers in the numerous actions they will take over the life of the plan. It is important that the plan sets realistic objectives for available management resources. To do otherwise encourages false expectations and begs failure.

Each Management Plan should include a mechanism for evaluating effectiveness and a schedule for its own revision. As a general rule, plans should have a life span of three to five years. Plans should be flexible enough for managers to modify certain activities based on their experience and on new data received during the implementation phase. A model outline for a Site Management Plan is shown in Table I-1. This outline is more of a guide to the basic elements of a management plan rather than intended as a prescription. It will need to be adapted to each site depending on purposes, scope, and who is implementing management. In cases of community-based management, for example, simpler outlines that are more directly focussed on the control of specific uses (like fisheries) will be ample.

2.4 Boundaries and Optimal Size

A major problem in conserving coastal and marine ecosystems is identifying their ecological boundaries and using these in the protected area design. In the past, protected area boundaries were based mostly on geological features (such as headlands that provide a "natural" boundary), political districts (national, provincial, or district borders), or costs (smaller areas may require less money to maintain). In general, there has been too little ecological reasoning behind the demarcation of coastal and marine protected area boundaries. Failure to recognize and use appropriate ecological boundaries may lead to inappropriate boundaries and zoning of the protected area.

There is no general rule for the optimal size and design of MPAs. There are proponents of "disaggregation" (establishing a number of small protected areas) and of "aggregation" (establishing fewer larger areas). The arguments for "disaggregation" are best applied to the terrestrial protected areas for which they were formulated; they do not seem to hold so well for underwater areas, where aggregation seems the best approach coupled with an effective use zoning scheme (see Box I-4).

Box I-4. Opinions Favoring Disaggregation

The arguments for disaggregation (advantage of selecting numerous small areas) are given below and answered in light of the special characteristics of the marine environment.

1. A number of small areas may support more species. There is no conclusive evidence that this rule is true for underwater areas. Besides, the total number of species may not be as important a parameter as the composition of species. Thus, species should be evaluated, not simply enumerated. Many inconsequential species may not be as valuable as fewer important ones. Also, certain species, such as predatory or non-territorial fishes, may have large area requirements, especially if they are poor at dispersing among separated habitats, and may be absent in smaller habitat areas. In fact, in the Chagos Archipelago certain corals were found only on reefs larger than a minimum size, which varied by species (Salm, 1980b, 1984).

2. A number of small areas may ensure survival of more species in a competitive group. Many coastal and marine habitats normally behave as clusters of areas. They are not continuous, but comprise numerous spatially discrete components that may be divided by headlands, creeks, and river mouths (like mangroves), or surge channels, deep passes, bays, and sandy patches (like coral reefs). These components function as small "islands of habitat" and could provide survival opportunities to different members of a set of competitive species in the context of a larger MPA.

3. A catastrophic event is not so likely to destroy all of a number of small areas. Considering the dispersal ability of many marine species with larval forms, scattered protected areas would seem to be of little consequence in preventing total infestation by disease or hostile species. For example, the way the crown-of-thorns starfish spread from reef to reef over hundreds of miles suggests that a system of small reserves or a single large one, like Australia's Great Barrier Reef Marine Park, would have been equally vulnerable.

2.5 Zoning

It is often difficult to accommodate all the interests and needs of local residents, tourism development, and the conservation values and needs within an MPA. Tourism in MPAs may be compatible with conservation in all but the most ecologically sensitive areas (Figure I-25) if properly managed. Nevertheless, damage may be caused by the construction of tourist facilities around wetlands and beaches that border the MPA.

MPAs are typically designed to permit several controlled and sustainable uses within their boundaries. But often particular uses need to be confined to particular zones within the MPA where they are appropriate or where their uses do not conflict with other uses. Zoning is a widely accepted method to keep people out of the most sensitive, ecologically valuable, or recovering areas, and to limit the impact of visitors.

As an example, MPAs may border on inhabited coasts whose residents are heavily dependent on fish, shellfish, and other marine resources for food and livelihood but who damage coastal habitats or deplete resources in their pursuits (e.g., dynamite and cyanide fishing). However, simply denying such residents access to the MPA is seldom a viable or desired option for control of the damaging activities. A better approach is a form of management that enables both continued local use and the safe-guarding of ecologically valuable elements. Zoning can help accomplish these aims.

In Kenya, for example, the four Marine National parks are adjacent to or surrounded by Marine National Reserves. Tourism activities (glass-bottom boats, snorkeling, diving) are permitted in the Parks, but all extractive activities are prohibited. The Reserves are open to fishing by traditional fishers using approved methods.

FIGURE I-25.

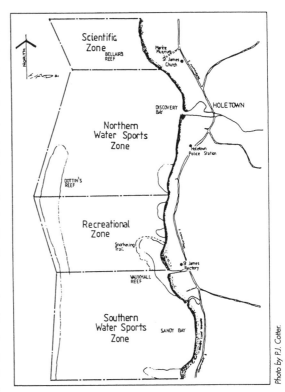

Conflicting uses are separated by a tourism-based zoning plan for the underwater park at Holetown, Barbados.

The Parks function as no-take zones for replenishment of fishing grounds in the adjacent Reserves and beyond. By way of additional compensation for their loss of access to fishing grounds now in the Parks, local fishers have *exclusive* rights to fish in the Reserves (recreational, tourist and non-resident fishing is prohibited in the Reserves and enforced by the management authority).

The following are some specific uses of zones:

– They permit selective control of activities at different sites, including both strict protection and various levels of use.

– They can establish core conservation areas (sites of high diversity, critical habitats of threatened species, and special research areas) as sanctuaries where disturbing uses are prohibited.

– They can be used to separate incompatible recreational activities (bird watching vs. hunting, or waterskiing vs. snorkeling) to increase the enjoyment and safety of the different pursuits.

– They enable damaged areas to be set aside to recover.

- They can protect breeding populations of fishes and other organisms for the natural replenishment of neighboring fishing areas and devastated or overfished areas nearby.

- They are cost-effective means of managing different uses, since manpower and maintenance needs are minimal.

In summary, an MPA may include a variety of habitats that are more suited to one type of activity than another. It is usual to zone areas so that: 1) sensitive habitats are protected from damaging activities, 2) intensive use is confined to sites that can sustain it, and 3) incompatible activities are separated to avoid conflicts.

2.6 Zoning Methodology

Management zones are identified according to the extent of multiple uses to be encouraged. Activities within these zones are planned in accordance with the objectives of the reserve as defined in the strategy document. Certain zones may require intensive management while others may require very little.

1. *Defining the core zones, or sanctuaries.* Habitats that have high conservation values, are vulnerable to disturbances, and can tolerate only a minimum of human use should be identified as "core zones" (or sanctuaries) and managed for a high level of protection. No disturbing uses should be allowed.

The first step in designing a protected area would normally be to delineate the core zones. The sizes of these zones can be most important in determining their usefulness as sanctuaries. Small areas of habitat generally have fewer species than larger ones. For example, a 300-ha coral reef of the Chagos Archipelago in the Indian Ocean contained 95 percent of all the coral genera found in the archipelago (Salm, 1980b, 1984), but smaller reefs or sections of reefs had lower coral diversity. The number of coral genera decreased as reef size decreased. Also, certain genera were found only on reefs larger than a certain minimum area that varied from genus to genus.

It is essential to delimit an area large enough to sustain a breeding population of the key species and their support systems including key habitats. This holds for conservation objectives as well as for replenishing depleted stocks. A core zone should be designated to include as great a diversity of habitats as possible, which is most easily done when there is extensive data (a rare occurrence).

The following categories of information may be helpful:

- The number of species and genera present in a given area.
- The distance of the site from human settlements.
- The levels of use and dependence by people.
- The migratory patterns of key species.
- The feeding patterns and ranges of key species.

– The distance from sources of seeds and larvae for species replenishment.

– The available prototypes, that is, successful designs from apparently similar situations elsewhere.

2. *Defining the use zones.* Sites that have special conservation value but that can tolerate different types of human uses, and that are suitable for various uses are candidates for dedicated zones in a protected area.

Different neighboring habitats are to be mapped and the protected area boundary extended to include as many of these as is practical.

The types and locations of required zones must be determined to fit the range of activities planned for the protected area (water sports, recreational fishing, commercial fishing, research, education, and special protection zones). Areas remaining among and around these use zones can be classified as general conservation zones.

3. *Defining buffer zones.* There may be need for a buffer zone wherein a more liberal, but still controlled, set of uses may be permitted. The buffer surrounds the protected area and is established to safeguard the area from encroachment and to manage processes or activities that may affect ecosystems within the protected area. Because nutrients, pollutants, and sediments can be transported over great distances by currents, buffer zones may be important in protecting MPAs from external influences.

An external buffer would be administered differently from the MPA, requiring cooperation of authorities outside the MPA, perhaps as part of a designated "Zone of Influence".

4. *Information.* It will be helpful to map any watersheds, rivers, streams, lagoons, and estuaries that influence the MPA. If these open directly into the protected area, they should be included in the buffer zone or Zone of Influence management category (see below). It will also be helpful to map currents and human settlements to identify upcurrent sources of potential stress, such as sewage outfalls, polluted and silt-laden rivers, ports, dredged shipping lanes, oil and gas exploration/production sites, and ocean dumping areas. If the protected area is to be sustained, such current-linked areas must be controlled.

The above zoning procedures delineate representative habitat types that are important to biodiversity protection and economic resource conservation. Most MPAs are comprised of core zone sanctuaries and other zones to enable the simultaneous preservation of critical sites and the continued enjoyment and sustainable economic use of appropriate areas by people.

Diagrams of core and buffer zones in Section I-5 illustrate some applications in the design of coastal and marine protected areas. In Part III, several case studies illustrate planning principles and the planning process.

2.7 Control of External Influences

Successful management of an MPA may depend on how much the influence of adjacent areas can be controlled, as discussed above and as articulated in the following situations:

– All areas that may be linked to the park or protected area should be examined carefully and monitored regularly—activities in remote areas can sometimes affect coastal or marine systems (e.g., deforestation leading to increased sedimentation, or pollution by inland industries along major rivers).

– Buffer zones with controlled multiple use can be established to control certain activities, reducing pressure on the core of the protected area.

– Mechanisms (such as management coordinating committees) can be created to correct unfavorable conditions in adjacent areas.

– Conflicting uses can be controlled if the protected area is incorporated into a general plan for coastal or marine resource uses (e.g., a Coastal Zone Management programme).

In the absence of a Coastal Zone Management (CZM) programme to assist with addressing transboundary effects from pollution (Figure I-26) and other impacts, the MPA planner or manager can attempt to establish a coordinating network composed of agencies with authority in surrounding areas of the land or sea which lie within the Zone of Influence (ZOI) of the MPA (Clark, 1998).

Figure I-26.

As examples, Spain has established a defined ZOI along parts of its coastal zone (Boelart-Suominen and Cullinan, 1994) and the Gulf Of Mannar Marine Biosphere Reserve (Tamil Nadu, India) has established a type of ZOI coordinating network (Neelakantan, K.S. 1994) to solve transboundary problems (see Part I-5).

Pollution can be a severe problem for MPAs.

2.8 Advisory Committees

Advisory committees (see Table I-1; F,2,a) may be appropriate for any given MPA. They should be established prior to or during site planning. It is less beneficial to activate them after a management plan is completed and ready for implementation. Such committees may be utilized for periodic consultation, for evaluation of the effectiveness of a plan, to review progress and approve work plans, and to authorize budgets or specific expenditures. Clearly, it is best to activate the Advisory Committee early on for advice in management and site planning.

Advisory committee members are usually appointed by the MPA administration. Some members should be selected from among the local community. In any case, they should represent the spectrum of stakeholders. They serve a useful function in keeping the local population informed of activities within the protected area, and very often they provide management with useful information and recommendations. Once advisory committee members become involved, they also help ensure support for the protected area since it tends to become "their" reserve or park. Administration and management must take great care to be candid with committee members and ensure they believe their advice is valued and is heeded (see also Section I-3).

The committee's role should be carefully planned and limited because once such committees are established it is very poor public relations to attempt to dissolve them. Committees should remain in their advisory capacity and not play an active role in management. If not they may become immersed in trivia, paralyze needed actions, lose appropriate national or international perspective, and preempt the manager's job.

Management decisions by a committee of village representatives may be required in collaborative or community-based management cases. It is important in these instances to ensure equitable representation on these committees by different subgroups of the community; e.g., women, men, elderly, poor, wealthy, fishers, farmers, and other concerned user groups. Where appropriate because of religious doctrine, females may meet separately from males. Also in caste dominated cultures, various castes may need special consideration.

Whatever the nature and composition of the advisory committee, it should be supported and empowered by adequate legislation. In Tanzania for example, the Marine Parks and Reserves Act, 1994, specifically provides for the establishment of an Advisory Committee for each marine park. The functions of the Committee as provided for in the Act are:

– To advise the Board [of Trustees] on the management and regulations of marine parks;

– To oversee the operation of marine parks;

– To consult with the Warden on technical, scientific and operational matters concerning the marine parks; and

– To propose names to the Board for the purposes of appointing a Warden.

See Box I-5 for details of Advisory Committee composition, tenure, and other details. Note that no arrangements are made specifically for women, fishers, and other groups (although women's input was arranged in the field; see Case III-25).

Box I-5. MPA Advisory Committee defined by the Tanzania Marine Parks and Reserves Act of 1994.

1. The Advisory Committee shall consist of members whose number shall not be less than nine and shall not be more than eleven including
   a. one representative of the ministry for the time being responsible for fisheries;
   b. two persons who are members of village councils whose villages are in the vicinity of or affected by a marine park;
   c. one representative of a local authority from an area containing all or part of a marine park;
   d. two representatives from these business entities:
      • a private commercial concern currently operating in the fish or marine products industry in the vicinity of the marine park;
      • a private commercial concern currently operating in the tourism industry in the vicinity of the marine park or reserve;
   e. an officer dealing with natural resources at a district level of the district which includes at least part of the marine park;
   f. two representatives from among the following institutions and organizations-
      • a scientific institution with expertise in the field of marine conservation;
      • non-profit organizations concerned with marine conservation;
   g. one representative of the regional authority with jurisdiction over the area of the marine park; and
   h. one member to be appointed by the Director.
2. The members of the Advisory Committee shall select from among their number, a chairman and a vice-chairman who shall hold office for three years respectively unless otherwise their membership is terminated, and shall be eligible for re-election.
3. Members of the Advisory Committee shall hold office for three years and unless their membership is otherwise terminated due to misconduct or any other reason, they shall be eligible for re-election.

2.9 Physical Management Strategy

In the MPA Site Management Plan, the discussion on resources and existing uses (see Table I-1; B, C) should provide concise descriptions of area resources and past and present uses and their effects. This material should be limited to that relevant to management for evaluating conservation values, needs, and alternatives or for making user impact analyses. The bulk of data collected during the planning phase can be placed in appendices or made available in a separate report.

The discussion on threats and their management implications (Table I-1, E) considers resource vulnerability in the face of existing and potential exploitation. Compatible and incompatible uses are identified and management solutions or mitigating measures for problems are briefly outlined (e.g., in the sections on boundaries and zoning, new regulations, the resources studies plan, and the interpretive plan).

Living resources are usually conserved by regulatory controls or by habitat manipulations. Uses can be controlled also by concessions and permits for users. Fish stocks are largely managed by harvest controls; that is, the regulation of fishing such as gear limitations, area closures, or catch limits. Physical management techniques employed in the MPA could include managed flooding to maintain wetland habitat, mangrove planting, restoring eroded sand dunes or cliffs, or even rebuilding of some special coral reefs.

Whenever possible, techniques should be used that alter nature the least. To ensure that natural processes are left alone is in itself a management technique. To work with nature is another. This is especially important in the marine environment, where people still depend largely on natural productivity to sustain resources. This applies in principle to both extractive uses (e.g., recognizing exclusive fishing rights for local people, in the case of fisheries) and non extractive uses (e.g., permitting charter operations to transport limited numbers of tourists into protected areas as at Buck Island, U.S. Virgin Islands). Another example is beach restoration and the safeguarding of shorefront property using natural means such as native plants to stabilize dunes, which can be more effective and sustainable in achieving long-term shore stability than concrete and stone engineering works.

The suggested resource management strategy (Table I-1; F,2,f) should detail specific management activities required to maintain or restore the value of different resources. Typical activities might include any of the following:

- Restoring a damaged habitat, as through replanting dunes;
- clearing blocked mangrove creeks;
- closing sections of the MPA to enable natural recovery;
- special stewardship of vulnerable resources, as by establishing turtle hatcheries; or
- controlling extractive activities, as through limiting catches of fish species or the taking of shellfish (Figure I-27).

FIGURE I-27.

Photo by R. Salm.

Living specimens of the giant clam *(Tridacna gigas)* have been eliminated from the reefs of the Seribu Archipelago in Indonesia. The shells of dead clams in the fishermen's craft have been dug from the reef flats and are on their way to Jakarta to be turned into flooring tiles. T. gigas is an example of a lost resource and a species threatened with extinction. Its large size and location on the reef flat render it easy to find and collect.

The impact of damaging uses can be mitigated by providing such facilities as fixed boat moorings, docks, and walkways. Interpretive programmes can help users understand why limiting and controlling uses are essential management tools (Figure I-28). Continual monitoring of the effects of use is required for corrective measures.

FIGURE I-28.

Controlled tourism can be accommodated in coral reef and other special areas without significant impacts on the resource if properly controlled. A ranger at Florida Keys National Marine Sanctuary in Florida offers educational materials to divers.

2.10 Information Base

Site planning requires a variety of information. The following are examples:

1. The types and locations of valuable habitats and their characteristics such as species diversity, size, degree of naturalness, uniqueness, and representativeness, and degree of species dependence on them.

2. The types, locations, and amounts of human use (recreational, commercial, subsistence activities, etc), their effects on the biota and habitats of the site, the degree of dependence of local inhabitants on these uses, and possible alternatives for activities that degrade habitats and deplete species stocks below sustainable levels.

3. The present and potential threats to the site's resources from activities outside the immediate area of concern in the Zone of Influence.

Effective protected area management will depend greatly on specific data generated from research, monitoring, and social and environmental assessment (Table I-1; F,2,e). A site-specific plan should first identify critical data gaps (i.e., data necessary for management decisions). For example, reef fish populations may be at very low levels, and the manager may suspect the cause to be fishing pressure. Rather than arbitrarily prohibiting fishing without adequate data, the social and resource studies plan would identify the information needed and suggest a study designed to obtain it (Figure I-29). Such a study would focus on determining who depends on which products from the MPA through monitoring fishing activities (pressure points, activity levels, gear types, size and species of catch, economics). Analysis of the data should enable the manager to propose and support any necessary controls on fishing or actions to spread the fishing pressure or direct it into alternative pursuits (e.g., from reef fishes to pelagics or from fishing to farming seaweed). It may be valuable to temporarily close a portion of the study area to fishing and monitor the recovery of reef fish populations and safeguard breeding stocks.

The social and resource studies plan should rank the data gaps and studies needed in accordance with management information priorities. It should be emphasized that in many cases the managing agency will not be able to fund all of the needed studies. It will fund those it can and seek other funding sources for the remainder. One inexpensive way to obtain what is usually good data is to interest graduate students in working on studies pertinent to both their needs and those of the protected area manager by paying their out-of-pocket expenses. A second method is to provide small grants to university professors to undertake small projects needed by managers. Also, once researchers have worked in an area, they are more likely to spend other research money at the site, which would generate additional data of use to the manager. But the manager must understand the academic nature of researchers and the problems of getting them to focus on practical issues of direct value to managers.

FIGURE I-29.

The stakeholders are being consulted as part of a government plan to create a marine protected area in Anse La Raye and Canaries in St.Lucia.

Other management points that might be studied include the carrying capacity for particular activities, the adequacy of buffer zones, and the status of resources. Finally, the plan should specify mechanisms for the manager to coordinate and follow other relevant research, review proposals and permit requests, stimulate information exchange, and contribute new data to the management and interpretive plans.

2.11 Carrying Capacity

It is clear that resources are finite and cannot resist unlimited use. Already, in the late 1990s, many coral reefs are degraded, fisheries depleted, and beaches eroded away. The idea that there *is a limit*—a "carrying capacity" for human use—has to be embraced to ensure that natural resources are not destroyed. MPA managers may ask themselves, "How much use can this area stand?" Many researchers have addressed this puzzle trying to find a technical answer, but success has been limited. The answer usually lies in a civil and political process backed by data.

Carrying capacity analysis was created (in the 1960s) as a method of prescribing the limits to development using numerical, computerized, calculation with cold objectivity. It has not achieved much success in influencing government policy because of the complexity of the parameters and because politicians, managers, and administrators are reluctant to have their judgement preempted by a computer. Nevertheless, a non-prescriptive and more qualitative and participative concept of carrying capacity has been useful in influencing control of development, particularly tourism (Clark, 1991b).

With carrying capacity, as with other biological analogies, human nature complicates the procedure for estimating limits (Chua, *et al.*, 1992). Some of the key components—such as tourist or user satisfaction—change when the users themselves or their preferences shift. Therefore, in spite of simulation models, the actual carrying capacity limit—in numbers of users or any other parameter—may be a judgement call based upon the level of change that can be accepted (Clark, 1991b). But an analytic approach conditioned by semi-subjective factors can be useful (Part III, Case No. 5).

2.12 Mapping

It is expeditious to organize the database so that essential information can be mapped and also to display as many categories of data as possible on maps, using approaches ranging from simple handwork to complex GIS technology. The first step in information gathering should be preparation of good base maps at appropriate scales. For example, Goeghegan *et al.* (1984) state: "It has been found time and again that perhaps the most useful way for the environmental planner to discover trends, conflicts, and problem areas that can otherwise be easily overlooked, is by mapping information". Photographs and maps are easily read, interpreted, and transcend language and cultural barriers to communication and analysis.

Maps found most useful will be at a scale of 1:50,000 or larger. But sometimes maps at 1:10,000 are needed for specific studies. In either case, it is more effective if the gathering of information is based on objectives set in advance. These objectives may reflect areas of known management concern, or suspected resource importance or sensitivity.

Most modern large-scale mapping (to show considerable detail within small areas) now relies in part on aerial photography. Aerial photographs can be used to pre-plan field surveys and sampling strategies to reduce cost, improve efficiency, and ensure adequate sampling of all relevant habitats and environments.

"Overlay mapping" is simple and especially useful in MPA programmes, whereby multiple theme maps are used to spatially analyze environmental components, to derive new parameters, or to select "least impact" alternatives. The method was originated by Ian McHarg (1969) as portrayed in his classic, *Design With Nature*.

In this technique, a typical base map is prepared at an appropriate scale and transparent overlay maps are prepared for each of the environmental components or attributes to be compared or analyzed (Classen, 1989). For example, transparent maps of depth, habitats, bottom types, etc can be overlaid and placed on the base map in order to identify areas where nature protection coincides with heavy uses—housing, mining, fishing, etc. Any other mapable information could also be overlain, such as, dive spots, beach erosion susceptibility, or pollutant discharge (Figure I-30).

One can add more environmental components and/or development constraints/attributes as required (e.g., critical habitat, endangered or rare plant communities, historic buildings) until satisfied that all essential aspects have been covered and an optimum scheme (or set of alternatives) has been identified to reduce use conflicts (Classen, 1989).

The same approach could be used to combine maps of shellfish beds, wetlands, and endangered species habitats into a single map of sensitive biological resources (Sorenson and McCreary, 1990). The resulting maps give planners and managers tools to guide the type and intensity of uses to be permitted or denied.

FIGURE I-30.

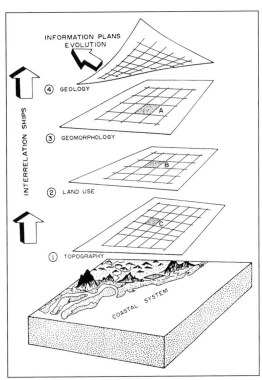

Overlay mapping can be done with GIS technology or manually, employing transparent sheets.
Source: Principles and Concepts of a Coastal Management Methodology. University of Sao Paulo, Brazil (1989).

2.13 Interpretation

MPA programmes address the need to manage human activities that degrade the environment or deplete species stocks. Gaining the cooperation of people (local residents, students, and visitors) through interpretation is an important management tool in this endeavor (Table I-1; F,2,g). Interpretation—explanation of the MPAs resources and functions and management issues and needs—enhances public awareness, understanding, and appreciation of different marine resources and of the need to conserve them. An effective interpretive plan often decreases the need for policing the protected area and reduces the cost of management because when people understand the reasons for management they more willingly comply with regulations (Figure I-31).

MPA interpretation programmes are based on circumstances specific to the site. In designing the programme, primary consideration should be given to how the MPA site can be maximally used without depleting its resources. Thought should be given to whether the resources are most suitable for direct visitor involvement —guided activities in or under the water on in the shorelands—or for indirect involvement—through remote television, glass bottom boats, lectures, slide shows, posters, and movies.

FIGURE I-31.

Providing clear instructions to visitors is an important part of MPA interpretation programmes, as here at Xel-Ha, Quintana Roo, Mexico.

Nature interpretation can communicate the complexities of issues facing the MPA manager, such as user conflicts and the effects of pollution. Interpretation methods that translate research into information that is understandable to the public may be particularly useful.

2.14 Public Support

The success of conservation management very often depends on local public support. Such public support, which can be regarded as a sign of understanding conservation objectives, leads to adherence to the protected area rules by the local population. Personnel constraints will also often require the help of volunteers. Local public support can be secured by sharing benefits with the local people. Some aspects of community participation are:

– Exclusive user or access rights to particular resources can be one of the strongest incentives to secure local public support, responsibility for specific management activities and compliance with regulations.

– Local communities can be given exclusive rights to certain types of use through appropriate zoning and through issuing permits for these uses only to community residents.

– Once a protected area has been established, local communities that have traditionally managed their marine resources for sustained use can be given responsibility for continued resource management under the general supervision of the conservation authority.

- In local communities with traditional resource management practices, the village heads may by definition become law enforcement officers.

- Job opportunities can be created for local people, both directly and indirectly, in the protected area and in related facilities and services.

- Local user groups can help carry out surveys and monitoring under the supervision of protected area personnel.

- Local tourist guides can be trained as park interpreters (Part III, Case No. 16).

Trained extension or social workers can help influence people's attitudes to conservation and marine park development. They can work inconspicuously, identifying local opinion leaders and overcoming opposition to conservation management. But local communities will want a piece of the action not just fast talk from the MPA agency. The public must be honestly consulted and not just patronized, placated and propagandized.

2.15 Public Awareness

Awareness plays a major role in public support and in the general success of conservation. *General* conservation awareness is needed among all stakeholders—communities, managers, politicians, administrators, and the private sector. The most important goal is to explain, through public information and education, the long-term, sustainable benefits that conservation can provide (Figure I-32). Environmental education aims to provide the community with information and a conservation ethic so that its members can make informed decisions about the use of their resources. Honest efforts to inform the public are essential; education should not be used just as propaganda to promote MPA programmes.

The first step in designing a *specific* education programme is to identify the main audience; for example, artisanal fishermen, dive operators, tourists, hotel owners, port directors, and/or politicians. In educating any group of stakeholders, it is important to use familiar language and concepts.

A particularly important function of an awareness programme is to inform stakeholders what the management authority can and cannot do. In parts of East Africa, for example, community programmes that

FIGURE I-32.

Photo by John Clark.

On-site discussion about MPAs in St. Lucia.

experimented with benefits sharing led stakeholders to expect far too much material benefit from management authorities, often seeing them only as a source of funds and technical expertise. These expectations were unrealistic; they left some stakeholders feeling let down by the authorities and antagonistic toward them.

A multifaceted approach, combining printed materials, audio-visual presentations, and face-to-face interaction is probably the best way to start a *specific* education programme. For a *general* education programme, a variety of additional options can be employed: mass media (press, television, radio), fixed exhibits, tours, training workshops, the sale of promotional items such as T-shirts, and informal recreational activities with an educational focus.

2.16 The MPA Manager

As an MPA professional, you become an advocate of good conservation practice based on accurate technical input. Clarity and specificity of programme elements are needed to convince policy makers to make a strong commitment to the MPA. This effort should continue through all stages of development and management.

Through the various stages of planning, the manager is often faced with a shortage of funds or qualified personnel. Sometimes there will be an inadequate legal basis for MPA management or too little detail in the Management Plan for the site. The site manager inherits these deficient products, but nonetheless is expected to manage the site effectively, whether or not the information, materials, and support are adequate.

Regardless of your past experience, as an MPA manager you will become a planner of sorts too. The planner's role is to deal with great complexity and reduce it to simple concepts and programmes that are politically and administratively viable. Typical administrators, engineers, politicians, and most economic planners are not usually well informed about the sea and the seacoast, consequently they will depend on your special expertise.

The MPA manager will need to keep a database and to update it. All modern data handling facilities are electronic. With the advent of reliable low-cost computer systems, computer storage and analysis of geographically oriented databases are now widely available. These computerized GIS databases are now available on PCs (personal computers) and simple workstations, putting the equipment within the budget of many agencies (see Section I-5).

The site manager is responsible for achieving management objectives through the efficient use of funds, staff, and equipment. He or she must participate in evaluating conservation needs, in identifying visitor use conflicts, in defining realistic management objectives, in requesting adequate budgets and equipment, and in selecting suitable staff.

The role of the government should be to fulfill commitments to safeguard both the national and the global heritage. However, governments often fail to show the long-term thinking needed to meet this obligation. Thus, more often than not, MPA managers will have to lobby intensely to obtain sufficient funds. Furthermore, trained coastal and marine protected area managers are rarely available—managing coastal and marine protected areas is a developing, challenging, and exciting field.

2.17 Administration

A section of the management plan describes how the protected area will be administered (Table I-1; F,3). The administrative plan should be carefully coordinated with management goals and objectives for the site to ensure that these can be attained within specified periods. The administration should develop over the life of the management plan. Even when money is no object, two or three years are generally required to reach optimal operation. The first year of operating marine protected areas has sometimes been a one-person effort. When this is the case, it should be made clear that very limited progress can be made.

Adequate personnel are necessary to perform the variety of functions of creating and managing the MPA site, particularly:

– To interpret relevant policies and objectives

– To direct the management of the MPA

– To prepare updated management plans

– To assess logistical requirements

– To undertake field operations, including surveillance and maintenance

– To perform activities related to research, monitoring, visitor use, education, and training

The size of the site management staff depends on circumstances of the particular MPA (see Case Histories in Part III for examples). Staff should be well trained for their responsibilities, so they can carry out their tasks effectively. Managing protected areas effectively calls for an understanding of the resource being protected, an ability to communicate this to local people and visitors, and competence in many other specialized areas.

2.18 Logistics

Certain minimum equipment is needed to ensure proper protection of an area. The equipment needed for any MPA is usually specific for that particular site—binoculars, boats, radios, vehicles, computers, or etc.

Marking marine protected area boundaries in the sea is usually difficult and expensive to do and to maintain and is often unnecessary. Installing buoys may be expensive and difficult. These buoys require regular and costly maintenance and vigilant surveillance against theft. In such cases, the site's boundary can be described by the distance from some discernible feature (beach or reef crest) to control encroachment and poaching. Colour-coded buoys can be used to mark navigation problems (e.g., dangerous reefs) and identify boat channels. Mooring buoys are useful to demarcate snorkeling and diving sites and to prevent anchor damage (Figure I-33).

In tourist zones, however, strategically placed markers, signs, or buoys can contribute to enforcement by encouraging visitors to follow trails and reminding them of zoning regulations. Sign boards above water are often essential (turtle nesting beaches, bird nesting or roosting colonies, dangerous marshes, and vulnerable sand dunes) to which the public would normally have ready access. They remind people of entry restrictions, inform people of behavior codes, carry educational information, and warn people of potential hazards (Figure I-34). It may be necessary to fence off particularly sensitive habitats to discourage public entry.

FIGURE I-33.

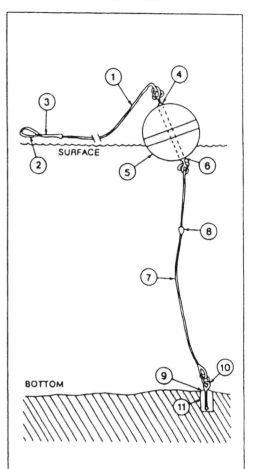

1) 15 Fl. 3/4" Polypropeline Line
2) 2' x 7/8" Rubber hose (chafing protection)
3) Eye Slice
4) 3/4" PVC Pipe through buoy with reducing bushing on ends. 3/4" line with eye splice at both ends put through pipe.
5) BUOY: 18" Diameter white polyethylene plastic with blue stripe. Buoy filled with polyurethane foam.
6) Short piece split hose for protection.
7) 3/4" polypropelene line 10ft. longer than depth of water.
8) 1/2 lb. lead weight to keep extra scope from floating to surface.
9) 18" x 4" Core into bedrock filled with concrete (or concrete block).
10) Eye splice with rubber hose shackled to eyebolt.
11) 18" x 3/4" stainless eyebolt.

FIGURE I-34.

A sign warns people of stinging jellyfish in Townsville, Australia.

Photo by Erkki Siirila.

2.19 Surveillance and Enforcement

An enforcement programme (Table I-1; F,4) is especially important in the early stages of establishing a protected area, before the interpretive programme begins to take effect. Depending on the circumstances of each site and each country, reinforcement officers should initially employ the "soft glove" approach if possible, with explanations and warnings for first offenses. The surveillance and enforcement section of the management plan should describe (in phases if appropriate) the enforcement approach and the number of rangers. Of course, specific areas and timing of patrols should not be revealed. This section should also contain a statement of enforcement policy.

Legislation must be followed by sensitive measures to ensure that its provisions are carried out. The experience of the Gulf of Mannar Marine National Park is a case in point (Box I-6). Some general guidelines are given below (adapted from Kelleher and van't Hof, 1982).

Box I-6. Enforcement in the Gulf of Mannar National Park

The coral formations in the Gulf of Mannar (Tamil Nadu, India) were fast deteriorating due to human disturbance, especially in the four islands of the Chidambaranar District coast. Before the Forest Department of Tamil Nadu took charge of the islands now within the Gulf of Mannar Marine National Park, illicit removal of corals was rampant. The Forest Department made earnest efforts to enforce laws against the illicit removal of corals, with good effect as shown below; from the violations, fines of 183,000 rupees (US$ 6,100) were collected:

Period	Cases Booked		Number Accused	
	Tuticorin	Mandapam	Tuticorin	Mandapam
Dec. 91 to March 9	4	2	111	2
April 92 to March 93	4	7	109	8
April 93 to September 93	40	–	56	–

Source: Neelakantan, K.S. 1994.

Sharing the burden of enforcement with coastal communities can be effective in controlling miscreants through social pressure. Local-level laws (bylaws) developed by the communities are more likely to be respected as they result directly from within the community in response to a perceived need, rather than being imposed from above.

Major measures in compliance should be public education and enlisting the help of user groups in management. Generally, more indirect, subtle, and less regimenting measures should be employed before police actions and sanctions. Regardless of public support, regulations must still provide adequately for enforcement by protected area staff as well as for suitable penalties.

MPA staff need to be carefully trained to carry out law enforcement functions effectively but without unnecessary public antagonism. Consistent guidelines should be developed for staff charged with enforcement on how to act depending on the type of offence encountered (e.g., when arrest would follow without exception and when a warning is sufficient). In many cases, rotating enforcement officers away from their home communities may be necessary to maintain consistent enforcement standards.

Public attention can be drawn to regulations through local news media, community leaders, brochures, and visitor information centers. Where MPAs are new, community suspicion of management may be high. It is therefore especially important that the first enforcement exercise in the MPA be conducted by the highest professional standards. The first arrest (or other enforcement effort) will leave a lasting impression on the community and must be done to elicit respect, not resentment or animosity.

The autonomy of customary leaders in determining and carrying out enforcement by whatever means should be preserved where this contributes to the objectives of the protected area. But customary law is generally only respected by members of the community to which it applies and needs to be backed up by national legislation and enforcement by government officers when challenged by outsiders. Honorary citizen officers can be used to detect and counsel offenders (but not to carry out legal enforcement). These officers should be trained regarding rights, risks, and proper procedures, and when they detect and report offences they should be fully supported through official means so that offenders are brought to justice.

An important component of enforcement in some countries is inspection of boats, cars, and bags. A system of inspection can lead to marked improvements in compliance with regulations. There can be value in authorizing coast guard, navy, or fisheries officers to enforce the protected area regulations (Figure I-35). They often have more equipment than the MPA authority, they are often better trained in law enforcement procedures, and have the authority to make arrests. Park staff will then not be regarded solely as law-enforcement officers and can devote more time to the public relations and education aspects of their job.

The sophistication of the equipment required for surveillance will depend on the types of incursions likely to be made into the reserve and the help that can be obtained from other law enforcing authorities.

FIGURE I-35.

Ranger is assisted by coast guard officer in patrolling the Key Largo National Marine Sanctuary, Florida, USA.

Photo courtesy of U.S. National Oceanic and Atmospheric Administration.

2.20 Monitoring and Evaluation

Evaluation (Table 1; F,5) should be continuous and should begin with the start of management implementation, if not before. It is the basis for managers' daily decisions and is one of the reasons that plans should be flexible enough to enable necessary shifts in direction. In most instances a formal evaluation mechanism or procedure is desirable. One approach is to require the Advisory Committee to conduct a major review of the effectiveness of the plan at the end of its lifetime and to recommend any needed revisions of management procedures. Brief evaluations can be conducted at the end of each year if circumstances warrant them (e.g., where budget proposals have to be submitted annually). In general, the more detailed the plan, the more it will need revision.

Evaluation by an external team can provide useful insights to on-site staff who may be too close to the problems or reluctant to acknowledge them; too preoccupied with day-to-day issues and activities; or too set in their ways to recognize the need for change and improvements. These external teams can also bring in the experiences from other areas to provide fresh perspectives on how to overcome obstacles and resolve issues.

In addition to involving the public, the management agency may wish to establish an evaluation team of managers from other protected areas for a more technical and objective review of management effectiveness. Whatever the mechanisms utilized, evaluation and revision are essential to a responsive management system.

2.21 Budget and Business Plan

Adequate resources for investment and annual costs (Table I-1; F,3,d) must be made available on time for the proper management of protected areas over the long term. Though some funds may be raised locally through fees and other devices, it has usually been necessary to get most support from government. Developing countries have often been successful in seeking international donor assistance to meet the costs of protected area management and to set up systems designed to achieve self-financing.

Providing incentives for the private sector, NGOs and communities to share in the burden of management through effective partnerships is one way to reduce dependence on revenue subsidies for park management. Several of the MPA Case Histories in Part III speak of experience in cost recovery through collection of user fees.

The budget will need to be divided into start-up capital costs and recurrent expenses for running of the MPA. Capital expenses cover such one-time costs for buildings, other infrastructure, office and field equipment, and recruitment and/or relocation of personnel. The recurrent budget covers the costs of wages, insurance and other staff benefits, services and utilities, office and vehicle (including boats) running and maintenance, and project activities. These costs are linked directly to the annual operational or work plans.

The business plan takes a long-term view and aims to generate revenues or in kind contributions and services to support the running of the MPA. Its aim should be to achieve financial self-sufficiency, or close to it, for the MPA by reducing dependence on annual subsidies. Revenues collected through this plan should be placed in a special account or established as a trust fund that is managed by an independent board comprising representatives of different stakeholder groups.

Community Engagement

In the past decade it has become obvious that coastal resources conservation benefits from decentralization of authority. This approach has been variously termed "community based management", "joint management", "the partnership", "collaborative management", or "co-management". The approach, whatever its title, succeeds because empowering communities always works better than commanding them (Clark, 1998). Collaborative management requires networking, forging linkages to community leaders, local law enforcement officers, private business, and national agencies like tourist authorities and environmental and fishery agencies.

3.1 Participation

Any move toward a democratic approach to implementing MPAs must itself be commended, but there are more than socio-political advantages to be gained. Most importantly, where a community has management responsibility, there is a good chance that more care will be exercised in the use of resources. For example, the quantity of fish or shellfish removed will be controlled, abstinence may be practiced during spawning periods, and less destructive fishing methods may be used. Also there may be a greater willingness to curb pollution and conserve habitats.

MPA managers have come to realize over the fifteen years since this book was first written that coastal communities should be closely involved with planning and management of MPAs. Local people are not now so easily displaced and disenfranchised by regional or central governments in the creation of protected areas nor marginalized in the planning process.

Community participation may be perceived by some environmental interests to entail compromising conservation objectives to achieve public support. On the contrary, where an area of high conservation value and a coastal community coexist, there are patterns of resource use or traditions that could form the basis for cost-effective conservation action through the community to achieve both conservation and community objectives. If, on the other hand, patterns of resource use are unsustainable and resource depletion is the result, the communities will be well aware of the problem and could welcome conservation interventions that bring them measurable benefits, again achieving both conservation and community objectives.

Community participation has many different interpretations and applications, ranging from just informing communities to encouraging full partnership in resource assessments, planning and management. Beaumont (1997) reviews international perceptions of and approaches to community participation in marine protected area establishment and management, providing descriptions of these and some specific examples (Box I-7).

The effectiveness of traditional, or customary conservation at the community level, has been recognized in studies in Nova Scotia (Canada), Brazil, Palau, the Solomon Islands, and elsewhere. However, this can be fully successful only where the communities have *exclusive rights* to resource areas they customarily use.

For detailed descriptions of participatory methods, principles and tools see Borrini-Feyerabend (1997a, b), Davis-Case (1989), Davis-Case *et al.* (1990), Odour-Noah *et al.* (1992), Pretty *et al.* (1995), and World Bank (1996). White *et al.* (1994) provide a range of case studies on collaborative and community-based management approaches for coral reefs.

3.2 Understanding the Community

It is important to understand the structure of communities, and the concerns and feelings of security of different groups and individuals for effective collaboration. The participatory rural appraisal, PRA, process is useful in this regard. Participatory surveys are a good way to identify all stakeholders and learn of their concerns. Some key considerations are listed below.

– Reorientation of management authority staff is important in enabling them to build rapport with communities. Training management authority staff in participatory rural appraisal so that they can conduct socioeconomic studies is a very useful step in improving relations between them and the community. By learning from and with villagers, they develop respect for the knowledge of the villagers who will in turn be encouraged that management authority staff want to listen and learn from them.

– Participatory socioeconomic and resource assessments at the beginning of site identification and planning form a good foundation for starting work with a particular community (Figure I-36). This helps people to clarify the critical issues and identify their priorities.

Box I-7. Types of participatory approaches

Persuasion or passive participation: Public involvement techniques are used to change attitudes without raising expectations of public participation in the planning and decision-making process. This is the old type approach that planners and managers are moving away from toward one of those listed below.

Participation through consultation: User-groups provide input to the government agency on proposals for a conservation area, or on management plans for the area. External agents define the problems and information gathering processes. Such consultative process does not concede any share in decision making, and professionals are under no obligation to utilize the information that has been gathered. This was the approach taken until recently by the Great Barrier Reef Marine Park Authority which offered little opportunity for indigenous people to provide information, and none to participate in decision making. This too is fast becoming an outdated approach.

Participation for material incentives: People participate by contributing resources, for example labour, in return for food, cash or other material incentives. People have no stake in prolonging the technologies or practices when the incentives come to an end. This is not a sustainable approach and does not lead to effective partnership in marine protected area management.

Functional participation: Participation is seen by external agencies as a means to achieve project goals, such as reducing resistance to the establishment of a park. People may participate by forming groups to meet predetermined objectives related to the project. Such involvement may be interactive and involve shared decision-making, but tends to arise only after external agents have already made major decisions. In the Mafia Island Marine Park in Tanzania local communities participate through Village Liaison Committees which have roles in maintaining equipment allocated to each village, recording meetings and information relevant to each village, and providing information concerning resource use and access. However, they have no power in decision making.

Interactive participation: People participate in joint analysis, development of action plans and formation of local institutions. Participation is seen as a right, not merely as a means to achieve project goals. The process involves participatory methods that yield the perspectives of different community groups, structured learning processes and problem solving approaches. As groups take control of local decisions and determine how available resources are used, so they have a stake in maintaining structures or practices. Good examples of this approach are provided for Tanga in Tanzania (Makoloweka *et al.*, 1996) and San Salvador Island in the Philippines (Christie & White, 1994). In both cases village level committees have been established to work with government in facilitating partnership between local people and government for area management, including enforcement.

Self-mobilization: People take initiatives independently of external institutions. Pacific islanders probably have the longest tradition of community management of marine resources, including area protection, through self-mobilization. Examples of erosion of traditional resource management caused by commercialization exist in the Maluku Islands of Indonesia, where they are being revived as more interactive management systems by government (Zerner, 1994a, b).

Source: Modified from Beaumont (1997) and IIED (1994).

– Participatory surveys provide a means to fully involve interest groups. Survey is the initial stage of the planning process. Community members who participate in surveys can advise other users and village committees on resource status during the planning process.

FIGURE I-36.

An extension officer talks with villagers who are part of the Tanga Coastal Management Project in Tanzania. The project has resulted in several protected areas based on issue identification and priorities set by the villagers.

Photo by Erkki Siirila.

– The structure of any community can be quite complex, and can be masked by those whose livelihood is more secure as they may have more time to participate in meetings, or may be more confident to speak out. The priority issues of those who are very poor may differ from those who are better off. The use of wealth ranking and poverty profiling can help identify the poorest and their priorities.

– Socioeconomic and resource assessments need to be gender sensitive and recognize that the resource uses and activities of men and women differ, as do their access to and control over resources, and their abilities and vulnerabilities. Assessments should profile these differences. Gender disaggregated data will enable the impact of actions on both men and women to be monitored.

– Rapid assessments produce critical and sufficient information for management, but require calibration with long term studies.

– In using rapid assessment techniques it is necessary to validate findings by "triangulation", i.e., using different methods to corroborate findings. Secondary sources of information, statistics and direct observations are very useful and are independent of villager perceptions.

– Management issues identified at community level do not differ markedly from those given by resource managers. Consequently, community-perceived issues, their causes and solutions can be used to define overall objectives, results and activities for management action planning.

– Semi-structured interviews, focus group discussions, participatory mapping, and ranking are all useful tools. It is necessary to continuously monitor and modify these tools during assessments to verify that they are yielding the required information.

– Selecting useful socioeconomic and biophysical indicators, which can be reliably measured at a later stage, is difficult. To be really useful, indicators need to be closely linked to the objectives of management.

– Community boundaries often correspond to resource (forest or reef) use boundaries. Therefore, conflicts with community boundaries need to be resolved early when attempting to establish protected area management responsibilities.

3.3 Lessons from Tanga

In the Tanga Region of Tanzania, coral reefs have often deteriorated from among the finest in Tanzania in 1968 (Ray, 1968) to wastelands of broken coral with few fishes. Overfishing accompanied by the use of increasingly destructive fishing methods (including dynamite) destroyed these reefs and left fishers increasingly desperate. The fishers knew the problem, but were reluctant to address it because of their need for food and income, no matter how little, on a daily basis. Shifting to alternative livelihoods carries too large a burden of risk for these people whose needs are immediate and who live at or below the poverty level (Part III, Cases 24 and 25).

A programme to address the needs of the local people as well as the environment was designed and implemented with the assistance of IUCN at the request of local government authorities (Makoloweka & Shurcliff, 1997). Once the government extension workers and communities had overcome their mutual suspicions and perceptions, and were able to work effectively together, the communities demonstrated a willingness and capacity to invest time and effort into dealing with difficult issues of enforcement and management.

The villagers have developed their own management plans for areas of sea and mangrove that include restrictions on harvest and closure of certain areas to establish community-based protected areas. In return these areas and the related bylaws have been officially recognized and gazetted by local and central government, thereby securing exclusive access for members of the community implementing management according to prescriptions they have imposed upon themselves. This concept of user or access rights in return for management responsibility is a strong incentive for community participation in protected area management. In most respects, the Tanga experience mirrors the Orion (Philippines) experience reported by van Mulekom (1999) and the following concepts apply generally to both projects.

A participatory approach to management of marine and coastal resources may require reducing the negative perceptions held by communities of management authorities and *vice versa*. The communities may view the management authority staff as tax collectors, police, useless, corrupt and indolent; while the management authority officers may view the communities as self-indulgent, ignorant and greedy. It takes time to change these perceptions and create a good relationship of mutual trust and collaboration. Creating this relationship in Tanga, Tanzania, took eighteen months and was time well invested. The need to build a realistic time frame for this activity is a major lesson learned.

Other lessons learned through the Tanga programme concerning participatory issue identification, assessment of resource use and management structures, and formulation of action plans and management agreements are listed below:

- *Start small, with only a few priority issues that stakeholders consider most important.* Learn to be effective on one or a few matters before trying to deal with every important issue, or all aspects of a single issue. The villagers themselves should have a major role in selecting priority issues.

- *Start with listening.* Who and where are the resource users (defined as those who are causing the problem, affected by it, or part of the solution), what are they doing, what do they want to achieve. This is fundamental to building effective partnerships.

- *Work to achieve an effective partnership with the community.* They have important roles to play. For example, villagers can effectively carry out routine patrols and inspections of gear, when most resource users come from that community only. Management officers may be needed when more than just a few resource users come from outside a community.

- *Use participatory approaches throughout, including resource assessments, issue identification, priority actions, decision-making.* Participatory approaches between the management authority and communities are an effective way of listening and building the partnerships discussed above. In this way, knowledge from resource users and managers is used to help identify issues and possible feasible actions.

- *Verify conclusions reached through participatory appraisals by feedback to resource users and independent observation and measurement.* Both approaches are needed at the same time.

- *Use transparent processes and decision-making throughout and at every level of programme activities, including routine administration as well as policy.* This approach is fundamental to improving management and community institutions.

- *Take an action-learning approach.* Test to see if proposed actions will work before turning them into policy or strategies. New ways of dealing with the issues are needed, since existing methods are obviously not working, and collaborative management approaches are new and yet to be shown to be effective.

- *Monitor all actions to test if they are having the desired outcome, or unexpected outcomes on both the environment, species and people's well being.* This is an important tenet of action-learning. If not sure of the best solutions, test them. Regular monitoring may show up mistakes before too much time and effort is spent on pursuing them.

- *Assume a pyramid of actions, whereby local people can take most actions without assistance from government or outside experts or donors.* There are fewer actions that require assistance, and fewer still that need to be done by outside experts. This approach will improve empowerment and local institutions. It assumes that funding from local and central government for protected area management is limited in the foreseeable future—a stark reality in most developing countries. While surveys are useful, even more challenging, however, is securing the participation of these stakeholders in project activities.

- *Deal with both the environment and people's well being.* Especially deal with those aspects of people's well being affected by the state of environment and its resources. This is an important policy imperative of central government and donors. It addresses the fundamental motivation for people's use of coastal resources.

- *Strengthen capacity of the management authority and in the community.* Working with only one or the other will not give satisfactory results.

The phasing of protected area planning into the listening-piloting-demonstrating-mainstreaming cycle (Piccotto & Weaving, 1994) is an effective means to constructively engage communities and facilitate their interactive participation. Thinking the planning/management process through and presenting it in this four-cycle approach greatly improves the focus, execution and evolution of activities, and helps to preempt some of the potential misunderstandings between the major partners (community, private sector, management authority and other concerned government agencies). An actual example of the application of this approach over three funding phases in Tanga, Tanzania, with the duration of each phase is listed below.

First Phase (July 1994 to June 1997)—understanding the issues and testing solutions.

1. LISTENING to ensure that the primary issues and actions are those of the beneficiaries themselves—in this case, the coastal resource users and managers. Listening starts from the assumption that we don't know all the answers at the start:

   – socioeconomic assessments
   – involving a wider range of players within affected communities (women, men, elders, fishers, farmers, wealthy, poor)
   – identify priority issues
   – resource assessments
   – improved relationship between government and other stakeholders
   – concept of community-based management of resources and protected areas (access/ownership rights in return for management responsibility) promoted at all levels of government.

2. PILOTING to test how well proposed actions work, and to try alternatives. The following activities implemented in three pilot villages:

   – coral reef management alternatives tested

- control of dynamite and other destructive fisheries implemented
- alternative uses/income generation option trials undertaken
- restoration of reefs and mangroves started
- woodlots for firewood and building poles established
- improved sanitation and pollution control tested and implemented
- bylaws formulated and accepted at all levels of government
- land/sea use plans and zoning (including protected areas) formulated at village level and accepted by all levels of government.

Second Phase (1997-2000)—leading to integrated resource management plans

3. DEMONSTRATION to fine-tune and adjust processes and actions to a wider range of cases, and to develop cost-sharing arrangements. The lessons from pilot villages applied in additional villages to:

- test strategies and approaches
- fine-tune strategies and approaches
- investigate cost-sharing mechanisms
- investigate suitable financing options
- increase number of experienced/skilled participants
- demonstrate visible and widely accepted benefits.

Third Phase (2000-2003)—spreading successes to more communities and handing over the project to local authorities.

4. MAINSTREAMING to adapt processes, actions, and methods as normal practice throughout the region. The actions anticipated for this phase include:

- lessons learned and successful applications spread widely throughout all villages
- network of community-based protected areas established and functioning
- institutions changed, if and where necessary, to support community managed areas
- collaborative management activities become part of normal government practice under broader CZM framework
- programme is self-sustaining.

3.4 Issue-Action Analysis

A community forum is one effective way to open up a participatory discussion on management issues and a series of specific actions to resolve them.

Issue-action analysis is the process of defining *issue-specific actions*, i.e., specific remedial actions for any management issues in the protected area, and assigning these to a responsible party (management authority, government agency, community group, or individual) for implementation. The process enables all concerned stakeholders to be brought into the discussion of priority management needs and to share among themselves the burden of protected area management.

It is also a means to focus management planning on the priority issues, whether these are specific conservation interventions, such as control of exotic species, installation of moorings, or reforestation, and on aspects of public relations, such as building community institutions, forums for feedback and dialogue, interpretive centers, and so on.

The process of *issue-action analysis* varies greatly according to the situation and the type of participatory approach (see Box I-7 above). For community-based protected areas, an interactive approach is used that requires local villagers to identify issues and actions. For other approaches, where objectives of more national or global significance dominate, the following process may be more appropriate.

On the basis of field and social surveys, identify the main areas of conservation value, human use and threats to both. These can be mapped to produce three separate maps showing the concentrations of conservation values (e.g., reefs, mangroves, and species feeding, spawning or nesting sites), the concentrations of human uses (e.g., fishing, recreation, tourism, bee-keeping, pole cutting, and medicinal plant extraction), and concentrations of threats to these resources and uses (e.g., turtle or bird egg harvest, pollution sources, poaching, illegal timber extraction, and illegal fishing). Overlay of these maps show the locations of potential conflicts (e.g., tourism activities in sensitive habitats, fishing in critical turtle habitats, and pollution in shellfishing areas). This defines the geographic scope of issues to be addressed in the management plan, and is a first cut of the issues to be addressed.

The *issue-action analysis* extracts the issues identified through the preceding step and other issues that are not mapable (e.g., deficiencies perceived in the policy, legal and administrative arrangements for protected areas) to list a series of actions for each. A practical approach for this is to write the management issue at the top of a page and list the actions beneath it that are required to resolve the issue. Keep renumbering the actions into a logical sequence and repeatedly go through the list while asking the question: *Will this lead to resolution of the management issue?* If not, add another action until the final answer is: *Almost certainly.*

The resulting series of actions can be grouped into a series of themes (e.g., those relating to policies, legislation, resource use opportunities, creation of special protection or pursuit zones, and conservation interventions) that form the basis for the management plan. These steps are summarized in Figure I-37.

FIGURE I-37.

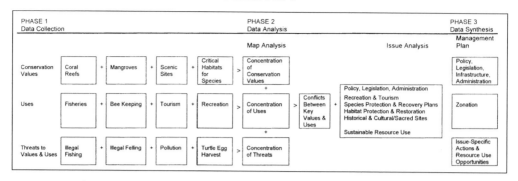

Issue-Action Analysis Approach to Protected Area Management Planning.

3.5 Winning the Support of Communities

Securing the support of local communities requires more than simply raising their awareness of issues. In fact, when/if asked they are likely to demonstrate a very profound awareness of the issues and to have some good ideas for the resolution of these (often to the surprise of management officers and consultant advisers). The communities need confidence that the management authority and protected area are there to help them (not just to place restrictions on them or to extract more license fees, taxes or bribes from them). They also need confidence that the risks involved with change are manageable and worthwhile in the time context of their needs (which may be very short). Empowerment is another important aspect of gaining community support. The communities need to know that their efforts will be rewarded by support from the management authority, provision of exclusive rights to resources under their management, and formal recognition of their role in resource management and harvest.

The communities should be shown how to manage their activities, and empowered to organize a village based system to plan, manage and reconcile their activities in a sustainable way, and provided with effective means to control non-local groups that exploit resources unsustainably adjacent to their village or management area. This is critical to provide the necessary climate for establishing protected areas, multiple resource use areas, and ability to derive economic benefits from the coastal resources as they recover and are rehabilitated. In the interim alternative practical, inexpensive, resource uses must be found so that the villagers are not tempted or forced to revert to their previous unsustainable resource use practices.

– Communities should participate in all stages of planning including resource assessments, identifying problems and defining actions to resolve them, and formulating and approving management plans, to ensure a sense of ownership.

- Participatory resource assessments, done jointly with managers and community resource users, can be influential in changing attitudes and building better relationships between them, and in initiating dialogue.

- It is important to verify resource users' perceptions of resources; independent observations should be made for different resources, e.g., both coral reefs and coastal forests.

Fishermen and other community resource users can display considerable knowledge and awareness of the state of health of their coastal resources, but they often lack suitable alternatives to their harmful practices.

Focusing on a small number of priority issues is very important in gaining the support of the community and in concentrating on the critical actions to address them. Setting clear objectives for community-based management plans is critical for ensuring that everyone knows what they are trying to achieve and in directing activities to reach them.

As women are often among the poorest people in coastal communities, specific strategies are needed for targeting them and ensuring their participation.

Ongoing monitoring and regular evaluations (i.e., every six months) are needed to check how well anticipated impacts match reality. Modifications are needed to actions that do not lead to the desired outcomes. Guidelines are:

- Regular feedback meetings between the management authority and communities are useful in participatory monitoring of progress and in sharing ideas and experiences to solve problems.

- Back-up management support is critical to provide good technical and policy advice, to monitor progress, and to ensure effective enforcement.

- Periodic checks are needed to assess the effectiveness of committees or other management structures within communities and whether they have the broad support of different community interest groups.

- It is important to have transparency in decision making and ensure that as many stakeholders as possible are aware of what is happening.

3.6 Fostering Partnership

A sense of substantive interaction by all partners should be encouraged. This in turn helps develop a sense of ownership, especially in communities concerned with collaborative management of protected areas. This sense of ownership provides incentive to fully embrace the assigned management or compliance activities and commitments and facilitates their evolution into a full-fledged partnership—a key element in achieving sustainability of the protected area. A few actions that assist the sense of community ownership in a government or NGO led process include:

– involve the community in all stages of protected area planning, and facilitate plan development by the villagers themselves wherever possible (Figure I-38)

– involve the community in final review and approval of the protected area management plan (including location of zones, boundaries and controls)

– integrate the protected area into the village institutional structure, using existing committees and customs as much as possible, and aim to reinforce these—at all costs avoid developing parallel structures

– have clear definitions of community and management authority roles and responsibilities, and establish these through formal agreements

– place community representatives in the forefront of public activities related to the protected area (planning workshops, meetings with donors and other institutions and media events)

FIGURE I-38.

An extension officer of the Ministry of Agriculture takes notes at a village consultation for a coastal nature trail project in St. Lucia.

Photo by Erkki Siirila.

– to secure central government support for community based initiatives, get these officials out into the field and participating in meetings with villagers, committing themselves publicly to follow up, and reporting back at appropriate (annual) intervals

– training villagers as "specialists" in a variety of skills so that they can train or advise a larger number of villagers is effective in getting villagers on board and saves time and money for cash-strapped management authorities

– use simple methods and start small—once something is found to work it should be simplified to the critical elements only, so that it can be easily understood and taken up by villagers without being excessively (and unnecessarily) demanding of their time, e.g., action plans and monitoring indicators should be simple and straightforward.

The concept of collaborative management may be anathema to some management authorities and individuals. It will be seen as a threat to revenues (even personal income in some societies) and erosion of power and influence. If the collaborative management structure we help build is to last, we need to demonstrate that it can work to everyone's advantage and achieve the goals of resource conservation and sustainable development. Collaborative management systems for marine resources and protected areas have been reviewed by Beaumont (1997), Christie & White (1994), Dyer & McGoodwin (1994), Horrill & van Ingen (1997), Salm (1998), Wells & White (1995), White (1989), and White *et al.* (1994).

3.7 Using Maps

It has been shown often that "sketch maps" of the project area at a scale of about 1:10,000 can be effectively used to organize participatory discussion. In this approach all participants are encouraged to add items to the sketch map and to propose alternatives and issues to be assessed. Flows of materials, energy, and people can be indicated on the sketch map (Figure I-39). Potential negative impacts can be shown. Ecologically sensitive areas (e.g., lagoons, coral reefs, flood plains, and wetlands) can be located. The knowledge exchanged serves to enhance understanding within the community and build the interest of authorities.

FIGURE I-39.

For initial scoping and information gathering, neatness is not required—the purpose is to capture all reasonable ideas and comments. Later, a fresh version of the sketch map may be prepared. Specific sites may be sketched at a larger scale to allow portrayal of more detail.

An interesting example is an initiative in St. Lucia (Soufriere Marine Management Area) during which Renard (1996) advocated the value of preparation of a map of marine resources, issues, and conflicts made by a mix of participants, which (during a boat inspection of the area) was "particularly important" to the success of the MPA programme, not only because it produced valuable data but also because it drew the data providers (fishers, divers, scientists, managers) together and "credentialled" them to the other participants including government officials. The success with the mapping led to a detailed zoning programme (see also Part III, Case No. 11).

A sketch map is being completed by the stakeholders during the first stage of an MPA project in St.Lucia. The characteristics, uses and user conflicts are marked on the map during a boat trip along the coast.

3.8 Enforcement and Prosecution

Lack of enforcement is an important factor in eroding a community's confidence in the management authority and in frustrating management interests and undermining their self-esteem. Although communities will generally need law enforcement officers to keep non-village "poachers" out of their exclusive management zones, they can be very effective at controlling illegal activities through the existing community mechanisms. Prosecution systems can be streamlined by the following:

- Increasing awareness among the judiciary: including them in technical workshops and providing specially designed training courses is an effective way of sensitizing them to the seriousness of specific illegal activities, such as poaching, dynamite fishing, deforestation and coral mining.

- Increasing awareness among the community: villagers need to understand the constraints on management or other enforcement agents in cash-short societies, and generate realistic expectations of what they can achieve. These will help motivate villagers to take up some responsibility and establish realistic partnerships with the enforcement agency.

- Improving prosecution: when there is confusion about what procedures are to be followed when making arrests or when suspect boats refuse to stop, there need to be clear guidelines on arrest procedures for community and enforcement officers, as well as training on how to implement the procedures. Arranging specialized training in evidence recording and presentation, and for a few management officers as prosecutors can enhance the success of prosecution.

- Funding enforcement: a portion of revenues from license fees and fish landing levies or whatever means are in place locally should go into supporting enforcement activities directly, without the need to transit the national treasury.

- Monitoring enforcement: use of log books to monitor patrols can be a useful method to assess the effectiveness of the patrols, demonstrate performance of officers in the field for evaluation purposes.

- Formalizing enforcement responsibility: formal agreements help ensure that each of the collaborating partners is clear on their respective authority, roles and responsibility, and is essential to ensure the smooth operation of patrols.

3.9 Collaborative Monitoring Approach

In addition to supporting enforcement, the management authority can assist communities to design and implement monitoring systems for measuring the impact of management actions. An example of a collaborative monitoring system is provided in Table I-2.

Table I-2. Example of a Collaborative Monitoring System

Indicator	Means of Verification	Who Does	Does What	Interval
Income *and catch* of resident fishers increased	Monitor fish catches for catch per gear per fisher; income earned	Users, Village Management Committee, Fisheries Officers	Deliver catches/record data Compile & analyse data Feedback information to fishers & District.	Daily Monthly Six months
Increased stocks on all reefs within management area.	Simple stock assessments of key species from catch statistics which record type & number of gears, area fished, species caught, number of fish per size class, weight of catch. Underwater census of key species	Users, VMC, FOs Same as above	Record data Analyse data Feedback information to fishers & District Same as above	Daily Six months Six months Every six months
Reduced number of incidences of illegal fishing e.g., dynamite, seine nets and sticks (kigumi), poison, spears and spearguns.	Patrol logs which record number and type of complaints/reports of illegal fishing and action taken.	VMC, FOs, Village Militia	Record complaints, incidences, responses & results Evaluate effectiveness & report to District FO & Village Government.	Daily Monthly
All vessels and fishers using area licensed.	District Fisheries Licensing records.	District FO	Compile licensing records	Yearly
Reduced number of incidences of legal but destructive fishing.	Patrol logs recording instances of extractive use & action taken.	Users, VMC, FOs	Record data Analyse data Feedback information to fishers & District	Daily Six months
Management controls in place.	Bylaws, regulations	VMC, Village Government, District Government	Formulate bylaws/regulations Approve bylaws/regulations	As required
No extractive use of closed reef.	Patrol logs recording number of reported instances and what action taken. Legal gazette of reef closure specifying restrictions and penalties	Users, VMC, FOs	Record data Analyse data Feedback information to fishers & District	Daily Six months Six months
Catch information recorded	Catch statistics recording fishing effort & catch from each device	Users, VMC, FOs	Deliver catches/record data Compile & analyse data Feedback information to fishers & District	Daily Six months Six months
Reduced number of visiting vessels.	Catch statistics recording fishing effort of residents & visitors	Users, VMC, FOs	Deliver catches/record data Compile & analyse data Feedback information to fishers & District	Daily Six months Six months

(Source: Horrill and van Ingen, 1997)

Selection of Marine Protected Areas

For those countries that have the resources to do so, it is most useful to organize MPAs by a national system rather than creating them on a case-by-case basis. The prospect of planning a national system of marine and coastal protected areas may appear to be daunting (Figure I-40) yet the job is not as difficult as it may first appear. MPA system planning is seen as most desirable for the full development of a country's marine and coastal protected area programme. This has been recognized at high levels by some governments that have mandated the systems approach to MPAs (e.g., Indonesia, Mauritius).

FIGURE I-40.

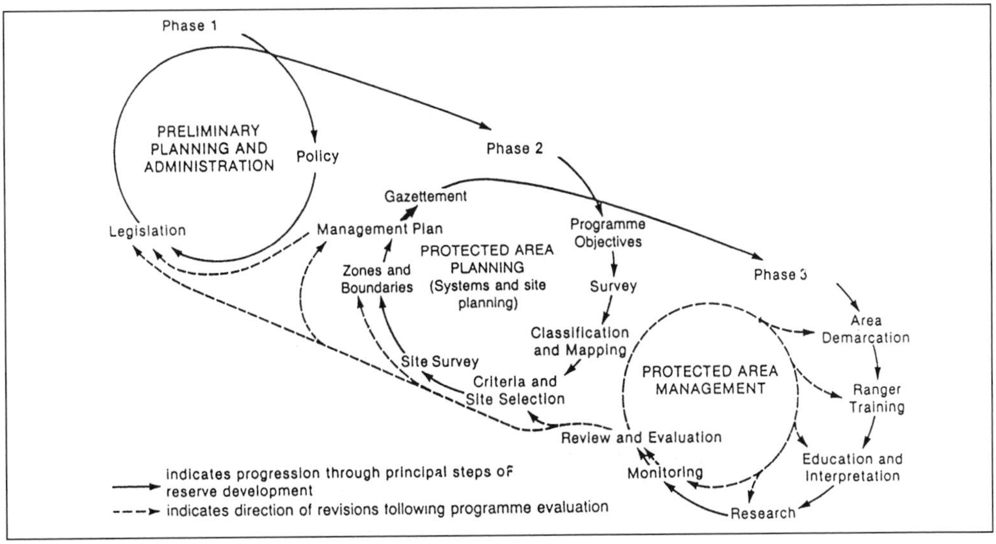

Interrelationships among various phases of protected area development.

4.1 The Selection Process

Selection of sites for conservation management is but one of many elements in the process of building an integrated system of marine protected areas. Thus, many of the essential steps of this system planning process, such as goal identification, site survey and data collection, data analysis, and data synthesis and plan formulation, apply to site selection as well as all other elements of the marine protected area programme.

While selection of marine protected areas through a systematic MPA planning exercise is preferable, in actuality MPA selection is most frequently determined by opportunity (a strong show of public and/or government support) or crisis (a high level of threat to a site that is considered important for any reason).

Selection of sites according to some well-laid plan that includes clearly understood goals and objectives, and a list of focused, practical criteria to guide site selection is preferable to selection by *ad hoc* means, such as by opportunity or crisis. Opportunities and crises are likely to arise at intervals, but one needs to try to get ahead of them if selection is to proceed along systematic and programmatic lines.

In the selection planning exercise, guidelines are usually defined to help fulfill the overall goal of the planning exercise. These guidelines are applied to evaluate candidate sites for selection, which should include samples of social, economic, ecological, regional, and pragmatic criteria that are applied to evaluate candidate sites for selection. In the latter case, popular pressure or urgency imposed by threat promotes action that may raise the priority for protection of a particular site.

Initiatives for establishing protected areas can come from local governments or communities outside of any objective selection criteria. Sites protected in this way have high local significance, but often may contribute less to the national conservation objectives. Nonetheless, because they enjoy strong local support and may require modest amounts of personnel, time, and money to manage, they should be viewed as useful contributions to conservation. These should be endorsed if not counted as substitutes for larger more extensive sites that might contribute more significantly to national objectives for biodiversity conservation and development.

A useful application of selection criteria is to evaluate and identify, among inherited, traditional, and locally established protected areas, those that contribute to national conservation objectives. In any event a national set of criteria for choosing MPAs is recommended.

In this section we propose some basic principles and list criteria that may help to guide selection of marine protected areas. The criteria and approach for their application have evolved relatively little from their original sources as reported in the first edition of this book in 1984 (see Salm & Price, 1996) and are similar to those published more recently (e.g., Kelleher & Kenchington, 1992; Nordiska Ministerrådet,

1995). Nilsson (1998) provides a valuable comparison and comment on these various criteria and their applications for different conservation objectives. Nilsson's report is highly recommended reading for those interested in the choice and application of criteria for selection of marine protected areas.

4.2 Guiding Principles

First principle: The needs, priorities, and abilities of the country define the objectives and scope of the marine protected area programme.

It is easier to list principles and criteria from the theoretical perspective, than it is to apply them in the real world. Thus common sense and sensitivity to the true needs and abilities of the country and its people should be applied to the selection of sites.

Second principle: The objectives of the marine protected area programme provide the foundation for the selection process.

It is extremely important to have clearly defined and focused objectives for the system of marine protected areas. For example, an objective may be to establish a system of conservation areas for certain endangered species. In this case, the planning process would focus on identification of critical marine habitats associated with the life functions (breeding, feeding, migration areas) of the target species (Figure I-41). Criteria would emphasize ecological, regional, and pragmatic parameters, and play down social and economic ones (see discussion on application of specific criteria below). If the objective were to protect critical habitats of fishery species, the selection criteria would include social and economic parameters, and possibly place less importance on regional ones. An integrated goal that includes the needs of all sectors of society (e.g., fisheries, recreation, tourism) as well as those of the environment (wildlife, productive marine habitats, ecological process) is more ambitious, but may be easier to enter into national development planning.

FIGURE I-41.

Researchers locate humpback whales and record their vocalizations near Lahaina, Maui, Hawaii.

Third principle: The scope of the marine protected area programme (national, provincial, numbers and size of marine protected areas) defines the limits of the selection process, and is an important determinant of the selection criteria.

It is increasingly difficult to select small areas in isolation of their surroundings, especially in the sea where winds, currents, and species movements ensure a great deal of linkage or connectivity between far distant areas. For this reason, management of small "hot spots" of activity needs to be built into that of the larger system of which they are a part (Salm & Dobbin, 1993). Establishment of marine protected areas in the broader context of coastal zone management planning has been recommended as an effective technique for management of upstream and other interactive processes and activities (IUCN 1987a, b, c; Salm, 1987). Coastal zone management plans can achieve a vast multiple use reserve for the entire coastal zone of a nation. Within the coastal zone all valuable resource areas (critical marine habitats) can be managed to avoid damaging activities and pollution through development policies controlled by Coastal Zone Management legislation, or contained by zoning plans.

Fourth principle: Because each nation has different social, political, economic, and environmental parameters, there can be no one definitive model for site selection.

Past experience has resulted in the evolution of a planning process with sets of criteria that can be adapted as appropriate to individual cases. The application of these criteria forms the main thrust of this chapter. Nilsson (1998) gives an excellent account of the application of criteria to meet different conservation objectives in Sweden.

4.3   The Site Selection Process

In developing a systematic logical approach for selection of marine protected areas, four steps can be identified as essential to site selection. These are the collection, analysis and synthesis of data leading to the identification of candidate sites, followed by the application of criteria to select specific sites for protection (Salm & Price, 1995).

Powerful statistical techniques (e.g., "principal components analysis" or "cluster analysis") can be applied to graphically portray the relative similarities and differences between the sites based on the selected criteria. The different types of criteria (e.g., economic, social, ecological, and so on) can be analyzed either separately or jointly for a more integrated picture. The result is that sites are arranged into groups. The members of a group share the greatest number of similarities, and differ substantially from members of other groups. The different groups can then be assigned a priority rating that takes into account the geographic spread of the candidate sites, the extent of popular support, and the urgency or schedule for establishment. Representative sites from some or all of the groups then can be selected for protected area status.

Data collection from all available sources, including literature searches, interviews, and field studies, is the first step in the identification and selection of marine protected areas. It is likely that existing data are incomplete (Figure I-41). There may be detailed information for a small part of the country and sparse or no data for the rest. Thus a detailed plan for a series of field surveys will be required to provide essential social, biological, and ecological information focussing on habitats and species (Tables I-3, and I-4).

Table I-3. Model Habitat/Ecosystem Data Sheet to Accompany

Habitat/Ecosystem Maps

Habitat/ecosystem: type (e.g., salt marsh, ocean trench, atoll)

Distribution: general environment and specific locations

Area estimates: table of estimated areas by location

Support systems: general notes on probable nutrient and energy subsidy sources

Legal status: legislation that controls uses or protects the habitat or ecosystem

Importance to people: role in fisheries production, other industry, research, recreation, coastline protection, etc.)

Threats:

> Natural (natural forms of habitat/ecosystem degradation)
>
> Human-related (specific forms of use that result in habitat/ecosystem alteration or degradation)
>
> Potential (proposed developments or activities that may encroach upon or degrade the habitat/ecosystem)

Specific conservation needs, including survey, research, protection, management, legislation, enforcement, and public awareness programs

Socioeconomic problems of habitat/ecosystem protection: existing or potential conflicts between habitat/ecosystem uses and their control

Persons contacted: list of people who provided useful information

References: literature consulted.

Data should be collected, evaluated for consistency and adequacy, and stored in easily retrievable form for analysis, such as on maps and in custom designed computerized databases (GIS) that are linked by coordinates to the maps (Price, 1990).

Once data collection is complete, the information is analyzed to show areas with concentrations of resources, human activities, and threats to resources, or any other required information, such as areas of conflicts among activities and other interests, or sites of specific interest (e.g., fish spawning areas). Areas with concentrations of resources are all obvious candidates for conservation. However, the specific objectives of the system planning process may call for strict protection of specific sites with high value for only one interest, such as the breeding site of an endangered animal.

The simplest way to achieve this analysis is by map overlay. First, a base map is prepared to an appropriate scale. Individual data elements (turtle beaches, seabird islands, fishery activities, coral reefs, pinniped rookeries, and so on) are then mapped onto transparent overlays of this base. Next, the transparencies are overlaid to show the areas with resource concentrations. These, together with any sites with specific interests can then be identified as candidates for selection. Overlay analysis can be most efficiently done by GIS systems.

Table I-4. Model Data Sheet for Species Distribution Maps

Species: both scientific and common names

Distribution in territorial or regional and neighboring seas

Location of national or regional populations: location of each isolated population

Estimate of national or regional stocks for each population

Life history information:

Feeding grounds (general notes on feeding habitat and location of known feeding areas)

Preferred food (list of usual food items)

Breeding grounds (general notes on breeding habitat and location of known sites)

Calving grounds (whales, dolphins, dugongs), *nesting beaches* (turtles, terns), *spawning grounds* (milk fish, mullets, groupers, shrimp, etc.), *seabird cliffs or islands* (boobies, frigates, terns) (general notes on habitat and location of known sites)

Nursery sites (shrimp, fishes) (general notes on habitat and location of known sites)

Resting beaches (turtles, pinnipeds), *shelters* (dolphins, manatees, dugongs), *roosts* (seabirds) (general notes on habitat and location of known sites)

Migration routes (general notes on migration habits and location of known routes)

Legal status: details of legislation that protects the species and its habitat and/or prohibits or controls trade in the species or its products

Threats:

Natural threats (natural predators or causes of mortality)

Human-related threats (specific forms of hunting and fishing or habitat encroachment and destruction, pollution)

Potential threats (proposed developments or activities that may affect the organism or its habitat)

Specific conservation needs, including, for example, identification of areas for survey, protection, and management, research requirements, necessary legislation and enforcement, and public awareness programmes

Socioeconomic problems of species protection: existing or potential conflicts between species and habitat protection and activities, such as mangrove cutting, which degrade habitat

Persons contacted: knowledgeable people consulted for species or habitat information

References: Literature consulted.

Maps (graded if possible into high, medium, low levels) of activities, threats to resources, or conflicts between resource protection and developments can be combined with the composite map resulting from the preceding analysis to refine the identification process. This synthesis helps to impose a measure of priority for protection on the candidate sites. For example, the level of dependence by people on a fishery could be used to indicate priority among candidate sites to safeguard fishery resources. Similarly, the vulnerability to some form of threat posed by an activity or a proposed development may determine the choice between two similar candidate sites.

Another application of data synthesis is to develop an understanding of spatial relationships among biological factors (e.g., species), ecological processes (e.g., nutrient transport), and human activities. Overlays of ocean currents, nutrient sources (such as estuaries), and resource distributions can be combined to show the specific support systems for species or ecosystems—all of which are candidates for protection. Also, by combining overlays of human activities, and particularly proposed developments, a picture can be synthesized of potential conflicts between resource management and developments, and of priority areas for action (Ray *et al.*, 1978).

The overlay mapping technique has limitations, and it is important to apply common sense to the interpretation of results. For example, candidate sites for protection will tend to be aimed at those without significant levels of human activity. As a result, there will be a tendency to overlook the great potential some exploited sites may have for restoration.

As another example, the overlay technique can mislead planners into excluding a site because of a perceived conflict between protection and powerful commercial interests. For example, an industrial fishery in a critical spawning ground may seem like too big a problem to tackle. However, protection during the critical spawning season, and fishing during the remainder of the year can be mutually reinforcing activities.

It can be very revealing to compare the candidate sites resulting from data synthesis with the range of established MPAs. As well as indicating the needs for additional MPAs, this comparison may show that some sites do not correspond to critical areas at all.

The identification procedure outlined in the data analysis and synthesis steps above will provide a long list of candidate sites for protection. Selection of the specific sites for protection from this list will require the application of a carefully compiled sample of focussed criteria.

4.4 Using Selection Criteria

Urgency, opportunity, and political or popular pressure often make the first areas for protection so obvious that there is no need to apply criteria except in selecting an appropriate management category, including potential zoning. However, the identification and selection of other candidate sites from a list of potential areas requires the application of criteria.

Criteria have two functions. They initially serve to assess the eligibility of sites for protected area status. Their principal role, however, is to order eligible sites according to priority in the selection process. The final determinants of how many sites are selected for protection are such factors as national policy, the urgency for action, the availability of financial and personnel resources, and, in the case of some developing countries, the extent of international concern and assistance.

The application of selection criteria helps to ensure objectivity in the choice of sites for protection. Criteria for identifying and selecting coastal and marine protected areas depend principally on the overall objectives of the conservation programme (see Nilsson 1998 for a clear application of this process). If, for example, the objectives are mainly to safeguard areas for tourism and recreation in wilderness settings, the criteria could emphasize accessibility, safety factors (such as the absence of currents and large waves), scenic value, the presence of such other interests as cultural or archaeological sites, and carrying capacity; i.e., the number of visitors the area can sustain without degrading the environment or destroying the quality of the wilderness experience by crowding (Figure I-42).

If economic goals (such as coastal protection, maintenance of fisheries, and development of tourism and related industries) are the main interest, the criteria might emphasize intensity of resource exploitation, the present and potential economic value of resources, and the degree of threat to them. Criteria stressing naturalness, uniqueness, and habitat or species diversity are likely to be applied to select sites when maintenance of genetic diversity, safeguarding of ecological processes, and species replenishment are the primary objectives.

FIGURE I-42.

Photo by Bill Keogh.

A boatload of snorkelers visit the Florida Keys National Marine Sanctuary.

The list of criteria on the following pages is long and complicated. However, it illustrates some applications of criteria and is intended to facilitate the task of defining a focussed, shorter sample of these. Every effort should be made to keep criteria few, practical, and well targeted so that the selection process meets the specific objectives of the marine protected area programme.

In using the criteria, it is important to appreciate that the lists provide examples that are meant to help the compilation of an appropriate sample and you should select only those that help to focus on identified conservation objectives.

For each site under consideration, the different criteria can be quantified or scored. In the simplest application, a set of carefully selected criteria is scored (e.g., on a scale of 1 to 5 for lowest to highest value) for each site. The scores are summed for each site, compared, and priority areas identified based on the highest scores.

The following examples of criteria for the selection of marine protected areas are based on IUCN (1981) and Salm & Price (1995), with minor modifications.

4.5 Social Criteria

Social and cultural benefits can be assessed in the following terms:

1. **Social acceptance:** the degree to which the support of local people is assured. Every effort should be made to nurture local support. An area that is already protected by local tradition or practice should be reinforced, and the area should receive a higher rating. An "official" protected area designation may still be necessary, even if local support is high, to ensure government recognition of the area. For example, central government planners gave out part of a sacred forest on Chale Island in Kenya to a hotel developer, despite its protection at the local level for possibly hundreds of years.

2. **Public health:** the degree to which the creation of a marine protected area may serve to diminish pollution or other disease agents that contribute to public health problems. Granting protected status to contaminated areas, such as shellfish beds or bathing beaches, may result in reduced pollution as the polluting source is identified and controlled as part of the plan for site management.

3. **Recreation:** the degree to which the area is, or could be, used for recreation by country residents. Sites that provide the local community the opportunity to use, enjoy, and learn about their local natural environment should rate highly for this criterion.

4. **Culture:** the religious, historic, artistic, or other cultural value of the site. Natural areas that also contain important cultural features should be given high ratings as they will benefit from a high level of local support, and their protection may help to maintain the integrity of the adjacent ecosystems.

5. **Aesthetics:** a seascape, landscape, or other area of exceptional scenic beauty (Figure I-43). Natural areas that also contain features of natural beauty should be given higher ratings since the safe-guarding of such features often requires that the integrity be maintained of adjacent coastal and marine systems. However, where species diversity and the biological conservation values are low, such areas retain a high value for recreation and tourism

6. **Conflicts of interest:** the degree to which area protection would affect the activities of local residents. If the area is to be used for recreation purposes, for example,

FIGURE I-43.

Photo by John Clark.

The Seventy Rock Islands MPA of Palau is a place of exceptional beauty.

the site should not be a major fishing area and should have few dependent fishermen. In some instances, careful zoning can minimize such conflicts.

7. **Safety:** the degree of danger to people from strong currents, surf, submerged obstacles, waves, and other hazards. The principal users will often be swimmers, snorkelers, divers, and boaters. It is important that they are able to pursue their activities safely.

8. **Accessibility:** the ease of access across both land and sea. Areas to be used by visitors, students, researchers, and fishermen must be accessible to them. The more accessible, the greater the value, but the greater the level of use, the greater the likelihood of conflicting interests, and the greater the impact of users. Accessibility is most important for marine protected areas with predominantly social objectives, fairly important for those with economic goals, and low for those meeting ecological criteria.

9. **Research and education:** the degree to which an area represents various ecological characteristics and can serve for research and demonstration of scientific methods. Areas that clearly demonstrate different habitat types and ecological relationships and are sufficiently large both to serve conservation and to accommodate teaching (i.e., field trips or on-site learning centers) should receive a higher rating.

10. **Public awareness:** the degree to which monitoring, research, education, or training within the area can contribute knowledge and appreciation of environmental values and conservation objectives. Areas that can combine such activities as pollution monitoring and education should receive a higher rating.

11. **Conflict and compatibility:** the degree to which an area may help to resolve conflicts between natural resource values and human activities, or the degree to which compatibility between them may be enhanced. If an area can be used to exemplify the resolution of conflicts in the region, it should receive a higher rating. Protected areas that demonstrate the benefits, values, or methods of protection or restoration should also have higher ratings.

12. **Benchmark:** the degree to which the area may serve as a "control site" for scientific research, i.e., a largely undisturbed site in which natural processes can proceed without manipulation and which can be used to measure changes elsewhere. Benchmark areas are essential components of an ecological monitoring programme, and should receive a higher rating.

As an example, say an area to be set aside for recreation involves criteria 1-3 and 6-8, and should score highly on these. It may not be necessary to consider criteria 4 and 9-12 in the analysis and selection process. Areas that focus on the conservation of cultural heritage, on the other hand, should involve criteria 1 and 4, with 3, 7 and 8 also important (if access and recreational use form part of the objective).

4.6 Economic Criteria

Economic benefits can be assessed by the following criteria:

1. **Importance to species:** the degree to which certain commercially important species depend on the area. Reefs, estuaries or wetlands, for example, may be critical habitats for certain species that breed, rest, shelter, or feed there, and that form the basis of local fisheries in adjacent areas. Such habitats need management to support the exploited stocks.

2. **Importance to fisheries:** the number of dependent fishermen and the size of the fishery yield. The greater the dependence of fishermen on an area, and the greater its yield of fishes, the more important it becomes to manage the area correctly and to ensure sustainable harvest (Figure I-44)

3. **Nature of threats:** the extent to which changes in use patterns threaten the overall value to people. Habitats may be threatened directly by destructive practices, such as fishing with explosives and certain bottom trawls, or by overexploitation of resources. Areas traditionally harvested by local fishermen become important to manage. The number of fishermen on these grounds may increase, bringing extra pressure to bear on stocks and habitats. Even if the numbers do not change, the traditional capture methods may be replaced by others that yield more per unit effort (an extreme example is the use of explosives). The stocks of some species may not be capable of withstanding such increased exploitation of their breeding populations. In this way whole species have disappeared from fishing grounds or have become exceedingly rare.

FIGURE I-44.

Photo by John Clark.

Family fishing activity near Sanur Beach, Bali, Indonesia.

4. **Economic benefits:** the degree to which protection will affect the local economy in the long term. Initially, some protected areas may have a short-lived, disruptive economic effect. Those that have obvious positive effects should have higher ratings (for example, for protecting feeding areas of commercial fishes or areas of recreational value).

5. **Tourism:** the existing or potential value of the area to tourism development. Areas that lend themselves to forms of tourism compatible with the aims of conservation should receive a higher rating.

As an example: say an area to be set aside in support of fisheries will need to include an analysis of criteria 1-4, while one for tourism purposes would include criteria 2-5.

4.7 Ecological Criteria.

The values of ecosystems and their species can be assessed by the following:

1. **Biodiversity:** the variety or richness of ecosystems, habitats, communities, and species. Areas having the greatest variety should receive higher ratings. However, this criterion may not apply to simplified ecosystems, such as some pioneer or climax communities, or areas subject to disruptive forces, such as shores exposed to high-energy wave action.

2. **Naturalness:** the lack of disturbance or degradation. Degraded systems will have little value to fisheries or tourism, and will make little biological contribution. A high degree of naturalness scores highly. If restoring degraded habitats is a priority, a high degree of degradation may score highly.

3. **Dependency:** the degree to which a species depends on an area, or the degree to which an ecosystem depends on ecological processes occurring in the area. If an area is critical to more than one species or process, or to a valuable species or ecosystem, it should have a higher rating.

4. **Representativeness:** the degree to which an area represents a habitat type, ecological process, biological community, geological feature or other natural characteristic. If a habitat of a particular type has not been protected, it should have a high rating. A biogeographic classification scheme for coastal and marine areas is desirable in applying this criterion.

5. **Uniqueness:** whether an area is "one of a kind". Habitats of endemic or endangered species occurring only in one area are an example. The interest in uniqueness may extend beyond country borders, assuming regional or international significance. To keep visitor impact low, tourism may be prohibited, but limited research and education permitted. Unique sites should always have a high rating.

6. **Integrity:** the degree to which the area is a functional unit—an effective, self-sustaining ecological entity. The more ecologically self-contained the area is, the more likely its values can be effectively protected, and so a higher rating should be given to such areas.

7. **Productivity:** the degree to which productive processes within the area contribute benefits to species or to humans. Productive areas that contribute most to sustain ecosystems should receive a high rating. Exceptions are eutrophic areas where high productivity may have a deleterious effect.

8. **Vulnerability:** the area's susceptibility to degradation by natural events or the activities of people. Biotic communities associated with coastal habitats may have a low tolerance to changes in environmental conditions, or they may exist close to the limits of their tolerance (defined by water temperature, salinity, turbidity, or depth). They may suffer such natural stresses as storms or prolonged immersion that determine the extent of their development. Additional stress (such as domestic or industrial pollution, excessive reductions in salinity, and increases in turbidity from watershed mismanagement) may determine whether there is total, partial, or no recovery from natural stress, or the area is totally destroyed.

As an example: say conservation of biodiversity is the objective, then criteria 1-5 are most important, while factors behind criteria 6 and 8 will drive the focus of management activities.

4.8 Regional Criteria

The contribution of an area to the conservation of shared resources and to a regional network of protected areas can be assessed in the following terms:

1. **Regional significance:** the degree to which the area represents a characteristic of the region, whether a natural feature, an ecological process, or a cultural site. The role the area plays in contributing nutrients, materials, or support for species (especially migratory ones) to the region as a whole should be evaluated. Both ecological processes and natural resources are often shared among nations, so areas contributing to the maintenance of species or ecosystems beyond national boundaries should have higher ratings.

2. **Subregional significance**: the degree to which an area fills a gap in the network of protected areas from the subregional perspective. This contribution may be assessed by comparing the distribution of protected areas with subregional characteristics. If a type of area is preserved in one subregion, that type should also be protected in another subregion.

As an example, Criterion 1 is extremely important in the development of regional collaboration for the conservation of shared resources, and would be a determinant in the selection of sites in marine protected area components of the UNEP Regional Seas Programme, for instance.

4.9 Pragmatic Criteria

The feasibility and appropriate timing of protection can be assessed in terms of the following:

1. **Urgency:** the degree to which immediate action must be taken, lest values within the area be transformed or lost. But lack of urgency should not necessarily be given a lower rating since it is often best, and least costly, to protect well in advance of the threat.

2. **Size:** which and how much of various habitats need to be included in the protected area. Size is an important factor in designing protected areas. It has often been overlooked in the design process, resulting in severe degradation, even total destruction, of protected areas. The protected area must be large enough to function as an ecological unit to receive a high rating.

3. **Degree of threat:** present and potential threats from direct exploitation and development projects. The farther the protected area is from potential sources of accidental poisoning (such as large ports or petroleum deposits) the better are the survival prospects of species and communities. However, if an important habitat is severely threatened, it may be important to implement an urgent management plan to reduce the threats to tolerable levels.

4. **Effectiveness:** the feasibility of implementing a management programme. A site that satisfies many criteria, but cannot be adequately managed (i.e., monitored, patrolled and defended) is not of much use. Higher ratings should go to sites that are more manageable.

5. **Opportunism:** the degree to which existing conditions or actions already under way or a ground swell of popular support may justify further action. However, extension of an established protected area should have a higher rating.

6. **Availability:** the degree to which the area is available for acquisition or can be managed satisfactorily by agreement with the owners or custodians. The problem of individual tenure rarely applies to the sea. Beaches also often belong to the central or provincial government. Thus, acquisition of aquatic areas, wetlands, and seashores may not be necessary. However, adjacent lands and islands may be privately owned or leased. Generally, to secure long-term control over these areas, the title or lease will need to be bought from current owners. Higher ratings should go to areas owned by state or national governments.

7. **Restorability:** the degree to which the area may be returned to its former natural state. Areas that can increase in productivity or value to important species and processes should receive higher ratings.

As an example: practical reality gives high prominence to these criteria and numbers 1, 3, 5 and 6 are often determinants of site selection and establishment. Low values for criteria 2-4, 6 and 7 may often argue against the selection of a particular site.

Although they can be useful, criteria often simply show what is intuitively obvious. Often their greatest benefit is that they allow us to justify what we already know and to build up a case for proposed site selection or zoning plans. Rigorous application and quantification of criteria generally does not apply in sparsely populated areas. However, this is important near urban centers and fishing communities where existing uses would be displaced or modified to suit new objectives.

Strategies and Tools

The design and management of MPAs is a constantly evolving field relying on both traditional approaches and newly available methods and technologies. In today's world, MPA formulation and operation require, and benefit from, higher levels of technology in information handling and onsite management than ever before. Also our base of experience is growing rapidly. This section presents examples of tools and strategies that are now available for use by MPA interests.

5.1 Geographic Information Systems

Computer assisted mapping tools, used in storing, retrieving, processing and displaying spatial data may be particularly useful. The most popular of these are a class of computer-assisted mapping tools called Geographic Information Systems (GIS). Previously requiring large computers, GIS are now available on personal computers and inexpensive workstations (Figure I-45). This increasingly puts them within the budget of most institutions which deal with resource data [Pheng and Kam, 1989].

GIS computers can be programmed for direct production of resource maps, including overlay maps. Most coastal features that have spatial attributes can be stored, analyzed, and printed out as maps using simple electronic methods. Decisions in resource use often depend on the spatial distribution of the resource in relation to other factors such as transportation. FAO has prepared a useful guide, "Marine Resource Mapping: An Introductory Manual" (Butler *et al.*, 1987).

Most resource data with spatial information are readily inputted as points, lines and areas, with attributes tagged onto these entities. The analyses for GIS are transformations of geographical data and attributes in the form of a map or referenced to a map. For example, GIS can overlay two map layers showing the extent of mangrove forests of two different years within the same study area and show with

FIGURE I-45.

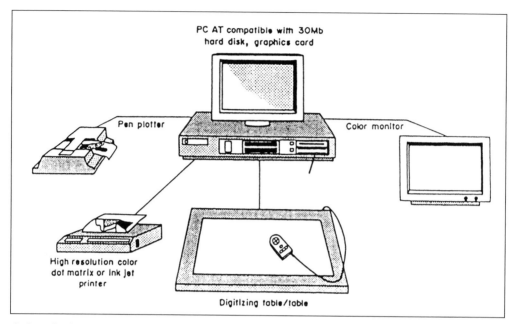

The basic hardware configuration for an inexpensive microcomputer-based GIS system.
Source: K.S. Pheng and W.P. Kam.

precision where mangrove forests have increased or have shrunk. Automatic calculation of the area of any defined parcel (hectares, acres, etc.) is another feature of most GIS (Pheng and Kam, 1989; Butler, *et al.*, 1987).

The role of the GIS as a tool in processing and displaying resource data is extensive. Also GIS are open-ended and can easily receive new data or integrate old data. Therefore, the GIS data bank can easily be updated. Then too, GIS systems work well in conjunction with remote sensing, including satellite images. The major difficulty is to acquire the data by which to do this.

Merging marine ecosystem maps with other environmental information, such as long-term monitoring data or land use information, in GIS is revolutionizing our ability to conserve, manage, and protect MPAs. The GIS becomes a tool for evaluating the condition of the ecosystem. Data collected in the past can be compared to current conditions to measure change.

Thematic map layers, such as the land use activities, locations of industrial discharge pipes, water quality monitoring stations, river inputs of fresh water, navigation routes, and commercial and non-commercial marine species distributions can be incorporated into the GIS. The result is a powerful, flexible decision support tool for coral reef ecosystem research, conservation, and management. For example, such a tool can be used to: develop better marine environmental education programmes that stress the importance of coral reef ecosystems and their conservation; identify and evaluate areas where coral reef management efforts are needed immediately; characterize and evaluate the status of the essential habitat of commercial and non-commercial marine species; develop management strategies for marine protected areas; predict and model the potential damage to populated areas caused by severe weather; and support activities that evaluate and develop capabilities to conduct long-term monitoring and change analyses. Since the information is maintained in a computer, new data can easily be added. If maps of different scales are needed for specific activities or areas, these too can easily be incorporated into the system. In addition, GIS-based maps can be inexpensively distributed on CD-ROM or over the Internet.

5.2 Remote Sensing

Remote sensing—by satellites such as LANDSAT (USA) and SPOT (France)—can be helpful, but the images are often very expensive. The high spatial resolution of multiband radiometers on LANDSAT and SPOT, well proved for land survey, also works moderately well for shallow-water survey (where waters are clear and cloud cover is low). Remote data have their best use in coastal zone planning and management when coupled to digital mapping and GIS technology. The US satellite, LANDSAT 7, features an advanced Thematic Mapper and the output is said to be relatively inexpensive.

The light you see when you look into the water is the same light used to map coral reefs. Sunlight penetrates the water and is reflected back. The light reflected back can tell you about the makeup of the bottom - areas that reflect brightly might be sand; areas that reflect less brightly might be seagrass or coral reef areas. Just as your eye sees these dark and light patterns in reflected light so does a camera. Colour film in a camera is composed of emulsions that are sensitive to different portions - red, green , and blue - of the visible light spectrum. Factors, such as altitude (when an aircraft carries the camera, the water depth, and aerosols in the atmosphere affect the amount of reflected light that hits the film. Unfortunately, no single remote sensing technology is capable of mapping all components of a marine ecosystem. Water depth is the primary limiting factor. As a result, complete ecosystem mapping requires merging the capabilities of several technologies.

Remote Sensing Platforms: Light reflectance-based remote sensing technologies can generally be grouped according to the resolution (pixel size) of the resulting data. This resolution is affected by both the altitude of the platform from which data are collected and the design of the instrument or camera. Low-resolution satellite platforms such as NASA's SeaWIFS (Sea Viewing Wide Field-of-View Sensor) and NOAA's AVHRR (Advanced Very High Resolution Radiometer) produce images where each pixel represents an area of 1 to 10 sq. km. Moderate-resolution satellite platforms such as LandSat, SPOT, and human-occupied spacecraft (e.g., the Space Shuttle or International Space Station) produce images where each pixel represents an area of 10 - 30 sq. meters. Instruments mounted on fixed wing aircraft and helicopter platforms produce images where each pixel represents an area of 1 - 5 sq. meters. Classified remote sensing platforms from the National Technical Means (NTM) Programme produce images where each pixel represents an area of less than 1 sq. meter.

Aircraft Platforms: High-resolution benthic habitat maps of extensive coastal areas have been produced from colour aerial photography. An important advantage to using colour photographs is their widespread availability and ease of analysis. Photographs of 1:12,000 to 1:24,000 scale can be used to identify features of 0.5 to 1 meter in size. Using textures and colours in the image and their own knowledge of the distribution of benthic habitats, photointerpretation experts identify polygons of 10 to 20 sq. meters in size from these images. An alternative approach is to digitally scan the image and classify the digital file using computer-based image-analysis software. While typically faster than photointerpretation in producing maps, this technique is affected by the ability of the software to discriminate subtle variations in colour patterns for certain features of water depth, turbidity and light penetration. Aircraft-based multi- and hyperspectral remote sensing systems offer the advantage of increased spectral discrimination over colour aerialphotography.

Multispectral systems: (typically, four colour bands) have been successfully used to map coral reef ecosystems. Hyperspectral sensors (typically, 10-277 colour bands) have been used in small geographic areas to map benthic habitats, including coral reef features.

Satellite Platforms: Satellite imagery has been used to map benthic habitat types (e.g. sand, seagrass, coral, hard substrate) in coral reef environments. While lacking the spatial or spectral resolution of aircraft-based imagery, satellite imagery offers the advantages of increased frequency of coverage, extensive coverage at low cost, archival data, and fast results.

Other Technologies: Rather than depend on reflected sunlight, some remote sensing technologies use "active" systems to characterize marine environments. For example LIDAR (Light Detection and Ranging) uses a laser to measure bathymetry. Multibeam sonar, also used to characterize bathymetry and seafloor composition, uses an acoustic out-beam. LIDAR can measure bethymetry in water to depths of 20-50 meters. Multibeam sonar can measure bathymetry in waters from 20-4000 meters or more in depth.

Mapping Requirements: Field validation of maps derived from remotely sensed data sources is essential. Any map produced from a remote sensing platform must be validated by field observation ("ground truth"). Because of the highly variable nature of the marine ecosystem, visiting as many areas to be mapped as possible is important. If some areas are difficult to access, extrapolating from maps of known areas to unknown areas may be required but is risky.

Habitat Classification: In order to produce digital marine ecosystem maps, a marine habitat classification scheme must exist. Such a scheme should have biological and physical parameters for the ecosystem. The scheme should be hierarchical and nest highly detailed habitat descriptions into more generalized habitat descriptions. The scheme should provide sufficient detail for research, conservation, and management needs. Finally, the scheme should recognize the limitations of the remote sensing technology to discriminate features in the marine environment. An accurate, high-resolution shoreline is the base map upon which all other map layers are superimposed. Shoreline links terrestrial ecosystems to marine ecosystems. In addition, datum adjustments must be applied to the shoreline to properly place this key feature on the earth. Efforts must continue to develop accurate, high-resolution, datum-corrected digital shoreline maps.

Bathymetry: This is a critical thematic data layer for many mapping activities. Bathymetry depicting water depths of less than 100 m is needed to identify and locate navigation hazards and shipping channels, predict and manage the damage from floods and storms, identify and monitor critical fish habitat, and document the location and extent of shallow coral reef ecosystems. Bathymetry also is required to fully utilize remotely sensed data to correct for light attenuation. Light received by the sensor is affected by the distance that it must travel through the water column. Fortunately, most corals are found in shallow-water environments of less than 30 m.

Remote Sensing Costs: Data acquisition accounts for about 25 percent of the total cost of producing marine ecosystem maps. The remaining 75 percent goes to georeferencing the imagery, calibrating the imagery, validating the draft maps, and producing the final map products.

Airborne LIDAR costs range from US$900 to 1,800 per sq km depending upon the horizontal spatial resolution needed. Deep water (> 50 m) bathymetry also is crucial for many mapping activities, including coral reef ecosystem mapping. Ship-based acoustic surveys using multibeam depth sounders have successfully produced bathymetric maps with vertical accuracies of +/- 15 cm from depths 10 m to 500 m and greater. In addition to providing highly accurate bathymetric maps, the system provides backscatter, which can be used to map the roughness of the seafloor. Costs of multibeam range from US$1,000 to 4,000 per sq. km depending on the type of boat required. When assessing airborne remote sensing technology, the cost is most affected by the altitude flown and the "footprint" of the resulting imagery. Typically, aerial photography costs about US$125/sq. km.

Due to their large footprint, satellite imagery costs range from $100/sq. km. for IKONOS to $6/sq. km. for LandSat 7.

5.3 Participatory Rural Assessment

Participatory Rural Assessment (PRA) is a process for gathering and analyzing information from and about rural communities in a brief time period (weeks). Sometimes called Rapid Rural Appraisal (RRA), the approach is somewhere between formal survey and unstructured interviewing. Used in the MPA context, PRA sets out to create a dialogue with folks in rural coastal communities.

PRA collects information mostly by interview (group or single) on social values, opinions, and objectives and local knowledge as well as "hard" data on social, economic, cultural and ecological parameters. The value of the data produced depends largely on the collecting team's skill and judgement. A participatory approach, rather than a researcher-subject relationship, is the goal. Some of the advantages of PRA methods for learning the needs of communities are: they are cost-effective; sampling errors and bias are reduced; close discussion with rural people is enhanced; and there is flexibility to make adjustments during fieldwork (Pabla *et al.*, 1993). Goeghegan *et al.* [1984] state: "It has been found time and again that perhaps the most useful way for the environmental planner to discover trends, conflicts, and problem areas that can otherwise be easily overlooked, is by mapping information".

Participatory mapping is particularly important for PRA. Mapping can include many items, including: (1) social; like village layout, infrastructure, population, households, chronic health cases, size of family; (2) resources; like fisheries, land use, land and water management, watersheds, degraded resources, etc.; (3) transects; like walks and boat rides to see indigenous technology, resources, and fishing practices. Guidance manuals on PRA are available by contacting international donor offices.

5.4 Education and Outreach

Civic awareness plays a major role in the success of coastal conservation. In countries where MPAs are effective, conservation awareness is usually high among communities, managers, *and* the private sector. The most important goal is to explain to the people the long-term, sustainable benefits that conservation can provide through public information and education. Honest efforts to inform the public are essential, but education should not be used as propaganda for "selling" conservation programmes.

Environmental education aims to provide the community with information and a conservation ethic so that its members can make informed decisions about the use of their resources (Clark, 1991). Then too, the place where the land ends is also the place where the knowledge and experience of most administrators ends. Planners, managers, engineers, and politicians alike need to be informed about the sea and the seacoast. In educating politicians and economic planners, it is important to use language and concepts with which they are familiar.

The first step in designing an education programme for capacity building is to identify the main audiences; for example, artisanal fishermen, dive operators, tourists, hotel owners, port directors, and politicians. Because most politicians monitor their constituencies, public awareness and sensitization is important to success of coastal conservation.

For example, Hudson (1988) recommends the following for Australia's Great Barrier Reef:

Target Group	Message
General Public:	Nature of coral reef environment Need to protect reef areas
Local Fishermen:	Economic benefit of proper management Provisions of plan regarding fishing
Tourist Operator:	Suggested tourist activity on reefs Provisions of plan regarding tourism
Govt Agencies:	How plan interacts with their mandates

Next, specific objectives must be established in terms of knowledge, attitudes and behavior to be changed or influenced within each target group. For example, in the Central Visayas project of the Philippines, fishermen who were educated about artificial reef construction and use were able to increase their catches and abandon dynamite fishing at the same time.

Initially, a multifaceted approach, combining printed materials, audio-visual presentations, and face-to-face interaction, is probably the best way to start an education programme. Depending on the target audience and budget, a variety of additional options can be employed: mass media (press, television, radio), fixed exhibits, tours, training workshops, the sale of promotional items such as T-shirts, and informal recreational activities with an educational focus (Clark, 1991a).

Evaluation of techniques that can be used to get the conservation message across follows (Hudson 1988):

1. Television: Has general audience, raises general awareness of situation and can motivate people to do something about an issue which they may not have known about before. It is a passive medium for the receiver but handled well can be of great benefit in general public education.

2. Video: This has many benefits to the environmental educator. You can make your own specific television programmes using your environment and people to get your message across to your target groups. The equipment needed is relatively cheap and easy to use. With a little experience one can make short programmes quickly (but it is advisable to secure professional advice).

3. Radio: An excellent medium, it is available in most countries and is extensively used by schools and other teaching institutions. Radio series on environmental issues, especially if there is a strong story line, are often appealing to children and not only children listen to school radio, often their families do as well.

4. Print media: Newspapers and magazines can reach either general or specific target groups. Careful analysis must be made of the type of material needed for each, how it fits into your education programme and goals and the gains you hope to make from it. Journalists must be dealt with carefully but can be most helpful in environmental education work.

5. Books and pamphlets: Each type must be evaluated for suitability. Books are expensive to produce but can be useful in schools and for sale to a selected adult audience. Pamphlets and leaflets can help in specific cases, e.g., rules for management.

6. Posters: They are attractive, easy to make, salable, and are a general educational tool. They can be useful in schools and other institutions, but are not so effective for specific target groups.

7. Printed clothing: T-shirts may be a very good educational tool with specific target groups, especially those in remote areas and where people interchange belongings within the groups regularly. They can become prestige items, showing that the wearer is fashionable and part of a 'new movement'. They are cheap to produce and can be sold to support conservation.

8. Badges: Many of the things said about T-shirts are applicable. Badges are cheap to produce and make in quantity. Young people like wearing them and they can be used as rewards with school groups. Teenagers and even older people often like badges. They are highly visible and a good talking point.

9. Entertainment: Messages in locally acceptable forms of drama are one of the best ways of getting your message across to your audience. People like to be entertained and if they can be made aware of issues and motivated at the same time, all the better.

10. Open meetings: They are most often held to discuss specific issues concerning developments in government plans and may be aimed at soliciting ideas from the public. Such meetings should encourage interactive participation. Meetings that are held just to propagandize the people should be avoided.

Changes of basic attitudes are difficult and not often affected by short-term awareness campaigns, according to Hudson (1988), who advises that it may be possible to sell soap powder in crash campaigns, but to cause fishermen to use less destructive techniques for fishing, for example, would take much longer. But such changes of public opinion are possible in the long run, especially where the coastal management staff have a good relationship with the people affected and where the need to change attitude can be backed by facts and is reinforced by the experience of the people themselves.

An important part of awareness work is "feed-back" to determine programme effectiveness. Feedback provides a conduit that can tell planners and other management staff what is really happening in the real world. Field staff interact with the people constantly and therefore are in the best position to gauge the actual effects of the programme.

5.5 Scientific Input

In project assessments, scientists have important roles to play. In particular, they should advise on the relevance, reliability and cost-effectiveness of scientific information generated by research and monitoring and advise on the suitability of control data. Scientists should also provide monitoring methods to estimate the extent to which observed changes in managed environments and practices can be attributed to conservation measures as opposed to other factors. A United Nations (UN) report lists eight major opportunities for scientific and technical input in coastal conservation (GESAMP, 1996):

1. Environmental impact assessment

2. Resource surveys

3. Simulation modeling

4. Economic assessment and valuation

5. Legal and institutional analyses

6. Social and cultural analyses

7. Management methodologies

8. Public education materials

Some good advice to scientists involved in planning coastal management programmes appeared in the UN report. Such scientists were advised to design their research by "...preparing concise statements of objectives for research and monitoring, clearly defining what is to be measured and why, and in identifying methodologies, facilities and personnel needed for the studies to be cost effective and successful." That is, for each priority issue to be addressed, scientists should work with conservation managers to formulate specific questions that are to be resolved through subsequent scientific investigations.

The UN report notes that scientists can help bring together the information required by managers and politicians. But often the reward system for scientists encourages them to concentrate on research which is not relevant to management, which could be a real problem for MPA planners (GESAMP, 1996).

5.6 Restoration

Ecosystem restoration is an important objective of many MPAs. The MPA planners should survey and identify the special habitats that have been degraded and that can be repaired at reasonable cost and effort. These should be mapped, priorities assigned, and strategies for rehabilitation created.

While all coastal resources that have been degraded cannot, in a practical sense, be returned to full productivity, some of them can. Mangrove forests can be replanted, coral reefs can be started toward gradual renewal and normal circulation to wetlands can be restored.

If a wetland is covered with fill behind a concrete bulkhead, it would be unrealistic to plan to restore it to its original condition; but if a wetland has been diked for rice culture or aquaculture, it would be relatively easy to remove dikes, restore circulation, and reconvert it to a nearly natural wetlands condition.

If a coral reef has been damaged by pollution, hurricanes, mining, natural bleaching, or boat anchoring, it would be difficult, but not impossible to rehabilitate it (Figure I-46). Such rehabilitation can be costly and the time of recovery very long, but for certain reefs of high value for tourism, fish breeding, or shore protection, the investment could yield a high payoff (Clark, 1988).

FIGURE I-46.

Photo by Erkki Siirila.

This coral colony from the western coast of St.Lucia was damaged by land runoff during a tropical storm. The soil particles and an algal bloom reduced sunlight penetration into the sea for days, resulting in the loss of the symbiotic algae.

Hundreds of thousands of hectares of mangrove have been planted in restoration and shore protection initiatives, globally (Figure I-47). There have been great successes and disappointing failures but on the whole the projects have been successful. A clear message has arisen from these initiatives: Plantings should not be wasted in environments that would not *naturally* be colonized by mangrove.

Community based restoration projects may be far less expensive than those done by hired labour; for example, in a Philippines analysis, community-based mangrove plantings cost about US $80/ha while contractor plantings cost more than US $400/ha. Also, the new mangrove area is also better cared for when the community plants it and has special rights to it.

Degraded dunes and beaches can be rebuilt using the approach of the "sand budget" (Charlier and DeCroo, 1991) whereby the beach is treated as a bank account with inputs and outputs, credits and debits, along with cash reserves. The parameters are as follows:

FIGURE I-47.

Mangroves are restored in Marigot Bay, St. Lucia, to stop shoreline erosion, which had resulted from mangrove removal.

Photo by Erkki Siirila.

1. **Debits**: longshore downdrift transport, offshore transport, deposit in submarine gullies, mining, aeolian (wind) transport, and solution and abrasion (withdrawals).

2. **Credits**: longshore transport onto beach, river transport, sea cliff erosion, onshore transport, biogeneous deposition, hydrogenous deposition, and beachfill (deposits).

3. **Sand Storage**: dunes, berms, sandbars (reserves).

5.7 Coastal Zone Management

Marine and coastal resource reserves, national parks, and other types of MPAs are better protected if they are integrated into an unified Coastal Zone Management (CZM) programme. Estuaries are an example of habitats that often present such a complex of problems that they are more appropriately managed within a CZM programme than as a completely independent MPA. A large lagoon or estuary is often the locus of such complex development activities (many originate at a considerable distance from the lagoon or estuary) that it would not make a suitable MPA site without external protection.

Managing a nature reserve or marine park in isolation from surrounding land uses and peoples, and without wide cooperation from agencies, stakeholders, and impacters, may not fully succeed. The reason is that protected areas alienated from a wider programme of coastal resources management exist as "islands of protection" surrounded by uncontrolled areas of threat where pollution, habitat destruction, and over fishing may exist. CZM provides an appropriate framework for incorporation of protected areas into a larger system of protection and a method of consensus building for their support.

CZM programmes can be organized to control uses in the Zones of Influence adjacent to protected area boundaries (see Section 5.8) and thereby prevent encroachment into these areas as well as reduce pollution from external sources, limit destruction of special "nurturing" habitats, and minimize other types of external impact that could be damaging to the protected area. CZM programmes can be of either national or regional scope.

The additional protection afforded by CZM regulatory mechanisms can be beneficial where, for example, harsh impacts to MPAs come across MPA boundaries from external sources such as industrial or urban pollution (Figure I-48) or storm runoff over which the MPA has no jurisdiction but which could be subject to unified CZM controls. CZM can address many other transboundary impacts such as adverse shoreline development and aquaculture intrusion. CZM programmes are primarily directed at *development management* rather than resource management (Clark, 1996). In this way CZM is the twin of MPAs which do focus on *resource management*.

FIGURE I-48.

Photo by Don Engdahl.

Visitors to MPAs should be protected from pollution.

Protection of species and their habitats is a necessary part of CZM and is an important aspect of biodiversity maintenance. Effective programmes will include *both* regulatory and custodial (protected areas) components. On one hand, the regulatory component provides a broad framework for controlling uses of coastal resources, including regulations, permits, environmental assessment, and development planning, operating through administrative process and police function. On the other hand the custodial component provides special protection for natural areas (reserves, national parks, etc.) of special resource value, operating through the owner's or custodian's exercise of proprietary rights. By combining the two, there is created both 1) an "umbrella" regulatory scheme for resource conservation and orderly development, and 2) a specific custodial scheme for high level protection of ecologically important areas. (Clark *et al.*, 1987).

CZM addresses protection for natural habitat types known to be especially valuable; for example, mangrove forests, coral reefs, submerged seagrass meadows, kelp beds, oyster bars, beach-dune systems (Figure I-49), and lagoons, estuaries and other embayments. While it is useful and practical to focus on individual habitat types,

FIGURE I-49.

Photo by Erkki Siirila.

The conservation of the natural vegetation keeps the beach dune systems stable near the town of La Paz in the southern Baja California, Mexico.

one must not forget they exist only as components of wider coastal ecosystems. Custodial protection of special habitats is integrated into CZM programmes so that managing a nature reserve or marine park does not have to be done in isolation from surrounding sources of pollution or troublesome land uses, nor without interagency collaboration.

MPAs support the broad objectives of CZM by conserving special nurturing habitats for fish species, enhancing tourism revenues and recreational benefits, preserving biodiversity, and promoting baseline scientific studies. Also a coral reef reserve could be established to both conserve the reef habitat and protect the beach from wave attack during storms.

There are two main purposes for identifying special habitats and providing for their protection: conservation of the economic resource base (fisheries, tourism, etc) and preservation of biodiversity (the whole range of species and natural habitats). Of particular importance in biodiversity conservation are the habitats of species that have been designated as especially valuable or in danger of extinction (Figure I-50).

Such special habitats are often designated for protection in CZM programmes. This can best be done in a three tier approach using a combination of regulatory and custodial approaches that provide an optimum approach for protection of special habitats. This approach includes both a regulatory scheme for conservation and a programme for establishing resource reserves (conservation) and marine national parks (recreation, education).

Planners might consider a mixed approach combining MPAs with CZM whereby: 1) *all* mangroves systems or *all* coral reef systems in a country are designated as off limits to disturbance-causing activities under special CZM laws; 2) ecologically special sites are designated for MPA protection; and 3) particular named sites, such as certain bays or stretches of coast that are not designated as MPAs are nevertheless spared from heavy impacts by development controls (see Box I-8).

For example, the following three categories are defined in the Puerto Rico (USA Territory) CZM programme:

FIGURE I-50.

Coastal conservation often requires adjustment of building locations and other land use arrangements. Above, structures on the beach with restricted turtle nesting areas suffered heavy storm damage. A turtle nesting site here was abandoned probably because the turtle was unable to dig through the storm-tossed debris in the sand (Hawkes Bay, Pakistan).

Box I-8. Special Habitats

CZM should recognize three types of particularly valuable habitats by identifying the following three categories:

1. **Generic types of habitats**: Those that are widely recognized as highly valuable and that should be given a high degree of protection through *regulatory* mechanisms— wetlands, seagrass meadows, coral reefs, species nesting sites. All should be mapped and publicized. In the CZM process of project review, developers would be required to avoid these types of habitats; therefore, developers must be informed ahead of time (before they design projects) that restrictions exist. In addition to ecologically valuable areas, other types of areas should be identified, such as sand dunes (which stabilize beaches) and flood-prone lowlands (those that are regularly flooded) both of which would be included in a "natural hazards prevention" category.

2. **Specific sites**: Those that are identified as Special Habitats and should be identified for *special regulatory protection*. These would include certain specific (named) lagoons, estuaries, islands, mangrove forests, river deltas, coral reefs, and so forth. Each would be described, mapped and announced for the knowledge of all interested parties. The CZM authority would strongly constrain development in these site-specific habitats by regulation. As "red flag" areas, they would get special analysis in the development review process.

3. **Resource Reserves and Other MPAs**: This category includes critical marine and coastal resource areas that need the additional safeguard of the type of *custodial protection* that is awarded to terrestrial parks and reserves. Such MPAs would be assigned to the country's existing conservation agency for management. Proprietorship (whether through ownership or custodianship) generally confers a higher level of autonomy than does CZM regulation through the "police power" (as in (2) above).

Source: modified from Clark, 1998.

1. *Generic habitat types*: all mangrove forests are included in a "special planning areas" category.

2. *Specific sites (critical areas)*: numerous bays, lagoons and other coastal features are included in a list of site-specific special planning areas.

3. *Protected Areas*: numerous coastal areas of exceptional natural value are identified as potential Natural Reserves.

CZM uses the current concepts of sustainable use, multiple use, rights to the commons, biodiversity, zoning, protection of special habitats, public participation, capacity building, institutional strengthening, co-management, situation management, and integrated management. The key is *unitary management* of the zone, which treats the shorelands and coastal waters as a *single* interacting unit and coordinates the interest of all stakeholders (Clark, 1998). Full participation of stakeholders is a necessity (Box I-9).

Box I-9. Public Participation in CZM

It is an axiom of CZM that only a truly unified programme (i.e., one that includes all the major sectors and interests affected) can accomplish all the needs; for example, port authorities, housing departments, tourist industries, fishermen, tribal chiefs, economic development planners. Therefore, a major function of CZM is to provide a framework for coordination of a wide array of interests.

Coastal communities and their leaders must be directly consulted about the formation of new coastal policies and rules on resource use if they are to support them. According to Renard (1986) public consultation is an opportunity available to the entire management community to ensure the quality and the effectiveness of the management solutions that will be implemented. He emphasizes that involvement is also a *duty* because "...the issue remains, above all, one of human development" and because "...people are not the object of development but the subject of development and the makers of their own history".

Encouragement of public participation is not supposed to lead to predetermined outcomes nor to change the ideologies or views of the fishermen, the government officials, the planners or citizens. Nor is it supposed to be a means to get a particular group or sector "aligned" to the needs of another group. Participation's only purpose is to unite people in open discussion and sharing of needs and ideas and in the working of solutions. Participation should lead to true consultation with ideas growing in both directions. Planners and managers too often resort to public consultation only when they encounter some form of opposition.

Kelleher (1996) states that "...participation that is not actively encouraged is not real participation. You've got to go out there. You've got to go through the process of distrust before you get to the process of trust... be prepared to be insulted, contradicted, even threatened. You have to prepare yourself psychologically."

According to White (1987) personal and community involvement come from wanting to support common values to gain some real or perceived benefit for the individual and the community. Without it, marine resources can never be conserved, because external enforcement of laws in the marine commons is not usually practicable.

Source: Clark, 1998.

CZM attempts to guide *future development* as a main purpose (Figure I-51) while also trying to correct environmental mistakes of the past as a parallel purpose (Clark, 1996). CZM is a powerful mechanism for allocation of natural resources and control of bad development if based upon sound environmental and socioeconomic planning and evaluation. It requires networking among all relevant government activities, including national economic development planning, and communities and NGOs. A primary strategy of CZM is to regulate construction and other actions in the coastal zone, often through a project review and permit letting process.

FIGURE I-51.

Photo by Erkki Siirila.

Environmental impact assessments are necessary to prevent shoreline crowding, such as this hotel construction in Cabo San Lucas, Baja California, Mexico.

Because enhanced economic development is typically perceived as the necessary first step in a nation's social development, coastlines often receive much economic development in the form of tourism and urban, agricultural, and industrial development. Unfortunately, the price of short-term benefits—from wetland reclamation, drainage, or conversion to rice fields, fishponds, coconut plantations, or pasturage—is pollution and the depletion of natural resources.

Certain damaging activities, such as dredging, landfill, coral mining, fishing with explosives, dumping at sea, and pollution, are direct and easy to recognize. Other effects are not so obvious, especially when they are far removed from the activity causing them (for example, hydroelectric schemes on rivers, irrigation projects, and forest cutting in watersheds). Thus, even inland activities must consider the coastal environment and its complement of interacting and interdependent habitats (Figure I-52).

The demand for coastal space and resources is usually so great that no one activity can be given exclusive use. The use of a particular coastal resource for a single economic purpose is discouraged by CZM in favor of a balance of *multiple uses* whereby economic and social benefits are jointly maximized and conservation and development become compatible goals.

FIGURE I-52.

Photo by John Clark.

Uncontrolled upstream activities can pollute the coastal zone, such as gravel mining here in Klung Kung, Bali, Indonesia.

While CZM can assist the MPA, the reverse is also true when, for example, a coral reef reserve helps to protect the beachfront from wave attack during storms. MPAs do support the broad objectives of CZM by conserving special nurturing areas for fish species, enhancing tourism revenues and recreational benefits, preserving biodiversity, promoting baseline scientific studies, etc.

In the evolution of MPA approaches, some holdings now resemble "resource management areas" more than "protected areas" and thus come close to resembling unified CZM programmes. These management areas may be run by a "management authority" of some type rather than a wildlife or national park type agency and are organized to yield a wide variety of uses and thus are really "multiple use" areas. Examples are, the Great Barrier Reef of Australia and the Florida Keys Coral Tract of the United States. It is particularly important that such areas be closely coordinated with the CZM programme (Clark, 1998).

5.8 Zones of Influence

In the absence of a Coastal Zone Management (CZM) programme or other means to assist the MPA with addressing transboundary effects from pollution and other impacts, the MPA planner or manager can attempt to establish a cooperative programme within a Zone of Influence (ZOI) beyond the boundaries of the MPA.

The Everglades National Park case in Box I-10 shows that no matter how large and seemingly complete a preserved area may appear, there will always be larger scale influences that affect its resources. Everglades, like so many other managed areas around the world, is not a closed ecosystem and will always be subject to effects from adjacent unmanaged ecosystems (see also Part III, Case No. 8). Therefore, MPA planners and managers must look to agencies in the "Zone of Influence" outside MPA boundaries for help in controlling external impacts.

FIGURE I-53.

Photo by John Clark.

While it would be conceptually valid to include within an MPA all areas that have an influence on the targeted coastal area, this definition could be politically self-defeating if it attempts to encompass all impacting coastal plains and the watersheds of all streams and rivers that drain into the sea, which at times extend hundreds of kilometers inland.

But, it is necessary to have some input into how resource uses are controlled in watersheds that are the sources of excessive siltation and chemical pollution of coastal waters. This can be accomplished by the designation of a Zone of Influence (ZOI). The ZOI would be accompanied by a formal method of negotiating MPA conservation needs with

Control of fishing access is an important function of the Gulf of Mannar Marine Park.

Box I-10. Everglades National Park

The state of Florida (USA) provides several useful examples of large-scale preservation. The Everglades National Park was established in south Florida in 1947 and currently encompasses more than 500,000 ha of land and water. Although much of this area is composed of upland plant communities, a significant portion is mangrove, sea grass beds, and coastal marshes. All of these habitat types provide nursery areas for the extensive commercial and sport fisheries that operate in contiguous coastal waters.

The great strength of Everglades National Park is that it includes almost the entire gradient from upland freshwater, through the estuary, to offshore many kilometers. The nearby Biscayne National Monument similarly includes coastal wetlands and mangroves, sea grass and macroalgae beds, barrier islands and passes, and offshore coral reefs. Together these two MPAs are designed to protect and nurture many commercial and recreational species like the gray snapper in all the various stages of their lives. The Everglades system also guarantees unimpeded natural production of detritus, which forms the basis of a complex food web that supports stocks of fishes.

Unfortunately, some factors cannot be totally controlled, even in a preserved area as large as the Everglades National Park (Morehead, 1984). For example, the watershed draining into the park extends far beyond the park boundaries so that activities outside the park, but within the watershed—irrigation, water diversion, and introduction of pollutants—have caused ecological damage to the park, but are beyond the control of park managers. For example, fish and shrimp populations within the Everglades estuary fluctuate in response to annual patterns of freshwater inflow. Without control of this inflow, it is impossible to properly protect and manage these fishery resources. And while the park has been allocated a total freshwater inflow of 430,000,000 m^3 (350,000 acre-feet) annually it has not been successful in getting the correct portions at particular critical times.

a variety of hinterland interests. The ZOI approach in the Gulf of Mannar is used to formally negotiate cooperative management actions *outside* the boundaries of the official coastal reserve and which affect the reserve, such as uncontrolled fishing (Figure I-53).

The ZOI approach could also work for offshore waters that extend past the statutory Coastal Zone boundary in order to cover some of the remote waters of the continental shelf (as defined by the 1982 Convention on the Law of the Sea) or the Exclusive Economic Zone (which extends to 320 km offshore) if important water use issues extend that far seaward.

5.9 Categories of Marine and Coastal Protected Areas

In its most recent treatment of protected area categories, IUCN (1994) identifies over 140 different names for marine and terrestrial protected areas from around the world. This variety of names underscores the need for and value of using names that have local meaning: this is as it should be—names should conform to their national or local relevance and to promote understanding and acceptance, rather than conforming to some international scheme.

However, this variety of names makes it difficult to communicate and compare protected areas on the basis of names alone, and creates the need for a standard terminology that is designed to facilitate understanding, communication, comparison, and assessment of global conservation achievement. While IUCN categories may be of slight relevance to an MPA site manager in his daily work, they may be of interest to national planners and academics.

While criteria help select protected areas, categories define their management regimes. For example, management category Ia, Strict Nature Reserve, may be appropriate for safeguarding critical habitats of fish or for coastal protection, while category VI, Managed Resource Protected Area, permits most uses, as long as they are sustainable (see below listing).

Conservation categories provide a means for clearly incorporating conservation into development. Each category relates to one or several major goals of a country's development plan: nutrition, environment, health, education, housing, water supply, science, technology, defense, national identity, and international obligations. Viewed in this way, conservation categories become the basis for sustainable development.

The six IUCN protected area categories, their management objectives and selection criteria as presented by Davey (1998) are defined below:

Category Ia—Strict Nature Reserve, protected area managed mainly for research.

Definition:

Area of land and/or sea possessing some outstanding or representative ecosystems, geological or physiological features and/or species, available primarily for scientific research and/or environmental monitoring.

Objectives of management:

- to preserve habitats, ecosystems and species in as undisturbed a state as possible
- to maintain genetic resources in a dynamic and evolutionary state
- to maintain established ecological processes
- to safeguard structural landscape features or rock exposures

- to secure examples of the natural environment for scientific studies, environmental monitoring and education, including baseline areas from which all avoidable access is excluded
- to minimize disturbance by careful planning and execution of research and other approved activities
- to limit public access

Guidance for selection:

- The area should be large enough to ensure the integrity of its ecosystems and to accomplish the management objectives for which it is protected.
- The area should be significantly free of direct human intervention and capable of remaining so.
- The conservation of the area's biodiversity should be achievable through protection and not require substantial active management or habitat manipulation (c.f. Category IV).

Category Ib—Wilderness Area: protected area managed mainly for wilderness protection

Definition:

Large area of unmodified or slightly modified land, and/or sea, retaining its natural character and influence, without permanent or significant habitation, which is protected and managed so as to preserve its natural condition.

Objectives of management:

- to ensure that future generations have the opportunity to experience understanding and enjoyment of areas that have been largely undisturbed by human action over a long period of time
- to maintain the essential natural attributes and qualities of the environment over the long term
- to provide for public access at levels and of a type which will serve best the physical and spiritual well-being of visitors and maintain the wilderness qualities of the area for present and future generations
- to enable indigenous human communities living at low density and in balance with the available resources to maintain their lifestyle

Guidance for selection:

- The area should possess high natural quality, be governed primarily by the forces of nature, with human disturbance substantially absent, and be likely to continue to display those attributes if managed as proposed.
- The area should contain significant ecological, geological, physiogeographic, or other features of scientific, educational, scenic or historic value.

- The area should offer outstanding opportunities for solitude, enjoyed once the area has been reached, by simple, quiet, non-polluting and non-intrusive means of travel (i.e., non-motorized).
- The area should be of sufficient size to make practical such preservation and use.

Category II—National Park: protected area managed mainly for ecosystem protection and tourism

Definition:

Natural area of land and/or sea, designated to (a) protect the ecological integrity of one or more ecosystems for present and future generations, (b) exclude exploitation or occupation inimical to the purposes of designation of the area, and (c) provide a foundation for spiritual, scientific, educational, recreational and visitor opportunities, all of which must be environmentally and culturally compatible.

Objectives of management:

- to protect natural and scenic areas of national and international significance for spiritual, scientific, educational, recreational or tourist purposes
- to perpetuate, in as natural a state as possible, representative examples of physiographic regions, biotic communities, genetic resources, and species, to provide ecological stability and diversity
- to manage visitor use for inspirational, educational, cultural and recreational purposes at a level which will maintain the area in a natural or near natural state
- to eliminate and thereafter prevent exploitation or occupation inimical to the purposes of designation
- to maintain respect for the ecological, geomorphologic, sacred or aesthetic attributes which warranted designation
- to take into account the needs of indigenous people, including subsistence resource use, in so far as these will not adversely affect the other objectives of management

Guidance for selection:

- The area should contain a representative sample of major natural regions, features or scenery, where plant and animal species, habitats and geomorphological sites are of special spiritual, scientific, educational, recreational and tourist significance.
- The area should be large enough to contain one or more entire ecosystems not materially altered by current human occupation or exploitation.

Category III—Natural Monument: protected area managed mainly for conservation of specific natural features

Definition:

Area containing one, or more, specific natural or natural/cultural features which may be of outstanding or unique value because of its inherent rarity, representative or aesthetic qualities or cultural significance.

Objectives of management:

– to protect or preserve in perpetuity specific outstanding natural features because of their natural significance, unique or representational quality, and/or spiritual connotations

– to an extent consistent with the foregoing objective, to provide opportunities for research, education, interpretation and public appreciation

– to eliminate and thereafter prevent exploitation or occupation inimical to the purpose of designation

– to deliver to any resident population such benefits as are consistent with the other objectives of management

Guidance for selection:

• The area should contain one or more features of outstanding significance (appropriate natural features include spectacular waterfalls, caves, craters, fossil beds, sand dunes and marine features, along with unique or representative fauna and flora; associated cultural features might include cave dwellings, cliff-top forts, archaeological sites, or natural sites which have heritage significance to indigenous peoples).

• The area should be large enough to protect the integrity of the feature and its immediately related surroundings.

Category IV—Habitat/Species Management Area: protected area managed mainly for conservation through management intervention

Definition: Area of land and/or sea subject to active intervention for management purposes so as to ensure the maintenance of habitats and/or to meet the requirements of specific species.

Objectives of management:

– to secure and maintain the habitat conditions necessary to protect significant species, groups of species, biotic communities or physical features of the environment where these require specific human manipulation for optimum management

– to facilitate scientific research and environmental monitoring as primary activities associated with sustainable resource management

– to develop limited areas for public education and appreciation of the characteristics of the habitats concerned and of the work of wildlife management

- to eliminate and thereafter prevent exploitation or occupation inimical to the purpose of designation

- to deliver such benefits to people living within the designated area as are consistent with the other objectives of management

Guidance for selection:

- The area should play an important role in the protection of nature and the survival of species (incorporating, as appropriate, breeding areas, wetlands, coral reefs, estuaries, grasslands, forests or spawning areas, including marine feeding beds).

- The area should be one where the protection of the habitat is essential to the well being of nationally or locally important flora, or to resident or migratory fauna.

- Conservation of these habitats and species should depend upon active intervention by the management authority, if necessary through habitat manipulation (c.f. Category Ia).

- The size of the area should depend on the habitat requirements of the species to be protected and may range from relatively small to very extensive.

Category V—Protected Landscape/Seascape: protected area managed mainly for landscape/seascape conservation and recreation

Definition: Area of land, with coast and sea as appropriate, where the interaction of people and nature over time has produced an area of distinctive character with significant aesthetic, ecological and/or cultural value, and often with high biological diversity. Safeguarding the integrity of this traditional interaction is vital to the protection, maintenance and evolution of such an area.

Objectives of management:

- to maintain the harmonious interaction of nature and culture through the protection of landscape and/or seascape and the continuation of traditional land uses, building practices and social and cultural manifestations

- to support lifestyles and economic activities which are in harmony with nature and the preservation of the social and cultural fabric of the communities concerned

- to maintain the diversity of landscape and habitat, and of associated species and ecosystems to eliminate where necessary, and thereafter prevent, land uses and activities which are inappropriate in scale and/or character

- to provide opportunities for public enjoyment through recreation and tourism appropriate in type and scale to the essential qualities of the areas

- to encourage scientific and educational activities which will contribute to the long-term well-being of resident populations and to the development of public support for the environmental protection of such areas

– to bring benefits to, and to contribute to the welfare of, the local community through the provision of natural products (such as forest and fisheries products) and services (such as clean water or income derived from sustainable forms of tourism)

Guidance for selection:

• The area should possess a landscape and/or coastal and island seascape of high scenic quality, with diverse associated habitats, flora and fauna along with manifestations of unique or traditional land-use patterns and social organizations as evidenced in human settlements and local customs, livelihoods, and beliefs.

• The area should provide opportunities for public enjoyment through recreation and tourism within its normal lifestyle and economic activities.

Category VI—Managed Resource Protected Area: protected area managed mainly for the sustainable use of natural ecosystems

Definition: Area containing predominantly unmodified natural systems, managed to ensure long term protection and maintenance of biological diversity, while providing at the same time a sustainable flow of natural products and services to meet community needs. The area must also fit the overall definition of a protected area.

Objectives of management:

– to protect and maintain the biological diversity and other natural values of the area in the long term

– to promote sound management practices for sustainable production purposes

– to protect the natural resource base from being alienated for other land use purposes that would be detrimental to the area's biological diversity

– to contribute to regional and national development

Guidance for selection:

• At least two-thirds of the area should be in, and is planned to remain in, a natural condition, although it may also contain limited areas of modified ecosystems; large commercial plantations are not to be included.

• The area should be large enough to absorb sustainable resource uses without detriment to its overall long-term natural values.

• A management authority must be in place.

The first step in identifying a category is defining the management objectives for the site. Once this is done, you may compare these with the objectives in Table I-5 and match them with the ones they most resemble. The table lists categories and example objectives ranked according to their relevance to each of the categories.

Examining Table I-5 along a specified row indicates categories that have a given primary objective and thus are suitable choices. If tourism development is a

Table I-5. Protected Area Categories and Management Objectives

Management Objective	Ia	Ib	II	III	IV	V	VI
Scientific research	1	3	2	2	2	2	3
Wilderness protection	2	1	2	3	3	–	2
Preservation of species and genetic diversity	1	2	1	1	1	2	1
Maintenance of environmental services	2	1	1	–	1	2	1
Protection of specific natural/cultural features	–	–	2	1	3	1	1
Tourism and recreation	–	2	1	1	3	1	3
Education	–	–	2	2	2	2	3
Sustainable use of resources from natural ecosystems	–	3	3	1	2	2	1
Maintenance of cultural/traditional attributes	–	–	–	–	–	1	2

Key: 1= Primary objective; 2 = Secondary objective; 3 = Potentially applicable objective; – = Not applicable

primary objective, for example, the choices would be categories II, III or V. However, the objective could also be accommodated by any of categories Ib, IV or VII, but not by category Ia, which specifies strict protection. If the site could serve both tourism and preserve genetic diversity equally, the best choice would be category II or III.

5.10 Economic Innovations

Traditionally, marine conservation has been based on ecological concerns and goals. But, as the human pressures on marine and coastal ecosystems have intensified, so economics approaches have come to play an increasingly important role in the establishment and operation of MPAs. In particular, it is now recognized that questions of financial viability and economic sustainability are of central importance to the success of marine protected areas. This chapter describes some of the innovations which have taken place over the last decade in the application of economic tools and measures to marine management problems, especially their use to justify the existence of protected areas, to guard against marine degradation and loss, and to raise the funds necessary to conserve the marine environment.

Valuation: a means of justifying the existence of marine protected areas

It has become increasingly difficult to justify the existence of marine protected areas on biological and ecological grounds alone. Coastal communities need to earn a living, marine-based industries need raw materials and other infrastructure, and governments need to generate income, employment and foreign exchange, as well as to win votes. The needs of these producers and consumers often provide powerful arguments—and form influential lobby groups—against the reservation of land and sea areas, or against the protection of marine resources against exploitation. Approval for the establishment of MPAs does not depend just on the decisions of conservationists or environmental protection agencies. It has become apparent that they must also be acceptable to other political and economic interests, and have the potential to compete against the development imperatives that apply to most coastal and marine areas.

In order to be politically and economically acceptable marine protected areas must be able to demonstrate themselves to be a worthwhile use of funds and natural resources, as entities in themselves as well as in comparison to any opportunities for exploitation, production or consumption that their establishment precludes (in economic terms, this is known as their "opportunity cost"). MPAs must be seen as financially and economically attractive options to other government sectors, to private companies and to the human populations who live in coastal and marine areas. The need to justify MPAs in social, economic and developmental terms has become almost universal. It is however particularly intense in developing countries, where coast-dwelling communities typically have few sources of income and subsistence aside from the exploitation of marine resources and where government budgets are particularly low.

Economic valuation has proved to be an extremely useful tool in providing this broader justification for the establishment of MPAs. Just as conservationists have been slow to see the importance of taking economic factors into account in marine management, so economists have, conventionally, had a very blinkered view of the value of marine resources. Slowly this view has been broadened, and applied to marine management problems. Traditionally, economic valuation of marine ecosystems has focused almost entirely on commercial fisheries and tourism which can easily be measured in monetary terms. Although these sources of income still play an important role in economic valuation, it is now increasingly recognized that marine economic benefits extend far beyond these direct values. Looking at fisheries and tourism alone hugely underestimates the economic importance of marine and coastal ecosystems.

Economic views of marine areas have gradually come to rely on a much broader definition of benefits and productivity—that of total economic value (Figure I-54). Total economic value includes, as well as the direct use of marine products and areas for income and subsistence (for example through fisheries, tourism, and the exploitation of other resources such as shells and corals), the "indirect economic values" associated with marine ecosystem services (such as coastal protection, storm control, carbon sequestration and the provision of breeding grounds and habitat for fish, bird and mammal species), their "option value" (the premium placed on maintaining coastal and marine ecosystems and their component species for possible future uses and developments) and their "existence values" (their intrinsic value, irrespective of use, including cultural, aesthetic, scientific, bequest and heritage significance).

FIGURE I-54.

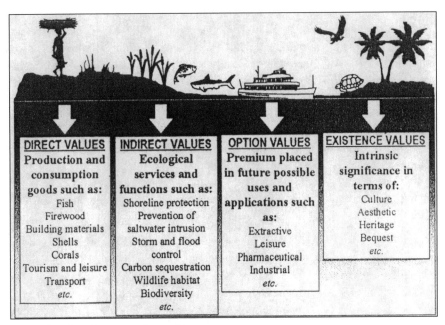

DIRECT VALUES	INDIRECT VALUES	OPTION VALUES	EXISTENCE VALUES
Production and consumption goods such as:	Ecological services and functions such as:	Premium placed in future possible uses and applications such as:	Intrinsic significance in terms of:
Fish	Shoreline protection	Extractive	Culture
Firewood	Prevention of	Leisure	Aesthetic
Building materials	saltwater intrusion	Pharmaceutical	Heritage
Shells	Storm and flood	Industrial	Bequest
Corals	control	*etc.*	*etc.*
Tourism and leisure	Carbon sequestration		
Transport	Wildlife habitat		
etc.	Biodiversity		
	etc.		

The total economic value of marine and coastal ecosystems.

As perceptions of the economic value of marine ecosystems have moved forward, so have a range of new methods been developed to quantify these economic benefits and express them as monetary values (Box I-11). In turn, these values have provided an extremely convincing—and much needed—way of demonstrating the desirability of MPAs in social, economic and development terms,. Economic valuation highlights that marine protected areas are much more than a static biological or ecological pool of resources, but should rather be seen as stocks of natural capital which if properly managed can yield a wide range of economic benefits to human populations—often to a value which is far higher than the income accruing from unsustainable exploitation and development.

Economic instruments and incentives: guarding against marine degradation

The preceding paragraphs have described the important role that economic valuation plays in justifying actions to conserve marine and coastal environments. However, even if conservation is broadly justifiable to government policy-makers and decision-makers, the establishment of MPAs often does not make economic sense to the people whose activities have the potential to impact negatively on the integrity of marine and coastal ecosystems. Although marine degradation incurs high social and economic costs, it may still be economically desirable to individual producers and consumers. It is frequently more profitable for people to degrade marine ecosystems than to conserve them, because they feel no private cost—and may even be able to generate higher profits—from doing so (see Box I-12). Fishermen, the harvesters of mangrove poles, shells, corals, seabirds and other resources, the people

Box I-11. Marine Valuation Methods

Market prices are often a poor guide to the real economic value of marine resources. As well as the fact that many marine products have no market at all (for example products which are used for subsistence purposes only, or services which cannot be bought and sold such as beach protection or carbon sequestration), market prices often underestimate their true worth (for example the aesthetic and cultural significance attached to marine protected areas is far higher than the entry fees people pay to enter and use them, the patent fees paid for the development of marine resource-based pharmaceutical or industrial applications only represents a tiny proportion of the potential value of these developments, a wide range of taxes and subsidies distort the prices of marine products in many countries). It has become necessary to find alternative valuation methods which are capable of capturing the full worth, and total economic value, associated with marine ecosystems.

Many advances have been made in the economic valuation of marine goods and services. This includes the use of costs saved as a proxy for the value of marine goods (for example the valuation of coral rag in Mafia Island, Tanzania at US$ 140/tonne—the price of the next best substitute building material, imported cement (Dulvy *et al.*, 1995)), or marine ecosystem services (for example valuation of the shoreline protection services provided by coral reefs, coastal marshes and mangroves in the Seychelles at some US$ 0.8 million a year in terms of the costs of their replacement with artificial groynes and barriers (Emerton, 1997), or the US$ 0.3 million a year global warming-associated damage avoided by carbon sequestration functions of Djibouti's coral reefs (Asrat and Emerton, 1998). Another way of calculating values is to look at the way in which marine resources are associated with other production and consumption processes (for example the beneficial effect of the Anolis lizard on agricultural production in the Antilles was estimated terms of the value associated with its control of crop pests, for the whole population worth a maximum of over US$ 450 million (Narain and Fisher, 1994)).

Where people do not pay to consume marine resources, or pay a price that is obviously lower than total utility gained, travel cost methods provide a particularly useful way of estimating values (for example the total tourist value associated with the Great Barrier Reef Marine Park was estimated by looking at the travel, accommodation and other costs incurred, some A$ 800 million a year (Craik, 1994)). Finally, economic valuation may be based on people's responses to hypothetical "what if" questions, carried out regardless of any actual markets in marine goods or associated resources and production processes (for example by the use of contingent valuation methods to assess residents' support for actions to conserve the Batangas Bay in the Philippines based on their stated willingness to increase garbage collection and sewage treatment charges, or to pay fees to maintain fisheries and coral reefs (Tejan and Ross, 1997)).

who wish to develop marine and coastal areas for tourism, settlement, industry and mariculture, as well as all the ultimate consumers of marine products, often continue to contribute to marine degradation through their economic activities. Even the very people who are attracted by MPAs, most notably tour operators and their clients, may contribute to marine degradation.

Box I-12. The Private Profits and Economic Costs of Marine Degradation

All too often marine degradation makes perfect economic sense to individual developers or producers, regardless of the long-term economic costs it imposes on the rest of society or the economy. Although many examples exist, those associated with destructive fishing practices epitomise many of the trade-offs between the private profits and economic costs arising from activities which degrade the marine environment.

A range of destructive harvesting practices bring high profits to fishermen operating in the Indo-Pacific region. For example in 1997 some 20,000 tonnes of live fish were exported into Hong Kong, bringing profits to fishermen of up to US$ 1.8 million and earning restaurateurs nearly US$ 4 million (Barber and Pratt, 1998). Many of these fish were caught using cyanide, a method which has devastating effects not just on the health of fishermen themselves, but is also extremely destructive to coral reef ecosystems. Similarly blast fishing, although highly illegal and destructive to coral reefs, provides both food and income to a vast number of fishermen who have few alternative sources of living open to them. Blast fishing brings in some of the highest income to coastal communities in Indonesia, despite leading to broader net economic costs after 20 years in excess of US$ 300,000 per km^2 of coral reef (more than four times higher than the total net private benefits accruing to fishermen (Pet-Soede *et al.*, 1999).

All too often the need to make marine protected areas economically desirable, or to make marine degradation economically non-viable to these other groups has been ignored. Although many countries have a complex body of laws relating to fisheries, resource utilization and to the implementation of developments in marine and coastal zones, without supportive economic measures these prohibitions are difficult to enforce. The legal establishment of MPAs, and restrictions on the utilization of marine resources, is frequently seen as an end in itself, rather than as a means to an end, to the detriment of marine conservation. By themselves command and control measures are often ineffective in ensuring that marine protected areas stay protected because they provide no positive encouragement or inducement, and are often difficult and costly to enforce. It is increasingly being realized that people are far more likely to conserve marine resources if it is more profitable, or economically desirable, for them to do so, or if a personal cost accrues to them from degrading the marine environment.

Here again economics plays an important role in MPA management. Unless there is a clear benefit, or a clearly enforced financial penalty against doing so, there is no reason why people should limit profitable production and consumption activities that harm MPAs. It simply does not make economic sense to do so. Setting in place economic incentives for conservation forms an important strategy for marine protected area management. Incentives can be defined as specific inducements designed and implemented to influence government bodies, business, non-governmental organizations, or local people to conserve marine ecosystems or to use their components in a sustainable manner. This involves not only setting in place positive economic incentives, or rewards, for marine conservation (see Box I-13), but also overcoming the disincentives and perverse incentives which encourage people to degrade the marine environment. These disincentives and perverse incentives typically result from much broader social and economic forces which cause marine resources to be under-valued, over-consumed and under-conserved—for example subsidies and concessions made to industrial development on coastal strips, the promotion of commercial fisheries or mariculture development, or tax breaks provided for the development of export fisheries.

Box I-13. Positive Economic Instruments for Marine Conservation

Economic instruments for marine conservation can take many forms, including reforming the policies and institutions which create a perverse incentive structure and encourage people to carry out activities at levels and in ways which harm the marine environment as well those which present disincentives to marine degradation by penalising them for carrying out particular activities or consuming particular products. The most effective instruments for marine conservation are, however, usually those which set in place positive incentives and reward people for good behaviour. As well as being relatively easy to transact and enforce, they are more likely to be taken up (because they provide a means of increasing personal gain (at the same time as benefiting society and the environment), they are far more attractive and acceptable to producers and consumers. Some examples of positive incentives for marine conservation are given below.

One very important positive incentive for marine conservation (which is often also a prerequisite to the application of other economic instruments (is to make individuals or groups responsible for resources and areas, and to thereby set in place a clear mechanism for them to benefit from marine conservation, or to personally bear the costs associated with degradation. For example steps are underway to grant a consortium of local fishermen and tour operators the rights to use and manage a marine protected area on the Kenya coast, Diani-Chale Marine National Reserve, for their own benefit (ICAM, 1999). Here, granting private property rights is seen as a means of ensuring that these groups, whose activities currently contribute to marine degradation, have a clear stake in the conservation of marine resources for their own benefit and profit. Another example of the granting of property rights is provided by the case of the Akamas Peninsula in north-west Cyprus. Coastal areas of the Akamas Peninsula have a high level of biodiversity, as well as containing several rare and endemic plant species. Part of the Akamas Peninsula has been zoned by the Government of Cyprus as a non-development area. So as to save costs in its conservation, raise funds and avoid conflicts with potential developers, a system of transferable development rights has been proposed (Panayotou, 1994). Under this scheme developers, rather than being compensated with cash for activities foregone, would retain their rights to development but not be able to exercise them on-site. Development rights could be traded for property in other areas, or sold to groups concerned with the conservation of the Akamas Peninsula.

Marine conservation is often unacceptable to local coastal communities, especially those who have been displaced or whose productive opportunities have been reduced as a result of an area gaining protected status. The development of new products and markets, geared specifically towards replacing unsustainable activities and adding value to marine protection, can provide a strong positive incentive for supporting conservation, or for avoiding degradation. For example in the Bazaruto Archipelago of Mozambique, one of the country's most valuable and fragile marine ecosystems, a number of activities have been started which aim to stimulate sustainable use by local communities (Reina, 1998). These are focused on eco-tourism and artisanal resource utilisation, which are being promoted specifically to compensate local villagers for the loss of land and fishing resources resulting from the establishment of a National Park. Simultaneously a range of new activities are being promoted, including permaculture and vegetable farming, which aim to take pressure of marine resources.

A broad range of economic instruments have been suggested for the Seychelles which have the goal of encouraging commercial and industrial producers to avoid marine biodiversity degradation in the course of their economic activities (Emerton, 1997). It is proposed that beach waste deposits be levied on hoteliers, refundable against cleanup, and that a mooring bond could be set for tour operators against the use of designated anchors and buoys so as to guard against reef degradation. A variable scale of fishing licence fees according to target species and fishing methods aims to promote sustainable fishing practices, and a series of tax concessions and waived import duties on waste disposal equipment and clean technologies are proposed for industries operating in the coastal strip.

Financing mechanisms: making marine protected areas sustainable

Proving the total economic value of marine ecosystems and setting in place economic incentives for marine conservation, although necessary, do not usually by themselves provide sufficient conditions to ensure that marine protected areas are practically viable, or can be sustained over the long-term. Showing that marine protected areas benefit the wider economy and society, or can be made to be profitable to individual producers and consumers, is not the same thing as capturing these benefits as real cash values. The establishment and maintenance of marine protected areas incurs tangible cash expenditures, as well as giving rise to more intangible opportunity costs in terms of resource uses and productive opportunities foregone or diminished. Making sufficient funds available to cover these costs is a major issue in marine protected area management.

It is commonly and optimistically, but often mistakenly, assumed that a combination of central government subventions, donor grants and loans and tourist revenues will provide adequate funds to cover the costs of running marine protected areas. This is rarely the case (see Box I-14). Just as many of the economic benefits associated with marine protected areas have traditionally been underestimated and underemphasized, so have many more of the more imaginative and sustainable ways of raising finance also been ignored.

Box I-14. Problems with Conventional Funding Sources for Marine Protected Areas

It is becoming more and more difficult to raise the cash necessary to maintain protected areas from conventional funding sources. Both government and donor budgets are falling in most countries, tourism is often highly variable, and there is stiff competition for private investment funds from other sectors of the economy which are seen to generate higher, and more immediate, returns than marine conservation.

The case of Kisite-Mpunguti Marine National Park epitomises many of these funding constraints. Throughout the decade, as public sector budgets in Kenya have fallen and expenditure has been rationalised and focused on priority areas for social development such as health and education, central government subventions to environmental conservation activities have been falling. The amount of programme and project aid being granted to Kenya from external donors has also decreased substantially. Since 1990 all national parks in Kenya have been under the management of the parastatal Kenya Wildlife Service, meaning that as well as being accorded a much greater degree of autonomy, parks have been expected to become increasingly financially self-supporting.

However, relying almost entirely on tourist revenues for income, the Kenya Wildlife Service has been hit hard by the drastic downturn in tourism to Kenya over the last 5 years which has resulted from political unrest and civil insecurity in key tourist areas of the country, including the coastal strip. As a whole the Kenya Wildlife Service's revenue base has been undermined, and budget allocations to Kisite-Mpunguti have also fallen substantially (from an average of US$ 400,000 a year at today's prices during the late 1970s to only US$ 20,000 in the last financial year (Emerton, 1999)). Conventional funding sources are proving inadequate for Kisite-Mpunguti, which is having difficulties financing even its most basic management operations.

Over recent years a wide range of more innovative financing mechanisms have started to be used to raise funds for marine conservation (Box I-15). These are mainly based on capturing as real income some of the economic values associated with the consumption of marine goods and services. Although many groups and individuals benefit from marine goods and services, for which they would be both willing and able to pay, mechanisms do not exist by which they can be charged for their consumption, or can invest in the provision of marine goods and services.

Box I-15. Innovative Financing Mechanisms for Marine Management

The private sector often has a huge interest in marine resources and ecosystems. Under proper management arrangements, and with safeguards against commercial and environmental malpractice, these interests can be used to raise funds for conservation. For example private investment has been used in Tanzania to raise funds for marine protected area management. New environmental legislation in Zanzibar allows for protected area management to be delegated to private entities. Chumbe Island Coral Park, off Pemba, is now managed by a company formed specifically for this purpose. Incentives were provided by the government by allocating a lease and management contract to this company, and the running costs of the park are now almost entirely covered by private income generated (Riedmiller, 1998). International commercial interest can also be translated into funding, as evidenced by the use of payments for coral reef prospecting rights as a means of generating income for marine conservation. A number of useful applications of coral reef species for medical and pharmaceutical applications have been discovered, and many more are under development (for example compounds against cancer, treatments for heart disease, sunscreens and bone graft substitutes. There is a high level of international commercial and industrial interest in this potential. In line with this interest Imperial Chemical Industries has acquired the rights to develop a number of reef pigments for use as sunscreens for humans, and in 1992 the Coral Reef Foundation entered into a five year contract worth US$ 2.9 million for the supply of reef samples to the US National Cancer Institute for use in cancer and aids screening programmes (Spurgeon and Aylward, 1992).

More innovative ways have also been found to channel or administer conventional sources of finance, including those raised from donor and government funds. For example the Jamaica National Parks Trust Fund was established in 1991 and capitalised in 1992 with money from a debt-for-nature swap, under which a portion of the country's debt was purchased at below face value with cash provided by USAID, the Conservation Trust of Puerto Rico, the Smithsonian Institute, Fidelity Investments and The Nature Conservancy and redeemed against local currency (IUCN, 1994). Additional contributions have also been received from domestic companies and individuals. The fund is managed primarily as an endowment trust, paying its expenses through investment income and leaving the principal untouched. Grants are made to two National Parks, including contributing to the operating costs of the Montego Bay National Marine Park. New arrangements have also provided a means of ensuring not just that funds are raised for marine conservation, but they accrue to the groups who are actually responsible, or bear the costs associated with, marine protected areas. For example in St. Lucia a collaborative management agreement has been established between government and a community institution with the capability of managing a marine protected area and administering a fee system. Fees raised will be placed in a separate government fund, which will make quarterly payments to the community institution for the management of the protected area (Geoghegan, 1996).

Institutional and Legal Framework

Modern protected areas were first established on land. Institutional and legal frameworks originally were formulated to suit these land areas, first for national parks and then for other types of protected areas. In many instances the same approaches were applied to coastal and marine environments, with varying success, and did not necessarily account for the particular aspects of marine resources. Among these characteristics, Agardy (1997) identifies the fact that marine systems: are not as well understood as terrestrial ones; have nebulous boundaries; exhibit wider geographical and spatial scales in which environmentally induced changes are common and almost immediate; are driven by largely changeable and unpredictable processes; have largely unstructured food webs; are characterized by varying degrees of linkage between communities of organisms in the water column and those of the benthos; and are generally more non-linear than terrestrial systems. All these differences point to the necessity ultimately of designing protected areas in marine and coastal systems differently than terrestrial protected areas.

6.1 The Legal Basis of Coastal and Marine Protection

The establishment of a marine protected area more often than not requires the drafting and adoption of appropriate supportive legislation. Marine area protection has sometimes been accomplished through existing legislation that regulated other uses; for example, programmes for marine fisheries, forestry (of mangroves), and land use (of barrier islands and salt marshes). Yet, experience has shown that laws established specifically for land areas do not usually address the specific characteristics of marine and coastal environments, or the peculiarities of their use. It should be noted that in the past some MPAs might have been set up before legislation was passed but this state of affairs is not sustainable. By definition, the designation of an area as an MPA will restrict activities, which will ultimately call for some degree of enforcement and such measures are impossible in the absence of a legal text that recognizes the authority vested in the managers of the MPA.

Any authority in charge of establishing, and maintaining, an MPA will need to achieve the following:

1. Define institutional responsibilities and relations
2. Establish priorities and mechanisms for selecting, establishing, and developing marine protected areas
3. Protect species and their critical habitats adequately
4. Conserve threatened, rare, endemic, and commercial marine species and threatened, unique, representative, and valuable marine habitats
5. Ensure permanent protection
6. Provide mechanisms for developing management plans for each protected area, based on scientific data
7. Enable the control of developments and activities outside the protected area that may adversely affect it
8. Regulate exploitation in protected areas and their adjacent buffer zones
9. Provide enforcement mechanisms
10. Restore damaged ecosystems

Attaining these objectives will provide a sound foundation for a protected areas programme. The law then becomes the instrument through which these objectives can be recognized, explained and respected (and to some extent, funded). This does not necessarily mean that the absence of new legislation should preclude the establishment of the MPA. In fact, in some cases where the need to act is pressing, it might be more appropriate to designate the area as protected, even if the enforcement of the protective measures is deferred until the appropriate law is passed. One of the first steps to be taken is to carry out an assessment of the laws that are already in place, and which may be adapted to incorporate the MPA elements. For instance, legislation for an MPA set up to protect important fisheries resources may well be incorporated within an existing fisheries law. Likewise, if the MPA is set up to preserve an area for tourism development, it could well be part of a broader tourism development law. The legal diagnosis stage will give an indication of the legal system in place and may suggest the appropriate approach to take when drafting new, MPA-specific, law. An important consideration in that regard is the legal and political state of the country in which the MPA is to be set up.

6.2 Diagnosis

The following is a list of questions that are useful to ask and that may ultimately determine the need for and type of legislation for the MPA to be initiated and maintained:

1. What is the objective of the MPA to be created? (and as a corollary, how large should it be?)

2. How urgent are the protection measures to be taken? Is there time to wait for legislation to be enacted or should urgent, temporary action be taken immediately?

3. Who does the area to be protected belong to? (central government, a state or province, traditional tenure system, etc.)

4. Who are the stakeholders/users of the resources in the area to be protected?

5. How do they feel about the need to protect the area and to restrict uses?

6. How can they be involved in this process? (importance of drawing from traditional knowledge and tenure when it is available)

7. What laws are already in place? (e.g., forest, fisheries, tourism)

8. What institutions are already in place? (governmental, traditional and non-governmental)

9. How can the existing laws and institutions be used?

Institutional arrangements will vary from one country to another according to traditional tenure patterns, colonial experience, and cultural heritage. Initially it may be best to experiment with one or a few protected areas as a trial toward evolving new administrative and management arrangements. International non-governmental organizations (NGOs) can offer advice, assistance, and specialists to help develop coastal and marine conservation programmes.

Recognizing the great variety of government approaches, this chapter does not suggest particular political or legislative methods to achieve the mandate for protected areas. Instead, it provides some background information of use to the policy makers, legislators, and administrators who must address different aspects of this task. The guidelines offered at the conclusion of this chapter are intended to help the planner, manager, and legislator formulate a full range of programmes for coastal and marine protected areas.

In summary, the form and extent of legislation for marine protected areas varies widely among countries. This applies particularly to community-based reserves in developing countries; e.g., the community reserves in the Tanga region of Tanzania where local level bylaws are used to protect and regulate use of certain reefs and mangrove stands. It also applies to sacred sites, such as the coastal kaya forests of Kenya that are protected by traditional law but not at the national level. Unfortunately, central government can override local interest, as happened at Chale Island in Kenya where an expatriate tourism developer was able to remove half a kaya forest despite strenuous objections of local elders and the Kenya Wildlife Service.

6.3 Different Laws for Different States

Mechanisms to implement MPA programmes can then be incorporated in a legal system appropriate to each individual country. This section is based on the understanding that it cannot be too prescriptive since there are probably as many approaches to MPAs as there are coastal countries. Provincial or local planning and management can be more responsive to local needs and changing circumstances, but, in contrast, national agencies usually have access to greater financial resources and expertise and have a more comprehensive view of conservation needs. Resource protection is often, if not always, seen to be more stringent in national protected areas than in locally organized ones. In any event, national governments usually have jurisdiction over marine waters and will have to be involved in some way.

The legal/institutional arrangement chosen for a particular country or programme may depend upon many elements, including the form of government (for example, whether centralized or decentralized), available finances and other institutional resources, lines of jurisdiction and decision-making, commonly accepted practice, etc. The variations possible may include elements of the following:

- Strong central programme with delegation of staff and resources directly from headquarters on all matters

- Strong central programme with decentralized units at the regional or local levels to handle day-to-day operations of each protected area or region with supervision from headquarters

- Central programme which provides guidance and coordination to strong decentralized and independently operating institutions with their own staff and institutional resources for each region or unit.

Most coastal and marine waters (including wetlands) come under the public domain and are treated as a "commons." There are exceptions; such as in the Pacific islands where rights to fish certain areas are vested by custom with individuals. In principle, the public authorities have jurisdiction over the seabed and the surface of the sea. There are a number of traditional interests bound up with seacoasts that legislators must address: the livelihood of inhabitants of the protected area, water sports and recreational activities, and economic interests and shipping. (Box I-16).

Administrative, scientific, managerial, enforcement, financial, and other responsibilities may be delegated to various divisions of the appropriate authority structure. Advisory bodies and consultative organizations may be used to ensure representative participation and technical assistance by public, scientific, governmental, and other concerns. For example, in Tanzania a Board of Trustees established under

Box I-16. Historical Rights

It is widely accepted that once the right of people to reside permanently in a protected area is recognized, they should be allowed to lead a life in accordance with their customs to the extent possible. This may require relaxing rules that are too strict. In addition to the special measures taken on behalf of the aborigines in Australia and the Maoris in New Zealand, only one of the laws reviewed tackles this problem, namely the Seychelles Sainte Anne Marine National Park Regulations (1973). These give residents on private land within the park the right of access by boat to their property, to beach, careen, clean, scrape, or paint any craft or vessel within the park, and to take fish from the sea. The park commission issues each family licenses for taking fish in traps or on handlines and for collecting shellfish under very strict conditions and under the authority's control.

Pacific islanders in particular have developed and implemented effective community based (village) marine resource management systems that include closed seasons, closed areas, size restrictions, bans on fishing spawning aggregations, sea tenure—exclusive rights to fishing grounds (Johannes, 1978). However, these traditional systems are not universally practiced and, where they are, may be inadequate to cope with burgeoning populations, breakdown in community identity through immigration, and commercialization and diversification of fisheries into non-traditional resources (e.g., shark fins, sea cucumbers, lobsters, prawns, oysters, sea horses, aquarium fishes, and turtle shell). Often they need to be strengthened through regional or national government assistance.

For example, the coral reefs in Kimbe Bay, Papua New Guinea, are claimed by various clans. Under their traditional clan laws, four of these reefs have been closed to fishing and designated conservation areas. The clans realize that the authority of their traditional law extends to clan members only and sought gazettal of these reefs under appropriate national law in support of their initiative—the fear is that foreign fishers, especially the live reef fish traders and distant clans would not respect the closed reefs and undermine the conservation effort. The Nature Conservancy, which has been assisting the communities in Kimbe Bay with conservation of their coral reefs, was able to facilitate the gazettal of these reefs under fisheries law. Communities are now able to call on government enforcement officers to assist the protection of these reefs and, more importantly, the fisheries law has provisions for the communities to maintain ownership of the reefs despite their protection under national legislation.

McGoodwin (1990) argues that there is evidence that overfishing started occurring 3,000 years ago and that where resources used by fishers remained abundant, this did not mean that their traditional practices were necessarily effective. Clearly, we need to be cautious in assessing traditional practices to ensure that they remain relevant in contemporary fisheries. Nonetheless, protected areas that are designed and managed as partnerships between government and communities (collaborative management) can build on traditional practices, especially those supporting seasonal or area closure, limited entry and sea tenure. Building community resource ownership through this process can lead to diligent conservation.

the provisions of the Marine Parks Act oversees and approves the activities of a management unit (attached to the Fisheries Division) concerning the establishment and management of marine protected areas. The Board comprises members from government, private sector, NGO and scientific communities (see Box I-5).

Inexperience is a problem for any land-oriented agency whose responsibilities are extended to include coastal or marine protected areas (Gardner, 1982a, b). Such an agency must seek advice and information and must be open to new management approaches.

Newly formed governments and those just beginning marine conservation programmes will have the least management experience and scientific data, and are unlikely to have appropriate institutional frameworks for coastal and marine conservation. Laws and administrative arrangements handed down from colonial governments may not be suitable, especially in respect of traditional law and co-management. Young governments may be too concerned with other administrative and development activities to afford more than a low priority to conservation. At such times governments are most vulnerable to pressures for short-term schemes and quick solutions—factors that do not foster successful conservation programmes.

A potential solution in these instances is management of protected areas through partnership with communities, the private sector or NGOs to share the management responsibility and related financial and human resources burden. For example, NGOs have effectively managed the Cousin Island Reserve in Seychelles and the Soufriere Marine Management Area in St. Lucia. Also, the Chumbe Island Coral Park off Zanzibar is run by a private business enterprise. In these cases (see Part III, Cases 6, 7 and 11), government has allocated responsibility for management, including employment of personnel, revenue collection and distribution, conservation interventions, and enforcement activities to its NGO partner.

Administrations that have little experience in the establishment of MPAs have the opportunity to learn from the experience of other countries, and to avoid their mistakes. In this way they can begin with a more efficient and comprehensive system for coastal and marine conservation, one integrating both land and sea.

Further complications arise in national systems where resources seaward of the low water mark, or a boundary a few more miles seaward, are owned by the central government, while resources on the landward side are state or province controlled (as in Canada, the United States, Australia, and Malaysia). Such jurisdictional divisions hamper the establishment of protected areas spanning the land-sea interface. A potential solution to this situation is a Coastal Zone Management programme (see Section I-5.7)

It may be desirable to have state (provincial) or regional agencies to collaborate with national government in the implementation of conservation policies. States may do so willingly if the value of the national policies is apparent, and if financial incentives are offered for programme development and implementation.

The following are some working assumptions that relate marine protected area programmes to the institutional mechanisms for their accomplishment.

Centralization of Authority. In most cases the success of coastal and marine protected areas will be enhanced by designating a single agency with power, motivation, and resources to carry out the management task, or to ensure that the task is carried out effectively by the NGO, community, or private enterprise to which the task is delegated. A special agency created for the purpose can effectively manage very large projects in the long term. But it is usually more expensive to set up a single agency, and the agency will be slow in its initial achievements.

Selection. Nominating a suitable existing agency to lead an interagency management programme can be efficient in terms of time, human resources, and cost. But this agency must have the required human, technical, and financial resources, and it must be motivated to carry out conservation management (see Case Study 10 on the Great Barrier Reef in Part III). The lead agency must have clearly stated objectives, responsibilities, and powers, administrative and technical expertise, and clear definitions of its relationships with other agencies.

Consultative Requirements. Formally providing for consultation between the lead agency, other relevant agencies, user groups, and the public at large in some circumstances is essential from early in and throughout the planning and management process. Such consultation may be sought with the general community, or with community leaders, where they traditionally have decision-making rights. Legislative provisions for public participation must be implemented with conviction, not reluctance, for the process to be useful. If legislation does not specify mechanisms for public participation, the lead agency should nevertheless ensure them. Public participation and collaborative management (government-community partnership) is a rapidly expanding field in marine protected area establishment according to Beaumont (1997), Christie & White (1994), Dyer & McGoodwin (1994), Horrill & van Ingen (1997), Salm (1998), Wells & White (1995), White (1989), and White *et al*. (1994).

Research and Surveys. The lead agency should have the means (funds, mandate, and expertise) to undertake or contract out and supervise research and surveys relevant to planning and management (Figure I-55). Generally, it is unnecessary that the lead or responsible agency carry out or fund all of the necessary research because arrangements with research funding agencies can result in some necessary research being carried out at no cost to the lead agency. The lead or responsible agency should undertake or fund priority research and surveys that others will not carry out and encourage the participation of local resource users in these activities. The surveys should be management oriented and should include detailed socioeconomic analysis of neighboring communities undertaken by qualified social scientists.

FIGURE I-55.

Photo by Erkki Siirila.

Researcher from the Caribbean Natural Resources Institute (CANARI) performs a photographic reef assessment in the Soufriere Marine Management Area, St.Lucia.

Effectiveness of Control. The implementing agency must hold full control over management of the protected area. If legislation for control cannot be achieved, a special agreement between the owner and the responsible agency may allow effective conservation management of the area, an alternative that is being tested is the provision of access rights or resource ownership given in return for management responsibility.

Revenue. The revenues from certain types of use, notably tourism, are an important source of income to many parks and protected areas. But care should be taken that parks and protected areas do not become excessively dependent on these revenues, since this could result in a bias toward revenue activities and away from habitat protection (Box I-17). It would be desirable for much of the financial assistance for park management to come from the local government, with the local government and people also retaining the largest share of tourism and other revenues. It is becoming more common for MPAs to be self-sustaining, mostly from user fees (see Cases 7 and 11 in Part III).

It is important to note that the institutional arrangements selected will actually depend on the purpose of the MPA. Each MPA will vary in size and set-up, depending on whether it aims to protect a critical ecosystem, a traditional activity, tourism development or an important breeding or feeding ground. The key to the establishment of the MPA is that it represents a compromise between the uses that are permitted therein and the degree of protection afforded the resources. Depending then on the uses that will be permitted, different institutional structures become appropriate. The Authority in charge needs to balance conflicting interests and establish the required degree of protection, thus restricting uses that were customary prior to the enactment of the MPA. As a result of the diagnosis stage, MPA managers will have a better sense of what uses are already taking place in the area to be protected and will assess whether these uses are sustainable or not (Box I-18).

Box I-17. Funding MPAs through "Bioprospecting"

While financial resources for marine conservation are scarce, "biodiversity prospecting", or "bioprospecting" for sources of new products in MPAs that are rich in genetic resources could harness market forces to provide new sources of funds for conservation and sustainable development. Many MPAs were created in the hope that they would support multiple uses compatible with conservation. Bioprospecting, like specimen collection for biological research, ordinarily involves very low level harvesting in the initial phase, making it an appropriate use of sanctuary resources. Bioprospecting differs from other types of scientific research because the information and resources gleaned from marine ecosystems have great potential to contribute directly to the development of marine biotechnology and other industries.

Managers, including indigenous communities, should consider options for marketing these assets and negotiating terms for access that ensure sharing of benefits and sustainable collection practices. Indeed, local people and governments could also create protected areas for the purpose of protecting and controlling access to natural concentrations of genetic and biochemical resources.

Scientists must generally apply for permits before they are allowed to conduct research in most parks. Park authorities should design permits that require researchers to both obtain prior consent from local communities and channel a part of any profits they derive back to the MPA and surrounding area, as support for continued conservation. (In many countries, establishing such mechanisms will surely require changes in authorizing legislation at the national level.) Such arrangements, often referred to as bioprospecting contracts, may take a variety of forms and should include provisions for employment of local people, scientific information and technology, training for and joint research with host country scientists, fees for samples and a share of any profits. In return for these provisions, industry would receive reliable access to protected concentrations of resources.

Source: L. Denno, Prospecting in the Park: New Opportunities for Genetic Resource Conservation and Development in the US MPAs, University of Delaware, 1995 (Master's Thesis).

Recreational activities, including water sports, are usually regulated by zoning the protected area and controlling people's movements. For example, the Sainte Anne Marine National Park Regulations (Seychelles) hold any person guilty of an offence "who uses or causes or permits to be used in the National Park any surf-board or water-ski."

The movement of vessels through the waters of coastal or marine protected areas is encompassed by most coastal and marine protected area legislation. The common purpose of this legislation is to allow free passage of vessels according to the rules of maritime law. "The right of the coastal state to restrict navigation by *foreign* flag vessels is circumscribed by international ocean law" (1982 UN Convention on the Law of the Sea). "But vessel traffic may be controlled by shipping lanes, speed limits, discharge restrictions and other measures, in accordance with international law." It

Box I-18. One Law, Several Uses, and Different MPAs: The Turks and Caicos Islands

The Turks and Caicos Islands, in the British West Indies are predominantly dependent on marine resources to sustain the islands' two main industries: tourism and fisheries. The TCI were pioneers of sorts in adopting early legislation that recognizes four kinds of MPAs: National Parks, Nature Reserves, Sanctuaries and Areas of Historical Interest. Each protected area is geographically defined in the law (with exact coordinates in longitude and latitude) and the Schedule to the Law even specifies the attraction of each area and the uses permitted therein. In addition, the Department of Environment and Coastal Resources has produced detailed maps of the areas that are covered under the legislation.

In practice, however, the local stakeholders are not always aware of the purpose of some of the parks and do not respect the use restrictions that are called for in the law. On South Caicos, Admiral Cockburn Land and Sea National Park is supposed to be closed to fishing but local fishermen are often caught fishing for lobster and conch within its boundaries. Some of the fishermen are under the impression that the park was designated for tourism purposes, while others do not know the exact boundaries of the park or fall victim to the "prisoners dilemma," whereby they will fish in the park because they fear that if they don't, others will.

could be noted that the power to regulate *foreign* vessels by the Great Barrier Reef Marine Park Authority is granted through the internationally-agreed International Marine Organization (IMO) "Areas to be Avoided." Similarly, with respect to regulating passage by *foreign* aircraft (airspace), this, too, is restricted by international law outside of national territory (and the territorial sea). Because of the damage anchoring causes to bottom-living plants and animals, it is expressly prohibited by Seychelles and New Zealand laws and is covered by the general power to regulate vessels given by the Great Barrier Reef Marine Park Act of Australia.

Control of some coastal and marine protected areas is empowered through direct legislation detailing restrictions, as in the New Zealand Marine Reserves Act of 1971. Other legislation, like the Great Barrier Reef Marine Parks Act of 1975, assigns this task to the rule-making authority. In the latter case the legislature may list in detail the restrictions and prohibited activities about which rules are to be made. The legislature usually also authorizes the administering agency to take any necessary steps to ensure observance of the legislative directives, thus safeguarding the agency's freedom of action.

More and more, MPAs are being designated as part of fisheries management policies to protect marine ecosystems critical to the fish stocks being managed. For instance, breeding grounds, feeding grounds or aggregation areas may need to be protected because harvesting of the species at that particular stage of their lives would be to harmful. Furthermore, considerable work has recently gone into studying the effects of "no-take zones" or fish refugia on the global health of the stocks. Several examples have shown that preserving a stock in one area can have beneficial effects outside that area (the so-called spillover effect). Fish refugia are mere complements to sound fisheries management, but if they are designated appropriately and strictly enforced, their impact can be substantial (Agardy, 1997).

Yet a new generation of MPAs is emerging, where not one single use is regulated, but rather where several, compatible uses are authorized and limited. In the Galapagos Island, for instance, a new *Ley Especial*, specifically targets a variety of uses to ensure that they remain sustainable and compatible. These MPAs tend to be more ambitious in scope in that the concerns that need to be addressed for each use (involvement of the stakeholders, the ownership of the resources, sustainability of use) must be assessed for all the uses. This also increases the odds of conflicts among users and may complicate the crucial involvement of the stakeholders.

Another important consideration can be whether the MPA is set up as a stand alone or within a network of MPAs. Whether or not the MPA is set up within a network will here again depend on the goal one aims to achieve. For instance, if the goal is the protection of an important reef or an ecosystem important to a given species, this network often needs to cross boundaries (de Fontaubert, 1998). There is mounting evidence from physical oceanography in the Caribbean that in order to protect coral reefs in some areas, seed sources of recruits need to be identified and protected in other areas, sometimes a hundred miles removed.

6.4 Importance of MPA Boundaries

The success or failure of an MPA may depend on the designation of its boundaries. Here again, the MPA manager must engage in a balancing act: the MPA must be broad enough to encompass the critical areas it aims to protect, yet must also be small enough that enforcement is possible. Once again, because an MPA represents a limitation of existing uses, these uses should not be hindered more than they need to be. This is based on an equity consideration, but also on a practical reality: the MPA will much more likely be accepted, and respected, by the stakeholders if they can understand the rationale of its designation. An MPA where uses would be unjustifiably restricted is bound to fail since ultimately it depends on the acceptance, and self-enforcement, of the stakeholders concerned.

Marine protected areas have horizontal and vertical components; both requiring clearly defined boundaries. The seaward extension of such protected areas may be confined by legislation to the limit of the territorial sea (as in the Netherlands and Trinidad and Tobago). On the other hand, it may extend to the outer edge of the continental shelf (as under the U.S. Marine Protection, Research and Sanctuaries Act of 1972), or there may be no specified limits.

New Zealand legislation limits the landward boundaries of marine protected areas to the high watermark, while the Marine Areas Act of 1970 of Trinidad and Tobago states that the term marine areas "includes any adjoining land or swamp areas which form within certain submarine areas a single ecological entity." Other texts refer to the "foreshore" (Seychelles, National Parks and Nature Conservancy Ordinance, 1973) or, less specifically, to areas that are part of a marine park (Australia, Great Barrier Reef Marine Park Act, 1975). It is worth repeating that MPAs must be extended landward when it is necessary to control activities that adversely affect the protected area.

Other legal powers can accomplish protection beyond the boundaries of the designated area of an MPA (see Section I-5.9). For example, a general mangrove protection programme may be coordinated with a lagoon-protected area. Or the MPA may be nested inside a CZM programme (see Section I-5.8). Another approach is to organize a coordinating entity for the zone of influence (see Section 5.9).

Coastal and marine protected areas are usually delimited by reference to geographical points, such as "landmarks," bearings and distance, or longitude and latitude (on the importance of these geographical points, see Box I-18). The most detailed provisions for delimiting vertical boundaries are those for the Great Barrier Reef Marine Park. The area of the park includes subsoils (extending to the depth specified in the proclamation declaring the parks), the air space above the site (extending to a height specified in the proclamation), the waters of any sea within the area, and the seabed beneath them.

A new (1998) law for the Galapagos Islands is hoped to achieve its goals and ensure the protection of the critical ecosystems of the Galapagos—it is one of the most innovative pieces of legislation covering an MPA. This ambition reflects the concerns of the government of the Galapagos and illustrates the variety of measures available to a government willing and able to take measures to protect a critical marine area (Box I-19).

6.5 Legislative Options

The general guidelines at the end of this section contain useful reminders of the essential elements that need to be included in any MPA legislation. Ultimately, however, there is no ideal legislation and each manager needs to think out the MPA strategy that best meets his or her particular needs. The importance of size, boundaries, traditional rights and use restriction has been explained in broad terms, but each MPA is truly a special mixture of all these elements. In addition to these technical considerations, whether or not to draft MPA legislation, and what kind of legislation, is also in part a political decision. The best legislation drafted in a non-consultative manner or that does not take into account some strong local concerns is doomed to failure. Likewise, an appropriate MPA could be established from the ground up, by the local stakeholders, long before legislation is enacted.

Box I-19: The Galapagos *Ley Especial,* Crucial Legislation for A Critical Area

The Galapagos Islands are under pressure. This remarkable archipelago lies 600 miles off the coast of Ecuador and is renowned for its biodiversity, which has evolved over millions of years in isolation from the South American mainland. Yet in spite of protective legislation that dates back to 1935, conservation and preservation in the recent years have been troubled. Tourism, fisheries activities and the introduction of alien species have all posed serious threats to the native fauna and flora. In response to this worrying situation, in 1998 the Government of Ecuador enacted the Special Law for the Conservation and Sustainable Development of the Province of Galapagos (*Ley Especial*).

This law is remarkable in several respects:

– First and foremost, this law, by virtue of its designation as "special," supersedes any other laws that may regulate uses such as fisheries or tourism. The Galapagos are clearly recognized as an exception in the Ecuador legal system;

– Second, the law is particularly broad in that regulates truly all aspects of development on the islands. For instance, the law goes so far as restricting immigration on the island: only permanent residents (i.e., those born in the Galapagos, their spouses and children and those who had lived in the province five years before the law) are entitled to work and engage in productive activities;

– Third, the boundaries of the area extend up to 40 nautical miles to sea from the island baselines. In addition, the transport of toxic or high-risk products is prohibited in an area that extends 60 nautical miles from the baselines;

– Fourth, the enforcement provisions can be quite strict: unauthorized fishing may result in imprisonment from three months to three years, harvesting of a species listed under CITES can lead to imprisonment of up to three months and a specific provision punishes the introduction of alien species or tourism activities by imprisonment of up to a year.

Source: Nina Eejima, Law Intern, IUCN.

If legislation is indeed needed, the legislative options of the MPA manager fit within a broad spectrum, from the short term, easier options (such as using an existing fisheries or tourism law) to the more detailed and tailored piece of legislation, designed specifically for MPAs and fitting within a broader MPA development plan.

The following is a simplified reminder of some of the options available, from the easiest to the most demanding:

– quick fix approach, adapt other legislation (e.g., forest of fisheries law) to authorize MPAs, or even establish an MPA in the absence of specific legislation;

– use existing terrestrial protected area legislation and adapt it to MPAs;

 – develop specific national MPA legislation, including broader management plans
 (with linkages to Coastal Zone Management, where available)

 – ultimately, regional and global integration into significant networks (including use
 of the relevant treaties, see below)

Behind all these options, however, lies the paramount issue of enforcement and
the danger of so-called paper parks. Enforcement is always the most sensitive aspect
of law making. This is particularly true in the case of MPAs because enforcement
operations at sea may be difficult, particularly for very large MPAs. At the same
time, the means of enforcement of the MPA managers are often limited. For this reason,
a significant portion of the enforcement needs to be carried out by the users themselves,
which requires genuine "buy-in" on their part. As indicated before, the users will only
respect an MPA if they understand its significance and if they believe that they will
ultimately benefit from it. This is particularly problematic in the case of fisheries no-
take zones where in the short term, fishers tend to see only that they are prohibited
from fishing in that area. Yet, if the same fishers believe that this will give the stocks
a much needed chance to recover, or even that the spillover will lead to higher catches
outside the MPA, they are more likely to abide by the restrictions imposed (see Part
III, Cases 1, 4 , 11 and 13).

In this regard, the way in which the MPA is set up will likely be much more
important than what the final product looks like. There are no bad MPAs, only MPAs
that have been set up the wrong way. For this particular reason, the MPA manager
must bear in mind all the options that are available and understand that a given solution
may not be appropriate in the short term but remain an option later on. The degree
to which the MPA manager or the legislating authority is able to "read" the situation
is a better forecaster of success than the ultimate MPA or enabling legislation.

The manager must be inherently opportunistic and ultimately flexible in order
to take advantage of favorable developments. A dramatic example in that regard is
the Red Sea Peace Park, an MPA established in cooperation between Egypt, Israel
and Jordan with considerable assistance from the United States. US assistance was
provided to encourage closer cooperation between the three middle-east countries
but beyond these realpolitik considerations, the marine environment of the Gulf of
Aqaba benefited from the protection of a well-designed marine protected area.

In the case of Mauritania, the MPAs have been established in the absence of
broader coastal management legislation but have also been fundamental building blocks
in that legislative construction. The Parc National du Banc d'Arguin in the North of
the country was created in 1976 with significant assistance from an international NGO,
FIBA (Federation Internationale du Banc d'Arguin). It is a site of critical ecological
importance, both from a terrestrial and marine standpoint. The traditional rights of
the local fishermen, the Imraguen, have been protected and the park is closed to any
industrial fishing. The Imraguen were encouraged to build traditional sail-powered

fishing boats and no motor boats are allowed in the park. Another successful park was also established in the south of the country in the Parc National du Diawling. Broader national legislation is currently being drafted by the Government of Mauritania, and encompasses a Coastal Zone Management plan that includes a zoning scheme, built around the two parks, buffer zones and other areas to which industrial uses (mining, shipping and industrial fishing) are limited. This represents a case where the parks were practically set up twenty years before the broader, more encompassing legislation was enacted.

6.6 International Tools for MPAs

Treaties that provide for protected areas in the marine environment are few. They can be grouped in two categories. First, some treaties are primarily designed to provide for protected areas on land, but can also be applied to marine areas under the jurisdiction of their parties. These include the Ramsar Convention of 1971 (the Convention on Wetlands of International Importance Especially as Waterfowl Habitat) and the World Heritage Convention of 1972, and regional treaties, such as the African Convention on Conservation of Nature and Natural Resources of 1968, the Convention on Nature Protection and Wildlife Preservation in the Western Hemisphere of 1940, and the South Pacific Convention on Nature and Natural Resources of 1976. Very few marine protected areas have been established under these treaties.

The second kind of treaty more specifically addresses the establishment of marine protected areas, for example, the regional seas conventions and especially the new protocol to the Barcelona Convention, which is concerned with establishing protected areas within the jurisdictions of Mediterranean coastal countries.

Awareness of the importance of marine protected areas is comparatively new, and national authorities whose experience has been limited to terrestrial protected areas are generally those charged with implementing the treaties. Even so, the new treaty on the southern ocean contains, for the first time in a fishery treaty, specific provisions on protected areas.

Whilst MPAs first evolved as a result of national initiatives, and thus depended on the awareness of their usefulness by governments, they have since been slowly incorporated in the growing body of international instruments negotiated to ensure the conservation of marine and coastal resources. These range from non-binding programmes of action (e.g., the Barbados Programme of Action on Small Island Developing States, the Global Programme of Action on Land-Based Activities—the GPA) to legally binding treaties (e.g., the Convention on Biological Diversity—the CBD— or the SPAW Protocol to the Cartagena Convention). The former are reflective of "soft law," while the latter constitute "hard law," but both sets of instruments reflect a clear understanding by the negotiating States of the value of MPAs. Other treaties, which at first did not focus on the protection of marine habitats, have slowly evolved into broader instruments that also recommend the establishment of MPAs (e.g., the Ramsar Convention). A short summary of each treaty and their relevance to MPAs follows (de Fontaubert *et al.*, 1996).

The UN Convention on the Law of the Sea (UNCLOS). The UN Convention on the Law of the Sea was adopted in 1982 after nearly 10 years of negotiation. It was dubbed "a new constitution for the oceans" because it aims to regulate practically all marine activities in any area of the sea. Agenda 21 (discussed below) declares that UNCLOS "provides the legal basis upon which to pursue the protection and sustainable development of the marine environment and its coastal resources." Though it was opened for signature in 1982, UNCLOS did not come into force until 1994 because of a controversial part of the Convention that deals with deep seabed mining.

UNCLOS provides that coastal States have exclusive jurisdiction for various matters over designated zones of the oceans along their coasts, including coastal zones (this area of jurisdiction usually extends up to 200 nautical miles from the baselines). At the same time, coastal States are obliged under Articles 192 and 61.2 to conserve and manage the living marine resources under their jurisdiction. States also have obligations to protect the marine environment and conserve its living resources beyond areas of national jurisdiction. In addition, States are obligated to share monitoring and assessment information and also to collaborate at the national level to undertake additional studies concerning the marine environment.

Under UNCLOS, therefore, coastal States have every right to designate marine areas as protected, so long as they aim to fulfill their obligations to protect and preserve the marine environment (Art. 192) or ensure that the maintenance of living resources is not endangered by over-exploitation. Furthermore, by calling on States to collaborate in areas beyond national jurisdiction on a global and regional basis to protect and preserve the marine environment (Art. 197), UNCLOS opens the door to the designation of areas of the high seas as MPAs.

The rights and obligations of States under UNCLOS are clearly and thoroughly reviewed in The Law of the Sea: Priorities and Responsibilities in Implementing the Convention (Kimball, 1995).

UNCED: Chapter 17 of Agenda 21. In the course of the UN Conference on Environment and Development (UNCED) all participating States negotiated and adopted Agenda 21, a blueprint for sustainable development. Agenda 21 is divided in 40 chapters. One of them, Chapter 17, addresses "Protection of the Oceans, all kinds of seas, including enclosed and semi-enclosed seas, and coastal areas and the protection, rational use and development of their living resources." One of the main sections of Chapter 17 deals with integrated management and sustainable development of coastal and marine areas and calls on coastal States to undertake "measures to maintain biological diversity and productivity of marine species under national jurisdiction, ... including ... establishment and management of protected areas."

Whilst Agenda 21 is not legally binding, it is widely recognized as a useful guide for developed and developing States aiming to achieve sustainable development. Its level of detail also ensures that States can refer to it for practical recommendations of concrete steps to take to that end. In that context, MPAs are clearly marked as a necessary tool for the protection of the coastal environment. One should also note that this recommendation is further taken up in two processes that were also called for in Chapter 17: the UNEP Conference on Land-Based Activities and the Barbados Conference on Small Island Developing States.

Convention on Wetlands of International Importance, Especially as Waterfowl Habitat (Ramsar Convention). The Ramsar Convention aims to stem the progressive encroachment on and loss of wetlands. While the Ramsar Convention focuses on wetlands that are important for migratory waterfowl, it recognizes the overall values of wetlands, including their fundamental ecological functions and their economic, cultural, scientific and recreational value. The Ramsar Convention defines wetlands broadly to include freshwater, brackish and saltwater marshes, including marine waters up to six meters deep at low tide and any deeper marine waters contained within the wetland area, as well as adjacent islands and coastal areas.

The Parties to the Convention have recently recognized the value of some coral reef ecosystems and are likely to protect such sites in the near future, including through the designation of MPAs.

The Convention on Biological Diversity and its Jakarta Mandate. The Convention on Biological Diversity (CBD) was open for signature at the UN Conference on Environment and Development (UNCED, or the Earth Summit), which was held in Rio de Janeiro in June 1992. The objectives of the CBD are the conservation of biodiversity, the sustainable use of biodiversity's components and the equitable sharing of benefits derived from genetic resources. State Parties are required, inter alia, to take measures to ensure the conservation and sustainable use of biodiversity, monitor biodiversity in their territories, identify and regulate destructive activities and integrate consideration of biodiversity into national decision making.

With regards to biodiversity conservation, it can be achieved though a combination of both *in situ* and *ex situ* conservation. The former is most important and the Convention provides that the Parties "shall, as far as possible and as appropriate, establish a system of protected areas or areas where special measures need to be taken to conserve biological diversity." The CBD does not refer specifically to marine or terrestrial ecosystems but in 1995, the Parties to the Convention adopted the so-called Jakarta Mandate, which outlined a programme of action for implementing the Convention with respect to marine and coastal biodiversity (de Fontaubert *et al.*, 1996). The Jakarta Mandate identifies five areas in which the State Parties can take practical steps to apply the Convention to marine habitats. They include: implementing integrated coastal area management, ensuring the sustainable use of coastal and marine living resources, implementing environmentally sustainable mariculture practices, preventing the introduction of alien species, and establishing marine and coastal protected areas. MPAs are therefore one of the five pillars of the Jakarta Mandate.

Global Programme of Action on the Protection of the Marine Environment from Land-Based Activities (GPA). The Washington Conference on the Protection of the Marine Environment from Land-Based Activities was also called for in Chapter 17 of Agenda 21 and was held in 1995. Its outcome, the GPA, is a non-binding instrument that specifies measures that can and should be taken at the national, regional and global levels. The GPA recognizes that the major threats to the health, productivity and biodiversity of the marine environment result from human activities on land and in coastal areas and further inland. It also highlights the fact the most productive areas of the marine environment are threatened by physical alteration of the coastal environment, including destruction of habitats of vital importance for ecosystem health.

At the national level, States are called on to identify critical habitats, including coral reefs, wetlands, seagrass beds, coastal lagoon and mangrove forests and "specially protected marine and coastal areas." They are then required to apply integrated coastal area management approaches and to take steps to protect critical habitats and endangered species. The need to establish MPAs therefore falls clearly within the scope of the GPA.

UNEP's Regional Seas Programme: The SPAW Protocol. The SPAW Protocol is the second protocol to the Cartagena Convention, adopted in 1983, which is the major legal instrument of the Caribbean Environment Programme, set-up under UNEP's Regional Seas Programme. Within the structure of the Regional Seas Programmes, the States of the Wider Caribbean collaborated on a substantive aspect through the adoption of an action plan, which was formally adopted by an intergovernmental meeting and then adopted an umbrella regional convention (Freestone, 1992). This approach reflects the realization by the member States of the importance of adopting regional approaches to the protection of the marine environment and sustainable use of marine living resources. The Cartagena Convention and the Protocol concerning Co-operation in Combating Oil Spills in the Wider Caribbean Region were negotiated and adopted concurrently and it was understood at the time that further negotiations would address other important aspects of the protection of the marine environment such as specially protected areas and wildlife and land-based sources of marine pollution and activities.

The SPAW Protocol refers specifically to the establishment of protected areas and includes a series of protection measures that can be adopted by the Parties to meet the objectives of the Protocol, but the implementation is to be carried out by the States as they see fit. There is, however, a major aspect of the SPAW Protocol, which indicates that the regional marine protected area regime it sets up could amount to more than the sum of its national parts. Marine protected areas serve a wide variety of functions and the Protocol recognizes the various objectives that can be pursued. The goal pursued through the designation of an MPA will actually often dictate its shape, size and the means of implementation. If, for instance, a Party intends to protect an endemic and particularly threatened species and the goal is the protection of a single vulnerable habitat type, the design and management of the protected area can be relatively simple. But if the goal of the MPA is to protect a wide range of habitats or resources, the protected area established will be more complex. In the case of protected areas where the goal is the protection of the ecosystem and its processes, the underlying ecology in the region dictates the outer boundaries of the area to be protected. In the case of the Wider Caribbean, and given the objectives of the Protocol, marine protected areas planners need to work towards conserving ecosystem integrity and thus to design networks of marine protected areas (de Fontaubert and Agardy, 1999).

Three approaches can be adopted in designating networks of protected areas: preserving ocean or coastal "wilderness" areas; resolving conflicts among users; or restoring degraded or over-exploited areas. In the case of the wider Caribbean, choosing one approach over another depends on the state of the resources one aims to protect (and thus whether the approach is proactive, interactive or reactive). There is mounting evidence from physical oceanography in the Caribbean that in order to protect coral reefs in some areas, seed sources of recruits need to be identified and protected in other areas, sometimes hundred of miles removed (Roberts, 1997). This in turn points to the importance of adopting a multilateral approach, which is likely to work more efficiently than the sum total of unilateral efforts that ignore the system dynamics. The SPAW Protocol provides the framework within which a regional network would allow for the protection at the ecosystem level.

Based on the example set by the Caribbean Regional Seas Programme, similar protocols will also be negotiated for conventions in other Regional Seas Programmes. Another strong protocol on MPAs was adopted in the case of the Barcelona Convention for the Mediterranean.

World Heritage Convention. The World Heritage Convention (Convention Concerning the Protection of the World Cultural and Natural Heritage) aims to create international support for the protection and maintenance of sites demonstrating outstanding cultural and natural heritage of outstanding value. It provides for identification and protection of those sites under international law and encourages public and official attention to the value and the need of to preserve such sites. Each of the 146 Parties to the World Heritage Convention assumes an obligation to identify, protect, conserve and transmit to future generations its unique cultural and natural heritage. In addition, the World Heritage Committee selects sites nominated by Parties to be placed on the World Heritage List. The criteria for selecting sites were revised in 1994 to provide for identification of sites that are the most important and the most significant natural habitats for *in situ* conservation of biological diversity (cf. The Convention on Biological Diversity, above). The World Heritage Convention provides for identification of World Heritage sites within the "territory" of its Parties. Thus, Parties may nominate sites within their internal and territorial waters (which can extend up to 12 nautical miles from the baseline).

The World Heritage Convention also sets up a World Heritage Fund to finance protection of World Heritage sites in developing countries. However, the amount of funding contributed by developed countries has been minimal, generally amounting to between U.S. $2-3 million per year.

Measures under the World Heritage Convention are related to the obligations under the CBD to identify and protect ecosystems of particular importance, including marine ecosystems. Whilst most sites protected under the World Heritage Convention have been terrestrial areas, marine areas can and should be designated under the Convention, particularly through the designation of MPAs.

UNESCO Biosphere Reserve Programme. The Biosphere Reserve concept derives from the Man and the Biosphere Programme (MAB), which aims to fill the need to preserve genetic resources systematically within representative ecosystems (Batisse, 1989). Biosphere reserves essentially serve three roles: a) a conservation role (providing protection of genetic resources, species and ecosystems on a world-wide basis; b) a logistic role (providing interconnected facilities for research and monitoring in the framework of an internationally coordinated scientific programme) and c) a development role (enhancing a sustainable use approach to the ecosystem). Biosphere reserves therefore clearly strike a balance between conservation and development, with core areas where uses are the most restricted and other areas (buffer zones) where more uses are permitted. The concept is clearly reminiscent of some MPA schemes where core areas are most protected and where other, adjacent areas more open.

While the concept of biosphere reserve was originally designed for terrestrial ecosystems, the concept has now been extended to marine areas, particularly in the coastal region. In work that dates back to 1974, Carleton Ray anticipated the application of that concept to marine and coastal areas when he drafted the UNESCO "Criteria and Guidelines for the Choice and Establishment of Biosphere Reserves" (UNESCO, 1974).

FAO Code of Conduct for Responsible Fisheries. The clear distinction that used to exist between MPA management and fisheries management is fading and nowhere is this more apparent than in a series of fisheries agreements or other instruments that increasingly recognize the importance of MPAs to protect key breeding and spawning grounds. The FAO Code of Conduct for Responsible Fisheries, in particular, places heavy emphasis on the link between fisheries management and integrated coastal area management. The Code was adopted by the Conference of the FAO in 1995 and is divided in six thematic articles on fisheries management, fishing operations, aquaculture development, integration of fisheries into coastal areas management, post-harvest practices and trade and fisheries research.

Whilst the Code is not a legally binding instrument, it is meant to reflect the optimum measures that States can take to manage their fisheries sustainably. In some respects it constitutes the benchmark against which a host of other instruments will be established. This is particularly important for regional fisheries arrangements where various habitats need to be protected to ensure the conservation of the stocks throughout their biological range.

At this point, the emphasis on integration of fisheries in coastal management has not yet been incorporated in legally binding instruments such as the various regional fisheries instruments or the UN Agreement on Straddling and Highly Migratory Fish Stocks. Yet, these kinds of measures are often first taken by States in soft law approaches (such as was the case in the Code of Conduct) because they may realize the necessity of such an approach but are still reluctant to be legally required to adopt it. Nevertheless, the Code of Conduct is a sort of road map that governments agree they will ultimately need to follow in order to address the global fisheries crisis and MPAs will probably become part of that arsenal of measures.

Barbados Programme of Action for the Sustainable Development of Small Island Developing States (SIDS). The sustainable development of small island developing States (SIDS) is another issue that was raised but not solved in the course of the UNCED negotiations. Consequently, Chapter 17 of Agenda 21 called for the convening of a conference to address this issue and it took place it Barbados in 1994 (de Fontaubert, 1994). Its objectives were to examine the nature and special vulnerabilities of these States and to define a number of specific actions and policies relating to environmental and developmental planning to be undertaken by these States, with help from the international community. The outcome of that conference is the Barbados Programme of Action for the Sustainable Development of Small Island Developing States (the Barbados POA).

The Barbados POA includes a number of measures that the small island States can take to manage their marine and coastal resources sustainably and also calls on developed States and the international community to provide them with financial and technical assistance to achieve this goal. The POA adopts a holistic approach and reviews comprehensively each of the essential aspects of the sustainable development of SIDS. The marine dimension of these islands is clearly emphasized and specific chapters of the Programme deal, inter alia with climate change and rising sea-level, coastal and marine resources, tourism resources and biodiversity resources. The adoption of an integrated coastal zone management approach is clearly identified as a required condition for the sustainable development of the island States, particularly to mitigate the effects of rising sea level. Likewise, at the national level, SIDS are called on to adhere to regional and international conventions concerning the protection of coastal and marine resources and are therefore encouraged to set up MPAs in application of other conventions (e.g., the Convention on Biological Diversity).

6.7 The New International Legal Regime

The new international legal regime now comprises a mosaic of various instruments, some of which aim to protect broad ecosystems (e.g., the biodiversity convention) while others are more targeted to various species (the Straddling Stocks Agreement) or specific impacts (the GPA). Nevertheless, each envisions (explicitly or implicitly) MPAs as useful tools to fulfill some of their objectives. This is particularly important for governments of States that are parties to these conventions because they represent both a justification and an obligation for setting up MPAs. This becomes relevant from an international assistance perspective because governments from developing countries are often justified under the terms of the conventions to obtain financial and technical assistance from developed countries. The obligations under the treaties often represent new obligations and are more broadly part of a new approach to sustainable development. All the most recent negotiation processes recognize that new obligations also call for new and additional resources for developing countries most in need.

To that end, the Global Environment Facility (GEF) was established specifically to help developing countries meet their new obligations related to biodiversity and climate change. Because MPAs are now in the realm of new international treaties they are no longer the sole responsibility of national governments (though of course they are responsible for their implementation), but rather of the international community as a whole.

Another important aspect of this "internationalization" of MPAs is the growing awareness that MPAs cannot be set up in isolation, but rather need to be integrated in networks. As the SPAW Protocol demonstrates, the responsibility of establishing MPAs can rarely be a purely national effort, but rather is better coordinated at the regional level, so as to maximize their expected benefits. Because this is enshrined in the new international regime, national governments can expect better cooperation from neighboring States and can make full use of the regional networks and organizations already in place (see the UNEP Regional Seas Programme, above).

This important aspect of MPAs was partly addressed by a joint exercise of the Great Barrier Reef Marine Park Authority, the World Bank and IUCN attempting to establish a global representative system of marine protected areas (Kelleher et al., 1995). This publication provides a basis for development and implementation of a global system of MPAs to protect and manage some of the world's most representative marine systems. The network is divided in 18 marine regions in which priorities are identified. It thus recognizes the need to adopt a proactive approach to MPAs and establishes a "road map" for identification of the sites that most need to be protected. This is still merely a preliminary stage in a long process in which all relevant entities are invited to participate. Ultimately it should lead to a process where the establishment of MPAs is decided on the basis of agreed upon priorities and where the connectivity between the MPAs in the network is optimized.

This evolving international cooperation, through the negotiation and implementation of targeted treaties or through the development of the global network of MPAs therefore constitutes a great opportunity for governments to multiply the effect of their national efforts. Realistically, integration of MPAs in the international system is still short of what it could be, but useful lessons are being drawn from some of the most successful examples. For instance, within the framework of the UNEP Regional Seas Programme, a protocol on protected areas was first adopted for the Mediterranean's Barcelona Convention. Based on relative success, this approach was then applied to the Cartagena Convention in the Caribbean Programme. So while much has been achieved, more remains to be done, but the international regime is more and more likely to be a useful supplemental tool for national governments.

6.8 General Guidelines

The guidelines below (based mainly on Kelleher and Lausche, 1982) follow one of several possible logical progressions toward the development of legislation for coastal and marine protected areas. Each country has its particular legal style and tradition, which may require some changes or additions to these guidelines.

The coastal zone approach. Where feasible, joint management of terrestrial and adjacent marine protected areas should be established by legislation in a coastal zone programme (Figure I-56). Under this umbrella, water and land components of marine protected areas can be joined by extending marine areas landward or terrestrial areas into the marine environment. If possible, the seaward boundary of a combined terrestrial and marine protected area should be far enough offshore to protect the principal features of the marine area from threats, such as pollution, generated outside the protected area.

FIGURE I-56.

Public interest. The active interest of citizens in planning, establishing, managing, and continuously monitoring marine protected areas is fundamental to the long-range success of the programme. The public should be involved as early as possible, while avoiding premature publicity that would spur land speculation or other actions likely to threaten the MPA proposal. One means of encouraging public participation at all levels is to take it into account explicitly in the legislation and,

Special requirements should be imposed on agriculture where fields are adjacent to coastal lagoons; e.g., here farms have vegetated buffer areas at their edges to reduce and filter runoff (U.S.A. east coast).

Photo by John Clark.

wherever possible, to specify the stages in the programme when and how the public is to participate. Legislation should also provide for strong programmes in public education. Providing benefits locally through operation of the protected area and responding to local needs and cultural values are two elements of public participation.

Equity. The interests of users and community groups should be taken into account when this facilitates attaining the objectives of the protected area legislation. Legislation should, where practicable, provide for alternative sources of income for people whose economic activities are displaced or reduced by establishing a marine protected area. The co-operation of customary or traditional users can and should be encouraged by providing enforcement responsibilities and necessary material benefits, such as reduced fishing competition or participation in economic activities associated with the protected area.

Existing rights in the area. The legal status, ownership, and use rights of the site to be designated as a protected area are primary considerations that may require different approaches in different countries. Public as well as private rights may be involved. The impacts of existing laws, traditions, and rights must be recognized and, where necessary, addressed through specific measures in the legislation, such as through appropriate acquisition or compensation procedures. Recognition of customary rights (e.g., for fishing and "ownership") may need to be supported by special provisions in national law, but should be linked to demonstrated management responsibility by user groups.

Multiple uses. Allowing the maximum variety of uses consistent with conservation is an important objective in protected area legislation, particularly where large areas are to be subject to the legislation, as in the Great Barrier Reef Marine Park.

Ecological ramifications. Legislation for establishing and managing marine protected areas should explicitly recognize the connection between sustainable use of living resources and protecting ecological processes and life history patterns, such as the transfer by water of larvae, nutrients, and pollutants, and critical aspects of marine animals' life cycles.

Formulating goals. Goals and objectives should be clearly defined in policy and legislation for any marine protected area programme. This provides valuable guidance for those who must select, plan, manage, and administer an area. All activities in an area must ultimately be judged according to whether they advance or defeat the objectives for both the programme and the area. The specific legal regime for an area must be designed to support and accomplish these objectives.

Management plans. Legislation on marine protected areas should require that management plans be prepared for each site and should specify the constituent elements and essential considerations of the plan. The legislation should require periodic revision of zoning and management plans and scientific surveys, research, and monitoring of relevant ecological and socioeconomic conditions and processes in establishing protected areas and in developing, applying, and periodically revising zoning and management plans.

Sharing of authority. Whenever different authorities have jurisdiction over different parts of a marine protected area, or over different activities within a protected area, new legislation should clearly identify its own relationship with existing legislation. In such cases the legislation must designate a lead agency with primary responsibility for meeting the objectives of the protected area legislation. For major long-term programmes, creating a new agency, such as a joint authority, may be desirable, provided it will have the governmental support, power, and resources necessary to perform its function. In other cases, an existing agency may be designated as the lead agency, provided it can be motivated to carry out conservation management, has clearly stated objectives consistent with the objectives of the legislation, and is given the necessary responsibilities, powers, and administrative and technical resources. In either case the relationship between the lead agency and other concerned agencies must be clearly defined in legislation, particularly with regard to potential conflict or overlap in different pieces of legislation. Processes for resolving conflicts and for consultation between relevant agencies should be defined in the legislation, which should additionally specify that the lead agency has ultimate authority over marine conservation and area protection.

Regulations. The legislation must provide authority for adequate regulation to control activities or, if necessary, prohibit them. Regulations are of three types: 1) those for the shoreland, coast, or MPA (with different degrees of protection being applied to different zones as appropriate); 2) those that are interim, maintaining the status quo until more complete regulation is in place; and 3) those required outside the coastal or marine protected area for activities that may adversely affect it.

Efficiency of legislation. Without deviating from the principal conservation objectives, legislation and administrative arrangements should be as flexible and cost-effective as possible and should adhere to the following guidelines:

– New agencies should be created only where existing agencies cannot be adapted, motivated, and empowered to carry out adequately the conservation task.

– Existing agencies with jurisdiction over marine activities should be involved by interagency agreement to the extent necessary and appropriate to meet the conservation objectives.

– Existing uses should be disturbed as little as possible.

– Continuing existing regulations and regulatory mechanisms should be considered when they are consistent with conservation objectives.

– Existing staff and technical resources should be used where possible.

– Unnecessary conflict with existing legislation and administration should be avoided.

– Regulations, zoning plans and management plans should be as simple as possible.

Legislative effectiveness. Legislation that creates an individual marine protected area must identify and where necessary establish institutional mechanisms with adequate authority and responsibility for managing and administering the area. Responsibility, accountability, and capacity must be specific and adequate to ensure that the basic purposes and benefits of an area can be realized. Institutional support involves not only government agencies, but also advisory bodies, fishery organizations, tourism interests, local institutions and individual citizens, conservation clubs, and other such non-governmental organizations.

Legislation for specific areas. Each protected area should be established by law, with approval and any subsequent changes, including abolition, being subject to endorsement by the highest body responsible for legislative matters in the country or region, wherever possible. Establishment also includes the requirement that the legislation contain enough detail for proper implementation and compliance, delineation of boundaries, adequate authority, and resources for support of infrastructure to carry out the required tasks. To ensure the permanence of coastal and marine protected areas, and thus the lasting conservation of species and ecosystems, it is necessary that full investigation of possible sites and maximum co-ordination of planning and designation be undertaken with the support of top levels of government.

Enforcement. A prerequisite for effective legislation is providing adequate enforcement duties and powers, including as many incentives as possible for the enforcement of rules and regulations by local people who use and benefit from the area. Special attention should be given to enforcement in offshore areas, including EEZs. Legislation should provide for strict penalties for breaches of regulations, including loss of access rights in cases of infringements by user groups empowered with management.

Comprehensiveness. Omnibus legislation (i.e., that serving several objectives simultaneously) based on sustainable use of large marine areas should be seriously considered. Such umbrella legislation can be justified on the grounds that world-wide experience has shown that piecemeal protection of small marine areas together with conventional fisheries management in unprotected areas usually leads to the overexploitation of resources and the collapse, perhaps irreversible, of fish stocks. Umbrella legislation can provide for the following:

- Conservation management over large areas, while maximizing economic use, recreation, public education, and research
- Different degrees of use and protection in different zones within large areas
- Continued harvesting, in some zones, of living resources at sustainable levels
- Specification of the uses and activities that can proceed in each zone and the conditions applying to these uses
- Multiple use

Financial aspects. Financing for coastal and marine protected areas should be identified or referenced in the legislation according to general practice. In addition, possibilities should be investigated for establishing special funds whereby revenue from these areas, for example from tourism, might be directed back to the protected area programme or to projects for local people without being deposited in or transiting through the national treasury.

International coordination. Legislation and policy for marine protected areas must take into account any international, regional, or other multilateral treaties of which the country is or will likely be a member. The legislation and corresponding institutional programmes should be consistent with present or possible multilateral commitments and obligations.

Levels of integration. Co-ordination and intergovernmental planning of protected marine areas is needed at four levels: (1) the transnational level where areas are located at an international border or next to an international zone, or where species protected in one country naturally migrate to critical habitat inside other national boundaries; (2) the national level, for general co-ordination with other development plans and policy; (3) the level of the marine programme, where different areas may need to be coordinated (regardless of whether they are operated through one mechanism); and (4) the specific activity level, where local level sector plans and activities and community interests require harmonization and collaboration.

Form and content of legislation. The form and content of legislation must depend on the legal, institutional, and social practices and values of the nations and peoples enacting and governed by the legislation.

Policy formulation. Each country should develop special policy on marine protected areas, as was done by Parks Canada (Parks Canada, 1983) and South Africa (Marine Reserves Task Group, 1997). This should be done at the national level for the country programme as a whole, at any appropriate sub-national level, and for each marine protected area. At each level policy should be based on ecological principles and also on economic, social, and political factors. Such policy should be an integral part of comprehensive economic and development policy.

PART II

Protected Areas
in Different Environments

Protected Areas for Coral Reefs

C oral reefs are popular for their beautiful variety of life, shapes and colours, and their great spiritual appeal. But in a material sense, they are important for the subsistence and security they provide to coastal communities in tropical nations. These nations' coral reef fisheries must be sustained at the highest levels of yield, a demand that can be met by protecting the physical habitats and ecological support systems of the reefs, as well as breeding stocks of fishes to replenish the fishery zones. The MPA approach has much to offer toward halting the degradation of reefs, facilitating the recovery of damaged parts, and supporting the sustainable use of reef resources. Coral reef management is a broad and complex topic in its own right.

This section discusses the value of coral reefs, the threats to their ecological vitality, and related planning guidelines. It does not discuss specific management activities, which are treated in detail in handbooks on coral reef management (Kenchington and Hudson, 1988; Salvat, 1987a; White et al., 1994) or survey methods for coral reefs and related habitats covered by English et al. (1997). Wells and Hanna (1992) give an excellent account of coral reef life, uses, threats and conservation.

1.1 Ecology

Coral reefs are tropical shallow water ecosystems that flourish best at temperatures between 25°C and 29°C (77° and 84°F). Because extensive reef development is seldom found where ocean temperatures fall below 20°C (68°F), coral reefs tend to be restricted to a circumglobal belt between the latitudes 30°N and 30°S, although coral assemblages are found at 35°N off Japan and at 32°S in the Tasman Sea.

The reef-building corals need sufficient light to grow well, which restricts significant reef development to water shallower than 30 m in the clearest seas and much shallower than that in turbid areas. For this reason, reefs are most often found close to land, frequently forming a continuous band parallel to the shore, the classical fringing reef, which is particularly vulnerable to pollutants and silt.

The true reef-building corals are animals that collectively deposit calcium carbonate to build ornate and sometimes large colonies. The polyps of most species remain retracted by day, but at night they protrude their tentacles and sweep the sea for the passing plankton on which they feed. With their polyps all protracted corals have a markedly floral appearance. The uniqueness of shapes and colours and the variety of life on a coral reef make the reef an experience that is hard to match on land or elsewhere in the sea.

Coral reefs rank among the most biologically productive and diverse of all natural ecosystems, sometimes supporting as many as 3,000 species. Yet the tropical waters that cover coral reefs are nearly devoid of life-supporting nutrients, such as nitrates and phosphates. The clarity of these waters attests to this, for if they were more fertile, they would support more plankton, which would cloud the water. Most remarkable of all the reef's features is the wealth of life it supports under such conditions.

The high productivity of coral ecosystems results principally from their flowing water, efficient biological recycling, and high retention of nutrients. The coral polyps have symbiotic algae, zooxanthellae, within their tissues, which process the polyp's waste products before they are excreted, thus retaining such vital nutrients as phosphates (Muscatine, 1973). It seems that these zooxanthellae utilize nitrates, phosphates, and carbon dioxide produced in the polyp and, through photosynthesis, generate oxygen and organic compounds that the coral polyp uses.

Coral reef communities obtain their supplies of fixed, or usable, nitrogen, which is essential to phytoplankton and algae for photosynthesis, from algae on adjacent reef flats and bacteria in reef sediments and sea grass beds. Blue-green algae fix nitrogen and flourish on the reef flats (Wiebe *et al.*, 1975). Surgeonfishes and parrotfishes graze these drab algal mats, return to the reefs, and deposit the nutrient there in their faeces. Also, fragments of algae containing fixed nitrogen break off the mats and are swept by currents onto the reefs as detrital food (Johannes and Gerber, 1974). In a similar way, fishes that feed in sea grass beds and return to the reefs carry fixed nitrogen produced by bacteria in the sediments there. Often overlooked, the reef flats and sea grass beds should be given a high priority for conservation (Figure II-1) as essential components of coral reef ecosystems.

FIGURE II-1.

Seagrass beds nurture many fishes and are an important component of coastal ecosystems (Florida Keys, U.S.A.).

Living corals exist as a veneer over a porous limestone base that accumulates mainly through two mechanisms: the active growth of organisms (corals, molluscs, and calcareous algae) and the cementation of calcareous debris (dead and broken corals and molluscs) by encrusting organisms (algae, bryozoans, and sponges). The great number of holes and crevices in a reef provide abundant shelters for fishes and invertebrates, and are important fish nurseries (Figure II-2). In addition, highly specialized creatures have become dependent for their survival on the reef environment. It provides a solid substrate for many bottom-living organisms (clams, sponges, tunicates, sea fans, anemones, and algae) to settle and grow.

Reefs show both high and low endemism. Those species that care for their young may be highly endemic; for example, "unique" subspecies of a gastropod mollusc may occur on two reefs separated by less than 10 km. The majority of species, however, distribute their young through the plankton via floating eggs. These species may have a recruitment line of many hundreds of kilometers and thus a low level of endemism.

FIGURE II-2.

Coral reefs provide an extraordinary variety of habitats and niches for sealife species.

1.2 The Value of Coral Reefs

It is the many subdivisions of food and space resources that support the high diversity of fishes on coral reefs (Smith and Tyler, 1972). Around the reefs, space is probably more limiting than food. Resident reef fishes have specific shelter sites that can be shared by diurnal and nocturnal fishes (Collete and Talbot, 1972; Smith and Tyler, 1972). During the day, many of the nocturnal fishes occupy these shelter sites, and others hover around the reef, while the diurnal fishes are out foraging for food (Figure II-3). At night they reverse roles and places. Many fishes leave the reef to feed over the adjacent flats, foraging up to 100 m away (Earle, 1972). This sharing of space allows a healthy reef to shelter two separate communities of fishes, greatly increasing the diversity of species and number of individuals the reef can accommodate. The standing crop of fish populations on reefs may reach 5 to 15 times the size of the crops of productive North Atlantic fishing grounds (Stevenson and Marshall, 1974) (Figure II-4). Further, the reefs and their surroundings may provide 5,000 kg per fishermen per year.

FIGURE II-3.

Photo by R. Salm.

Corals, such as this staghorn (Acropora) off Mauritius Island, offer sanctuary to humbugs (Dascyllus aruanus) and blue-green pullers (Chromis caeruleus), among a variety of other species.

High competition with other organisms has caused species that live in crowded conditions, such as reefs, to develop many kinds of interactions. One type of interaction particularly well developed on coral reefs is antibiosis, the production by one organism of substances that are harmful or repulsive to others (Burkholder, 1973). Some of these substances are highly active biocompounds whose applications in medical research are just now being discovered. For example, certain reef-dwelling sea fans and

FIGURE II-4.

Photo by R. Salm.

Foxface or painted surgeonfishes (Acanthurus leucosternon) schooling over the reef flat at Albatross Rocks, a proposed marine reserve in the Seychelles. They graze nitrogen-fixing blue-green algae and in this way transport nitrogen onto the reef, where it is introduced as faeces to the food web.

anemones have been found to possess compounds with antimicrobial, antileukemic, anticoagulant, and cardioactive properties (Ruggieri, 1976). Such species may be important in producing pharmaceuticals, such as anti-cancer drugs, or may serve as models for the synthesis of new and effective drugs. Since Ciereszko and Karns (1973) first stated that reef corals alone provide a vast source of novel compounds that have potential value "as drugs or as tools for pharmacological research," bioprospecting for valuable medicinal derivatives from reef organisms has blossomed into a big industry.

That coral reefs are a storehouse of potentially valuable species is demonstrated well by the successful transplanting of the commercial gastropod trochus (*Trochus niloticus*) from the Indian Ocean to the tropical west Pacific, where a trochus industry has now flourished for more than 70 years (Heslinga, 1980). Heslinga reports that this transplanting programme apparently proved to be "ecologically innocuous," that is, it did not unbalance the system.

An important function of fringing reefs along wave-swept shores is preventing coastal erosion and storm damage. This is particularly important for regions with low-lying coastal plains, where fringing and barrier reefs protect plantations and villages from the ravages of tropical storms and tidal waves.

Johannes (1975) states that fringing reefs "are self-repairing breakwaters which permit the continued existence of about 400 atolls and numerous other low tropical islands, as well as preserve thousands of miles of continental coastlines." Entire island archipelagos owe their existence to the reef-building processes of past millennia and the protective role of living sea-level reefs. In the Indian Ocean, for example, 77 percent of the isolated islands and island archipelagos are built exclusively of reef depositions, and 18 percent have coral islands in addition to the principal island type (Figure II-5). The Maldives Archipelago alone comprises 20 atolls and about 2,000 coral islands. Coral islands are valuable for tourist sites, permanent settlement, plantations (notably coconut and papaya), and a refuge for fishermen in stormy weather, temporary bases for itinerant fishermen, and recreation areas. They also provide sanctuaries to a number of species, including seabirds and turtles.

FIGURE II-5.

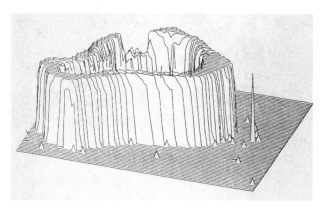

A satellite-eye view of Salomon Atoll (Indian Ocean) as digitally interpreted by computer graphing. Notice the characteristic ringlike reef on which islands form, the central lagoon, and the sheer seaward slope of atolls.

In summary, coral reefs are utilized for subsistence, income generation, research, and recreation. Their uses can be classified as either extractive or non-extractive. Extractive uses include the harvest of edible species (fishes, crabs, lobsters, snails, clams, octopus, sea cucumbers, sea urchins, and turtles), the harvest of ornamental products (pearls, coral, echinoderms. molluscs, and turtles), and the harvest of industrial products (bulk coral, sponges. and giant clams). Non-extractive uses include recreation, science and education, tourism, and shore protection. Cesar (1996), Cesar *et al.* (1997), and Spurgeon and Aylward (1992) have attempted economic valuation of these reef products and services.

1.3 Threats from Human Activities

Coral reefs are in trouble from both natural and human causes. The literature abounds with many cases of damage from careless development (see, for example, Bryant *et al.*, 1998; Endean, 1976; Johannes, 1975; Salvat, 1974, 1978, 1987a; UNEP/IUCN, 1988; Wells and Hanna, 1992; Wilkinson, 1998). Specific examples are discussed in the following paragraphs.

After the mining of coral reefs on high energy shorelines on the east coast of Sri Lanka (Figure II-6) the shoreline eroded, causing trees and coconut palms to fall into the sea (Salm, 1981a). After the loss of reefs, sand is washed into the sea to smother lagoon and reef life. Islanders certainly cannot afford to have the sand washed out from beneath their feet.

Sediments from dredging have killed portions of reefs off Florida (Voss, 1973), Guam (Marsh and Gordon, 1974), French Polynesia (Salvat, 1974), and Indonesia (Salm, 1982).

Sewage discharged near reefs has killed corals in the U.S. Virgin

FIGURE II-6.

Photo by T. Hoffmann.

Cause and effect are well illustrated in this photograph. Piles of coral mined from fringing reefs (upper left) lie behind a badly eroded beach that was once protected by the reefs.

Islands (Salvat, 1974, 1987b) and in parts of Kaneohe Bay, Hawaii, including those in the protected area around Coconut Island (Banner, 1974; Marszalek, 1987), and Florida (Marszalek, 1987). *Thermal pollution* from release of power plant cooling water has destroyed reefs off Hawaii (Jokiel and Coles, 1974), and had both positive and negative effects on corals elsewhere (Neudecker, 1987). *Siltation* by soil eroded from inland deforestation and other development ruined coral reefs off Hawaii and Indonesia (Salm, 1984) and St Lucia (Sladek Nowlis *et al.*, 1997). *Coral mining* to meet the demand for lime (particularly off Sri Lanka, India, Comores, and Indonesia) and increased *explosives fishing* (particularly off Tanzania and throughout Southeast Asia) are creating wastelands of once productive reefs (Guard, 1997; Guard and Masaiganah, 1998; Salm, 1981a, 1983, 1984) (Figures II-7, II-8, & II-9). *Chronic*

pollution from oil and phosphate fertilizer shipments killed a mile of reef in a reserve at Eilat in the Red Sea and has prevented the recovery of reefs damaged by unusual weather conditions (Loya, 1976; Mitchell and Ducklow, 1976).

Goats, by their contribution to dune erosion, were the major threat to Mozambique's southernmost fringing reef off Inhaca Island (Salm, 1976b), until the dunes were stabilized and goats kept away. Goats denuded dunes at Ponta Torres, Inhaca Island, which allowed the erosion of unconsolidated sand by strong southerly

FIGURE II-7.

Photo by R. Salm.

Lime production from coral at Kalkudah, Sri Lanka. First coral fragments are sorted into groups of similar sizes; next they are piled on firewood in the limekiln and stacked high; finally the lime is sifted, bagged, and transported to building sites. This is a process repeated at many places around the world.

FIGURE II-8.

Photo by R. Salm.

A. Corals mined for the carbide industry in India: boulder corals mined from around offshore islands are piled on the Tamil Nadu beaches. B. The coral is then smashed with axes at Vedali and trucked to the calcium carbide factory at Sankarnagar.

FIGURE II-9.

Photo by R. Salm.

A conflict of interests: islanders dry fishes attracted to the reefs around their island in the Seribu Archipelago (Indonesia), yet they also mine coral and destroy the reefs. The boats anchored offshore will not return to Madura Island until their holds are full of shells. They contribute little to the local economy but take much, leaving smashed reefs behind.

winds. The windblown sand formed a spit, which advanced across a channel to a shallow sandbank (seen exposed at low tide). The fringing reef borders the channel, through which it obtains its fresh supplies of seawater. If the spit were to fuse with the sandbank, the flow of water over the reef would be obstructed and the reef would almost certainly die. This is a good example of why protecting a target habitat alone is not enough: management must also extend to neighboring and linked habitats.

Unfortunately, those of us who visit reefs most often contribute to their destruction innocently by careless anchoring; for example, anchors have smashed 20 percent of a fragile staghorn coral reef in the Fort Jefferson National Monument, Florida (Davis, 1977) and in a range of other areas reviewed by Tilmant (1987). Snorkelers and divers often stand on reefs, walk over corals in the shallows, and collect coral and shell souvenirs. These activities are very damaging to the reef and may cause long-term alteration to its communities (Tilmant, 1987; Woodland and Hooper, 1977).

1.4 Global Status of Coral Reef Protected Areas

Over 100 countries now have some form of coral reef protected area. There are 14 of these areas in the Indian Ocean, 35 in Japan and the Association of Southeast Asian Nations (ASEAN) countries (Indonesia, Thailand, Brunei, Malaysia, Singapore, and Philippines), 17 in the Pacific, and 35 in the Atlantic. Information is available on about one quarter of these. Analysis indicates that these areas cover the geomorphological diversity of coral reef systems throughout the world (fringing reefs, barrier reefs, reef lagoon complexes, and atolls). However, many coral reef protected areas exist only on paper and have no administrative structure in the field. Without supervision and surveillance they may be of little value.

1.5 Avoiding Degradation of Reefs

The coral reef protected area manager has a number of special problems to address. Some of these have simple solutions through on-site rules and enforcement procedures: others are far removed from the protected area. A number of authors in Salvat (1987a) list recommendations for control of activities that damage coral reefs and White *et al.* (1994) provide a range of case studies concerning collaborative and community-based management of coral reefs. The following guidelines suggest some responses for managers in addressing certain problems.

Commercial and recreational activities may physically damage parts of coral reefs and over time may cause protected areas to deteriorate. The level of these activities should be regulated to enable natural repair of damage. They should also be confined to the least sensitive sites in designated zones and to where they can be easily monitored. If necessary, heavily used and damaged areas will have to be closed for recuperation. Some of these damaging activities and management responses are listed in Table II-1.

Fishing and collecting can considerably damage the physical structures and biotic communities of coral reefs (Alcala and Gomez, 1987; Guard, 1997; Gomez *et al.*, 1987). In general, controlled and ecologically sound fishing and collecting methods should be permitted in protected areas that are sufficiently large to sustain them, but they should be closely monitored. Table II-2 lists fishing and collecting activities that generally threaten coral reef communities, with comments on their management.

**Table II-1. Impacts of Commercial and Recreational Activities on Coral Reefs
and Possible Management Responses**

Construction (tourist facilities, research facilities, navigation aids, etc.)

Has immediate mechanical impact.

May alter water flow around the reef and thus change a major ecological factor.

May shade reef locally, reducing photosynthesis.

May become a point source of pollution and littering.

Should be the subject of prior environmental assessment.

Anchor Damage

Breaks or damages corals.

Some designs, notably plough anchors, are particularly destructive.

For small boats a sandbag can be an effective and relatively non-damaging temporary anchor.

At intensively used reefs compulsory anchoring areas or compulsory moorings may
be necessary.

Diver Damage

Almost all diving results in minor unintentional damage to corals and other reef
biota; at frequently dived sites this damage can become significant and can lead
to local loss of fragile species.

On intensively used reefs periodic closure to allow recuperation of dive areas may be
needed.

Small Boat Damage

Small boats and inexperienced boat handlers grounding on reefs can cause considerable
physical damage to shallow areas, particularly at low tide.

On intensively used reefs a system of designated boat channels and moorings to keep
boats away from shallow, fragile areas may be necessary.

Reef Walking

Walking on reefs at low tide is a popular method of reef viewing that inevitably causes
some physical damage.

In areas with a highly developed cover of fragile corals, severe damage to corals can occur.

Reef walking should be controlled and a system of periodic closure for recuperation
may be necessary.

Boulder Moving

Reef walkers move or overturn boulders to view animals beneath them; if the boulders
are not replaced these animals are likely to die.

Boulder replacement is an essential element of education and interpretation.

Shell collectors may use crowbars and hammers to break away pieces of reef when
hunting shells.

Boulder movement and damage to corals should be regulated.

Conservation staff should supervise education and interpretation activities.

Destructive shell collecting should be banned.

Introduction of Species for Commercial Purposes

Introduction of a commercially valuable species may offer temporary economic gain,
but may have a substantial impact on the preexisting natural system by displacing
original species from their earlier habitats and increasing competition for food.

The need for and the environmental impacts of introductions should be carefully
evaluated before they are permitted.

Table II-2: Fishing and Collecting Activities on Coral Reefs and Possible Management Responses

Collection of Corals and Shells by Tourists
Should be discouraged.

Collection of Corals and Shells for Commercial Purposes
May be a sustainable small-scale fishery designed around strictly protected zones.

Spearfishing
Use of SCUBA for this purpose should not be permitted.
Should be discouraged.
Conflicts with underwater photography and fish watching.

Collection of Aquarium Fishes
Needs careful control.
Can be a sustainable fishery.
In time may be replaced by mariculture or rearing of postlarvae collected near reefs.

Collection of Reef Materials (Coral, Sand, or Shell) for Construction
Needs careful control.
Unlikely to be a sustainable industry.

Commercial Line Fishing
Can deplete stocks of certain fishes (groupers, snappers, trigger fishes) and cause their
    local extinction.
Generally compatible with reef conservation objectives if restricted to open waters off reefs.
Needs careful control.

Commercial Trawling
Can cause severe local damage to non-target seabed communities and in particular
    to stocks of young fish.
Can cause severe local physical modification to the structure of the seabed.
Needs careful evaluation to determine a truly sustainable level.

Fishing with Explosives
Highly destructive to the reef structure and community.
Should not be permitted under any circumstance.

Fishing with Poison (including cyanide for the live reef fish trade)
Highly destructive to the reef system.
Use of "natural" poisons bears careful evaluation, but may be sustainable in stable
    traditional fisheries.
Should not be introduced.
Use of modern chemicals should not be permitted under any circumstance.

Fishing with Nets
Weighted seine nets, muro-ami and similar nets are highly destructive to corals and
    reef structure.
Should not be permitted under any circumstance.
Gill nets entangle corals and are destructive to reef structure,
Catch non-target species, including dugongs and turtles.
May be permissible in specific areas with careful control and monitoring.

New Fishing Techniques
Before being introduced, any new technique should be carefully evaluated to determine
    its ecological impact and sustainability.

Pollutants originating offsite have been demonstrated to have a number of effects: killing mature plants and animals, interfering with physiological—particularly reproductive—processes, aborting larval development, making areas unsuitable for recruitment or settlement of new individuals, and smothering or changing the texture of the habitat. Johannes (1975), Loya & Rinkevich (1987), Marszalek (1987), Brown (1987) cover this topic in detail. Forms of pollution that should be noted by the protected area manager are listed in Table II-3. Various methods of discharge that limit damaging effects to reasonable levels can be established for most pollutants. Initial assessment and constant monitoring of actual and potential pollutant discharges are important in selecting, planning, and managing viable coral reef protected areas. Gaining collaboration of offsite authorities and communities in the adjacent Zones of Influence could be helpful in controlling sources of pollution.

Table II-3. Pollutants and Their Effects on Coral Reefs

Herbicides
> May interfere with basic food chain processes by destroying or damaging zooxanthellae in coral, free living phytoplankton, algae, or seagrass communities.
> Can have serious effects even at very low concentrations.

Pesticides
> May selectively destroy or damage elements of zooplankton or reef communities; planktonic larvae are particularly vulnerable.
> May accumulate in animal tissues and affect physiological processes.

Antifouling Paints and Agents
> May selectively destroy or damage elements of zooplankton or reef communities.
> Not likely to be a major factor except near major harbors, shipping lanes, and industrial plants cooled by seawater.

Sediments
> Smother substrate.
> Smother and exceed the clearing capacity of some filter-feeding animals.
> Reduce light penetration, which may alter vertical distribution of plants and animals on reefs.
> May absorb and transport other pollutants.

Sewage and Detergents
> May interfere with physiological processes.

Sewage, Nutrients, and Fertilizers
> May stimulate phytoplankton and other plant productivity beyond the capacity of control by grazing reef animals and thus modify the community structure of the reef system.
> May cause eutrophication and consequent death of reef organisms.
> May favor coral growth if limited in quantity and where water circulation is good.

Petroleum Hydrocarbons
Have been demonstrated to have a wide range of potential damaging effects at different concentrations.

Heated Water from Power Station and Industrial Plant Cooling
Changes local ecological conditions; water temperature is a key factor in distribution and physiological performance of most reef organisms.

Hypersaline Waste Water from Desalinization Plants
Changes local ecological conditions; salinity is a key factor in distribution and physiological performance of many reef organisms.

Heavy Metals (e.g., mercury, cadmium)
May be accumulated by and have severe physiological effects on filter-feeding animals and reef fish, and be accumulated in higher predators.

Radioactive Wastes
May have long-term and largely unpredictable effects on the genetic nature of the biological community.

Responses to phenomena linked to *climate change* are less clear cut and beyond the reach of protected area managers, for example elevated sea water temperatures and coral bleaching (Brown, 1990; Glynn, 1998, 1990; Glynn *et al.*, 1988) and sea level rise. For this reason, they are not covered here, and the best we can do is to monitor the effects of global climate change, experiment with restoration activities and follow natural recuperation.

1.6 Design Principles for Coral Reef Protected Areas

This section is intended to help planners select reef components for protection and draw protected area boundaries.

The reef ecosystem extends beyond its physical boundary to include the neighboring habitats with which it interacts, especially sea grass beds and back-reef lagoons. They all need to be considered and managed as parts of a single functional unit.

Coral reefs are linked intimately by dynamic processes (currents, rivers, and species movements) to distant areas and may be influenced by the activities there. These activities require some form of control if reef communities in a protected area are to survive.

At a critical minimum reef area, the diversity of coral, and presumably of other reef taxa, begins to decrease. The core area of a protected coral reef should be as large as possible to preserve high diversity of reef biota.

Coral reef users like traditional fishers and other user groups should participate in coral reef protected area selection and design to ensure strong grassroots support for the site and partnership in management.

1.7 Design Guidelines for Coral Reef Protected Areas

The three main steps in preparing the site design for a coastal or marine protected area were discussed in the earlier section on site planning (Section I-2). The same procedure is followed in designing coral reef protected areas. For convenience, these steps are summarized and interpreted for coral reefs in Figure II-10.

FIGURE II-10.

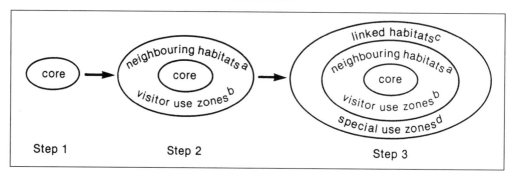

Simplified steps in the design of a coral reef protected area. 1. The core boundary is defined after determining the critical minimum core area. 2. The protected area boundary is defined to maintain ecological processes and support systems and to regulate visitor use. 3. A buffer zone boundary is determined in light of potentially damaging activities in linked habitats. (a. reef flats, sea grass beds, sand or mud flats, lagoons, mangroves, and estuaries; b. headquarters, ranger stations, and diving, fishing, research and education zones; c. beaches, dunes, watersheds, agricultural lands, and urban and industrial development; d. sea lanes, commercial fishing grounds, and intensive use zones.)

Source: Salm, 1984.

There are two basic questions to answer in determining ecologically sound boundaries for protected coral reef areas: (1) Which habitats should be included in the protected area? (2) How large should the protected area be?

To help preserve the diversity of reef biota, a coral reef protected area should contain many different habitats for a steady and varied supply of larvae to replenish naturally damaged areas and to replace dead or emigrated organisms. This is particularly important to help maintain a source of larvae to settle and help reestablish portions of coral reefs devastated by coral bleaching and related mortality. Table II-4 indicates the diversity of corals in one typical reef.

In practice, three kinds of habitats should be considered for inclusion in coral reef reserves: coral habitats, neighboring coastal habitats (i.e., submerged, intertidal, or above water), and distant linked habitats (Table II-5).

Coral Habitats. Different reef types or zones within reefs are characterized by different coral assemblages. There are corals in shallow water and those that begin below 20 m. Dominant corals and coral diversity differ in each assemblage; for example, sheltered reefs may have dense overlapping colonies of staghorn coral

Table II-4: Diversity of Corals on a Patch Reef in Pulau Seribu Marine National PARK

Patch Reef Type	Zone	Dominant Growth Form	Dominant Biota
Submerged	Reef flat	Branching, occasionally massive	Corals (*Acropora, Porites*)
	Reef slope	Explanate, massive	Corals (*Mycedium, Echinophyllia, Oxypora, Pachyseris*)
Sea level			
Sheltered habitats	Inner reef flat	Small branching, small massive	Sand and talus (coral debris)
			Corals (*Acropora, Porites andrewsi, Porites lutea*)
			Invertebrates (Holothurians, *Heliopora coerulea*)
			Seagrasses (*Thalassia*)
			Algae (*Padina, Halimeda*)
	Outer reef flat	Massive forming micro-atolls, branching	Corals (*Acropora, Porites andrewsi, Porites lutea*)
			Algae (*Padina*)
	Reef crest	Branching, tabular, massive vertical and vase-shaped plates	Corals (*Acropora* spp., *Clavarina, Pavona cactus, Pachyseris, Montipora foliosa, Echinopora lamellosa, Galaxea*)
	Upper reef slope	Branching, vase-shaped plates	Corals (*Acropora, Pachyseris, Turbinaria Echinopora lamellosa*)
	Lower reef slope	Explanate, massive	Corals (same as on reef slope of submerged reefs)
Exposed habitats	Inner reef flat	Same as in sheltered habitats	Same as in sheltered habitats
	Outer reef flat	Robust branching (bushy), small tabular; massive	Corals (*Acropora* spp., *Porites lutea*, Faviidae)
			Algae (*Turbinaria, Porolithon*)
	Reef crest	Tabular, large and small massive	Corals (*Acropora, Porites lutea, Coeloseris*)
			Hydrozoans (bracts of *Millepora*)
	Upper reef slope	Mixed, without dominant form	Corals (mixed, without dominant taxon)
	Lower reef slope	Same as in sheltered habitats	Same as on reef slope of submerged reefs

Source: Salm *et al.* (1982).

Table II-5. Connections Between Coral Reefs and Neighbouring and Linked Habitats

Habitat	Benefits	Potential Harmful Impacts	Linking Mechanisms
Neighbouring Reef flat	Introduces fixed nitrogen, dissolved and particulate organic compounds to reef food web As feeding ground and nursery for reef fishes, increases diversity and abundance of reef species		Transport by waves currents, fishes and sea urchins Nocturnal/diurnai migration
Sea grass beds	Introduce dissolved and particulate organic compounds to reef food web As feeding grounds and nurseries for reef organisms, increase diversity and abundance of reef species Consolidate sediments, protecting reef from smothering	Destruction of seagrass beds by repeated anchoring releases sediments into the water column and increases turbidity; reef organisms can be smothered, resulting in decrease of diversity and abundance of reef species.	Transport by currents, fishes and sea urchins Nocturnal/diurnal migration Transport by waves and currents
Sand or mud flats	As feeding grounds for reef fishes, increase diversity and abundance of reef species		Nocturnal/diurnal migration

Mangroves, lagoons, estuaries	Introduce dissolved and particulate organic compounds to reef food web As feeding grounds and nurseries for reef fishes, increase diversity and abundance of reef species Trap pollutants and silt, protecting reef from poisoning or smothering	Transport by tidal flushing and currents Nocturnal/diurnal migration
	Disturbance of substrate, release of trapped silt and pollutants can result in smothering or poisoning of reef organisms	Transport by tidal flushing, stream flow, and currents
Linked Beaches and dunes	Sand released by erosion or destruction of binding vegetation may smother organisms	Transport by wind, waves, and currents
Watersheds	Regulate stream flow Silt, floods, and dilution of seawater caused by deforestation and erosion can stress organisms	Transport by streams and currents
Urban or industrial Developments	Litter; domestic, chemical, and thermal pollution; increased freshwater runoff can poison or physically damage organisms or cause eutrophication	Transport by streams and currents
Agricultural development	Silt, floods, and dilution of seawater; pesticides, herbicides, and fertiliser pollution can smother organisms or cause eutrophication	Transport by stream: and currents

Source: Salm (1984).

(*Acropora*) that are aesthetically pleasing, but have few species (Figure II-11). Such reefs may be suitable for visitor use, but not for maintaining biological diversity.

FIGURE II-11.

Photo by R. Salm.

Staghorn coral (Acropora) can form large fields, which are attractive for snorkelers but low in species diversity (proposed Togian Islands Marine Protected Area, Indonesia).

Different reef types result from distinct processes (e.g., seaward reefs endure greater wave stress than lagoon reefs), as is reflected in variations in coral assemblages and zonation patterns (Sheppard, 1980, 1981). Some reef habitats are relatively unchanging, while others are constantly interrupted by wave stress or natural periodic exposure to air or freshwater. These habitats contribute different types and quantities of larvae to the reef system. It is important to identify the reef types and, as far as possible, the various coral assemblages, and to include examples of each in the protected area.

Neighboring Habitats. Including the following habitats in protected areas may often be incidental, but should be deliberate if reefs are to flourish.

Reef flats. Much usable nitrogen supporting the productivity of reefs comes from adjacent reef flats (Wiebe *et al.*, 1975). This nitrogen is introduced to the reef food web from faeces of fishes feeding on the reef flat and algal fragments washed onto the reef.

Sea grass beds and sand flats. Sea grass beds and sand flats surrounding coral reefs are important feeding grounds for nocturnal feeding fishes, such as snappers and grunts, which shelter on reefs by day (Ogden and Zieman, 1977). When they return to the reef these fishes deposit organic compounds in the form of faeces that become available to detritivores and are introduced to the reef food web.

Mangroves. Mangroves provide nurseries for juveniles of certain reef fishes (e.g., butterflyfishes, parrotfishes, and snappers). Where they are close enough to reefs, mangroves provide feeding grounds to fishes that shelter on the reefs. They also introduce fixed nitrogen and organic detritus into the trophic system of reefs, as do reef flats and sea grass beds.

Beaches and dunes. Coastlines are dynamic zones. Disturbances to them may cause beach erosion and alteration of the natural cycle of accretion and erosion of sand along the shore. The result may be the smothering of living reefs by excessive sediment.

Linked Habitats. Influences that are not obvious, that is, not highly visible, may be difficult to control, including watershed disturbances. While watersheds are not obvious candidates for being included in coral reef reserves, coastal streams and marine currents may intimately connect them to reefs, their distance notwithstanding. Deforestation and development in a watershed can decrease the absorptivity of land bordering rivers and streams, accelerate erosion, and contribute damaging quantities of freshwater or silt or both to reefs, such as happened in Malindi, Kenya, Kaneohe Bay, St. Lucia, and elsewhere (Figure II-12). These effects are best controlled by Coastal Zone Management approaches (see Section I-5).

FIGURE II-12.

Sorokin (1973) has suggested that dissolved organic compounds originating in the Antarctic enhance productivity on West Indian coral reefs. But of course a management plan for Antigua would not extend to Antarctica. The fact still illustrates the far-reaching consequences of distant events in the ocean realm and emphasizes the need to manage reefs as one of many integral parts of reasonably larger ecosystems, rather than autonomous units.

Road construction has exposed the soil to natural forces on Roatan, the Bay Islands of Honduras. The result may be soil runoff to the reefs of the Sandy Bay MPA.

1.8 Sizes of Coral Reef Protected Areas

In theory, we know that we could help prevent loss of species within an MPA if we maintained a balance between the rate of species loss and the immigration rate of replacement species. It is this balance, or whole-reef equilibrium, that maintains the *status quo* of general reef species composition. If the balance is tipped in favor of extinction, the protected area will lose species. There are many natural stresses such as tropical storms, from which reefs recover naturally with time. Human activities increase the burden of stress and may prevent normal recovery by increasing the extinction rate or decreasing the immigration rate.

To maintain the balance between immigration and extinction rates we need to ensure a steady source of propagules (eggs, larvae, and juveniles) to replenish stressed areas. Large reefs may be self-replenishing. They manage to achieve this because their large size allows portions of reef damaged by slumping (collapse of the reef slope), storm surges, prolonged exposure to air, heat, or freshwater, bleaching, crown-of-thorns starfish, or other stresses to be recolonized by propagules from undamaged parts of the same reef. Such large reefs are mosaics of patches in different stages of community development and redevelopment (Connell, 1978).

We have previously stated that, on balance, fewer large protected areas are to be favored over a greater number of smaller ones. This principle applies in selecting and delineating coral reef protected areas.

The optimal size of a protected reef area is designed around a strictly controlled sanctuary zone or core, which encompasses sufficient reef to be self-replenishing for all species. This is particularly important if preserving biological diversity is the principal management objective. This design is less important for other objectives— for example, maintaining the area's value for recreation, tourism, research, and education—or safeguarding specific breeding populations of particular species, like giant clams (*Tridacna gigas*), that have smaller area requirements (Figure II-13).

The critical minimum core size for protected coral reefs is that smallest reef size in which all species in the general vicinity are virtually certain to be found. For example, core areas encompass at least 300 ha for each reef type in the Chagos Archipelago (Salm, 1980b, 1984). The remainder of the reserve (including reef flats, land, and intervening and surrounding waters) functions as a buffer and is zoned for different uses. In addition to the core area, there may be research zones, education zones, visitor zones (perhaps used on a rotational basis), and fisheries zones. All may be planned within a single reserve.

One possible way to determine the critical minimum core size of coral reef protected areas is outlined below. However, if urgency or lack of funds and

FIGURE II-13.

Photo by R. Salm.

Tridacna derasa is an endangered giant clam species, an animal whose survival depends on the protection of suitable reef habitats (identified protected area, Taka Bone, Rate, Flores Sea, Indonesia).

suitable personnel prevent studies from beginning immediately, a core area of about 450 ha should be designated, if possible, until the estimate can be verified by studies (the value of 450 ha derives from the estimate of 300 ha for Chagos reef with an arbitrary 50 percent safety factor added). Also, select the critical core so that it encompasses reef habitats as diverse as possible. A single reef is preferable but a cluster of small reefs will do. This portion of the core zone should be managed as IUCN category Ia or IV (Strict Nature Reserve or Habitat Management Area).

The design team (see Section I-3) should choose carefully from the many objectives for protecting coral reefs—providing for recreational activities, contributing to fisheries, preserving biological diversity, or protecting endangered species or the breeding stock of other valuable species. Objectives are the basis of design. Table II-6 lists examples of specific management objectives for protected coral reef areas.

If preserving biodiversity is the main objective, it is especially important that habitat and species diversity is high. The protected area should be designed, and the minimum core area determined, with this principle in mind. The following procedure for determining critical minimum core area assumes that biodiversity is valued. However, other objectives (such as safeguarding recreational value) may not require that biodiversity is high, and the minimum core area might be reduced. Many reefs smaller than 450 ha suit recreation, education, research, and fisheries objectives and merit conservation management. Keep in mind, however, that, in general, larger areas should be selected where possible, particularly to preserve biodiversity.

If time, funds, or personnel are short, or in cases of great urgency, determining a minimum core area is not immediately essential, as we have said. In the long term, however, a well-designed protected area with an appropriate core zone is a prerequisite to the success of the reserve. As mentioned above, 450 ha should be a sufficient minimum core area for each reef type, at least initially. It is important to secure the protection of a designated area around the core, whose boundaries can be adjusted if necessary after appropriate studies. An outline for such a study is presented below (Salm, 1984).

1.9 Estimating the Number of Coral Genera and Subgenera

Choosing the reefs. The greatest variety of coral genera and subgenera will occur on the largest reefs with the greatest morphological diversity. Reefs with the greatest irregularity of shape, contours, and depths probably have the greatest variety of microhabitats. Hence they offer survival opportunities to a greater variety of corals. This should be borne in mind when selecting a core area on more or less continuous reefs, such as those fringing continental shores. Different reef types (e.g., those lagoonal and seaward) will need to be sampled separately.

Arrangement of transects. Experience on reefs of the Chagos Archipelago (Salm, 1980b) showed that sampling from four transects per reef of at least 3 ha and at the

Table II-6. Examples of Management Objectives for Coral Reef Areas

To preserve a representative sample of the coral reef ecosystem and a variety of its component and associated habitats, biotic communities and species (biodiversity)

To protect endangered, depleted, or rare species (e.g., hawksbill turtles, giant clams)

To preserve the ecological processes and support systems on which the integrity of the coral reef ecosystem depends

To control upstream activities that may damage or destroy all or part of the value of the area for conservation and development

To promote uses compatible with conservation and sustainable development objectives

To separate incompatible activities and resolve conflicts among user groups by zoning

To maintain the social and economic benefits of the area

To preserve the natural character and scenic value of the site

To control access to biologically and environmentally sensitive habitats

To restrict snorkeling and SCUBA diving activities into readily monitored locations

To prohibit anchoring, poling, and beaching of boats on reefs

To restrict forms of commercial, recreational, and subsistence fishing to those that cause least physical damage to the environment

To prevent access by all except surveillance personnel or scientists to certain areas that will function as sanctuaries for valuable or endangered species

To safeguard the breeding stocks of fishery species for replenishment of depleted areas

To encourage and facilitate research compatible with the protected area's objectives

To monitor the effects of all activities in the protected area

To monitor natural processes and responses to climate change (including bleaching, sea level rise, UV radiation)

To prevent dredging or other manipulations of the environment and control construction activities within the protected area

To protect critical sand-binding vegetation on beaches

To enable successional and other ecological processes and species interactions to continue unimpeded

To protect ecosystems, biotic communities, and individual species from disturbance or alteration by people

To regulate all activities inconsistent with the objectives of the protected area

To enable recuperation of damaged habitats or depleted stocks

To control access by land, sea, and air

To facilitate interpretation by special lectures, films, publications, guided tours, and underwater trails

To secure tenure of necessary land areas to permit siting of essential facilities and to protect sensitive habitats

minimum from 4 to 18 m deep will yield 75 percent of the coral genera and subgenera characteristic of that reef environment (i.e., lagoon or seaward reef). After four transects, the yield of additional genera and subgenera drops markedly. Assuming that the Chagos results have wider applicability, one can estimate the total genera and subgenera on a reef of greater than about 3 ha as the number of genera and subgenera counted from four transects, divided by 0.75.

Transect location is important. Transects should be placed over widely different parts of the reef (e.g., areas of low and high exposure to wind and waves, and gentle and steep slopes). Also, transects should be laid in areas of abundant growth. Avoid sandy, talus, and dead coral areas. A line may be laid down the reef slope to mark the transect, but this is generally unnecessary. The location of the transect can be buoyed at some convenient shallow depth. Start at the greatest depth and work up the slope. Sampling need not be confined to strict linear transects.

Sampling depth. Surveys will be limited by such practical factors as the length of time a SCUBA diver can remain at depth without going through decompression. To get the most from underwater work, sampling should be limited to 18 m (60 ft) and shallower since most corals are found at less than this depth. Sampling should be made at 6, 9, 12, and 18 m along each transect. Four transects are made per reef type, so 16 would be sampled on each reef.

Sampling procedure. Coral genera or species are identified and recorded visually, or small pieces are collected (where underwater identification is difficult) and placed in bags labeled with transect number and depth. The highest yield of corals at each depth is obtained by careful search and identification from a 2 X 2 m patch of reef followed by a search for different corals away from this site at the same depth. Thirty minutes should be enough time for both collections.

The above method may have to be modified to suit local conditions; for example, during studies on the reefs of the Seribu Islands in Indonesia, a higher yield of coral genera was obtained with less time and effort. In this case, 15 minutes sampling between 10 and 18 m followed by 15 minutes between 0 and 10 m on each of two transects per reef yielded an average of 79 percent of total genera and subgenera.

1.10 Estimating Critical Minimum Core Area

Critical minimum core area is determined by the following six steps:

1. Following the methods described above, sample along the transects on a reef of about 300 ha.

2. Increase the number of transects until 95 percent of the total estimated genera and subgenera are obtained, or until no new coral types are found. (The 95 percent limit is arbitrary and selected to save effort. If time and funds are not limiting, continue until no new corals are found).

3. If 95 percent of the genera and subgenera are not found, select a larger reef and begin again at step (1). If 95 percent of the estimated total is reached, select a discrete reef of similar area and repeat steps (1) and (2).

4. If the two reefs do not both have 95 percent of the genera and subgenera common to them, two larger reefs must be selected and the entire procedure repeated from step (1).

5. If the reefs do have the required 95 percent of genera and subgenera in common, a third reef of similar area is selected and steps (1) and (2) are repeated.

6. If the three reefs do not have the required 95 percent of the genera and subgenera in common, the procedure is repeated with larger reefs until three discrete reefs are found with at least 95 percent of the total estimated genera and subgenera common to them. The average area of these reefs is taken to be the critical minimum core area.

It should be clear that establishing and successfully managing coral reef protected areas has two prerequisites: designating the area based on ecological and social parameters, and controlling activities with potentially harmful effects within the boundaries of the site and those outside but linked by rivers, currents, or winds. These rules apply equally to protected estuarine areas, as we will see in the following section.

Protected Areas for Lagoons and Estuaries

C oastal lagoons and estuaries are exceptionally important for sustaining marine resources and biodiversity. These productive habitats support important sealife communities through their role in seafood production and their nurturing of many valuable marine organisms, not to mention their benefits for recreation, aesthetic appeal, suitability as harbors, and importance to wildlife. Moreover, delta environments are often an important extension of the estuarine system.

But the extent of economic development and intensity of use often deters selection of lagoons and estuaries as MPAs because they are often the locus of substantial economic activity and may be highly impacted by port development, land reclamation, heavy industry, housing, upstream agricultural practices, sewage disposal, and dumping. These activities degrade productive habitats, the quality of estuarine waters, the production of organic detritus, and feeding and nursery habitats of fishery species.

It may be possible to offer protection to entire *small* lagoons or estuaries and to assign management to a single MPA authority. But for large ones, MPA protection needs to be supported by a wider conservation programme such as Coastal Zone Management (CZM). With this approach, the entire lagoon/estuary would be the management unit, with management of MPAs, pollution control, dredge and fill regulation, fishery management, upstream land use planning and management, and port, navigation, and boating control being the responsibilities of different authorities coordinated by a single lead agency (see Section I-5).

2.1 Definitions

An "estuary" is an embayed coastal water basin diluted by freshwater flow and therefore characterized by a salinity gradient diminishing with distance from the sea. Technically, "an estuary is a semi-enclosed coastal body of water which has a free connection with the open sea and within which seawater is measurably diluted with freshwater derived from land drainage" (Pritchard, 1967). "Lagoons" include coastal embayments that are partially open to the sea but lack freshwater dilution from rivers and tend to be quite brackish (Figure II-14); they are sometimes seasonally closed to the sea by a sandbar deposited by wave action—this definition does not include those shallow inshore areas enclosed by coral reef barriers that are open systems rather than embayments but are often referred to as coral "lagoons" (or "moats"); these are discussed Section II-1, "Protected Areas for Coral Reefs."

FIGURE II-14.

Photo by R. Salm.

Small fishing boats (background) and mangroves (foreground): a dependent relationship.

2.2 Values

Both lagoons and estuaries maintain exceptionally high levels of biological productivity and play important ecological roles such as: 1) creating and "exporting" nutrients and organic materials to outside waters through tidal circulation; 2) providing habitat for a number of commercially or recreationally valuable fish species; and 3) serving the needs of migratory nearshore and oceanic species which require shallow, protected habitats for breeding and/or sanctuary nurture areas for their young. To give one example, over 90 percent of all fish caught in the Gulf of Mexico are reported to be "estuarine dependent" to some degree (Clark, 1996).

Estuaries are ecologically vital, vulnerable, and valuable. They are the buffer zones between silt-laden freshwaters of river systems and the sea, and exemplify the interdependence of terrestrial and marine systems. They provide the filtering systems and settling basins for silt brought down rivers and are the sites where salt water mixes with fresh.

Estuaries provide a variety of products of direct use to people: fishes, crustaceans, shellfish, birds, mammals, reptiles and reptile skins, amphibians, insects, timber and wood products, fodder, clay, oyster shell, sand, and cooling water for industry purposes. The list of mangrove wetland products from lagoons and estuaries is impressive (Table II-7).

These wetland habitats provide spawning grounds and nurseries for numerous commercially valuable species such as shrimp, crabs, fishes, and oysters (Figure II-15). Both salt marshes and mangroves export nutrients and organic detritus, which form the base of a complex food web supporting estuarine, coastal, and some offshore fisheries (Figure II-16). Coastal fisheries supply the majority of animal protein in dozens of countries. In 1978, for example, at least 550,000 tonnes of fish, worth US$ 194 million, caught in Indonesia were species directly linked to mangroves and estuaries during some stage of their life cycles (Salm, 1981b). Probably an equal quantity is caught for subsistence and never enters the fisheries statistics.

FIGURE II-15.

Mangrove wetlands help coastal communities by reducing coastal erosion, flooding, and storm surge; dampening waves and high winds generated by tropical and subtropical storms; and perhaps lessening the ravages of tidal waves (*Tsunamis*) in seismically active areas. Like coral reefs, mangroves provide no-cost, self-repairing, and natural "breakwaters." In a similar way, mangroves help stabilize riverbanks, preventing erosion and protecting adjacent lands. Mangroves, reed beds, and salt marshes often function as silt traps, slowing the flow of silt-laden rivers and streams and enabling the particles to settle out, then afterwards holding the silt in place. In this way they help to maintain the quality of coastal waters.

Photo by Erkki Siirila.

Prop roots of the red mangrove provide shelter to juvenile fish at Ramrod Key, the Florida Keys National Marine Sanctuary.

Table II-7. Products of Mangrove Ecosystems
Mangrove Forest Products

Fuel

Firewood for cooking, heating
Charcoal
Alcohol

Construction materials

Timber, scaffolds
Heavy construction timbers
Railroad ties
Mining pit props
Boat building materials
Dock pilings
Beams and poles for buildings
Flooring, paneling, clapboard
Thatch or matting
Fence posts, water pipes,
chipboards, glues

Fishing equipment

Poles for fish traps
Fishing floats
Fuel for smoking fish
Fish poison
Tannins for net and line preservation
Wood for fish drying or smoking racks

Textiles and leather
Paper products
Synthetic fibres (e.g., rayon)
Dye for cloth
Tannins for leather preservation
Other products

Food, drugs, and beverages

Sugar
Alcohol
Cooking oil
Vinegar
Tea substitute
Fermented drinks
Dessert topping
Condiments from bark
Sweetmeats from propagules
Vegetables from propagules,
fruit, or leaves
Cigar substitute

Household items

Furniture
Glue
Hairdressing oil
Tool handles
Mortars and pestles
Toys
Matchsticks
Incense

Agriculture

Fodder, green manure

Paper of various kinds

Packing boxes
Wood for smoking sheet rubber
Wood for firing bricks
Medicines from bark, leaves, and fruits

Other Natural Products

Fish
Crustaceans
Shellfish
Honey
Wax

Birds
Mammals
Reptiles and reptile skins
Other fauna (amphibians, insects)

Source: Saenger *et al.* (1983)

Wetlands provide opportunities for research, education, tourism development, and recreation like canoeing, bird watching, hunting, and claming (Figure II-17). For example, every year thousands of visitors go to Trinidad's Caroni Swamp mangrove area specifically to view the great numbers of birds (Saenger *et al.*, 1983), including the scarlet ibis *(Eudocinus ruber)* and other rare and endangered species (see Case 21 in Part III). During winter, hundreds of thousands of water-fowl (ducks, geese, and swans) and waders feed and roost in and around the salt marshes, mud flats, and sheltered inshore waters of the Chesapeake Bay and other wetlands of the U.S. coastal zone, Holland, Tunisia (at Lake Ichkeul), and the Sinai.

All these wetlands are important for species protection. Saltwater croco-diles *(Crocodylus porosus)*, their fresh-water counterparts, and the alligator *(Alligator mississipiensis)* frequent estu-aries and mangroves (Figure II-18). The endangered Bengal tiger *(Panthera tigris tigris)* survives in the mangroves of the Sunderbans in India and Bangladesh (Sanyal, 1983). Muskrats *(Ondatra zibe-thica)* are a valuable component of U.S. saltmarsh communities. Seals frequent the wetlands of the Wadden Sea. The proboscis monkey *(Nasalis larvatus)* is a mangrove inhabitant of Borneo.

Cooper, Harrison and Ramm (1995) show convincingly that both small and large estuaries along the KwaZulu-Natal coast of South Africa contribute signifi-cantly to the marine fisheries in the adjacent marine ecosystem. They provide essential nursery and seasonal feeding habitats for estuarine-dependent marine species and probably also support the

FIGURE II-16.

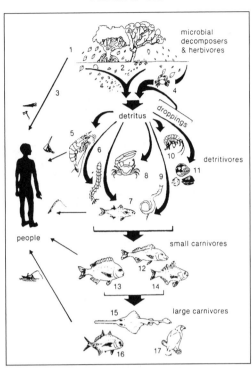

Interdependencies within the mangrove environment: (1) leaves; (2) algae; (3) fungi, protozoa, bacteria; (4) sesarmid and grapsid crabs; (5) shrimp; (6) insect larvae; (7) mullet; (8) fiddler crabs; (9) worms; (10) amphipods; (11) bivalve molluscs; (12) grunters; (13) emperors; (14) pony fishes; (15) sawfish; (16) trevallies; (17) sea eagle.

FIGURE II-17.

Photo by John Clark.

Nature tours provide good income for guides in Palau.

Figure II-18.

Alligators not only attract tourists but are a critical link in coastal ecosystems (Sanibel Island, Florida).

Photo by John Clark.

productivity and water quality of the adjacent marine system by nutrient inputs and filtering out sediments and pollutants.

2.3 The Need for Protection

Estuaries around the world have been degraded by poorly conceived development that failed to consider losses of natural productivity, such as loss of mangrove forests. Probably the greatest threat arises from construction and reclamation activities (Table II-8). Reclamation for industrial, urban, and airport development has seriously threatened mangroves in Australia, New Zealand, the United States and other countries (Saenger *et al.*, 1983).

Table II-8. Management Implications of Construction in Lagoons and Estuaries

Dredging of Channels, Marinas and Ports

　Creates the problem of dredge spoil disposal.

　Should be discouraged in small estuaries and through or near the critical habitats of valuable species.

　Should be preceded by environmental impact studies.

Channelisation and Diversion of Freshwater Inputs

　Generally increases channel bed and bank erosion, resulting in siltation of estuaries, and should be discouraged.

　Diversion of freshwater sources away from estuaries may cause increased salinity, stimulating widespread change in biotic structure and composition, and should be discouraged.

　Diversion of water into estuaries alters the water balance, decreasing salinity and often increasing siltation, and should be discouraged

Channelisation and Opening of Lagoon Mouths

　In most instances should be discouraged to allow natural cycle of closure and opening and related flushing.

　May enable intrusion of seawater and marine sands, which increases salinity and decreases depth.

　May necessitate periodic dredging of inlets to remove marine sands deposited there by longshore drift and tidal currents.

Reclamation for Industrial, Urban, or Agricultural Use, and Port Development

　Should be preceded by national survey and classification of wetlands by both natural values and best-use alternatives.

　Should avoid interference with freshwater inputs from streams, rivers, and sheet flow.

　Should avoid contamination of freshwater inputs.

Should be preceded by environmental impact assessments.

Should be sited in areas with suitable soil chemistry to avoid expensive remedial measures, crop failures, and low yields.

Should alternate with natural areas managed to provide nurseries (in many cases for seed stock), and the range of traditional uses maintained at sustainable levels.

Should be components of multiple use management and should be confined to zones in wetlands where it interferes least with critical habitats and coastal protection function.

Conversion for Mariculture

Has a mixed history of success, with some major and expensive failures from around the world, and should be generally considered non-sustainable.

Has limited potential because of acidification of soils.

May have severe impact on productivity of coastal waters and introduce poisons and disease to natural populations when conducted on grand scales.

May be more appropriate on small community level scales.

Loss of mangroves and other wetland plant communities results in loss of natural productivity.

Should be subject to comprehensive environment impact assessment and rigorous monitoring, and designed with the lessons learned from other failed enterprises.

Dyking and Construction of Retaining Walls, Groins, Docks, Piers, Causeways, and Roads

Should be preceded by studies of water and faunal movements.

Should be sited and constructed to avoid interference with the freshwater inputs from streams, rivers, and sheet flow (e.g., roads should follow the direction of stream flow and include adequate culverts).

Should be sited and constructed to avoid interfering with the tidal flushing of wetlands.

Should be sited and constructed to avoid interfering with movements of detritus and fauna (larvae, juveniles, and adults).

In many instances retaining walls may be inferior and expensive substitutes for barriers of natural vegetation.

If conservation countermeasures are not employed, the result can be rapid and severe degradation of the lagoon and estuary ecosystems and depletion of natural resources. But approaches other than MPA designation may be necessary for a successful conservation programme; for example, the Coastal Zone Management approach that includes pollution control and land use management.

In Gambia, India, and Bangladesh, conversion of mangrove stands of coastal lagoons to rice fields has caused considerable loss of natural productivity. In Indonesia, Ecuador, and Costa Rica, the cost of conversion has proved high and the yield generally low because of resultant acidic conditions. Coconut plantations have preempted mangrove forests in Sri Lanka (Salm, 1981a) (Figure II-19).

FIGURE II-19.

Photo by R. Salm.

Mangroves are cleared to allow access to boats, and wetlands are drained and planted with coconut in Negombo Lagoon, Sri Lanka.

Shrimp culture ponds have preempted wetlands in Bangladesh, Ecuador, Philippines, Indonesia, and dozens of other countries, where the cost of conversion has proved high and the yield generally low because of the acidification of soils. Despite this experience, the lure of potentially vast, quick profits from conversion of wetlands to shrimp ponds is threatening huge areas of the Tana and Rufiji deltas in East Africa and many other regions. Many of these abuses can best be corrected by combining MPA and Coastal Zone Management approaches (see Section I-5).

Considerable mangrove areas have been clear-felled, leveled, and diked to produce brine ponds for salt production in India, Benin, and Malaysia, with extensive loss of natural values. Reclamation of wetlands for farmland or industrial sites has been a major threat to the salt marshes of Britain (Nature Conservancy Council, 1979b).

Port construction generally requires obliterating the estuarine environment at the site and degrading surrounding waters through dredging, reclamation, and pollution.

Diverting freshwater has caused major changes to the ecology of the St. Lucia estuary in South Africa and the Laguna de Tacarigua National Park in Venezuela (see Case History 9 in Part III). In the first example, diverting a river away from a lagoon contributed to greatly increased salinity. In the second, diverting a river into a lagoon caused severe sedimentation. Siltation caused by inland erosion has altered part of the Laguna de Tacarigua National Park in Venezuela (see Case 9 in Part III).

A variety of harvest activities causes wide spread destruction of wetlands and estuaries, unless made sustainable. The worst is clear-cutting of mangrove trees for timber, pulpwood, firewood, chipboard and charcoal. However, under appropriate management rules, certain harvest activities can be allowed (Figure II-20). More than 200,000 ha of mangrove have been exploited in Indonesia (Saenger *et al.*, 1983). Mangrove felling is managed on a rotational basis in Malaysia and Thailand and is accompanied by replanting. Other harvest activities include fisheries of a variety of species; grazing of mangrove vegetation by camels, goats, and cattle and of salt marshes by livestock; and the harvest of vegetation as fodder.

Pollution can be very serious, causing pervasive and continuous degradation of coastal basins. Major sources are agricultural and industrial chemicals and sewage and industrial organic wastes. These basins are diminished when large areas of lagoons and estuaries are reclaimed (drained and/or filled) to create ports or real estate or agricultural land in land-scarce regions. Oil spills have resulted in the immediate death of mangrove plants and have decreased growth rates and increased stress and

FIGURE II-20.

Controlled mangrove harvest for charcoal is permitted in an MPA in St. Lucia.

mortality of mangrove biota through chronic poisoning; e.g., in Puerto Rico and Ecuador (Saenger *et al.*, 1983). Tables II-9 and II-10 list activities that may degrade lagoons and estuaries along with some management implications.

Table II-9. The Management Implications of Cities, Industries, and Agriculture on Lagoons and Estuaries

Extraction of Drinking Water (Groundwater and River Water)
  Requires prior investigation of freshwater inputs (streams, rivers, sheet flow, rainfall) and outputs (evaporation, evapotranspiration, seaward flow) of the system to determine the water balance.
  May be permitted in quantities that do not alter the water balance to the detriment of the system (such as by increased salinity) or cause the land to subside, producing flooding problems.

Irrigation
  Must be regulated to within predetermined limits to avoid alteration of water balance to the detriment of the system.

Plantations
  Must be buffered from waterways by belts (setbacks) of natural vegetation to avoid erosion and siltation of the estuary.
  Should contain species that make efficient use of water and bind soil on slopes.
  Should not encroach on critical habitats, including reed beds functioning as natural silt traps.

Uptake of Cooling Water and Discharge of Heated Water
  Must be preceded by studies to determine the maximum thermal load tolerable by estuarine communities.
  Should not alter the water balance to the detriment of the system.
  Must be carefully sited, regulated and monitored to avoid entrainment of planktonic forms.

Solid Waste Disposal
  Not an acceptable practice in estuaries.
  Must be prohibited in wetlands.

Liquid Waste Disposal

Biological wastes may be sustainable under certain conditions and within carefully determined limits.

Must be preceded by studies to determine amounts capable of being processed by wetland communities.

Must be carefully regulated and monitored.

Must be accompanied by monitoring of shellfish for accumulation of toxins and pathogens (e.g., hepatitis virus and cholera).

Navigation and Transport of Oil and Hazardous Chemicals

Must be carefully controlled and monitored.

Must be accompanied by oil spill contingency plan, including adequate containment and cleanup equipment which is rapidly mobilized.

Must be permitted under license.

Introduction of Exotic Species

Should be generally discouraged, including accidental release.

Should be preceded by careful research.

May alter natural community succession and composition with undesirable effects

Conversion to Mariculture and Salt Production

Salt production and mariculture may be acceptable in bare saline areas (salinas) inland from mangroves.

Mariculture has a mixed history of success and limited potential due to acidification of soil.

May be more appropriate on small scale.

Loss of mangroves results in loss of natural shrimp and fish production.

Should be subject to comprehensive EIA and rigorous monitoring.

Salt marshes in many countries have been destroyed by using them as refuse dumps. In Brazil solid wastes have been deposited at the rate of 130 tonnes per day in the Hacorobi mangrove swamp (Saenger *et al.*, 1983). Liquid waste in the form of industrial and domestic sewage has destroyed wetlands in Puerto Rico, Guadeloupe, and Martinique. Salt marshes and mangroves are able to process a certain amount of these liquid wastes. According to E. P. Odum (1971), estuaries have varying abilities to process degradable wastes, depending on their sizes, flow patterns, types, and climatic zones. Certain materials (e.g., treated sewage and pulp mill wastes, seafood and food processing wastes, petroleum wastes, and dredging spoil) can be decomposed and dispersed provided that two conditions hold: (1) the system is not additionally stressed by toxic pollutants, such as insecticides and acids; and (2) the rate of input is controlled at acceptably low to moderate levels and the estuary is not suddenly stressed by periodic dumping.

Impounding estuarine waters (i.e., cutting off their free connection with the open sea) probably has a strong negative effect on their functioning, including their ability to process waste and their value for food production (E. P. Odum, 1971).

Table II-10. Management Implications of Harvest, Hunting, and Mining Activities in Estuaries

Finfishing

Fishing gears and weirs that block the access channels to coastal lagoons or connecting channels between lagoons interfere with the spawning cycles and movements of fishes and shrimps; they should be removed and replaced by gears allowing free passage.

Active fishing gears that are dragged along the estuary floor, causing damage to the rooted vegetation and natural oyster beds, should be prohibited.

Must be regulated at sustainable levels.

Should be controlled by seasonal quotas and size limits to avoid interference with breeding stock.

Shellfishing

Should be regulated by permits and quotas.

Should be carefully monitored for impacts on substrates and stocks.

Crocodile Hunting

Can be a sustainable industry in areas that have abundant stocks.

May be replaced by crocodile farming.

Mining

Must be carefully regulated and monitored.

Should be preceded by impact assessment studies.

Must have adequate controls to prevent sedimentation of watercourses from spoil deposits and disturbed land surfaces.

Should be prohibited in the critical habitats of valuable species and all beaches.

Must avoid disruption of the hydrological regime in adjacent lands.

Should be discouraged or strictly controlled upstream of critical habitats.

Should be accompanied by rehabilitation of disturbed areas, including stabilization of spoil dumps.

Should have plans for the disposal of spoil in approved sites outside wetlands and other critical habitats.

Must avoid interference by pipes and service roads of water flow through the system.

Grazing

Must be prohibited in wildlife preservation areas as it limits the value to wildlife and can cause serious erosion of the creek margins.

May be permitted in specific zones and carefully controlled and monitored levels.

Forestry Operations

Need careful evaluation to determine truly sustainable levels for both selective logging and clear felling.

Should employ methods that cause least damage to the substrate.

Must be accompanied by replanting or natural regeneration of mangroves, if necessary through replanting with propagules, weeding of undesirable species, and disposal or other treatment of trimmings.

Should be confined to areas of least value to fisheries and danger of erosion.

Should be accompanied by research and monitoring studies to determine effect on fisheries.

Should be accompanied by strict protection of adjacent sites for general reference and for supply of propagules for both direct planting and natural reseeding.

2.4 Management Concepts

Lagoon or estuary ecosystems that are small and have little habitation and commercial development are the easiest case for designation as Marine Protected areas (MPAs). For these "pocket lagoons", the priority can be given to conservation of resources and maintenance of biodiversity. Conflicting uses are controllable. Economic benefits to a local population are evident. The whole of such a system can easily be managed as an MPA.

The other extreme is the heavily settled, industrialized, shipping port—e.g., New York, Jakarta, or Rotterdam—which common sense tells you would not be a successful MPA site. Yet there are numerous in-between cases of lagoons and estuaries where valuable natural habitats remain and where pollution and other impacts are controllable but, for which control is more appropriate to a Coastal Zone Management (CZM) approach (Section I-6) and management solutions are more institutional than ecological.

A solution is to use a joint CZM/MPA approach, where the desired MPA is nested within the broader protection of a CZM programme. The Negombo Lagoon in Sri Lanka is a good example of the joint CZM/MPA approach, whereby a CZM approach was taken to resolve use conflicts and general environmental degradation of the lagoon ecosystem and the wetland resources were set aside as protected areas. The Negombo case history (Part III, Case No. 3) shows the value of disaggregating the ecosystem into components and then giving protected status to those components that merit MPA designation, such as wetlands.

Negombo Lagoon is of international significance for biodiversity and as a refuge for migratory birds. But the lagoon and surrounding marshland area are beset by a profusion of socioeconomic and environmental problems. Here, an ecosystem-based approach was used to integrate environmental considerations into a Master Plan based on biological, geophysical and socioeconomic information and consensus building. The foundation of the Master Plan was zoning, which addressed the issues of development needs, conservation value and social equity. Four zones were delineated for the lagoon and surrounding area (a total of 10,700 ha) and endorsed at stakeholder workshops. The zones were: 1) Conservation Zone (91% of wetland), 2) Buffer zone (6.4% of wetland); 3) Mixed Urban Zone (2.5% of wetland); and 4) Residential Zone (42% of total planning area). The Conservation Zone is the equivalent of an MPA.

Planning an MPA programme for a small or undeveloped lagoon or estuary where it may be feasible may still require adjustments *outside* the MPA boundaries; that is, beyond the reach of MPA management authority. This can be aided by formation of a Zone of Influence (ZOI) coordinating entity. The ZOI entity is a network composed of agencies with authority in surrounding areas of the land or the sea, or both, that lie outside the defined Coastal Zone but which need management attention (see

Section I-5.8). This approach gives site management a formal mechanism for negotiating with the entities that do have control over activities outside the MPA boundaries.

Kapetsky (1981) discusses the management of coastal lagoon and estuarine fisheries in considerable detail. Some considerations in managing recreational activities in estuaries are listed in Table II-11. Other aspects of mangrove value, use, and management are discussed by Hamilton and Snedaker (1984) and Saenger *et al.* (1983). Detailed information on mangrove ecology and the principles and guidelines for a range of management options, including survey techniques, have been defined by FAO (1994).

Table II-11. Management Implications of Recreational and Educational Activities in Estuaries and Their Associated Habitats

Boating
  Generally acceptable but needs to be regulated by zones and speed limits.
  Speeding boats and large wakes may erode creek banks.
  May result in collision, propeller lacerations, and death of endangered manatee or dugong.
  May disturb roosting and nesting birds if inadequately managed.
  Needs to be diverted from critical bird habitats during the nesting season.

Fishing
  May cause social problems through conflict between recreational, subsistence, and industrial activities.
  Generally acceptable within sustainable limits.
  May be zoned, regulated and monitored.

Hunting
  Should be discouraged.
  Conflicts with other nonconsumptive pursuits, such as bird watching and photography.
  When permitted should be zoned to areas that do not conflict with other uses (water sports, fisheries), and must be regulated at sustainable levels.

Swimming, Diving, Nature Viewing, and Relaxation
  Generally acceptable.
  Should be subject to safety regulations.
  Should be prohibited in particular critical habitats of sensitive species.

Walking on Tidal Flats and Through Wetlands
  May cause compaction of the substrate and mortality of sessile life along frequently used trails and may alter drainage patterns.
  Should be monitored and if necessary routes should be changed.
  May be effectively controlled by confinement to boardwalks supported above the substrate; boardwalks offer numerous opportunities for efficient environmental interpretation.

Research and Education Programmes
  Should be encouraged.
  May require regulation and monitoring in sensitive environments.

2.5 Design of the Marine Protected Area

Regardless of how small or how large the portion of the lagoon or estuary that is intended for an MPA, it is necessary to address the *entire estuarine ecosystem*. When you cannot designate a whole estuary as an MPA, we suggest using one of the techniques mentioned above and either 1) attempt to invoke CZM for the whole estuary, or 2) attempt to set up a ZOI coordinating entity.

The policy of the planner should be to design the protected area following procedures like those described herein. First a strategy should be worked out and a Strategic Plan created. Second a Site Management Plan should be created with specific mechanisms for periodic review and any needed revisions of design based on new management studies. Assuming no initial expert assistance and little knowledge of the life histories of estuary-dependent species, the protected area should be designed to encompass as many habitats as possible.

The actual design work should follow the procedure in the earlier chapter on site planning (Section I-2). The objective is to design the lagoon or estuarine protected area around its principal habitats as revealed by field surveys of flora and fauna. The number of zones, if any, and the size of the protected area will depend on management objectives, examples of which are listed in Table II-12. Conserving estuary-dependent commercial species may require protecting a range of critical habitats both inside and outside the estuary.

2.6 Identifying Critical Habitats

Managing an estuary requires protecting the critical habitats of estuary-dependent species. The identification of these sites and processes requires knowing the geographic biology, particularly the life histories of key estuarine organisms. Each species has a characteristic requirement including substrate type, water depth, water clarity, dissolved oxygen content, and type of habitat (e.g., mangrove prop roots, marsh grass, or sea grass stems). And each key species has critical habitats that it uses during its life cycle. Such critical habitats are numerous and diverse (Box II-1).

Many habitats, perform special nurturing functions for certain species, including low intertidal marshes, high marsh tide pools, mangrove swamps, swamp and marsh creeks, mud and sand flats, passes or openings to the open ocean, open beaches, sea grass beds, macroalgae beds, rocky shores and tide pools, and many types of coral reefs, from patch reefs to extensive barrier reefs.

If the MPA is nested within a CZM area, special habitats may be identified for different categories of management, not just MPA management. Examples of three such categories previously discussed in Section II-5.8 are: 1. *Generic habitat types*; 2. *Specific sites (critical areas)*; and 3. *MPAs*.

Table II-12. Sample Management Objectives for Estuarine Protected Areas

To preserve a representative sample of the ecosystem and associated habitats, biotic communities, and species

To maintain the value of the area to resident and migratory species

To honour international obligations through protection of the critical habitats of shared resources

To maintain the value of the area as a nursery, feeding ground, or other critical habitat for fishery and other species

To maintain the production and flow of organic detritus from the wetlands to the feeding grounds

To prevent encroachment (landfill, felling of trees, cutting of marsh grasses, dredging) and degradation (pollution, sedimentation) of valuable habitats

To maintain the water balance

To promote research, recreation, and education

To control access by land, sea, and air to biologically and/or environmentally sensitive habitats

To promote interpretation through special lectures and films, interpretative publications, guided tours, and the construction of boardwalks

To maintain the value to fisheries production

To preserve the ecological processes and support systems on which the integrity of the ecosystem depends

To control upstream activities that may degrade or destroy all or part of the value of the area to conservation and sustainable development

To promote uses compatible with conservation and sustainable development objectives

To separate incompatible activities and resolve conflicts among user groups by zoning

To preserve the natural character and scenic value of the site

To limit uses to within sustainable levels and to regulate all activities

To enable successional and other ecological processes and species interactions to continue unimpeded

To review and revise periodically the management needs and procedures

To monitor all activities in the area and the outcomes of management

To enable recuperation of damaged habitats or depleted species stocks

To secure tenure of essential lands for the appropriate management authority (central, provincial, district, or village government, NGOs, or private sector)

Here we address the third category, the MPA. To start the process for a particular MPA site, it is recommended that you obtain a small scale base map of the estuary extending from a distance perhaps 10 km offshore and extending inwards through coastal waters and inland to include the main water catchment of the estuary/lagoon. It is essential that the base map include depth contours and topography along with the locations of critical habitats (refer to Box II-1).

These habitats can be identified by remote sensing and aerial, boat, and automobile surveys, then plotted on an overlay of the base map. You can draw on the base map locations of all wetlands (mangroves, reed beds, or salt marshes). For large estuaries, or those with poor databases, it may be necessary to survey the

Box II-1. Types of Critical Habitats

Sea grass, kelp, and algal beds are sources of primary productivity and detritus production. These are important feeding grounds for certain fishes and waterfowl and nurseries for shrimp and fishes.

Mud and sand flats are the habitats of bivalves and the feeding grounds of shrimp and crabs. They are particularly important to over-wintering waders and shorebirds, the substrate for nitrogen-fixing blue-green algae, and a storage unit for important dissolved substances.

Salinas (barren salt flats) may be important in flood control and, in some areas, harboring valuable species, such as the brine shrimp *(Artemia)*.

Creeks and Meanders are the critical habitat of many species, and during certain seasons may be replete with juvenile shrimp and fishes. They are a source of algal and phytoplankton productivity and serve as the course of tidal and freshwater supplies and the routes of access to different parts of the wetlands complex for aquatic organisms.

Oyster reefs are valuable in their own right for the harvest of their biomass and for providing a special habitat.

Coral reefs are connected to estuaries/lagoons in many ways: e.g., as the spawning places of fishes that seek refuge as juveniles in the mangroves.

Reed beds (Phragmites) at stream or river mouths and deltas are important silt traps that help control the turbidity of waters flowing into the estuary, and they may also be important factors in flood control. They also provide nesting habitats for a variety of birds.

Sand dunes, barrier islands, and beaches are dynamic habitats. They are sensitive to overuse and prone to erosion, which alters natural cycles of accretion and erosion of sand supplies along the seashore. This may result in the sea breaching the coastal barrier and flooding wetlands with salt water, the smothering of wetland habitats by wind-blown sand, and the choking of lagoon and estuary mouths by increased longshore drift of sand. These beaches and barrier islands often provide valuable nesting habitat for sea turtles (e.g., Tortuguero National Park in Costa Rica)

Alluvial bars are unstable dynamic habitats formed of water-borne silt. When disturbed, they are prone to resuspending fine alluvial particles that cloud the water, reducing phytoplankton, sea grass, and algal productivity.

Mangroves have multiple roles, including shoreline stabilization, trapping river-borne silt, detritus production, and providing nursery habitats for fishes and shrimp and safe roosting and nesting sites for birds.

estuary by air to locate and map critical habitats like wetlands. If recent aerial photography (or satellite imagery in the case of very large areas) can be used, it should be spot checked ("ground truthed") by walking or boat surveys. It is convenient to use computers for storage, retrieval, and display of data; for example through Geographic Information Systems (GIS) as discussed in Section I-5.1.

You can enter on the base map—manually or electronically—known critical habitats of species both inside and outside the estuary, including submerged sea grass and algal beds, as well as connections to the sea (lagoon mouths, deltaic channels). Some critical habitats may overlap others, for example the nesting and roosting sites of shorebirds and seabirds in mangroves may overlap the habitat of muskrats in marshes (Figure II-21). Designated habitats should include those of commercial species, showcase species, and endangered species.

Highlight the selected critical habitats --whether using manual methods of mapping or GIS—and indicate the recommended management approach for each on the map. Be aware that the areas chosen may be subject to multiple use, not exclusively assigned to protection, and the recommended extent of such uses has to be clearly indicated so that zones can be designated.

You will need to investigate the pattern of human use and settlement in the estuary and record significant sources of impacts. In larger inhabited estuaries where there has been some use and alteration of wetlands and

FIGURE II-21.

A muskrat house on a transitional brackish tidal marsh next to a small creek (Pautuxent River, Chesapeake Bay, Maryland, U.S.A.).

other coastal habitats, identify the remaining areas of high conservation value, which generally will be those in a natural state, removed from human settlements, or currently managed for recreation, research or education, or as private nature reserves.

Depending on the extent and location of settlement and commercial use, a larger estuary can be zoned for different MPA management approaches, or as mentioned above, allotted to CZM protection if there is an effective CZM process for the lagoon or estuary. In this case, the most valuable and vulnerable critical habitats should be given the fullest protection that MPAs can afford through zoning or other means.

2.7 Delineating the Zone of Influence

Water supply is vital to the estuary's functioning. Sources of water include the catchment, rivers and streams crossing the watershed, groundwater seepage and sheet flow (runoff), rainfall, and intrusion of salt water from the sea. These water sources link estuaries to agricultural and development activities that are tens, even hundreds, of kilometers away. Disturbance of these sources--including their reduction, diversion, and pollution—may have disastrous consequences for estuarine ecosystems. Such distant activities are difficult to monitor, but must be controlled if an estuary and its valuable components are to survive. When the main catchments that discharge to the estuary lie close at hand and are not heavily settled, the two may be protected as single "source-to- sink" units.

To accomplish understanding and control of catchment areas and coastal plains that are settled or cultivated and *lie outside MPA boundaries* in the Zone of Influence (ZOI), the following specific techniques to identify and manage linked habitats may be helpful if funds are available and the organized ZOI consortium cooperates:

- Using remote sensing, topographic and land use maps, and surveys, identify permanent and seasonal streams and rivers draining into the estuary; agricultural, urban, and industrial zones; primary and secondary roads; dams and irrigation schemes, and production forests and farmlands. Plot these on an overlay of the small-scale base map. Note that much of this information may already be available.

- Try to persuade the ZOI consortium to take action on erosion controls (such as brushwood or hay-bale dykes) for all construction sites, developments, and farms in the watershed where ground clearing or earth movement is taking place. Also try to incorporate erosion control guidelines for farms and road construction (Figure II-22).

- Estimate from hydrologic studies the minimum requirements for freshwater flow to the estuary. Based on this, estimate the minimal seasonal flow of freshwater that the estuarine MPA needs and that you want provided by dam operators, irrigators, water suppliers, and others who draw on the water resources. This amount will normally be a high percentage of the flow and should come at the appropriate season of the year.

FIGURE II-22:

Photo by Erkki Siirila.

- From aerial or ground survey, determine how, and where stream flows to the estuary may be impeded. From findings, recommend remedial measures to the ZOI consortium, such as clearing obstructions and constructing a certain number and size of culverts under a road.

- Identify the banks of rivers and major streams as exclusion zones that may not be settled, developed, cultivated, cut, or altered. These fringing zones will vary depending upon local configurations, but should include all the designated floodplain; they may range in size from 20 to over 100 m.

- Where any of the above conditions lie within the ZOI boundaries, the same corrective actions should be taken.

A road engineer presents measures to prevent soil runoff into the sea at an MPA in St.Lucia. The group comprises environmental planners from several Eastern Caribbean states.

2.8 General Information Needs

Planning for MPAs in estuaries or lagoons requires detailed ecological knowledge. The protected area manager should have a thorough knowledge of the physical, chemical, and biological parameters of the estuarine ecosystem and when possible participate in research in the field (see Boxes II-2 and II-3). Research and monitoring studies and periodic management plan revisions are the basis for the most successful management of lagoons and estuaries. But only occasionally has sufficiently detailed research preceded protected area design.

Box II-2. Physical Information for Lagoon and Estuary MPAs.

Geomorphology of a basin reveals a wealth of information on the likely functions and characteristics of the ecosystem. Classifying the estuary by type requires little more than visual inspection.

Bottom topography can yield features of ecological significance (shape of bottom affects currents; shallow areas have higher photosynthetic rates, etc.). Depths can be taken by a cheap electronic meter or simple lead line.

Bottom types reveal biological activity types that are particularly diagnostic for estuaries. Samples of bottom sediments are easily obtained by simple methods; a bamboo tube would be sufficient in many cases to distinguish among sand, mud, gravel, and ooze.

Salinity gradient (seasonal and sporadic) is easily determined with a direct reading salinometer (see Chemical in Box X), although "presence or absence" can be learned from the "taste test."

Tidal flux in most estuaries is a dominant hydrological force. Measure diurnal changes by use of water level gauges (marked stick), tidal velocities (movement of a float) and extent of substrate exposed and flooded. Tide tables are usually available for navigable estuaries.

Current patterns influence the degree of mixing between seawater and sedimentation. Currents may be powered by tides, external marine currents, rivers, and wind. Surface currents can be plotted with floating objects, like bottles or coconut husks.

Turbidity results from suspended particles of silt, organic detritus, and plankton. It influences light penetration and photosynthesis. Turbidity can be measured with a Secchi disc (a white-and-black painted, weighted disc lowered from the surface by cord).

Geomorphological dynamics indicate stability of different substrates in the basin which may be shifting or filling. An outlet may silt up or a sandbar form or a new outlet may open, seasonally, over a few years or overnight during storms. The MPA manager can monitor these dynamics using trees, buildings, etc as visual benchmarks, or stakes driven into the ground. More sophisticated survey techniques (remote sensing) may also be used.

Seasonal considerations, including rainfall, air and water temperatures, insulation (sunshine), tides, and hydrology are all important.

Source: Carr, 1982b.

Box II-3. Chemical Information for Lagoon and Estuary MPAs.

Salinity distribution (horizontal, vertical, tidal, and seasonal) can explain the presence and distribution of many estuarine plants and animals.

Indicators of community metabolism, including oxygen, carbon dioxide, biological oxygen demand (BOD), and others, reflect the functioning of an estuary and should be monitored.

Plant nutrients, including phosphate and nitrogen compounds, require elaborate procedures to be tracked through the aquatic system. Where the manager gives way to scientists depends on the training and terms of reference of the manager, and the facilities available.

General chemistry of an estuary is a topic of which the manager should have some basic knowledge. For example, the absence of silica in the water may explain the paucity of diatoms in the plankton community.

There should be an inventory of plants and animals for the estuary or lagoon MPA. Of particular importance are critical habitats of commercial, endangered, or otherwise valuable species (feeding, roosting, resting, nesting, spawning, nursery sites, and migration routes) which need to be located and carefully managed and zoned (Figure II-23).

FIGURE II-23.

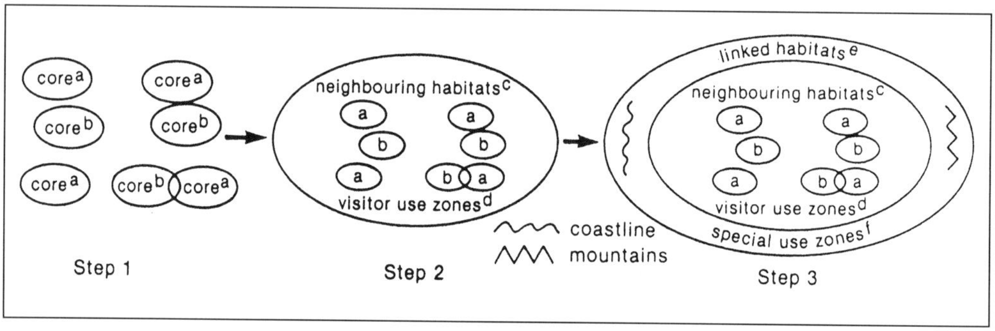

Principal steps in the design of an estuarine protected area. (a. Wetlands, salt marshes, and mangroves; b. wetlands, sea grass beds, grasslands and other critical habitats of species, channels, and openings to the sea; c. sea grass beds, algal beds, tidal flats, salinas, creeks, oyster or coral reefs, reed beds, sand dunes, barrier islands, beaches, and alluvial bars; d. protected area headquarters, ranger stations, and recreation, traditional fishing, research, and education zones; e. water catchments, watersheds, rivers, streams, agricultural lands, agricultural and urban developments, and dammed waters; f. shipping lanes, commercial fishing grounds, and intensive use zones.)

In addition ecological processes should be understood, particularly major food chains which can be analyzed at various levels of complexity, all with useful results. Ideally, the MPA manager should attempt to understand energy flow through the system and to quantify this flow where feasible. For example, in Tortuguero Estuary there is a shift from an algae-based photosynthetic production to a detritus-based production according to season (Nordlie and Kelso, 1975). Yet in Malaysia phytoplankton productivity never contributes much to the estuary relative to the huge inputs from mangroves.

Without too much trouble the various compartments of the food chain can be identified. Knowledge of the following elements will be useful:

– Photosynthetic, (a) producers (phytoplankton, rooted submerged aquatic plants, and attached algae), (b) consumers, (c) detritivores

– The detrital food chain, (a) sources (mangroves, salt marshes, and other wetland and terrestrial sources), (b) transport to and through the estuary, and (c) the resulting food chain or web

– Overlaps between the two food chains

– Seasonal and diurnal patterns (noting that photosynthesis stops at night)

– Correlations with major physical and chemical features

2.9 Design Principles

It is worth repeating that the estuary hydrological regime and water quality characteristics determine the basin's ecosystem and hence its biodiversity and value for fisheries and wildlife. Salinity gradients determine the distribution of plants, animals, and whole communities in estuaries, so activities outside estuaries that alter the water balance must be carefully managed. Consequently, maintaining water cycles and water quality are an important part of estuary management. As an estuary's watershed (or catchment) may cover many hundreds of square kilometers, the effective design and management of its protected areas can be a difficult task and one the MPA manager cannot accomplish alone.

Not all estuaries/lagoons and wetlands habitats within them are equally valuable for all activities. Establishing protected areas in these environments should follow surveys classifying particular habitats according to different values and appropriate uses. An MPA or several MPAs for the basin can then be chosen that are most suited to management objectives, with priority to those that suit both economic objectives and resource conservation objectives.

Management should extend over the largest area practicable (Figure II-24). This may be done through multiple use management, protecting the most critical areas strictly, and confining different uses to specific zones. Large estuaries should be managed as multiple use areas, optimally through combined CZM and MPA designation (Clark, 1998).

2.10 Design and Management Guidelines

The following guidelines are meant to help the site planner in fulfilling the objectives of a lagoon or estuarine MPA:

1. Conserving estuary-dependent commercial species requires protecting a range of critical habitats both inside and outside the estuary.

2. Conserving estuarine habitats depends on controlling direct impacts (reclamation, dredging, logging, and grazing) and on maintaining the water balance and the quality of the water supply. The water balance of an estuary is a function of forces acting on it from outside and within the limits of its shorelines.

FIGURE II-24.

Photo by Erkki Siirila.

Entire estuaries should be managed as multiple-use areas.

3. Not all estuaries and wetlands or zones within them are equally valuable for all activities. Establishing protected areas in these environments should follow surveys classifying areas and habitats according to different values and appropriate uses (Figure II-25). Protected areas can then be selected that are most suited to management objectives, and developments can suit both their own objectives and those of resource conservation.

4. Large estuaries should be managed as multiple use areas. Conflicting uses should be reconciled in the interest of the welfare of the whole system.

5. Protecting an estuary requires detailed ecological planning, possibly more than for any other environment, to determine the boundaries of the functional unit. Because such planning is often too lengthy to undertake before implementing initial management, the following principles should be borne in mind:

   – Wetlands contribute significantly to the production and value of lagoons/estuaries and should be afforded high management priority.

   – Salinity gradients determine the distribution of plants, animals, and whole communities in estuaries, so inland activities that alter the water balance must be carefully controlled.

– Management plans for lagoons/estuaries will inevitably be based on limited data and should be accompanied by detailed research programmes.

– The protected area manager should have a thorough knowledge of the physical, chemical, and biological parameters of the estuarine ecosystem and should participate in research in the field.

FIGURE II-25.

Research boat used to survey marine habitats to determine their values and characteristics.

6. A larger lagoon/estuarine wetlands area clearly has greater potential to support higher numbers of waterfowl, reptiles, and mammals. Management should extend over the largest possible wetlands area. This may be done through multiple use management, protecting the most critical areas strictly, and confining different uses to specific zones or species (Figure II-26).

FIGURE II-26.

Shorebirds need protected wetland habitats to prosper (Ballona Wetlands MPA, California).

7. The entire lagoon/estuary should remain the management unit even where an MPA includes only part of the basin. Management must extend beyond the shorelines to streams, rivers, and the water catchment, and where possible to the limit of the functional boundaries of the lagoon or estuary ecosystem.

Protected Areas
for Small Islands

T he approaches to protecting small island ecosystems are as diverse as the islands themselves. Still, some generalizations can be made about conserving their resources based on their particular structures and functioning. Islands are molded by their isolation from other landmasses and enclosure by an environment quite different from that supporting continental life. The isolation of islands both limits the variety of their native plant and animal species and renders them vulnerable to human activities. Yet most of the same basic MPA management principles apply. A special factor is that the entire area of small islands is often included in an MPA.

The approach to MPA creation and management varies according to the status of the particular small island and may be different for each of the following types of islands:

– Islands uninhabited and seldom visited by humans

– Islands uninhabited but regularly visited by humans

– Islands inhabited by people with traditional economies (and possibly exploited only on a subsistence basis) (Figure II-27)

– Islands inhabited by people with trading economies and relying on the sale of exports to support a cash economy.

In this section we consider some basic principles of establishing protected areas on populated islands, but will stress design and management strategies for protecting small, uninhabited islands and remote sparsely inhabited islands (see Ogilvie and Wace, 1982, and Wace, 1982).

FIGURE II-27.

Photo by John Clark.

Seaweed farming is a major industry at Nain Island in the Bunaken National Marine Park, Indonesia.

Those interested in conservation of islands should be alert to opportunities for regional cooperation in historically uninhabited or seasonally inhabited islands. Consistent with unclos (see section 1-6) such cooperation can reduce the potential for conflict, through the establishment on trans-boundary Peace Parks.

3.1 An Overview of Islands

Two important principles for protecting island habitats are: first, to establish upper limits for their permanent human populations, and for tourists where possible; and second, to integrate protected habitats into the economy of the islanders so that they have a vested interest in protecting and conserving habitats and resources. This integration may entail various forms of exploitation, such as tourist viewing of wildlife or scenery, or taking of fish, seabirds, or other native biota. Alternatively, it may provide helpful services, such as water catchment and stabilization of steep slopes in forested areas, or beach and anchorage protection by coral reefs.

According to the classic work of Alfred Russell Wallace (1880), islands have been considered either "oceanic" or "continental." Oceanic islands are volcanic or coralline, with few exceptions (e.g., the granite islands of Seychelles). They are separated from continents, and usually from one another, by deep water and have never been connected by land to any continent, or, as is the case in Seychelles, have been separated for more than 100 million years. They have therefore recruited their native floras and faunas by overseas dispersal. Most oceanic islands are of mid-Tertiary age (35 million years B.P.) or younger, having formed since the continents became arranged more or less as they are now, and the oceans began to reach their present configurations. Many are now extremely remote from all other lands.

Table II-13 compares some of the major features of oceanic and continental islands and continents as they affect the size, stability, and human use of their native

Table II-13. Characteristics of Oceanic and Continental Islands as Compared to Continents

Oceanic islands	Continental Islands	Continents
	Geographical Characteristics	
Remote from continents	Close to continents	–
Bounded by wide seas	Bounded in part by narrow seas	–
Small areas	Large or small areas	Very large areas
Equable air temperatures	Less equable air temperatures	Often very large seasonal and/or diurnal temperature ranges
Climates often unlike those of nearest mainland	Climates similar to nearest continents	
	Geological Characteristics	
Volcanic or coralline generally	Sedimentary or metamorphic	Sedimentary, metamorphic or igneous
Mid-Tertiary or younger	Young or old	Young or old
Few valuable minerals	Some minerals	Minerals
Permeable soils	Various soils	Various soils
	Biological Characteristics	
Impoverished overall biodiversity	Less impoverished biodiversity	Broad range of biodiversity
High turnover of species	Lower species turnover	Usually low species turnover
Mass breeding of marine vertebrates	Often mass breeding of marine vertebrates	Few marine vertebrates breeding ashore
Morphologically and anatomically primitive leaf structure of endemic species	Normal and primitive leaf anatomy	Normal and primitive leaf anatomy
	Historical Characteristics	
Late discovery by humans	Often early discovery	Early or late discovery and settlement by humans
Recent settlement	Early or late settlement	
	Economic Characteristics	
Few terrestrial resources	Wider range of terrestrial resources	Wide range of terrestrial resources
Marine resources important	Marine resources important	Marine resources often unimportant
Distant from major markets	Nearer to large markets	Markets relatively accessible

Source: Wace (1982).

ecosystems. There are exceptions to all of these usual characteristics in some islands, but together these characteristics define the major differences underlying insular and continental habitats. The biological characteristics result directly or indirectly from the operation of geographical, climatic, and geological features over time. Similarly, an island's historical and economic characteristics result from the operation of all the previous characteristics, among which remoteness, small size, and impoverished biotic variety are probably the most important.

The native terrestrial floras and faunas of oceanic islands have fewer forms compared to those of similar areas on continents. However, older oceanic islands may have large numbers of unique or endemic species of singular scientific interest that are undergoing evolutionary radiation. An important consequence of the "impoverished" biota of oceanic islands is that their food chains tend to be shorter than those of continents or continental islands. Lack of native mammalian herbivores (and probably few herbivores generally and an impoverished range of decomposers) and lack of mammalian carnivores render the native biota of ocean islands particularly vulnerable to such animals when they are introduced by people. Many endemic plants on oceanic islands display primitive features of leaf anatomy and are particularly palatable to such herbivores as goats.

The terrestrial flora and fauna of oceanic islands may have high turnover (colonization and extinction) rates, even under natural conditions. This is particularly true of small islands independently of direct or indirect human effects. MacArthur and Wilson (1963) affirm on both theoretical and empirical grounds that the turnover rate of species varies inversely with island area. Oceanic islands frequently support enormous populations of marine birds, mammals, and reptiles that feed at sea but rest and reproduce ashore (Figure II-28 and 29). Such congregations of marine creatures have direct effects on insular ecosystems during certain seasons because of their import of plant nutrients and their disturbance of plant growth in turning over the soil (notably burrowing seabirds).

FIGURE II-28.

Photo by R. Salm.

A red-footed booby chick (Sula sula) in the branches of a Rhizophora mangrove, Aldabra Atoll strict nature preserve and World Heritage Site.

Diamond (1976) demonstrated that the boundary shapes and dispositions of nearby reserves in relation to one another, as well as their sizes, are important in minimizing extinction rates of birds. Temple (1981) advocated the transfer of some endemic species of land birds from one island to another in the Mascarene Islands because they were supposedly endangered by competition with other native species from crowding in the reduced forests of Mauritius. This transfer of endemic birds species among the granite islands of Seychelles has proved effective in the conservation of island birds threatened by encroachment of their critical habitats.

FIGURE II-29.

Sea lions find a suitable nearshore resting place in Puget Sound, Washington, U.S.A.

The biota of continental islands, although lacking some continental plants and animals, are seldom as impoverished as those of oceanic islands. However, they often harbor relict endemic species that have been extinguished on nearby continents, whether or not through human action (e.g., the Irish Elk and Tasmanian Tiger).

The "inhabited" islands shown in Table II-14 are distinguished from islands where parties of scientists, meteorologists, or military personnel may reside, but do not normally raise families, and rely on imported supplies of food and fuel for their sustenance.

Table II-14. Oceanic Islands of the World

Ocean	Inhabited Islands*	Uninhabited Islands	Unknown	Total
Atlantic Ocean				
Arctic/north temperate	36	11	–	47
Tropical	16	4	44	24
Southern temperate/sub-Antarctic	1	15	–	16
Totals	53	30	44	87
Indian Ocean				
Western tropical	100	50	100	250
Eastern tropical	23	35	–	58
Southern temperate/sub-Antarctic	–	20	–	20
Totals	123	105	100	328
Pacific Ocean				
East Pacific (temperate/tropical)	5	38	7	50
Polynesia (mostly tropical)	155	18	114	287
Micronesia (tropical)	109	22	30	161
Melanesia (tropical)	148	89	104	341
Nontropical (including sub-Antarctic)	15	66	28	109
Totals	432	233	283	1,463
World totals	**608**	**468**	**387**	**1,463**

Sources: Wace (1982); Douglas (1969); Snow (1970); Elliott (1972); Central Intelligence Agency (1976)
* "Inhabited" means settled by a self-sustaining human population.

The proportion of definitely inhabited islands in the Atlantic appears to be higher than in the other two oceans, but only the southern temperate and sub-Antarctic zones appear to have more than half of their oceanic islands still uninhabited. The remoteness and inhospitable climates have prevented settlement, but not the destructive exploitation of some of their wildlife. Almost all oceanic islands dominated by flowering plants (and probably fewer such continental islands) have been more or less disturbed by human activities (Wace, 1979). As has long been the case on the continents, the conservation of plant and animal life on islands is increasingly about managing and influencing the ongoing activities of people, rather than controlling their initial invasion or exploitation.

3.2 Threats to Island Habitats from Human Activities

Although most continental islands have been accessible for many thousands of years, people have reached oceanic islands (and thus disrupted their biota) mostly within the last millennium. Similarly, technological developments within the last few decades have greatly increased the accessibility of island and coastal habitats that were formerly protected by inaccessibility (Figure II-30), according to Wace (1982).

FIGURE II-30.

Nature tourists benefit from modern transportation and communication to get to faraway places (Palau).

Photo by John Clark.

If isolation and inaccessibility have hitherto been the great conserving forces in people's relations with wild nature, oceanic islands are the best examples we have of the catastrophic effects of the removal of these powerful constraints. Decline and extinction of endemic island species, such as the dodo, giant tortoises, and some plants, may be merely the last convulsions of those parts of wild nature that are unable to adapt to humans as they reach the least accessible areas of the planet.

Further threats to island and shoreline environments arising from human misuse of these areas, and ecological guidelines for compatible development are presented by McEachern and Towle (1974), W.E. Odum (1976), Clark (1977, 1996), and Clark *et al.* (1980). These documents are also relevant to establishing protected areas in estuaries and coral reef environments.

3.3 Site Selection and Island Biogeography Theory

It is evident that the design of protected island areas depends on whether the reserve is to be established to protect indigenous fauna, flora, or communities, or to protect transient species (migratory waders and shorebirds) or seasonal species (turtles, seabirds, and marine mammals).

The selection of a protected area may be determined by the presence or absence of an endemic species, of populations of indigenous species depleted or eliminated on other islands, of endangered species, or of intact representative samples of indigenous communities. In the case of endemic or endangered species, there may be no choice of site (Figure II-31). This also holds for new volcanic islands that are undergoing colonization and that consequently have high value for studies in geology, geomorphology, volcanology, ecology, and island biogeography.

Where there is an assortment of islands to select for the protection of insular biota, the choice can be more complex. In making it, the following principles of island biogeography theory generally apply to the design of protected areas (Diamond, 1975, 1976; Diamond and May, 1976; Goeden, 1979; May, 1975; Preston, 1962; Simberloff and Abele, 1976a, b; Terborgh, 1974, 1976; Usher, 1973; Whitcomb *et al.*, 1976; Willis, 1974; Wilson and Willis, 1975):

FIGURE II-31.

A green turtle swimming in the waters of the Great Barrier Reef Marine Park off Townsville, Australia. For reproduction, the turtle depends on beaches, often provided by islands.

– The number of species on an island is a function of extinction and immigration rates.

– There is a direct relationship between island area and the number of species present (larger islands have more species).

– Larger island protected areas are generally better because they harbor more species (with equilibrium between extinction and immigration) and have lower extinction rates.

The following characteristics of larger islands generally enable them to support more species:

– They have a greater variety of available habitats

– They have greater variability in the location and timing of available resources

– They have a greater number of sites of high resource production that can be utilized by different species.

3.4 General Principles and Premises

Islands have the following characteristics of importance to planners and managers of island MPAs:

- They are generally isolated, both biologically (with limited colonization by organisms and a tendency toward species extinction) and for management (being remote, difficult of access, and difficult to guard).

- Their small sizes may make even temporary habitation by enforcement or research officers difficult and render them vulnerable to natural disturbances (e.g., tropical storms) and human-related ones (e.g., trampling of vegetation and erosion).

- With the exception of continental islands, they are geologically young and dynamic environments.

- Their species diversity is generally low and species turnover may be high, so special care is needed to control activities that might impede immigrating species or accelerate extinction.

- They show well defined relationships among the parameters of habitat diversity (e.g., island area and altitude), degree of isolation (e.g., distance from mainland or other source of colonizing organisms and presence of stepping stone islands) and species diversity, which should be taken into account during the selection, design, and management of protected island areas. (See Diamond and May, 1976, for a discussion of island biogeography theory and the design of protected areas.)

- Islands are more or less genetically isolated, which creates the opportunity for evolutionary divergence. For this reason, they may be rich in endemic species, which increases their conservation value.

- Conversely, certain species using islands (notably seabirds, seals, sea lions, and turtles) are wide ranging (Figure II-32). Island species (both plant and animal) may have evolved without predators and hence are tame (in the case of animals) or without suitable defenses (in the case of both plants and animals) and vulnerable to introduced predatory or herbivorous species.

FIGURE II-32.

Photo by Erkki Siirila.

California sea lions sharing an intimate moment at Los Islotes, a small island MPA in Baja California, Mexico.

– Coralline islands are sensitive environments, which, when disturbed, may completely disappear as did Mawizi Island Reserve in Tanzania. Wind may erode beaches and dunes if sand-binding vegetation is trampled or removed (Figure II-33), and waves and currents may erode the entire island if reefs are damaged by coral mining or channels are dug through to the shallows.

– Islands often have high scientific value because of the opportunities they offer for the study of the above characteristics and the processes determining them.

FIGURE II-33.

Spinifex is an important sand binding plant and its spines are a deterrent to dune walkers in Sri Lanka.

Special attention should be afforded to the ocean-land interface in the planning and management of small island MPAs for the following reasons:

– Islands, particularly small ones, have a high ratio of shoreline to total land area.

– The shoreline is the area of dynamic contact between sea and land (through waves and currents) and wind and land, and serves as a buffer against the erosive power of these agents.

– Strand or seashore vegetation is quite sensitive to disturbance by trampling, offroad vehicles, and other sources of mechanical damage, and is very important in stabilizing the shore (Figure II-34).

– Beaches are especially attractive for recreation, where visitor activities concentrate.

FIGURE II-34.

Nesting sites for turtles need special protection.

– Facilities (seawalls, groins, and piers) alter current patterns and the natural erosion and accretion processes along shorelines, causing both severe erosion downstream and smothering by deposited sand upstream of their structures.

– Where practicable, protection should apply to the entire island to control exotic species (such as rats and cats on bird nesting islands) and to enable species that are seasonal residents to respond to changes in weather conditions or population size, by occupying additional areas.

Particularly on islands, protected areas should embrace both land and water for ecological and practical reasons. There is much transfer of material from reef to beach and of nutrients from sea to land by birds. Reefs also protect coralline islands from erosion by waves. Certain species mate, roost, rest, nest, or pup on land but feed at sea. Both the terrestrial and marine critical habitats of such species require protection. Protection of offshore areas is especially important along turtle nesting beaches, since turtles congregate and mate there and feed and shelter on fringing reefs or grass and algal beds (Figure II-35).

FIGURE II-35.

Photo by C. Zuber, courtesy of World Wide Fund for Nature.

Sooty terns (*Sterna fuscata*) are an island nesting species that congregates in colonies of up to many hundreds of thousands of individuals.

Protected areas on both uninhabited and populated islands can often be linked to areas or structures that have historical or cultural value. Entire islands may have been set aside for religious purposes and the harvest of island or adjacent marine resources strictly controlled by taboos. These naturally protected sites may often have a high conservation value.

Protecting islands with breeding seabirds, marine mammals, and turtle nesting beaches requires particular care and presents difficulties, especially where the breeding and nesting sites are easily accessible by boat. Where appropriate, visitors should be restricted by number, by season, by time of day, and to specific points at the periphery of the colony.

New lands formed by uplifting, or by emergence of submarine volcanoes, provide a unique opportunity for research into geological, geomorphological, ecological, and successional processes. They merit recognition for their scientific value and should be protected.

Supply of freshwater is often a critical factor limiting the carrying capacity of islands, whether for islanders or tourists. Great care should be taken to avoid depleting island water resources at the expense of native flora.

Garbage and waste disposal are severe problems for islands generally, and for tourist resorts and recreation areas in particular, especially because of the excessively packaged goods of developed societies.

On islands, as on continents, problems of nature conservation are largely (and inevitably) problems of land use, as noted by Wace (1982). Especially on small islands, land is a resource of prime importance.

It must be recognized that especially on small inhabited islands or remote populated islands people are a central part of the island ecosystem. Protection of areas in the traditional sense (i.e., by exclusion of people) may be impossible. Habitat protection is best achieved by managing islanders' activities rather than by managing defined areas. It may be possible to accomplish this through a multiple use approach whereby areas are zoned for different uses and such uses are controlled by season to regulate the capture of breeding organisms, and the use and management of resources is divided among villages toward their self-interest in the sustainability of harvest.

3.5 Design Guidelines and Considerations

The entire island should be protected if all of its area is important for conservation (e.g., a small island totally covered by nesting seabirds). If not, limited access and facilities may be appropriate in areas well separated and naturally screened from the conservation sites.

Managing visitor use and access require greater emphasis than details of design on protected islands. Nonetheless, it is important to buffer islands from upcurrent sources of pollution, particularly oil production and loading sites. Oil can be disastrous to species inhabiting the ocean-atmosphere and ocean-land interfaces.

One large island is generally a better choice than several smaller ones of the same total area, because the straits separating an island cluster may prove impassable barriers to many species.

If circumstances demand that one select a cluster of smaller islands rather than a large one, it is important that these should be as close together as possible to increase the chances of immigration.

A protected area on an island should be as circular as possible. This maximizes the area-to- perimeter ratio, which minimizes the dispersal distances within a reserve. Elongate protected areas and islands are likely to suffer "peninsula effects," for example, dispersal rates to outlying parts from central areas may be too slow to avoid local extinction.

Theoretically speaking, an island protected area should be as close to a source of colonizing species as possible (a mainland or large island) to maximize the immigration rate and the survival of a greater diversity of organisms. In practice, however, islands closer to human habitation are less likely to retain their pristine condition, and have greater poaching problems. The choice between a nearby island with a higher immigration rate of both organisms and people and a remote, more pristine island must be determined by the proximity of human habitation and the degree of threat posed by people.

Distribution of endemic species among protected areas on several different islands increases their survival prospects in the face of disease or accidental introduction of predators (rats, cats).

There are a few proponents of designing a protected area around a number of small islands rather than on one large island, citing several advantages:

–   Enabling protection of more species by enabling the survival of different sets of species on each island.

–   Being less susceptible to epidemic disease or similar disasters that could eliminate an entire species or set of species from a single island.

–   Enabling edge species, which thrive at the interfaces between habitats, to thrive on islands with a higher ratio of perimeter to area.

If one is designing protected areas for maximum "edge" for shore species, such as turtles, shorebirds, and pinnipeds, then a number of small islands would seem to best fulfil the objectives. Although, in general, a large island area can better protect samples of indigenous communities and biological diversity, since many edge species will survive outside the protected area and require no special management.

With these various ideas in mind, the following guidelines for protecting island habitats seem important.

Use natural limits for protected areas.

Islands are naturally divided from other lands by the sea. Since their biological peculiarities and their ecosystems' vulnerability are largely results of isolation, whole islands rather than parts of islands should be protected under different management regimes. The natural isolation of islands can thus be used to prevent or slow the dangers of alien plant or animal invasions. Where it is not possible to protect whole islands, natural boundaries, such as contour or climate boundaries or isthmuses that can be fenced off are the best boundaries for management regimes with different conservation objectives, just as they are for protected areas on continents. The best approach is usually to protect habitats rather than species, as elsewhere, and to exploit the natural isolation that islands present.

Enforce rigorous quarantine on all imports.

Imports of plants, animals and soils need to be quarantined. The more isolated a landmass, the more vulnerable are its native ecosystems to disruption by introductions of species. Smaller islands need to exercise quarantine control to exclude troublesome invading plants such as privet, guava and New Zealand flax, and animals such as mongooses, goats, and rats, which have become pests on many islands and destroyed native vegetation and fauna. Exotic diseases of domesticated animals have also been extremely destructive on islands, when they have infected wild stocks there, as ornithosis did in Hawaiian native land birds. The importation of any new species to islands should be regarded from the point of view of possible damage to native ecosystems and native species as well as to domesticated species. Effective quarantine control against species that may be aggressive on islands is difficult, but managers can exploit some of the natural advantages of island isolation by prohibiting the import of species that might be troublesome in comparable environments.

Managers of islands may have several kinds of difficulties in enforcing quarantine controls to protect their native ecosystems:

- Difficulties in policing any sort of import regulations in the relaxed and informal atmosphere of officialdom that is typical of small communities.

- Difficulties in predicting which species may be harmful in the ecological context of a particular island

- Difficulties in controlling imports, whether intentional or accidental, in the face of a large-scale tourist invasion that may, moreover, be an important source of revenue.

Despite such administrative difficulties, the protection of island habitats and their biota should always take cognizance of the biological factors resulting from isolation that may influence the persistence of native biota and the options for growth of crops.

Establish means of estimating the environmental impacts of tourist invasion of islands.

Tourism is seen as the fastest growing economic development in the Pacific islands, with enormous potential to change both the social lives and the environments of islanders (Turner and Ash, 1975) and is the mainstay of the economy of many island states, such as Seychelles (Shah, 1995; Emerton, 1997). Despite the large capital infrastructure needed, and the environmental change that mass tourism brings wherever it becomes established, tourist entrepreneurs are not required by governments to produce either social or environmental impact assessments of the results of importing large numbers of people into islands (or elsewhere) under tourist development schemes.

Changes brought by tourism may be lamented or admired retrospectively, but few attempts are made to anticipate them, so that the "carrying capacity" of fragile insular ecosystems can be defined in terms of tourist numbers, duration of stay, or modes of behavior. Tourists who travel in busloads from airport to motel to enjoyment sites have different environmental impacts than small parties of independent hikers. The management and development of national parks demand some assessment of the economic and environmental impacts of different types of visitors, as do islands, to determine their tourist carrying capacities and to protect island habitats (Figure II-36).

Integrate the management and conservation of terrestrial and marine resources on and around islands.

The sea has a direct influence upon the terrestrial ecology of small islands and on the economic systems of islanders that settle them. This interdependence should be recognized in the development and the conservation of islands for human benefit.

FIGURE II-36.

Photo by John Clark.

Visiting party to Perez Island in the Alacranes Reef complex take all wastes back to the Yucatan mainland.

Colonial breeding of marine-feeding species on islands, especially seabirds, leads to intensive eutrophication of many island ecosystems. Massive concentrations of phosphate in seabird guano deposits on some islands are valuable for mining of fertilizer. Following human contact and settlement, concentrations of seabirds decline rapidly, usually because of the import of predators, especially rats (Bourne, 1981), and direct harvest of eggs and birds. The network of ecological connections between land and sea is broken very early on many islands as a direct result of human contact. Fishing and the exploitation of other marine resources are important elements in the economy of many island peoples, either for subsistence or for export. This dependence on, and progressive depletion of, marine creatures at different stages of economic development is discussed for the Tristan da Cunha Islands by Wace and Holdgate (1976). The recent extension of ownership of fish stocks to 200 miles offshore has very greatly increased the marine resources owned and theoretically available to many island states, although they may find such resources difficult to exploit or conserve (Lawson, 1980; Kearney, 1980).

Because of the importance, both ecologically and economically, of marine-terrestrial interactions, it is particularly important in protecting island habitats to prevent the disruption on land or the overexploitation at sea of marine-feeding species. These links between land and sea are fragile, but are best preserved on uninhabited islands by rigorously preventing the introduction of predators, and on inhabited islands by encouraging the composting or other local recycling on land of waste products from fisheries. Soil fertility is better maintained in this way than through a total reliance on imported synthetic fertilizers.

Establish environmental monitoring and research in the natural sciences as a locally based activity.

Because of their proximity to continental coasts, many islands are used for monitoring the atmosphere for synoptic weather analyses and forecasting. Islands with substantial populations of breeding seabirds have also been used to monitor nearby seas for pollutants and are increasingly seen as valuable sites for estimating the size of nearby fish and other seafood stocks (e.g., fulmar counts in the North Atlantic and penguin counts in the sub-Antarctic islands and the Antarctic Peninsula).

Protection and management of island habitats themselves may also demand some baseline studies, so that changes in vegetation and animal life can be detected early enough to avert lasting damage. Establishing environmental monitoring on islands to protect their habitats is as essential as such monitoring is in national parks. Under the "user pays" principle, funding of such essential activities should be provided by those who enjoy the protected habitats-usually tourists-and by such mechanisms as airport taxes, hotel taxes, and taxes on exposed film at departure points.

Apply guidelines selectively.

Applications of the above suggestions for protecting island habitats must vary according to the degree that human activity has already affected them. Wace (1979) presents detailed suggestions for different islands worldwide.

All premises should be addressed, seeking especially to develop some resource- and energy-conserving agroecosystems, with small energy inputs and high nutrient reuse, incorporating the human population into the system. This may be progressively more difficult, according to whether the islands have one or more of the following features:

– Subsistence or local trading economies

– Large-scale developed plantations or single crop intensive agriculture

– Significant numbers of tourists or military bases or other high energy capital-intensive uses by outsiders

– Populations consuming imported products.

If island habitats and their native species are to be conserved, development must integrate wild nature with ongoing human activities, and preferably locally based activities. On inhabited or exploited islands, developments should integrate people with nature by favoring small-scale systems of local food and energy production, waste disposal, and recycling. Centralized energy generation systems that rely on a single energy source and long-distance transport (notably energy imports in the form of oil) are expensive to import, store, and distribute. Similarly, importing food and essential supplies to islands is expensive, and distributing supplies (like oil fuel) directly destroys terrestrial environments through highway and power line construction.

A central idea of this discussion is that protecting island habitats involves the social well being and the political realities of the human community living on or near the protected habitats. People are more obviously and immediately a part of nature on inhabited islands than they are on continents, but trying to arrange for their cooperation and understanding is not always easy, as shown by the Turtle Islands Case History (Part III, Case No. 17).

Given the limitations of islands for human population growth, decentralized, small-scale, dispersed systems of food and energy production and waste disposal are forms of development that are far less destructive of nature in the long term than large centralized systems (Schumacher, 1974). Most islands are small and poor in primary natural resources. If small is beautiful ecologically and socially, it may also be inevitable for the long-term stability of people-nature relations on islands. Agroecosystems in which energy ratios (energy out/energy at the farm gate) are greater than one (Simmons, 1980) should be favored in island development and conservation because they give a degree of independence to islanders and promote integration of human and natural ecosystems.

3.6 Management Guidelines

The following guidelines for managing protected island areas are based largely on the report prepared by Ogilvie and Wace (1982). For specific ecological guidelines on the development of islands and tropical coastlines, readers are referred to Clark (1974, 1977), Clark *et al.* (1980), McEachern and Towle (1974), and W.E. Odum (1976). For guidelines on the management of turtle nesting beaches, see IUCN (1979b). For discussion of the rational use of island ecosystems, see UNESCO (1973). For an example of the interaction between people and wildlife on the Tristan da Cunha Islands and a case study of an island management plan, see Wace and Holdgate (1976).

Construction of facilities. Where the whole island is a protected area, ensure that any management, research, and visitor facilities can be fully controlled. This rule applies to tourism in particular, since attempts may be made to exempt the land on which a resort is established from protected area status. The consequences of such action can be very damaging to the effectiveness of management.

Siting of facilities. On island protected areas, facilities should be placed well away from sensitive habitats (e.g., seabird and turtle nesting areas and seal and sea lion rookeries) and well landward of the high watermark. The latter precaution is especially relevant on coral cays, where natural erosion and seasonal rearrangement of beaches is common and where turtle nesting is widespread. Natural erosion and accretion cycles are a feature of many beaches (Figure II-37). The construction of seawalls and groins to modify this feature is generally discouraged, since it invariably transfers the problem to another location. The same is generally true of reclamation activities.

Design of facilities. Consideration should be given to aesthetics and the culture of the island or region. On Heron Island on Australia's Great Barrier Reef, for example, there is an agreement that no building will be constructed higher than the *Pisonia* forest canopy, that new buildings will be sufficiently landward of the high watermark to not interfere with turtle nesting, and that outside lights will be shaded to avoid disorienting hatchling turtles. Similar restrictions on the maximum height of buildings on the Seychelles Islands have enabled the islands to retain their natural beauty when observed from the sea, despite considerable construction.

FIGURE II-37.

A major purpose of the Gulf of Mannar Marine Park (India) is to protect the chain of islands that parallel the coast.

Groundwater supplies. Where groundwater is being tapped, particularly on small coral cays, water quantity and quality should be monitored carefully. In certain areas the freshwater lens may fluctuate widely. Care must be taken not to deplete the water supply to the point that dependent vegetation can no longer survive.

Sewage disposal. Sewage disposal should be carefully planned. Human wastes may affect the nutrient status of the soils on some islands, with the consequence that introduced species may be given a competitive edge over indigenous species adapted to the nutrient-poor conditions. Any sewage outfall to the sea should be carefully located in relation to tides and currents. Septic systems should be monitored for efficiency (particularly if saltwater is used and coral is laid in absorption trenches). Septic tanks and French drains should be placed at least 15 meters from wells to avoid contaminating freshwater supplies. However, this distance is soil-dependent and greater spacing (up to 45 m) should be required if land is available (see Clark, 1996).

Garbage disposal. Garbage disposal must be carefully planned. Biodegradable materials can generally be dumped at sea, as long as currents are moving seaward and garbage is dumped well off reefs and shoals. However, wherever possible, they should be composted and used to enhance agricultural production. Visitors should be discouraged from bringing glass containers and cans with tear-off tops. Managers should be encouraged to seek lightly packaged goods and to use biodegradable materials where possible. Dumping wastes on a large scale near islands may attract undesirable scavengers, such as sharks in tropical seas and skuas off Antarctic coasts. Expensive deepwater dumping in 200-litre (50-gallon) drums may be the only solution possible for clustered islands, even though it has its environmental dangers. On Rose Atoll, a wildlife refuge in American Samoa, visitors are allowed only by permission and in small numbers, and the complete removal of all wastes is demanded to prevent nutrient additions to the system. Such stringent controls are only possible in a few cases, and waste disposal poses serious problems when large numbers of people are involved.

Ecological interactions. Interactions between land and sea, which tend to be broken by the settlement of people ashore with their associated animals, can be re-established by recycling wastes on land instead of dumping them at sea. It is probably best to encourage such local eutrophication of island soils where the sea-land nutrient transfer regime has been disrupted, rather than to pollute the nearby seas.

Carrying capacity. Carrying capacity is the maximum number of people that should be allowed on the protected island at any one time. The physical carrying capacity (i.e., determined by island area, water resources, etc.) needs to be determined, but this is seldom done. Consideration should also be given to the "aesthetic carrying capacity" (i.e., the level of visitor use at which visitor enjoyment decreases because of too frequent contact with others).

Resource thresholds. Resource thresholds are one natural reference for delimiting the physical carrying capacity. When possible, the number of visitors should be restricted by the availability of island resources they utilize, for example, water. If water is not considered a limiting factor, its unchecked use will often be at the cost of other resources. Where relevant, care should be taken to determine the water dynamics and water requirements of biota on the island before tapping supplies for people. Low numbers of visitors can be accommodated by rainwater catchment, while greater numbers may require the tapping of groundwater supplies, desalination of seawater, or both. In times of particular stress these arrangements may need to be supplemented by supplying water shipped in from elsewhere by barge or boat.

Education and interpretation. The management programme should begin plans for education and interpretation very early in the life of any protected area (ideally, in advance of establishing it). An early activity, as for any protected area, should be to establish a corporate identity for the area managers (e.g., badge, logo, uniform, and a standard sign format). This establishes a corporate image in the eyes of the public and a healthy team spirit can develop among the management team. Particular user groups should be singled out for special attention and specific interpretative material and activities (e.g., brochures, talks, posters, self-guided trails, guided walks, audiovisual materials, information on regulations, and children's programmes). Where possible, emphasis should be placed on materials and activities for children, using the formal education system as much as possible. The mass media (television, radio, and newspapers) should be used to contact potential users and, probably more importantly, the public at large, since the public generally determines the actions of politicians. If the island is remote, there is more reason to provide the public with pictorial material.

Monitoring programmes. Monitoring programmes should be instigated as soon as possible after a protected area is established. They should specify tasks for both scientists and the area manager to carry out. Valuable information can be obtained from simple monitoring exercises, such as a series of photographs taken from the same location about every six months to show changes in beach structure and vegetation, counts of bird pairs or nests, and tagging of turtles and nest counts. A map of the whole island is a basic requirement.

The consensus planning approach. Where only a part of the island is protected, consensus planning can often resolve matters relevant to both the resident community or resort and the protected area managers. The approach requires frequent discussions and consultations between all parties and invariably benefits all. A plan formulated in this manner may have no legal status. Nonetheless, all agree to abide by resolutions, which are recorded and subject to review when required by any party. Such a plan was prepared for Heron Island.

Access to islands. Some forms of access (e.g., helipads, airstrips, marinas and jetties) may damage limited island habitats and interfere with the life functions of species. Air access to seabird nesting islands will often be inappropriate and will always need to be carefully planned and sited. Wind and waves erode shorelines in natural erosion and accretion cycles in monsoon and trade wind areas. Waves move diagonally up the beach carrying sand and fall back vertically down the slope. As a result sand is transported to the downwind side of the beach or island in one season and returns the next season when winds change direction. This can cause islands to change shape radically.

When jetties, breakwaters, groins, boat ramps, or other solid structures are built, they trap sand, which builds up on the upcurrent side and erodes from the other. For example, a pier built in 1948 on the south side of Ste. Anne Island in the Ste. Anne Island Marine National Park in the Seychelles blocks the seasonal movement of sand (Salm, 1978). During the northwest monsoon the sand moves east along the southern shore behind the fringing reef, and during the southeast monsoon it returns west. After construction of the pier, sand moving east piled up behind the pier and smothered the reef. Seasonal covering with sand prevents coral recolonization. At Heron Island a harbor was blasted through the reef crest and reef flat. Cyclones have breached the harbor walls so the harbor now acts as a giant drain through which sand is lost from the island.

Travel through island habitats. Special pathways may be required through sensitive island habitats (Figure II-38). These may take the form of boardwalks through fragile primary dune areas to avoid damage to sandbinding plants, or of hides and viewing towers beside seabird nesting areas.

FIGURE II-38.

Photo by R. Salm.

A trail through a dune forest should be placed in the valley behind the primary or secondary dune. (Umhlanga Nature Reserve, South Africa.) It should be stepped down slopes by pegging logs at intervals, and should be leveled and secured along inclines by planking that is partly buried and pegged in place.

Seasonally limited access to islands or island habitats. Human activities on islands should be timed to avoid disrupting species during critical phases, like turtles and seabirds during their nesting period and seals and sea lions during their mating and pupping season. Certain Great Barrier Reef seabird nesting islands are closed to visitors during the nesting season. Construction of earthworks that may disturb the nesting mutton bird or shearwater (*Puffinus pacificus*) are halted between October and May on Heron Island; the birds migrate after breeding.

Spatially restricted access. Where access to ground-nesting seabird sites is permitted, people should be restricted to the edge of the colonies and prohibited from moving among the birds, as on Bird Island in the Seychelles, islets off the windward coast of Oahu in Hawaii, and in the Daymaniyat Islands Nature Reserve in Oman. Forcing adult birds from their nests can affect breeding success: eggs and chicks are exposed to predators and intense heat; chicks flee their nests and are often attacked by adults as they attempt to return; food is regurgitated by both chicks and adults, affecting their nutritional intake.

Many ground-nesting seabirds, particularly the nearshore nesters, change their location in response to annual alteration in beach erosion and accretion and the growth of vegetation. The siting of permanent facilities must take this into account.

Alien species. On any island protected area, every effort should be made to prevent the introduction of alien species by people. This is difficult where only part of the island is a protected area. Introduced species should be eradicated. Goats, for example, have damaged numerous oceanic islands and coral cays (e.g., certain of the Galapagos Islands and Round Island off Mauritius) and compete with indigenous herbivores, like the giant tortoise on Aldabra World Heritage Site, Seychelles. To control the introduction of species in the New Zealand "island nature reserves" (the strictest category of New Zealand protected areas), visitors are required to do the following:

– Have permit issued by Director General of Lands and Survey

– Have themselves and their boats and equipment inspected for exotic plants, rats, and other materials

- Remove all wastes other than organic biodegradable material when leaving the island

- Not introduce flora and fauna to the island

Attitudes toward the introduction of exotic species must be influenced by whether the island is inhabited or not. It may be necessary to strictly prohibit some imports, even to inhabited islands, if parts of them have protected status. On Frazier Island, off Australia's Queensland coast, dogs imported by tourists have introduced diseases to the local dingo population. Prohibitions on keeping poultry on some oceanic islands and in the Antarctic is maintained because of the dangers of introducing avian diseases (especially Newcastle disease) to breeding seabirds. Quarantine should be applied to complete islands rather than to protected parts of islands alone.

Souvenir collection. The removal of natural objects from islands should be tightly controlled. Seashells and driftwood on beaches add greatly to the aesthetic quality of an island visit, and the first have considerable educational value. They can be quickly stripped from beaches if collection is allowed.

Litter. Visitors to uninhabited island protected areas should be required to remove all their rubbish with them. Pollution is a major problem on all islands since they have a limited capacity to absorb waste.

Tourism development. Tourism may greatly increase the number of people on islands and may alter the structure of island economies. Tourism is a fickle industry influenced by political circumstances, natural disasters, global economic conditions, and the attitudes of islanders. When Cuba became unavailable to U.S. tourists, the pattern of tourist movement changed throughout the Caribbean (Figure II-39).

FIGURE II-39.

Jamaica attempts to overcome the resistance of locals to tourism.

Culture. Culture itself is a resource that requires protection. Protected areas often attract tourism, which can engulf cultures, particularly those of small populations, and alter economies.

Permits. For entry to island protected areas permits often can reinforce the value of the resources being protected and earn needed revenue to subsidize management expenses. However, such revenues are unpredictable and should be factored into a business plan for the running of the site. In some cases they will form more of a bonus, rather than the primary source of management funds.

Communal land ownership. Where land is communally owned, efforts should be made to convince the local community of the value of a protected area (which may require economic arguments) and to seek their involvement. Ideally, they can be persuaded to establish and manage the area themselves within the framework of their own community, and benefit directly (jobs, revenue, and resource rights) from this responsibility.

Financial management. Examples of partnerships for island protected area management demonstrate that careful business planning can support conservation activities without the need for external revenues from government or international donors. Examples include Cousin Island Reserve in Seychelles which is run by the national NGO BirdLife Seychelles and the Chumbe Island Coral Sanctuary off Zanzibar which is run as a private venture (see cases X and Y in Part III).

These examples show that total delegation of management responsibility can be a successful formula to achieve self-sustainability of these areas. However, there are some essential prerequisites for this kind of delegated partnership to work:

- Security of tenure

- Tax breaks or similar incentives

- Total responsibility for hiring and firing, and revenue collection and disbursement

- Cooperation from government

See Section I-5 and also Hooten & Hatziolos (1995) for more on financing mechanisms for marine protected areas.

Appropriate technology. Protected area facilities should attempt to incorporate alternative energy sources (e.g., solar and wind energy) both as a long-term money-saving exercise and to educate others in the value of such devices. Import of expensive fossil fuels forces islanders to intensify their harvest of local resources, which in turn creates additional conservation problems. Use of alternative energy sources can reduce the dependence on imports.

Volunteers. Volunteers can be used to carry out certain unskilled jobs and interpretative programmes in protected areas.

Protected Areas
for Beaches

Numerous beaches around the world are protected by MPAs. A beach system may be protected as part of a larger, multi-habitat, MPA or as a stand alone MPA. A high percentage of existing small island MPAs include beaches. In the best examples, the MPA beach under protection includes the whole beach system or beachfront, including any adjacent dunes and berms and also submerged sandbars, and other nearshore features (Figure II-40). But wherever they occur in MPA status, beach systems require special management attention.

4.1 Values

Many important birds, reptiles, and other animals nest and breed on the berm and open beach, as well as feed and rest there. For example, sea turtles may come ashore during the spring and summer to lay their eggs in the "dry beach" (berm) above the high-water line (see Cases 2, 6 and 17 in Part III). Also, terns and other seabirds frequently lay their eggs on the upper beach or in the dunes.

FIGURE II-40.

Photo by John Clark.

A managed beach in Maryland (U.S.A.) provides a getaway experience for visitors.

Beaches also provide a unique habitat for burrowing species such as ghost crabs, coquina clams, razor clams, and others. There may also be a complex intertidal community of crustacean organisms that attract shore birds for feeding. The shallow waters of the adjacent surf zone provide habitat for shellfish of many kinds and a wide variety of forage species, which in turn attract fish and birds.

The plant communities of the beachfront thrive on the continuing stress of natural disturbances to which the grasses and other plant species living here are especially adapted. The vegetation plays a significant role in stabilizing the dune front, trapping and holding the sand blown up by the wind, and thereby allowing the dunes to build and stabilize (Figure II-41).

Photo by John Clark.

FIGURE II-41.

It may be necessary to control access to dunes to protect the beach ecosystem.

Beaches are used by more people than any other habitat in the coastal zone. Beaches are the focal point for international coastal recreation and tourism. People are willing to travel thousands of miles and spend thousands of dollars to lie, sit, or walk on the beach.

4.2 Beach Dynamics

Beaches are not stable. They are, instead, dynamic landforms constantly subject to erosion and/or accretion. Differences in beach form and position reflect the local balance or imbalance between sand deposition (gain) and erosion (loss). On a worldwide basis, erosion (natural and man-induced) dominates over deposition, which is partly due to the global rise in sea level and partly due to direct human activities. Consequently, there is serious loss of beach and beachfront in many parts of the world (Figure II-42).

The **beach** may be defined as an unvegetated part of the shoreline formed of loose material, usually sand, that extends from the upper berm to the low-water mark. The complete beachfront complex is composed of the following five parts:

1. **Bar**. An offshore sand ridge that is submerged permanently or at higher tides.

2. **Trough**. A natural channel running between an offshore bar and the beach, or between offshore bars.

3. **Foreshore**. The part of the shore lying between the crest of the most seaward berm and the ordinary low-water mark; it is ordinarily traversed by the uprush and backrush of the waves as the tides rise and fall.

4. **Backshore**. The part of the beach that is usually dry and that lies between the foreshore and the dunes, and that is acted upon by waves only during storms and exceptionally high water.

5. **Dunes**. More or less continuous mounds of loose, windblown material, usually sand, behind the berm (often vegetated). The first tier dune is termed the "foredune," or the "frontal" or "primary" dune; those behind the frontal dune are called "secondary," "rear," or "back" dunes. An active dune is one that is mobile, or in the process of visibly gaining or losing sand; such a dune is usually vegetated mostly with grasses rather than woody vegetation.

FIGURE II-42.

Photo by Erkki Siirila.

Sand and coral blocks have been mined from the offshore bars of the Rodney Bay beach in St. Lucia. The only solution is artificial sand replenishment because storm waves have eroded this tourist beach. Pigeon Island National Historic Park is visible in the background.

Two other terms that need definition are:

1. **Berm**. A ridge or ridges on the backshore of the beach, formed by the deposit of material by wave action, that marks the upper limit of ordinary high tides and wave wash; berms often have sharply sloping leading edges.

2. **Beach ridge**. A more or less continuous mound of beach material behind the berm that has been heaped up by wave action during extreme high-water levels; if largely wind built, the ridge is usually termed a "dune," and often is vegetated.

Under storm attack the dynamic response of a beach is to sacrifice some of the beach, and often the foredune, to provide material to an offshore bar. This bar helps to protect the shoreline from further erosion. After a storm or storm season, natural defenses may again be re-formed by normal wave and wind action. Following a storm there is a return to more normal conditions, which are dominated by low, long swells. These waves transport sand from the offshore bar, built during the storm, and place the material on the beach. Winds then transport the sand onto the dunes where it is trapped by the vegetation. The rebuilding process takes much longer than the short time span during which the erosion took place.

It is important to realize that the erosional and depositional cycles of beaches may respond to forces acting far from the beach itself. Of special importance are sources such as offshore shoals and currents, inland dune systems, and river outflows that bring sand to the sea.

Variation in foreshore slope from one region to another appears to be related to mean nearshore wave heights—the gentler slopes occur on coasts with higher waves. The inverse relation between slope and wave height is partly caused by the relative frequency of the steep or high eroding waves which produce gentle foreshore slopes and the low accretionary post-storm waves which produce steeper beaches (COE, 1984). In summary:

– Slope of the foreshore on open sand beaches depends principally on size of the sand grains and (to a lesser extent) on nearshore wave height.

– Slope of the foreshore tends to increase with increasing median grain size.

– Slope of the foreshore tends to decrease with increasing wave height.

FIGURE II-43.

Photo by N.W. Pammenter.

Outlet of a typical bar-built estuary (Umhlanga Nature Reserve, South Africa) which alternately opens and closes.

Natural channels through the beach may require special attention. Such channels may be *permanent*, allowing daily tidal flow, or *temporary*, allowing drainage of land runoff water during flooding periods (Figure II-43). Such channels often move laterally along the beach as a natural response to the forces of the sea or the runoff flow. Attempts are often made to fix the position and depth of such inlets to facilitate boat traffic.

4.3 Beach Protection

The natural forces at work are immense, making stabilization of beaches a difficult and often elusive endeavor. It is usually much better to not intervene with engineering works and to let nature prevail. Then, management may be needed to maintain the beach profile by protecting the natural processes that supply the beach with sand as well as the sand-storage capacity of the beach elements themselves.

It must be remembered that the key to the natural protection provided by the beachfront is the sand, which is held in storage and yielded to storm waves, thereby dissipating the force of their attack. Consequently, taking sand from any part of the beach—dry beach, wet beach, bar or the nearshore submerged zone—can lead to erosion and recession of the beachfront. Therefore, beach conservation should start with the premise that any removal of sand is adverse, whether for construction fill, concrete aggregate, or any other purpose, and should be prohibited or tightly controlled.

In addition to excavation of beach sand for construction, the worst impacts may come from destruction of protective coral reef systems (Figure II-44) or the building of seawalls or groins which deplete or eliminate the beach. If nothing is built on or next to the beach, it will remain as long as the process of natural replenishment continues. It may shift with the seasons, yield sand temporarily to storm erosion, slowly recede landward with rising sea levels, or accrete seaward with natural shifts in the flow of ocean currents, which bring more sand. Mobile and responsive, the beach can be expected to remain in place over the years under careful management.

Understanding the sand budget (erosion and deposition cycles; sources and quantities of new sand and causes and volume of sand loss) of beaches under conservation management is essential. Mining of sand from river beds, dams and flood control measures may rob the beach of critical supplies of river-borne material. This will decrease the volume of deposited material and lead to erosion of the beach.

FIGURE II-44.

Photo by John Clark.

Destructive coral mining in Bali; now prohibited except for religious purposes (e.g., temple reconstruction).

In summary, to preserve the natural beach profile, roads, buildings, utilities, and other permanent structures should be prohibited at the beach or in the frontal dune area. The mining of dunes for sand should also be completely banned and adjacent coral reefs protected from damage.

4.4 Sand Dunes

Behind the beach there may be one or more parallel rows of natural dunes, each built in response to forces of waves that pushes the sand high up the beach and to the wind that finally carries the sand grains up onto the dunefield. These dunes are an integral part of the beach system and must be managed as such.

If a dune is attacked by large storm waves, eroded material is carried onto the beach and then to an offshore deposit—often forming a sand bar parallel to the beach which absorbs or dissipates, through friction, an increasingly large amount of destructive wave energy that would otherwise focus on the beach. It is this capacity of the berm-and-dune system to store sand and yield it to the adjacent submerged bottom that gives this system its outstanding ability to protect the shorelands.

Dune vegetation promotes large-scale trapping of sand, whereby the sand reserves of the dunes expand. The frontal dune is elastic, alternately receiving and yielding sand. But the back dunes tend to become stabilized into more permanent features of the landscape. If any of the dunes are removed or diminished, the reserve sand in storage may be reduced to a level no longer capable of replacing sand losses from severe storms. The beach system then becomes unstable and slumps.

The main protection needed for dunes is to prohibit any removal of sand—no taking of sand should ever be permitted (Figure II-45). In addition the vegetation that binds the dune together needs protection. Vegetation that grows on shifting dunes is adapted to withstanding the rigors of wind, sand and salt, but not human feet, vehicles, or herds of grazing animals. Once a frontal dune is worn down by vehicles or foot traffic or by consequent loss of vegetation, it may be eroded by wind or wave action and no longer serve its unique protective role.

FIGURE II-45.

Photo by Erkki Siirila.

Sand mining continues in spite of being legally prohibited on the Vigie beach in St. Lucia.

FIGURE II-46.

Photo by Rod Salm.

Inexpensive techniques, such as flexible fencing, are a good approach to dune maintenance.

Two inexpensive and effective methods to protect beachfronts are simple fences (Figure II-46) and revegetation programmes. Fences have two initial advantages over vegetative planting that often warrant their use before or with planting: (a) sand fences can be installed during any season and (b) the fence is immediately effective as a sand trap once it is installed. There is no waiting for trapping capacity to develop in comparison with the vegetative method. But, It is not necessarily "either one or the other" because it is best to use both plantings and fences (Box II-4).

In revegetation, it should be noted that only a few plants thrive on the dunes and these are adapted to conditions that include abrasive and accumulating sand, exposure to full sunlight, high surface temperatures, occasional inundation by saltwater, and drought. They are long-lived, rhizomatous or stoloniferous perennials with extensive root systems, stems capable of rapid upward growth through accumulating sand, and tolerance of salt spray.

Box II-4. Stabilization of Sand Dunes.

Relatively inexpensive and available slat-and-wire fencing is used successfully in artificial, nonvegetative dune construction. Field tests of dune building with sand fences under a variety of conditions have been conducted in the U.S.A. The following guidelines are based on these tests (COE, 1984):

1. Fencing with a porosity (ratio of area of open space to total projected area) of about 50 percent should be used. Open and closed areas should be smaller than 5 centimeters in width.

2. Straight fence alignment is recommended. Zigzag alignment does not increase the trapping effectiveness enough to be economical. Lateral spurs may be useful for short fence runs of less than 150 meters (500 feet) where sand may be lost at the ends.

3. Efforts have been most successful when the selected fence line coincided with the natural vegetation or foredune line prevalent in the area. This distance is usually greater than 60 meters shoreward of the berm crest.

4. The fence should parallel the shoreline. It need not be perpendicular to the prevailing wind direction; it will function if placed at an angle to sand-transporting winds.

5. A 1.2 m fence with 50-percent porosity will usually fill to capacity within 1 year. The dune will be about as high as the fence. The dune slopes will range from about 1:4 to 1:7, depending on the grain size and wind velocity.

6. Dunes are usually built by installing a single fence and following it with additional single-fence lifts as each fence fills. Succeeding lifts should be parallel to and about 4 times the fence height of the existing fence.

7. The trapping capacity of the 1.2-meter-high fence averages 5 to 8 cubic meters per linear meter (2-3 cubic yds/linear ft.).

8. Fence-built dunes must be stabilized by planting vegetation or when the fence deteriorates it will release the sand. The rehabilitation of dunes with fencing should be only the first step in a two-step operation.

The hardiest species are native beach grasses and creepers, like morning glory (*Ipomoea*). In dune planting, plants are often gathered from the wild, trimmed, sorted, bagged, transported and replanted, as any plant might be. They are planted according to a design strategy for the dune rehabilitation project (COE, 1984).

A shore protection plan should include regulations to preserve the frontal dune intact by controlling foot and vehicular traffic (Figure II-47). Access to the beach should be limited to elevated steps and boardwalks over the dunes that allow unobstructed movement of sand beneath them and foot traffic should be limited to these walkways. Exclusion fences should be erected to keep grazing animals off dunes where this is a problem. Vehicular traffic anywhere on the frontal dune system should be prohibited. Dune buggies, trail bikes, and other offroad vehicles should be restricted to the "hard beach" below the berm and to places where traffic will not interfere with other beach uses.

4.5 Barrier Islands

The seacoast of some countries is edged, in part, by elongated sandy islands or peninsulas. These "barrier islands" and "barrier spits" are mobile, not fixed, geological features. They grow or shrink in response to storms and to fluctuations in sea level, currents, and sediment supply (Figure II-48). They also may move inland, seaward, or laterally, according to changing conditions. The changes are the net result of erosion and deposition. The multiple

FIGURE II-47.

Beach protection often requires control of visitors.

Photo by John Clark.

rows of parallel ridges (inactive dunes) that form the stable structure of barrier islands are often visible in the patterns of vegetation. While classified as islands they are functionally the edge of the continental coastline and the beach frontier where great battles between natural forces often take place. (Clark, 1991)

FIGURE II-48.

Photo by John Clark.

The barrier beach at Rio Lagartos in Yucatan, Mexico, was severed by Hurricane Gilbert in 1988, leaving some houses stranded.

The natural properties of barrier islands and their beaches provide a strikingly unique combination of values. A typical barrier island—with its ocean beach, sometimes jungle-like interior, and broad expanse of marsh—has scenic qualities unequalled in the coastal zone. Barrier islands enclose and protect lagoon and estuary resources and provide habitat and food for hundreds of species of coastal birds, fish, shellfish, reptiles and mammals.

4.6 Design and Management Guidelines Summary

The major design and management considerations for beach MPAs may involve the following: 1) species protection, 2) habitat protection, 3) erosion protection, 4) visitor control and safety, 5) visitor facilities and interpretation (Figure II-49), and 6) MPA boundaries. A summary of guidelines for these considerations is presented below.

Boundaries: If the beach alone is the MPA, the boundaries should extend far enough landward to include, and protect, the dunefield that lies behind the beach. The outer boundary should be far enough seaward to include any offshore bars or sand deposits that interact with the beach.

Facilities: Parking lots, snack bars, water sport stands, and other facilities should not preempt the dunefield or the beach berm.

Access: Boardwalks should be built for passage to the beach so that visitors do not trample the dunes. Vehicles should be prohibited except for hard beaches where vehicular use is long standing and can be limited.

Visitor control: Rules of behavior should be clearly displayed on signs. Decency should be upheld and courtesy required. Rangers should immediately eject miscreants.

FIGURE II-49.

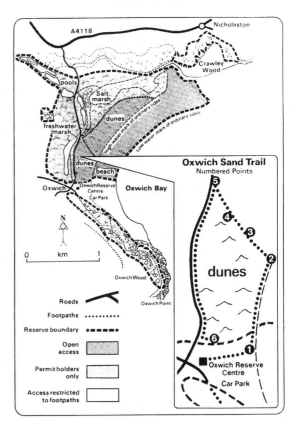

Nature trails at Oxwich National Nature Reserve, England.
Source: Nature Conservancy Council.

Safety: Visitor safety rules should be posted clearly and management should have well organized programmes to prevent drowning and to treat victims of jellyfish stings, shark bites, etc.

Animal control: Domestic animals should normally be prohibited and wild and feral animals controlled to protect the habitat and seasonal breeding activities of turtles, birds, etc.

Vegetation: Dune and berm vegetation should be protected and replaced with native plants if damaged .

Dune maintenance: Dunefields should be protected with sand holding plants and fences or other devices if dune erosion is a problem.

Species protection: The beach (or key parts of it) should be closed to unsupervised use during nesting of turtles and birds; signs should be placed to explain the purpose of the closure; lighting controls should be exercised and sometimes rescue of eggs undertaken. (Box II-5 and Figure II-50).

Box II-5. Mitigation Measures for Lighting Near Turtle Beaches

Measure 1: Low pressure sodium vapor lights

Current research on the effects of lighting on nesting and hatchling sea turtles demonstrates that certain lights deter emergence of adult turtles attempting to nest, and disorientation of hatchlings attempting to reach the sea. Low pressure sodium vapor lights have been shown to have minimal effects on turtles. These are readily available in the market place, being commonly used for street and security lighting.

Low pressure sodium vapor lamps should be a mandatory requirement for all external municipal and hotel lighting within three hundred meters of or directly visible from turtle beaches, whichever is further. For example, use 18-watt low pressure sodium vapor lamps activated at nightfall and turned off at a fixed time corresponding to shut down of activities in the associated facility (applicable especially to car parks).

Measure 2: Placement and orientation of light fittings

Care in placement and orientation of light fittings will reduce both the effects of direct and scattered lighting on turtles. This can be achieved by orienting lights inland away from the beach (e.g., street lights can be placed on the seaward side of roads so they cast their light inland), by directing lights downwards rather than horizontally, and by exercising care to avoid illumination of highly reflective surfaces such as white painted walls.

All public service, security, and private lighting within 300 meters of or directly visible from turtle nesting sites, whichever is further, should direct light away from beaches and downward. The lights should not be visible from the beach, and care should taken to avoid illumination of light-colored or reflective surfaces visible from beaches.

Measure 3: Lights screened on seaward side

A simple means to reduce the influence of lights on turtle beaches is to screen them on the seaward side. This can be achieved either by enclosing the facility in a perimeter wall or line of vegetation, or by blacking out the lights on the seaward side; e.g., by installing shields inside or partially surrounding light fittings).

All external lights within 300 meters of or directly visible from a turtle nesting site should be screened by shields or vegetation so that they are not visible from the beach. The option of surrounding structures with walls, trees or hedges should be evaluated on a case-by-case basis.

Measure 4: Height restriction

Positioning lights near the ground will, in many cases, prove perfectly adequate to achieve the purpose of illuminating footpaths and car parks while reducing the effects of direct and scattered light on turtles.

Light installations should be restricted to a maximum height of one meter for all car parks, and less than 50 centimeters for all footpaths near turtle beaches.

Measure 5: Time restriction

It is essential that all lights in view of important turtle beaches remain turned off after a fixed time during the nesting season.

> Within the constraints of hotel and personal security, and in the absence of compelling arguments to the contrary, lights of all new developments, camping sites, and existing facilities (where possible) adjacent to important turtle nesting beaches, particularly those in any existing or proposed nature conservation areas, should be turned off no later than 2030 during the nesting season.

Measure 6: Motion/sensor activated

> To avoid unnecessary use of lighting that is required intermittently, such as car park, footpath and washroom facilities, lights can be activated and timed by a sensor or push button. This restricts light use to the brief periods needed and reduces exposure to turtles.

> *All essential lighting for public car park, footpath and washroom facilities within 300 meters or direct line of sight of turtle beaches should meet above criteria relevant to the associated facility, and should be either sodium vapor, yellow-coated 15 watt standard vacuum-type incandescent lamps, or the "anti-insect" type. They should be sensor or push button activated and shut off automatically following a fixed fifteen minute interval (applicable especially to footpaths and washroom facilities).*

Source: Rodney V. Salm, The Nature Conservancy, Hawaii, USA.

Trash: Trash control should be included in the interpretation programme, sufficient trash containers provided, and rangers should remind visitors not to discard trash on the beach.

Collecting: Usually, no collecting of shells, vegetation, or live specimens should be permitted.

Fishing: Should be permitted unless it conflicts with the objectives of the beach MPA.

FIGURE II-50.

Protected loggerhead turtle hatchery at Terengganu, Malaysia, where a percentage of eggs are obtained from harvesters in a futile attempt to sustain the species.

Fires: Open fires are usually prohibited. The MPA management should provide barbecue and fire pits as needed.

Permits: Permits to visit sensitive or privately held adjacent areas normally off limits should be issued wherever justified according to specific rules.

Pollution: Check for all external sources of pollution which could degrade the beach ecosystem and take steps to reduce or eliminate the problem by negotiation with pollution authorities or other relevant agencies.

Sand removal: No extraction of sand should be allowed from any part of the beach from nearshore to foreshore to the dunefield.

FIGURE II-51.

Severe erosion of beaches results from coral mining at Mafia Island, Tanzania.

Coral reef protection: MPA management should make diligent efforts to protect coral and coralline algae reefs which, as natural breakwaters, shelter beaches from storm waves (Figure II-51).

Note that further important guidance for beach system management is included in Section II-3, "Protected Areas for Small Islands".

PART III

Case Histories of
Marine Protected Areas

Review of Highlights of the Case Histories

Highlights of the Case Histories are listed below by subject to assist the reader in rapidly finding cases of particular interest. The cases are identified by their location and their case numbers (1-25). More information is available from the authors via their e-mail numbers listed at the end of each case.

Carrying capacity: Diving visitor quotas recommended for Bonaire (No. 5).

Community engagement: Bad example, Roatan (No. 22); good examples, Tanga (Nos. 24 and 25), St. Lucia (No. 11), Bunaken (No. 1), Negombo (No. 3).

Coastal Zone Management approach: Negombo (No. 3), Florida Keys (No. 8), Laguna de Tacarigua (No. 9), Saudi Arabia & Oman (No. 15), Ras Mohammed (No. 14).

Self-financing efforts: Bonaire & Saba (No. 23); Chumbe I. (No. 7); Cousin I. (No. 6), Montego Bay (No. 12).

Fisheries: Examples of MPAs with particular fishery concerns are Bunaken (No. 1), Tanga (No. 24), Philippines (No. 4), Palau (No. 18), St. Lucia (No. 11).

International aspects: Sabah (No. 17), Indian Ocean (No. 20).

Local management: Examples of community controlled management experiences are Tanga (No. 24), Palau (No. 13), Philippines (No. 4).

NGO management: St. Lucia (No. 11), Cousin I. (No. 6), Montego Bay (No. 12).

Pollution: Montego Bay (No. 12).

Private management: Chumbe I. (7).

Species protection: Examples of conservation of particular bird (ibis) and reptile (turtle) species are Trinidad (21), Cousin I. (No. 6), Sabah (No. 17), Indian Ocean (No. 20), Celestun (No. 16).

Tourism & visitor control: Boca Grande (No. 2), Celestun (No. 16), Ras Mohammed (No. 14), Bonaire (No. 5).

Zoning: Great Barrier Reef (No. 10), Bunaken (No. 19), St. Lucia (No. 11).

1. Bunaken National Park: Participatory Management in Zoning

L ocated just fifteen kilometers off the coast of Manado, the provincial capital of North Sulawesi, Bunaken NP is an 89,000 ha reserve covering 6 islands and mainland coastline (Figure III-1). It has diverse coastal and marine habitats, including extensive coral reefs and mangroves, which are home to a number of protected species including dugong, marine turtles, giant clams, and the recently discovered new coelacanth species. Of stunning beauty and of vital importance to the local and regional economy, the park also offers some of the best scuba diving in SE Asia, and provides livelihood to a population of about 20,000 people living in communities in and around the NP. A recent study puts the combined value of fishing and tourism to the region at more than $8m/yr. At the same time, a staff of only 39 people, consisting of 16 administrative staff and 23 field-based rangers, manages the park. The autonomous management unit was only established in 1997, coinciding with Indonesia's economic crisis and corresponding government budget cuts. While the park staff has some basic facilities such as speedboats and diving equipment, the current annual budget is less than US$80,000, so operating, maintenance and infrastructure budgets are extremely limited. In order to effectively manage the conservation of

FIGURE III-1.

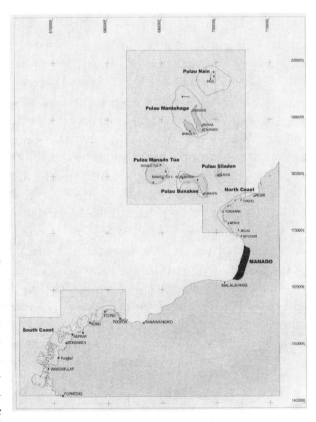

The North Sulawesi coast, location of the Bunaken National Park.

Bunaken, the National Park office has been facilitating a participatory management approach, developing strategic partnerships with government agencies, the private sector and local communities in order to access necessary technical and financial support.

Bunaken NP is an example of an MPA with established intensive use, and multiple stakeholders with potentially competing interests, in a country with high levels of corruption, limited state budgets, and where law enforcement is known to be patchy. In such an environment, effective conservation management requires the adoption of a multi-stakeholder participatory management process, with adequate balances between rights and responsibilities of stakeholders. Such a process creates a strong lobby against outside unilateral interests, and increases compliance to park regulations thus reducing the shared costs that are shared management costs. It is also necessary to balance sustainable economic development opportunities with broader conservation objectives. Finally, management must be adaptive as resource use pressures change over time, as demonstrated by recent changes in Bunaken NP.

The path to participatory management has been long. The main section of the park was declared a provincial park in 1980, followed by the southern coastal section in 1984. In 1991, both areas were combined and designated as the Bunaken NP. Detailed mapping and surveys of the park began in 1991 along with identification and engagement of user groups and other stakeholders. Four major stakeholder groups with competing interests in the park were identified, and early planning for the park was a process of sparring between three of these, the provincial government, the tourism industry represented by local dive operators, and the central government represented by the Ministry of Forestry (Box 1). The local communities, an important stakeholder, were left out. The provincial government's primary interest was tourism development and resultant revenue generation, supported by a long-held misconception that the tourism value of the park greatly outweighed uses such as fisheries. Further, there was a belief that the park was suitable for mass beach tourism similar to that of Bali, even though the beaches in the park are limited in size and unsuitable for this. The local dive operators were based outside the park on the mainland and had long lobbied for a ban on tourism facilities inside the park. Their primary motive was that whoever obtained permission to develop facilities in the park would obtain an unfair competitive advantage. The Directorate-General of Forest Protection and Nature Conservation (PHPA) of the Ministry of Forestry as the agency responsible for designation and management of conservation areas in Indonesia perceived the major goal of the park as conservation. Three stakeholders perceived the activities (mainly farming and fishing) of the fourth major stakeholder group, namely local communities, as incompatible with their perceived goals of the park. Therefore communities living in and around the park were largely unwanted pawns until the planning process begun in 1991 by a USAID project (the Natural Resources Management Project or NRMP) actively encouraged their participation.

Box III-1. The Relationship between National and Local Government

Local government still recognizes Bunaken as the major tourism attraction of North Sulawesi, and has been keen to see the tourism industry develop. Before management planning for the park began in 1991, there were plans to relocate communities living on the islands out of the park to enable tourism infrastructure development. However, following the designation of the areas as a National Park, management authority shifted to the Ministry of Forestry, leading to the perception that the province no longer controlled its major tourism asset. This has in the past led to friction, complicated by delay in the establishment of the PHPA management unit for the park. During the management planning process, the local PHPA conservation office was responsible for management of the park. The head of this office had a relatively junior rank in the government bureaucracy, making it difficult for him to liaise with more senior local counterparts. During the planning process, several large-scale tourism developers approached local government with plans to develop major facilities on the islands within the park, and the then Governor of North Sulawesi did in fact give a permit for an exclusive resort development within the park. There was no prior consultation with the PHPA office. The park management unit, with a more senior official in charge, was not established until 1997, after the planning process had finished. With the major political changes that have been occurring in Indonesia since 1998, including the recent passing of legislation devolving more authority to provincial and district governments, it is likely that local government will claim a larger role in management of the park. The current head of the park (still representing the Ministry of Forestry) is realistic about the limits of his power and is actively working towards greater participation among local government and other stakeholders in park management.

When management planning began in collaboration with the local PHPA conservation office, it was quickly recognized that because local communities had long-established use practices, their involvement in planning and management of the park was imperative. It was considered unfair that they be relocated out of the park as proposed by both local and national government, when, after more than 100 years of use, the coral reefs of the park were found to still be in good condition. Indeed there were strong arguments that, contrary to popular myth, much of the damage that had occurred since the "discovery" of the reefs in the mid-1970's, was in fact caused by tourism. Accepting that local communities had a legitimate right of access to the park's resources, a participatory planning and management approach was adopted. Thus local communities and the dive operators were engaged as part of the management solution rather than a management problem.

The participatory planning process involved identification of resource use patterns by local communities and dive operators (Box 2). This was greatly assisted by the detailed mapping of the park in the early 1990's. There was then a process of cross-consultation with the user groups to identify potential use conflicts. A *de facto* equilibrium had already been developed in the park between dive areas and fishing areas, so that there were relatively few conflicts between the two groups. However some conflicting use claims were made by different communities, and inter-community meetings were held to resolve these. During the participatory process, management issues such as defining acceptable and unacceptable practices were discussed and consensus achieved. This initial process provided the basis for the development of the participatory zoning plan.

Box III-2. The History of Dive Operator Participation in Park Management

When the management planning process began in 1991, there were 4 established local dive operators operating in the park. Attempts to involve the dive operators in the planning process met with mixed success. Individually operators demonstrated a commitment to conserve the park's resources, but rivalries between them thwarted attempts at developing an association to represent the industry and develop standardized good environmental practices. A mooring buoy programme begun in 1993 ultimately failed because of these rivalries. However, since 1996 a number of new 4-star hotels with professional dive operations have opened. These hotels and diving companies operating in and around Bunaken rely on a healthy national park to ensure their financial success, and are now working together to support conservation management of the park. Bunaken National Park management and the dive operators are developing a partnership to support a wide range of conservation activities. Starting slowly but quickly gaining strength, this partnership is based on the design and implementation of mutually beneficial activities such as development and dissemination of park information materials as well as a new mooring buoys programme. A formal user-fee system is being designed. In the meantime, the dive operators have started to collect monthly membership fees, which are then donated to the national park to cover specific operating costs necessary for regular patrolling by National Park ranger and marine police, and outreach.

The plan identified four types of marine zones: 1) core (or sanctuary) zones, 2) dive zones, 3) traditional use zones for limited use by local communities, and 4) use zones for small and medium scale industrial fishing enterprises. The latter covers open sea areas within the park at 200 meters distant from the reef crest. The majority of the reef flat areas were designated as traditional use zones for local communities only. Designation of core zones was done in conjunction with users, and there was strong pressure from communities to place these relatively close to villages, in contradiction of accepted practice. The reasoning behind this was that local communities could more effectively monitor and prevent violations of zone regulations.

Partnerships between park management and local communities developed during the planning process are based on sharing the rights and responsibilities for sustainable management of the park's resources through Community Conservation Agreements (CCAs). CCAs are used in buffer zone development activities to ensure an adequate link between community development and a corresponding commitment to park conservation. CCAs are taken a step further with the participatory zoning system described above. Traditional use zones covering reef flats are strengthened by community-based zoning plans. This ensures local responsibility in the conservation management of these important areas. In both cases, National Park management provides local communities with management and exclusive use rights (a major incentive) in exchange for a commitment to support conservation of the park's resources. The existence of the National Park provides the legal basis for the management authority to provide these management rights, which under existing law in Indonesia is not possible outside protected areas.

The resultant zoning plan for the park appears spatially more complex than the original zoning plan proposed in 1983 (see Case History 19). It has more, smaller zones, but by developing the zoning in conjunction with users, outreach and enforcement costs are much reduced, as users have already "bought into" the plan (Box 3). However, the need for active and adaptive management remains, as demonstrated by several recent developments. First, the rapid spread of seaweed farming in recent years within the park has led to dramatic changes in resource use patterns by local communities and local economic development. Positive effects have been the reduction of the fishing pressure on the reefs in the park, as fishermen have switched to farming seaweed due to a rise in international seaweed prices. However, negative effects include the excessive pressure on mangroves in and around the park, due to a growing demand for housing, seaweed drying floors, seaweed planting stakes and fuelwood, and the spread of farms from lagoons to more fragile habitats such as reef flats with live coral cover. In light of Indonesia's current economic crisis, it is essential for the park to accommodate economic development aspirations of local communities in order to ensure their support for broader conservation objectives. Therefore park staff are trying to reduce negative impacts while supporting positive ones. Park staff are working with growers and buyers to both discourage the use of mangrove wood in seaweed cultivation while providing alternative resources to offset further mangrove habitat damage.

A second development is the appearance of major new tourism operators, who were not involved in the initial planning process and must be incorporated into the management process. A third one is the economic crisis within Indonesia which has drastically reduced government conservation spending, and has lead to greater numbers of infractions by outsiders using destructive fishing practices. Fourth, the rapid political developments within the country and the move to decentralization may affect the legal status of the park. These factors mean that the current park management team has to remain active in public awareness, and play a role of facilitator in fine-tuning the zoning pattern to reflect potential changes in use patterns. The success or failure of the park will be determined by the level of compliance with the zoning, which itself will be the indicator of the success of the participatory planning and management system used for the park.

Box III-3: A Change of Approach to Zoning

The first zoning concept developed in the early 1980s had been designed to support tourism and reef biota. Based primarily on ecological criteria and tourism value, relatively large areas of the park were designated for tourism and conservation (See Case History 19 in Part III). However it did not reflect the realities of use patterns within the park, and assumed that use by local communities was incompatible with either conservation or tourism goals. This largely reflected "either/or" conservation thinking at the time, i.e. **either** an area is used, **or** it is conserved. While this may be relevant to forest systems, it is less applicable to coral reefs, where it has been consistently shown that reefs must be in good condition (i.e., conserved) if they are to support both sustainable fisheries and/or tourism. This initial zoning system provided a model of what should be conserved, but it did not address the more fundamental issue of the practicalities of managing conservation and capturing these conservation benefits. Quite simply, Bunaken NP does not have the human, technical or financial resources necessary to adequately manage a zoning system that does not accommodate non-destructive existing-use patterns. Therefore, the park has adapted a more realistic zoning strategy which involves greater stakeholder participation in design, implementation and monitoring of the zoning plan, as well as much smaller and thus more easily managed conservation zones.

Source: Graham Usher, Consultant on Marine Resource Management, 53 Melford Way, Felixstowe, Suffolk, U.K. and Reed Merrill, Protected Areas Management Advisor, USAID, Jakarta, Indonesia.

E-Mail Contact: reedm@cbn.net.id

2. Boca Grande Key: Management of a Wilderness Island

Boca Grande Key is an isolated 90-ha island in the Key West National Wildlife Refuge in Florida, USA. It is a federally designated wilderness area in the Florida Keys, situated some 14 miles west of Key West, a heavily populated international tourist mecca. Boca Grande Key harbors rare and endangered wildlife, including 3 nesting sea turtle species (Wilmers, 1994), and contains an important sand dunes tract (Kruer, 1992). Visitation to Boca Grande Key increased concurrently with burgeoning population growth in the Florida Keys, and the advent of large commercial tours from Key West.

Boca Grande Key's 1.2-km beach is narrow and bordered by extensive shallow seagrass flats. Public use is concentrated along 215m of the beach where a deep-water channel facilitates boater access to the beach and adjacent low-lying dune. In northern part of the beach, native vegetation has been damaged or destroyed by illegal campers and /or careless visitors, resulting in increased erosion and/or invasion of exotic grasses. This beach section has essentially no accretion (T.Kana, pers, comm.). Plant roots are exposed on scattered scarps of up to 1.5m high, with the dune highly unstable in such areas.

Because of the island's rare wildlife, significant plant communities, and increasing public use problems (crowding, loss of biodiversity), the southern half of the beach was closed to public entry in 1993. The north part remained open to provide boat access.

Dune erosion has impacted nesting sea turtles. Only two endangered green turtles (*Chelonia mydas*) nest on Boca Grande Key (Wilmers, 1994), and both nest only there. They dig deep body pits and clutch cavities, with most nests dug on the dune, not the beach. But the narrow dunes have eroded so much that some nests are laid beyond the dune crest, in salt marsh habitant where they are flooded at spring high tides.

Attempts to post regulatory signs had been futile because of vandalism. In 1991, a vandal deterrent signage system was implemented. Thick-wall steel signposts were placed in one-m² holes into which 300 pounds of concrete was poured. Steel plates were welded to each post to hold signs securely. This system eliminated signpost theft, and virtually eliminated vandalism to signs (Figure III-2). Posting, augmented by occasional presence of enforcement officers reduced illegal camping during the May-August sea turtle nesting season from a peak of ten violations in 1989 to only one in 1996.

FIGURE III-2.

Construction of vandal-proof signs at Boca Grande.

In early 1994, a 60-passenger commercial catamaran brought tourists to the Key without a required permit. Subsequently, a permit application was submitted, but was denied by the refuge manager following a compatibility assessment. Reasons included the large number of visitors involved, concerns over dune erosion, and loss of wilderness character. Several years of litigation followed, culminating in a 1998 court verdict that supported the refuge manager's decision.

In 1995, a camping site (10 X 40m), where several green turtles nests have been found, as posted "closed to all public entry." Reasons included severe erosion problems at an unstable 1.5 m scarp, and recurring instances of vandals shattering glass bottles. The latter likely caused lacerations to nesting green turtles; tracks through shards of broken glass were observed on three occasions.

In the summer of 1997, restoration of the clearing, including removal of about 45 kg of broken glass, planting of native species, erection of a wooden dune fence, and posting of "Area Closed for Habitat Restoration" signs was completed. One year later the plants were thriving, and no vandalism had yet occurred.

Erosion has continued, challenging managers to counter natural erosion while continuing to reduce anthropogenic impacts. Measures include: 1) increasing visitor awareness of the value and fragility of dunes; 2) enforcement of trespass regulations and rigorous prosecution of vandals; 3) immediate restoration of damaged areas; 4) limiting numbers of the visitors; and/or 5) closing the area to public use.

Source: Tom Wilmers, Wildlife Officer, U.S Fish and Wildlife service, Big Pine Key, Florida, USA.

References

Kruer, C.R. 1994. An assessment of Florida's remaining coastal upland natural communities: Florida Key. FL natural areas inventory, Tallahassee, FL 244p.

Wilmers, T.J 1994. Survey of nesting sea turtles in Key West national Wildlife Refuge: productivity and management recommendations. Unpubl. Rep. National Key Deer Refuge, Big Pine Key, Fl. 24 p.

Editor's Note: This case shows what can be accomplished when one dedicated person takes up the conservation cause.

3. Negombo Lagoon, a Protected Area Under Coastal Zone Management

With an area of some 7,000 ha, the Muthurajawela Marsh-Negombo Lagoon (MM-NL) lies on the west coast of Sri Lanka, 15 km north of its capital Colombo. The lagoon proper (3,200 ha) is connected to the Indian Ocean by means of a narrow inlet near the town of Negombo (Figure III-3). The lagoon supports about 3,000 fishing households and provides numerous environmental services with an annual worth of over US$ 23.5 million.

The lagoon is of international significance for biodiversity and as an refuge for migratory birds. But the lagoon and surrounding marshland area are beset by a profusion of socioeconomic and environmental problems. They include: 1) prevailing poverty of fisherfolk causing over-exploitation of the marine and brackish fisheries resource; 2) changing land uses in the catchment area which have altered runoff and sedimentation patterns and altered key hydrological characteristics of the lagoon; 3) rapid population increase in the North-Colombo suburbs which leads to illegal encroachment and puts pressure on the wetlands fringing land area and 4) land use decisions not based on the complex ecological systems of the lagoon.

An ecosystem-based approach was used to integrate environmental considerations into a Master Plan. The plan was prepared by a consultant team based on

FIGURE III-3.

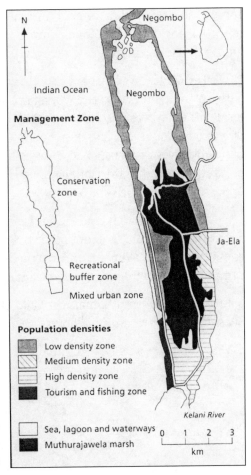

Zoning plan for Negombo Lagoon, Sri Lanka.

biological, geo-physical and socioeconomic resource information and consensus building among stakeholders. Support was provided by the Netherlands government during a period of over seven years.

The foundation of the Master Plan was zoning, which addressed the issues of development needs, conservation importance and equity. Detailed mapping at 1:10,000 scale was undertaken to facilitate zoning. For planning purposes, four zones were delineated for the lagoon and surrounding area (a total of 10,700 ha), endorsed by stakeholder workshops. The zones were: 1) Conservation Zone (91% of wetland), 2) Buffer zone (6.4% of wetland); 3) Mixed Urban Zone (2.5% of wetland); and 4) Residential Zone (42% of total planning area).

The Master Plan received Cabinet approval in 1991 and a Master Plan Implementation Steering Committee (MPISC) was established. By 1994, five main types of activities were identified for further planning: 1) relocation and community development package for 200 households who had encroached upon the Conservation Zone; 2) an EA requirement for proposed developments in the Mixed Urban Zone and a detailed land use and marketing plan; 3) a management plan for the conservation zone; 4) a land-use plan (after community consultation) and screening of investment proposals for the Buffer Zone, aiming at economically viable tourism development; and 5) development of a cost-recovery system for conservation management.

The MPISC was instrumental in ensuring community participation during the entire planning process. The workshops resulted in a common vision on the ways to tackle the main coastal zone management issues, obstruction of lagoon-water exchange due to heavy siltation, and destruction of fisheries nursery areas. It was agreed that basic objectives were sustainable use of the lagoon resources, community development, pollution control, enforcement of environmental legislation, and creation of job opportunities in tourism.

Success factors include: exercise of practicality, legitimacy, and equity; strong scientific and technical foundation based on ecosystem structure and functioning; community and stakeholder involvement and empowerment; and high level political commitment and inter-agency coordination.

Source: Adapted from Samarakoon, J., H. van Zon and W.J.M. Verheugt in Coastal Seas, the Conservation Challenge (1998), Blackwell Science, Oxford, 134 pp.

E-Mail Contact: wverheugt@compuserve.com

4. Philippines: Community-Based Management of Coral Reef Resources

Destruction of coral reef habitats, overfishing and a consequent decline in fish catches plague small-scale fishermen throughout the Philippines. The three island communities discussed below—Apo, Balicasag, and Pamilacan—were all suffering from deterioration of their marine environment in 1984. Destructive fishing methods in common use were explosives, fine mesh nets, scare-in techniques and poison. Increasing poverty was forcing people to use more efficient, but destructive, fishing methods.

This motivated the Philippines to experiment with various forms of coastal management. One experiment which has proved effective for coral reefs surrounding small islands is creation of marine reserve and sanctuary combinations which encourage local community responsibility for fishery and coral reef resources. The sanctuary was to provide an undisturbed place for fish to feed, grow, and reproduce.

This approach was applied to the three island communities in two-year community-based projects beginning in 1985. It included some protection for the coral reef and fishery surrounding the entire island but complete protection from exploitation for a reserve (or sanctuary) covering up to 20 percent of the coral reef area (Figure III-4). The results showed increased or

FIGURE III-4.

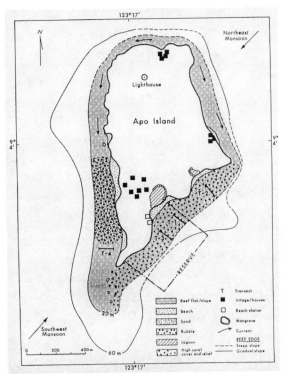

Apo Island (Negros, Philippines) where community-based conservation of coastal resources succeeded through integration, education, core group building, and institutional strengthening.

stable fish yields from the coral reef ecosystems. At present, the management regimes are supported by the community and are functioning without significant intervention.

Fishermen members of the three island MMCs confirmed in both 1992 and 1997 that the marine reserves and sanctuaries had significantly improved fishing by serving as *semilyahan* (breeding places) for fish. Fish yield studies in the reserves outside the sanctuaries indicated that yields have been at least stable and probably increased.

Comparison of baseline data of 1985 and 1986 with a survey made in 1992 showed an increase in fish diversity (species richness) and abundance (number/500 m² of reef, 19 families of fish) within the fish sanctuary at Apo Island as follows:

	1986	1992	% Increase
Species richness	52.4	56.0	6.8
Abundance			
Food fishes	1,286	2,352	83
Total fishes	3,895	5,153	32

Concurrently, the coral reef cover in the sanctuary and non-sanctuary areas of the three islands has remained stable and perhaps improved slightly since 1984, which is generally not the case for coral reefs of the Philippines.

Implementation at the three island project sites included the five types of community based activities described below:

1. **Integration into the community**. During a three-month initial period, field workers located in the community introduced the project, met with community leaders, attended community meetings and generally became acculturated to the island situation. Baseline data were collected for later evaluation. Also pursued were: socioeconomic/demographic surveys; pretest of environmental and resource knowledge and perceived problems of local people; and a survey to document the status of the coral reefs by means of substrate cover, species diversity and abundance, and several other indicators.

2. **Education**. Education was continuous throughout the project but emphasized in the initial stages. Most forms of education were non-formal, in small groups and by one-on-one contact. Focus was on marine ecology and resource management rationale and methods. During the education process, community problems and potential solutions emerged.

3. **Core group building**. It was clear that the correct way to implement management solutions was through community work groups with close ties to the traditional island political structure. Because funds were available for a community education center adjacent to the sanctuary, the first group activated was the one responsible for Center construction. Secondly, individuals interested in the conservation

programme formed a Marine Management Committee (MMC) to study problems of each island. Each MMC earned community respect once it decided to implement a marine reserve.

4. **Formalizing and strengthening organizations**. Other initiatives were aimed at providing continuing support, in real and symbolic terms, to the MMC such as helping it to: 1) identify enhancement projects such as reforestation, 2) place giant clams in the sanctuary for mariculture, 3) refine the marine reserve guidelines, 4) train MMC members to guide tourists to the island, 5) collect fees for visits to the sanctuary, and 6) try alternative income schemes such as mat weaving.

As a result, Apo Island became a training site where the MMC helps conduct workshops by sharing their experiences from the Apo success with other fishermen groups. This activity has truly strengthened the core group and solidified support for the marine reserve among the community.

The three island-wide marine reserves that were created receive municipal administrative support. Municipal ordinances, tailored by the communities to suit their particular needs, are posted in the local language. Enforcement varies from island to island, with mostly moral support from the Philippine police.

The reserves are, with some local variations, well marked by buoys and signs and managed by island-resident committees which patrol for rule infractions by local residents or outsiders.

Community Centers function and serve as meeting places for the MMCs and other groups. Diving tourism to both Apo and Balicasag Island has increased significantly in response to the sanctuaries which are teeming with fish.

Acknowledgment: This work was made possible by Silliman University and staff, particularly Angel Alcala and Nida Calumpong. Support was provided by the East-West Center in 1983, Earthwatch International in 1992, and USAID in 1997.

Source: Adapted from Alan T. White, in Coastal Seas, The Conservation Challenge. (1998). Blackwell Science, Oxford. 134 pp.

E-Mail Contact: prccebu@usc.edu.ph

5. Bonaire: Calculating Carrying Capacity

T he coral rich waters surrounding Bonaire in the Netherlands Antilles Marine Park are a major tourist attraction and all have been designated the Bonaire Marine Park (BMP). However, the steady increase in the number of divers visiting BMP caused concern about diver impacts and the sustainability of the coral based resource. The World Bank commissioned a study of the situation in 1991.

Fortunately, an extensive reef-mapping project conducted in 1981/82 provided good baseline data for comparison with the 1991 situation. The study focussed on a comparison of two heavily dived sites and one moderately dived site. Comparison of available 1981/82 estimates of coral cover with 1991 found that the percentage of live coral cover was significantly lower in the heavily dived sites, but not in the moderately dived site.

An informed assumption was made that the decrease in coral cover observed at the two heavily dived sample sites was not acceptable and exceeded the scenic carrying capacity of those particular sites. "Unacceptable" impact was found more at 100 m to 260 m from fixed mooring buoy locations. Dive statistics showed that the impact becomes unacceptable when a site receives over 5,000 dives per year.

The total "diveable" coastline was estimated at 52 km, and with moorings spaced 600 m apart, the Park could have a total of 86 dive sites. At 4,500 dives per year per site there could be 387,000 dives per year. Making corrections for unevenness of use of the various sites, the maximum carrying capacity was set at about 200,000 dives per year. Concurrent with Bonaire's recommended total tourist limit of 40,000 divers (of a total of 100,000 total tourists) the 200,000 dive limit would allow 5 dives per visitor.

An important lesson learned is that for the use of marine resources for tourism to be sustained, tourism interests must be warned early on that resource use may have to be limited at some stage. It is essential to assess carrying capacity at an early stage of development and to refine the assessment later.

Source: Tom v'ant Hof, *in* Coastal Seas, The Conservation Challenge. Blackwell Science, Oxford. 1998. 134 pp.

E-Mail Contact: vanthof@megatropic.com

6. Cousin Island, a Sea and Island Reserve Scientifically Managed by an NGO

C ousin Island is one of the 115 islands which comprise the Republic of Seychelles. It is a small (27ha) granite island. It lies approximately 4 km SSW of the Northeastern most point of Praslin the second largest island. It is physically dominated by a granite hill that rises to 69m, and is bordered by a broad flat plain of phosphatic sandstone fringed by beaches of sand. In 1968, the island was purchased by the International Council for Bird Preservation (ICBP), now BirdLife International, with funds raised through an international campaign. BirdLife International managed it from its UK office until the country office, BirdLife Seychelles, was created in January 1998. It was designated a Special Reserve under Seychelles national law in 1975. The National Parks and Nature Conservancy Act 1969, as amended in 1973, states that a Special Reserve is "an area in which the characteristic wildlife requires protection and in which all other interests and activities are subordinated to this end."

Activities on the island, since acquisition in 1968 have revolved around scientific research, conservation and education. The activities have been guided by a series of Management Plans. Approximately 125 scientific papers, articles and reports have been written on Cousin's biodiversity to date. Educational activities through tourism bring six thousand to eight thousand visitors a year. The Reserve was run by expatriate Scientific Wardens until 1984, when local staff took over. The management focus since then has been principally awareness-oriented and non-interventionist, the principal aim being to protect biodiversity.

The habitats present on the island include salt-tolerant woodland, rocky communities, a small mangrove system, sandy shores and coral reefs. The island has always been managed as a "sea and island reserve" and marine life is afforded equal protection to terrestrial biota. The Special Reserve area includes the surrounding marine waters up to 400 m offshore in all directions around the island. To the north and east there is high coral cover on the reef—although very severe coral bleaching occurred in 1998. In the Northeast the spur-and-groove formation has a rich coral community but different from that on the main reef front. Patch reefs are also found here. So far, 217 species of coral reef fish have been recorded within the Reserve boundaries. Recent comparative studies of marine protected areas in the granitic islands have shown the reef fish community on Cousin reefs to be far higher in diversity and biomass than any of the other areas investigated.

From 30 to100 hawksbill turtles nest annually on Cousin, and according to published studies is the most important breeding site in the Western Indian Ocean for this species. Small numbers of green turtles also nest. The transformation of the coconut plantation into a forest of indigenous species (notably *Pisonia grandis)* has taken place through BirdLife's restoration work. About half of the 129 plant species on Cousin are probably native to the Seychelles. Five terrestrial birds endemic to the Seychelles currently occur, including the recently translocated Seychelles magpie-robin. The seabird fauna is spectacular. Seven species of breeding seabirds nest in numbers exceeding 300,000 individuals. Another six species of seabirds regularly roost but do not breed there. Neither rats nor cats, which have wiped out many indigenous faunas, have been introduced to the island.

Thirty years after acquiring Cousin, BirdLife International facilitated the creation of BirdLife Seychelles in January 1998 as a locally registered and managed NGO and as its national arm. Under the new management there has been no significant change in conservation priorities, but practices and systems are being developed to be more in line with those used in protected areas and conservation organizations elsewhere. Since the management take-over new administrative and financial practices, as well as programmes of research and monitoring, education and public awareness, marketing and training activities are being implemented by BirdLife Seychelles. A new Management Plan finalized in May 1999 now guides all activities. The Management Plan contains a Vision for the Reserve, Goals and Objectives. An annual Work Programme based on a Logical Framework (LFA) is intended to put the Goals and Objectives into practice.

The island is open to visitors four times a week (Tuesday to Friday) but there is no overnight accommodation. Access is by sea. The Reserve's legal status means that the usual public domain access to any beach in Seychelles below High Water mark does not apply. Visiting parties are brought by private boats, local tourist operators, charter boats, yachts and cruise ships. Landing on the island is only permitted via the Reserve boat and only on open days. All non-resident visitors need to be in possession of a valid ticket (implemented in 1998). Wardens who provide interpretation and identification take visitors around the reserve twice a day. Entry to residents is free; foreign tourists pay a landing fee of about US$20. A colour brochure describing the Reserve is supplied free to visitors. Revenue generation, mostly from landing fees, has so far been sufficient to run the island, but any special projects need to be funded from outside sources.

Research, which was previously driven largely by the priorities of individual scientists, is now controlled by BirdLife Seychelles and based on the Objectives of the Management Plan. A research station, which can house about 4 scientists, is available. Housing, electricity, water, field assistance and transport to Praslin is supplied free of charge to those scientists whose work contributes to Management objectives.

Reserve staff consist of a Manager, Assistant Manager and five Wardens. The Manager reports directly to the Chief Executive of BirdLife Seychelles. The Programme Assistant, based on the main island of Mahe, assists the Manager with administrative work. All staff are Seychellois—BirdLife Seychelles preferentially hires nationals. All personnel are recruited through newspaper advertisements and hired by a Letter of Appointment and on the basis of a Job Description. A Staff Handbook which is signed by all the staff lays out policies and internal regulations. Staff are paid through salary transfers to their respective bank accounts on Praslin every month. Salaries include Social Security and Pension Scheme contributions.

A 6KW-diesel generator that runs for about 5 hours every evening currently supplies power for the island. It is intended to replace the generator with solar panels by the end of 2000 through project funding. Sewage is disposed of through deep-pit latrines. Grey water from sinks and showers is disposed of in soakaways. Composting toilets are being planned to replace the latrines. The tour operators remove most of the solid waste generated by their activities. Other solid waste is collected in refuse bags and taken off the island to Praslin on a regular basis in the Reserve boat. A commercial operator is then paid to transport it to the landfill site. The Reserve is provided with a radiophone link and a mobile (cellular) phone. Currently the Reserve has two locally manufactured fiberglass boats in good working condition. These are used for patrols, staff transport and for disembarking visitors.

The economic benefits of Cousin to surrounding communities and private sector are based on educational tourism. This is serviced by three large travel agencies, and many other locally owned small to medium sized operators and charter boat businesses based on Praslin. The employees of these businesses, apart from cruise ships are, in the majority, all Seychellois. It is estimated that about US$ 600,000 is generated from these activities through direct and indirect revenues. Unlike tourism in many other developing countries, much of the proceeds flow to local businesses.

Poaching of marine resources in protected areas is widespread in Seychelles. Nevertheless, human pressure on Cousin remains low. The main reason may be the small size of the Reserve, which has probably not deprived neighboring fishers of their livelihoods. Another reason is the local management of the island; over the years the Wardens have managed to forge good working relations with fishers who by and large avoid the Reserve. In addition, non-extractive economic benefits to locals are obvious (as described above). However, as the population grows and when neighboring areas are depleted of their biodiversity resources, poachers may turn their attention to Cousin and its seabird colonies, turtle nesting beaches, and well-stocked reefs.

The relations between the Seychelles authorities and BirdLife have always been cordial and professional. In the past Government has provided tax exemptions for equipment imported for Cousin, waiver of Gainful Occupation Permits (GOP) for expatriate staff, and free tickets on the national carrier for project staff. Mechanisms of reaching these agreements are through formal meetings and or are made in writing. Tensions however may arise because of differing priorities between the national environment authority and BirdLife.

Source: Nirmal Jivan Shah, Chief Executive, BirdLife Seychelles, Suite 202, Aarti Chambers, Mahe, Seychelles.

E-Mail Contact: birdlife@seychelles.net

7. Chumbe Island: Experiences of a Private Marine Conservation Project

Introduction

Chumbe Island Coral Park (CHICOP) in Zanzibar/Tanzania is an example of a small but increasing number of privately created and managed protected areas operating in an often difficult institutional and legal environment (Watkins *et al.*, 1996). The project has over seven years invested heavily in the conservation of Chumbe Island in Zanzibar/Tanzania, and has established it as an efficiently managed protected area. It was the first, and remains up to date the only functioning marine park in Tanzania.

The paper summarizes the background of the project and describes management experiences, problems and achievements in the legal, political and institutional environment of Zanzibar/Tanzania, a country that has after Independence embraced a socialist development model and only recently encouraged private investment. Finally, some lessons are drawn for the commercial viability of tourism based on marine conservation in similar cases.

The legal and institutional environment

At the start of the project in the early nineties, liberalization of the economy had been initiated. However, the still predominantly socialist legal and institutional environment of Zanzibar/Tanzania did not yet encourage private investment or non-governmental initiatives. NGO's were not legally possible before 1995. Concerning conservation of natural resources, there was no policy and legal framework or institutions for this.

While coastal communities depend on fishing for their survival, there is little evidence of traditional reef management or awareness about the limitations of the resource (Scheinman & Mabrook, 1996). The national language Kiswahili has no word for corals (referred to as 'mawe na miamba', stones and rocks). Also formal education does not yet provide environmental knowledge on this important natural resource— coral reefs are not covered in the syllabi of primary and secondary education. As a result, decades of destructive fishing methods (dynamite, smashing corals and beachseining) have met with little public or governmental concern (UNEP-RSRS, 19989; Horrill, 1992; Guard, 1997).

At the same time, Chumbe Island, a small coral island of ca. 22 ha presented a rare chance for coral reef conservation along an otherwise heavily overfished coast (Figure III-5). The island was uninhabited and seemed to face little immediate threat. Fishing was traditionally not allowed on its western side bordering the strategically important shipping channel between Zanzibar and Dar es Salaam, as small boats would have obstructed large vessels. For many decades the area surrounding the island was also a military area where the army routinely conducted shooting range exercises from the adjacent coast. In addition, few boatmen could then afford an outboard engine to go to this most distant of the islets surrounding Zanzibar town.

The Project

Chumbe Island Coral Park Ltd. (CHICOP) is a privately funded and managed reef and forest conservation project covering the whole of Chumbe Island and the fringing reef on its Western side. Conservation management was built up through capacity building and raising of awareness of local fishers (training of rangers and their interaction with fishers) and government officials (through an Advisory Committee), close monitoring and review.

FIGURE III-5.

View of the Chumbe Island Reserve, Tanzania. Photo by Guido Cozzi.

Though privately funded (with some minor donor inputs covering about a third of the investment costs), the project is non-commercial. Profits from ecotourism are to be re-invested in conservation area management and free excursions for local schoolchildren.

The Government of Zanzibar approved the project as a tourism investment based on the provisions of the Zanzibar Investment Protection Act 1986, and gave CHICOP the lease of the project site on Chumbe Island in 1993. After commissioning ecological baseline surveys on the flora and fauna and thus establishing its conservation value, CHICOP negotiated for conservation of the island and the Chumbe Reef Sanctuary was gazetted as a protected area in 1994, covering an area of about 300 ha along the Western shore of the island. Simultaneously, CHICOP was given management contracts for the whole of the island and the reef sanctuary. According to these, access to the Reef Sanctuary and the island is controlled by CHICOP.

After some rather 'political' challenges to the conservation status of the area (including press campaigns) in the early years, there are now no major problems with infringements from fishers or other users, and the project is well accepted by the local communities (Carter *et al.*, 1997). CHICOP is registered with the World Conservation Monitoring Center (WCMC) and has been chosen for presentation at the World Exhibition in Hanover/Germany for its achievements in private conservation area management and the innovative eco-architecture of all buildings.

As a result of successful management the coral reef has become one of the most pristine in the region, with 370 species of fish (Mildner, 1995) and over 200 species of scleractinian coral, at least 90% of all recorded in East Africa (Veron, pers.com. 1997). In addition, the coral communities in the sanctuary have survived the 1998 bleaching event much better than most other reefs in the region. The forest covering the island is one of the last pristine 'coral rag' forests in Zanzibar (Beentje, 1990) and has now become a sanctuary for the highly endangered Aders' Duiker (*Cephalophus adersi*) probably facing imminent extinction from poaching and habitat destruction (Kingdon, 1997). The island also has a large population of the probably endangered Coconut crab (*Birgus latro*) recorded as 'data deficient' in the IUCN Red data book and had in 1994 a large breeding population of Roseate terns (*Sterna dougalli*) classified as 'rare' (Iles, 1995).

In summary, project activities from 1992-1998 were:

Four former fishermen from adjacent villages were employed and trained as park rangers by expatriate volunteers from 1993, basically in interaction with fishers, monitoring techniques and tourist guidance skills;

Also with the help of volunteers and some limited donor funds, baseline surveys and species lists on the island's flora and fauna were conducted from 1993;

An Advisory Committee was established in 1993 with representatives of the Departments of Fisheries, Forestry and Environment, the Institute of Marine Sciences of the University of Dar es Salaam and village leaders of neighbouring fishing villages;

A Management Plan 1995-2005 was produced in 1995 and guides project operations since then; forest and marine nature trails were established from 1993 with informational material; rats were eradicated in 1997; a Sanctuary for the highly endangered Ader's duiker was established from 1997; the ruined lighthouse keeper's house rehabilitated as Park HQ/Visitors' Center; free excursions to the island are offered to local school-children during the off-season; seven visitors' bungalows ("eco-bungalows") and the Visitors' Center were constructed according to state-of-the-art eco-architecture (rainwater catchment, gray water recycling, compost toilets, photovoltaic power generation); tourism operations (day excursions and overnight stay) started in 1997, but have not reached economical levels yet.

Positive lessons learned: Private coral reef conservation can work

The Chumbe experience suggests that private management of marine protected areas is technically feasible and efficient even when the enforcement machinery of the State is not available or is ineffective. This is probably the case for reefs that are not yet over-exploited by communities depending on them for their survival.

A private protected area such as Chumbe can provide important community benefits, particularly in capacity building, biodiversity conservation and restocking of fisheries resources. The Chumbe Reef Sanctuary provides a safe haven for endangered species and breeding grounds for reef fishes and other organisms that are severely depleted elsewhere. With the predominantly northerly currents in the Zanzibar channel and the sanctuary being located South of all major fishing grounds off Zanzibar town, depleted areas downstream are potentially restocked.

The hands-on approach to capacity building and monitoring through inexpensive on-the-job-training of local fishers by volunteers has produced very competent and committed park rangers. They are stationed on the island and manage the Reef Sanctuary with no other means of enforcement than persuasion of their fellow fishers. Lacking Government support and policing power, the rangers interact with fishers by stressing the role of the protected area as a breeding ground for fish. This has proved to be very successful. Village fishers now generally respect the park boundaries and report that catches outside the boundaries have increased since the establishment of the sanctuary.

Any event or infringement is closely monitored by the rangers, and their reports provide daily data (from 1992), on the type, number and names of vessels involved, nature of the intended activity and the fishers' reaction to the rangers' intervention (Carter *et al.*, 1997). Also observations on any major change in the coral reef are recorded by the rangers, such as storm damage, coral bleaching etc.

The project has also helped to raise conservation awareness and understanding of the legal and institutional requirements among government officials. Seven government departments were involved in negotiating the project in the initial phase, followed (among other issues) by intense discussions on the "Management Plan 1995-2005" in the Advisory Committee. This has improved political support and prepared the ground for improvements in the legal framework. Recent legislation passed in 1997 on environmental management provides for private management of protected areas.

With an overall investment of approximately 1 million US$ over seven years, the cost of private management is probably considerably lower than would have been the case with a donor-funded project through the Government machinery. And, most importantly, there are better prospects for sustainability, as the incentives to struggle for commercial survival are much stronger for private operations than for donor-funded projects.

Negative lessons learned: High commercial risk

The regulatory environment is characterized by cumbersome bureaucratic requirements with wide discretionary powers for government officials. This encourages rent-seeking and delays operations, thus increasing investment insecurity and costs in general. This is particularly the case for innovative and environmentally friendly project designs that are generally not encouraged by existing regulations, e.g., concerning building permits, etc.

To date, CHICOP is regarded as just another tourism venture by the Zanzibar government and given no tax exemptions or other benefits for the conservation work. The up to US$ 10,000 annually to be paid for land rent, government fees and licenses represents a considerable burden on operational costs, compounded by the high and complex tax regime.

The logistical requirements of building on an island and particularly the innovative technology for water and energy provision, as well as the commitment to not cause any degradation of the island environment have also added to the development costs. A compost toilet, for example, which operates without any sewerage, costs about five times the price of a normal flush toilet. Water, sand and timber for the building operations, and even the firewood for cooking meals for the building workers and staff had to be purchased and transported to the island at a high cost.

The drastically increased investment costs and continuing burden of government taxes and fees have forced CHICOP to revise the price structure for tourist operations and go up-market. A financial analysis conducted in 1998 has established that overnight prices would have to be around US$300 per person per night for commercial viability. Access to this market requires further investment in marketing rather than in conservation.

As a consequence, Chumbe Island has now to be marketed primarily as an exclusive private island. While it is a challenge to train park rangers and local staff for the very demanding logistical and service expectations of that particular market, there is also a potential conflict with the non-commercial project component providing free education to local school children.

In addition, realistic price levels that reflect conservation costs are difficult to realize as long as unmanaged and donor-managed wilderness areas can be accessed at very low cost by the tourism industry (though still charging high prices). It can be said that Chumbe Island may face 'unfair competition' from 'cheap' destinations subsidized with donor funds.

As donor support in conservation is typically given as grants to government institutions that sometimes lack commitment, competence and accountability, there are few incentives to check wastage, misuse and mismanagement. This not only wastes precious resources but also crowds out private initiatives which have to operate commercially, and must thus be more cost-conscious and clearly show results on the ground.

Conclusions

It is suggested that particularly in a country like Tanzania, it is primarily commercial viability and long-term economical resource use that makes conservation area management sustainable. Investment in conservation is necessarily long-term and requires high security and a supportive legal and politico-administrative environment. Therefore, the overall conclusion is that before anything else, a favorable investment climate is required for private investment in marine conservation.

In some cases, this may require a revision of donor policies concerning the creation of conservation areas and the establishment of management structures. Instead of building up costly institutions that need long-term or permanent external funding, donor money would have longer-term impact when supporting improvements in the legal, institutional and regulatory environment for investment. Donor organizations should also consider sharing risks of private investment in conservation, support non-commercial project components or provide seed capital.

References:

Carter, E., Nyange, L., Said, Y. (1997). Management Experiences of the Chumbe Reef Sanctuary 1992-1996, Paper presented at the National Coral Reef Conference, 2-4 December, Zanzibar.

Iles, D.B. (1995). Brief preliminary survey of Chumbe Island Butterflies, Zanzibar.

Mildner, S. (1994). Benthic composition of transects of Chumbe Island Reef (Baseline survey).

Beentje, H.J. (1990). A Reconnaissance Survey of Zanzibar Forests and Coastal Thicket, FINNIDA-COLE, Zanzibar.

Guard, M. (1997). Dynamite Fishing in Southern Tanzania, Miombo 17, Wildlife Conserv. Soc. of Tanzania, Dar es Salaam.

Horrill, C. (1992). Status and Issues Affecting the Marine Resources around Fumba Peninsula, COLE-Zanzibar Environmental Study Series, Number 12.

Kingdon, J. (1997). The Kingdon Field Guide to African Mammals, Academic Press, 372-373.

Scheinman, D. & Mabrook, A. (1996). The Traditional Management of Coastal Resources, Tanga Coastal Zone Conservation and Development Programme, Tanga/Tanzania, June 1996.

UNEP-RSRS, (1989). Coastal and marine environmental problems of the United Republic of Tanzania. By M. Pearson. UNEP Regional Seas Reports and Studies No. 106.

Watkins, C.W., Barrett, M., & Paine, J.R. (1996). Private Protected Areas, A Preliminary Study of Private Initiatives to Conserve Biodiversity in Selected African Countries, World Conserv. Monitoring Center (WCMC), Cambridge, December 1996.

Source: Sibylle Riedmiller. Paper presented at the ICRI-International Tropical Marine Ecosystems Management Symposium (ITMEMS), Townsville/Australia, 23-26 November 1998.

E-Mail Contact: chumbe.island@raha.com, www.xtra-micro.com/work.chumbe

8. Florida Keys: Distant Influence on Coral Reefs

Background

Lying parallel to the Florida coast is a barrier reef more than 200 miles long. Parts of the reef system were designated as marine protected areas some time ago: John Pennekamp Coral Reef Park combined with Key Largo National Marine Sanctuary (103 square nautical miles) designated in 1961 and 1975; and the Looe Key National Marine Sanctuary (5.32 square nautical miles) in 1981. The management of these protected areas was focused primarily on various sources of direct, *in situ*, impact to the coral reef resources and depletion of reef populations. The idea was to prevent damage from boat anchors, boat groundings, harvesting, and diver impact—they proved to have some limited success in protecting the coral reefs. Other management strategies such as gear restrictions and prohibitions on spearfishing and the harvest of invertebrates have shown some success. However, something was missing from the protection scheme.

In 1990, the U.S. Congress expanded the coral reef programme greatly by designating an area of 2800 square nautical miles for conservation. This area—the Florida Keys National Marine Sanctuary—includes the previous protected areas and encompasses 220 miles of coral reef tract that parallels the island chain of the Florida Keys. Also contained within its boundary are vast seagrass communities, mangrove habitats, hard bottom communities, thousands of patch reefs, over two dozen shallow bank reefs, and a reef habitat (intermediate to deep) that runs almost continuously for the length of the reef tract.

Problem

The problem is that regardless of all the management arrangements, the coral reefs and coral reef resources of the Florida Keys are declining (Figure III-6). Clearly, the management programme for Key Largo and Looe Key was not sufficient to prevent the decline of the coral reef resources from impacts originating outside their boundaries. No matter how many mooring buoys were installed in the Sanctuaries, or how many times the education efforts helped keep boats from running aground, the health of the coral continued to decline.

FIGURE III-6.

Snorkelers enjoy the Florida Keys Sanctuary which extends from Miami to Key West. The sanctuary is affected by a variety of agricultural and urban pollutants entering from the north and by major changes in the amount and periodicity of flow through the Everglades National Park.

Management of Key Largo and Looe Key has been like managing "islands" in the ecosystem. Regardless of the intensity of management effort, scientists have documented a decrease in the amount of living coral cover, as well as recruitment of new corals. Following studies that characterized the flow of water in and around the Looe Key, it became clear that the potential for water quality impacts originating outside the boundaries of the Sanctuaries was very high.

Even after its great expansion, the Florida Keys marine protected area is dwarfed by the huge Central and South Florida ecosystem that drains into it. This system begins at the headwaters of the Kissimmee River, includes Lake Okeechobee, the Everglades Agricultural Area, Everglades National Park, and Florida Bay. There is extensive agricultural and urban activity in this area which is the source of directed pollution discharge (point source) and runoff pollution (non-point source), all of which runs south into the waters surrounding the Florida Keys.

Solution

The establishment of the much larger Florida Keys protected area made it possible for Sanctuary management (National Oceanic and Atmospheric Administration— NOAA) to look at holistic management of the coral reef community. In addition, the Act that established the Sanctuary also called for the Federal Environmental Protection Agency and the State of Florida, in coordination with NOAA, to develop a comprehensive water quality protection programme for the Sanctuary. The focus of this plan is mainly on land based sources of water quality impacts, including pollution that originates outside the boundary of the enlarged Sanctuary. Currently, there is a Federal Task Force that has been established to develop a plan to restore the South Florida ecosystem as it is described above. Although complete restoration may not be feasible, major hydrological linkages and ecological linkages can be restored to the point that a natural functioning ecosystem can be maintained.

Lessons Learned

Today, it is obvious that successful management of the coral reef resources of the Florida Keys depends on the ability of Sanctuary management to address impacts that come from outside the physical boundaries of the Sanctuary (which go only up to mean high water). In order to be successful in protecting the resources of the Keys, Sanctuary managers must be capable of influencing interagency activities that affect the quality of the water that flows through the Keys and out to the reefs.

In order to be fully successful in protecting the resources of the Sanctuary, it is important to be able to address the impacts affecting the entire South Florida ecosystem. Whereas eight years ago Sanctuary Managers felt they were managing the "coral reef ecosystem" of the Florida Keys, today it is recognized that the coral reef community of the Florida Keys is only a small portion of an enormous ecosystem.

Source: Billy Causey, *in* Coastal Zone Management Handbook. Lewis/CRC Press. Boca Raton, Florida (1996). 694 pp.

9. Laguna de Tacarigua National Park, Venezuela: Management Problems in a Protected Estuary

This case is based on the report of a 1980 study for the government of Venezuela on threats to the Tacarigua estuary and management options in the National Park, followed by a 1999 update.

With the establishment of the National Park at Laguna de Tacarigua (Figure III-7), the managers inherited several problems. Much of the lagoon itself is in good natural condition and continues to provide feeding, roosting, and nesting sites to a variety of birds, and feeding, spawning, and nursery areas to valuable shrimps and fishes. The lagoon supports a fishing industry based at the village of Tacarigua de la Laguna and, together with its neighbouring lagoons, sustains an important shrimp fishery offshore.

FIGURE III-7.

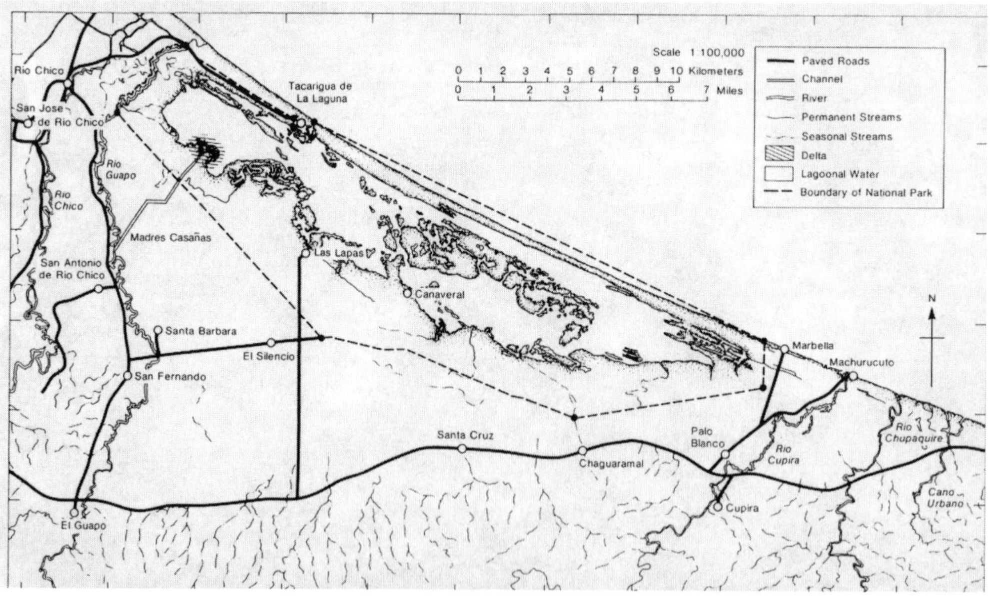

Parque Nacional Laguna de Tacarigua (in 1980).

There are some localised problems at the edge of the lagoon, such as encroachment into wetlands, dumping of garbage, and a marina development with clearing, felling, and filling 146 ha of prime mangrove and threatening effectively to destroy about 700 ha of productive habitat.

The National Park was designed around the unaltered parts of the lagoon. The village, the marina, and a second development close to the east end of the lagoon were not included within the management boundaries. Management was confined to boundaries that were determined more by convenience than ecological design.

The problems arising from activities outside the park's boundaries, but inside the lagoon's ecological boundary, are those that most threaten the ecosystem. These problems are outlined below.

The Functional Unit

The brackish water in Laguna de Tacarigua derives from mixing of freshwater—from streams, groundwater seepage, surface runoff, and rains—with seawater entering through the mouth and seeping in through porous areas of the coastal barrier. Lagoon water may range from almost fresh to hypersaline. In the dry season the lagoon level drops when water is lost through the mouth, and through evaporation and evapotranspiration when they exceed all inputs. At this point tidal currents dominate the estuarine currents at the mouth and salt-water flows into the lagoon.

If tidal flushing is insufficient to keep the mouth open, it is blocked by longshore drift of sand. When the water level of the lagoon is high, flow of water from the lagoon scours the inlet and maintains it open.

Clearly, the water balance of the lagoon is a function of forces operating on it from outside, not inside, the limit of its shorelines. The shorelines of watersheds delineate ecological boundaries of the Laguna de Tacarigua ecosystem. Similarly, surrounding swamps that act as natural filters of silt borne down rivers, and connected channels and waterways that influence overall lagoon productivity, are all part of the same functional unit.

The Siltation Problem

The gravest, most obvious and most urgent problem in Laguna de Tacarigua is siltation in the western zone called El Guapo. In 1964 the water from the Rio Guapo was diverted to the lagoon via a channel, called Madre Casanas, to avert flooding problems in low-lying villages on the Rio Guapo floodplain. Madre Casanas is much shorter and its slope greater than the meandering Rio Guapo. Hence the flow of water is faster and there is erosion of the channel bed, resulting in deposition of a vast amount of silt in the estuary. Since 1964 a delta of 225 ha has developed in El Guapo at the mouth of Madre Casanas.

Silt deposition accelerates the succession from productive lagoon to coastal plain. The turbid waters inhibit primary productivity, which adversely affects the production of commercial fishes and shrimps. Lower production of commercial species means lowered fishery yield. Lower fishery yield means lowered per capita income from fisheries with consequent effects throughout the community of Tacarigua de la Laguna village. Madre Casanas was built to avoid a flood problem, but it has created a new problem in the economic base of the fishing community.

Rainwater runoff and streams carry a great deal of silt to the river from such sources as the earthworks at the base of the dam on the Rio Guapo, small farms, and houses close to the river bank.

Obstruction of Freshwater Drainage

Adequate freshwater input is vital to the functioning of the brackish lagoon. Too little freshwater will cause a drop in lagoon water level, an increase in temperature and salinity, and a decrease in dissolved oxygen with potential massive mortality of fishes. Too much water may cause local flooding and, if sustained, drown mangrove vegetation.

Completion of the dam on the Rio Guapo will enable regulation of the flow of freshwater to the Laguna de Tacarigua. This has both advantages and disadvantages. Chief among the advantages is the ability to avoid the recurrence of massive fish mortalities during unusually dry periods by maintaining a flow of freshwater into the lagoon. Chief among the disadvantages is the ability to abruptly alter conditions in the shallow western part of the lagoon by sudden large differences in the volume of water released from the dam. For example, sudden increase in the volume of released water may cause a localised precipitous drop in salinity in the lagoon, stressing or even killing organisms in the affected area.

An east-west highway runs south of the lagoon, separating it from the southern water catchment. There are frequent bridges and culverts along this road, but it blocks drainage in some places.

The Controversial Inlet

The water level of the lagoon is variable and depends on the interaction of many factors. High water level in the lagoon maintains a strong flow of water to the sea and keeps the mouth open, so fishes and shrimps are free to enter or leave the lagoon. The juveniles of fishes spawning at sea enter the lagoon to feed and shelter in the mangrove nurseries.

In the past the mouth opened naturally once the lagoonal water level had risen sufficiently to break through the bar. However, people have settled in low-lying areas that flood before the water level rises high enough to open the mouth naturally.

Consequently, it now is opened both officially by the public works authority (MARNR) and unofficially by fishermen.

No obvious problems arise from artificially maintaining the mouth open until such time as tidal currents dominate the outflow from the lagoon. Then marine sands and seawater enter, leaving silt in the mouth area and flooding the estuary with salt water. The area in and around the mouth would need to be dredged periodically to remove sand deposited there by longshore drift and tidal currents. Salt water would intrude through the dredged channel as a wedge under the brackish lagoon waters and penetrate the lagoon or, when lagoon waters are low, flow in freely, increasing the salinity of the lagoon in even the freshest areas. The formation of a bar across the mouth when lagoon waters are low is natural insurance against massive influx of salt water.

Conclusion

This case illustrates a range of management problems resulting from the interplay of social, economic, and ecological requirements. Ultimately, the goals are to preserve the fisheries and recreational, flood control, and conservation values of the lagoon, and to perpetuate the benefits deriving from these to local inhabitants. However, there are still conflicts between the immediate demands of the local residents (opening of the mouth, inland water needs, local garbage disposal, flood control, village expansion, resort development) and the immediate ecological problems (altered water balance, siltation, opening of the mouth, encroachment of mangroves). These must be resolved before the lagoon can be managed with long-term goals in mind. It is clear that management will have to extend beyond the immediate environments of the lagoon to the catchment and beyond ecological parameters to social ones.

*Source:*Adapted from Rodney V. Salm. 1980. *Alternativas para el control de las perturbaciones provocadas por el hombre en el ecosistema de la Laguna de Tacarigua.* Caracas, Venezuela: Ministerio del Ambiente y de los Recursos Naturales Renovables. 27 pp.

Update on Laguna de Tacarigua—1999

Laguna de Tacarigua's management procedures and ecological situation since 1980 have not changed significantly. The need of extending the park's management decisions to the surrounding areas is still a must. However, in 1992, the marine boundaries that ended at the seawater's edge were extended 5 nautical miles offshore. The tourism developments toward the eastern part of the area have suffered a more strict control and the owners require that the park's authorities monitor any remodeling of the buildings.

Due to the work of NGO's on certain endangered species, the management actions have been rather successful in comparison with other coastal NP's in Venezuela. Inside the park's boundaries some management actions have been successful. Threatened species such as the Caimán de la Costa and sea turtles have been monitored constantly and their nesting areas protected. In the surrounding areas outside the park, INPARQUES has no authority as such control belongs to the Ministerio del Ambiente y de los Recursos Naturales, of which INPARQUES depends institutionally. On the marine side, INPARQUES coordinates actions with the Maritime Police of the Miranda State Government.

In the social aspects, INPARQUES has been conducting an environmental education campaign aimed at the local schools and, more recently, a voluntary rangers group is being formed among young local residents.

Regarding the Rio Guapo delta, some limited actions have been taken, mainly altering the watercourse at the Madre Casañas and directing the sediments to the low lands. However no data is available on this matter and such appreciation remains to be a very subjective one, drawn from the opinion collected from the different experts consulted.

Since some efforts are being done in order to change the fishing behavior of the local communities, mainly taking the pressure off the Laguna's resources and encouraging marine fisheries, the inlet has to be maintained open for the boats to go in and out of the Laguna.

Source: José Ramón Delgado, Los Chorros—Caracas, Venezuela.

E-Mail Contact: jrdelgadopvzla@hotmail.com

10. Great Barrier Reef Marine Park

The Great Barrier Reef in Australia is one of the World's very special places and is the largest marine park in the World. The Marine Park covers an area of 240,000 square miles, along the northeastern coastline of Australia. Its 2,900 coral reefs, vast range of inter-reef habitats, and 900 islands make up one of the most diverse ecosystems on earth.

Historically, Australian Aboriginal people have used the nearshore areas of the reef for thousands of years and continue to do so as part of their subsistence, culture and lifestyle. The Great Barrier Reef also provides employment for many through the tourism, fishing and shipping industries managed on an ecologically sustainable basis.

During the late 1960s and 1970s concern was raised about the changing density of human use of the Great Barrier Reef. Of major concern were proposals for oil drilling and limestone mining. Other concerns were increased land clearing and development along the adjacent coast as well as accelerated fishing, recreation and tourism.

To address these concerns, Federal parliament acted to establish the Great Barrier Reef Marine Park in 1975. The Park provides for multiple use consistent with the requirements for nature conservation. The Act banned oil drilling and mining as unacceptable threats to the coral ecosystem.

The establishment of a conservation regime that encompasses the entire reef ecosystem and provides for multiple uses is a special feature of the Marine Park. The empowerment of the Great Barrier Reef Marine Park Authority (the Authority), an independent statutory authority, to manage the entire area is a unique feature for marine protected areas around the world and has proven an important factor in the success of the Great Barrier Reef Marine Park.

Zoning plans provide a basic framework for management of the Marine Park (Figure III-8) that includes:

- Establishment of "representative areas" of protected habitats as flora and fauna refuges and scientific reference areas.

FIGURE III-8.

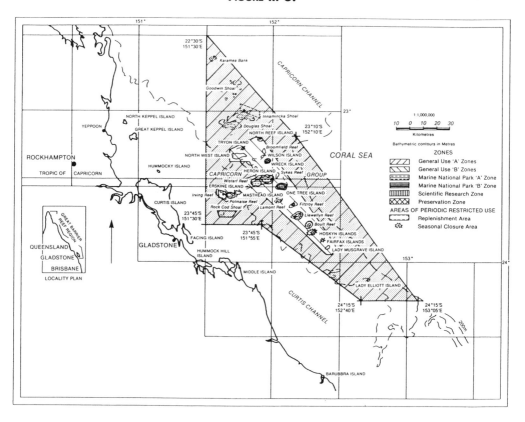

Great Barrier Reef Marine Park, Capricornia Section zoning plan.

- Protection of sensitive habitats and species from activities that might threaten them (e.g., trawl fishing is precluded from coral reef and seagrass communities, and species that may be particularly vulnerable to exploitation, such as dugong and turtle, receive appropriate protection).

- Provision for environmental impact assessment for new activities that may have significant environmental impacts, detailed management planning for high use and sensitive sites, and development of conservation strategies for threatened species.

The focus of the Authority has changed over time. For the first ten or so years the focus was on establishing the Park and management systems. Now the focus has shifted to resolving the following critical issues: (i) water quality impacts from coastal development and agricultural run-off, (ii) effects of fishing, (iii) management of tourism activities, and (iv) protection of biodiversity, particularly vulnerable species. Awaiting intensive effort is full integration into the programme of the needs of Aboriginal people whose lifestyle and culture have evolved over thousands of years of co-existence.

Public involvement is a cornerstone of the Marine Park. A formally constituted Consultative Committee was established by the act and advises the authority and the responsible federal and state ministers. The act also requires the authority to seek public input into the development of zoning plans. Specialist advisory committees are also established where appropriate, for example, to advise on strategies for addressing critical issues or to develop more detailed plans for management of intensively used areas.

A summary of important lessons learned from the Authority's experience include the importance of:

1. adopting an holistic approach to ecosystem management;

2. establishing an independent authority with strong legislative mandate to focus exclusively on management of the protected area;

3. establishing formal complementary management arrangements amongst all relevant levels of government and stakeholders and creating processes for reaching agreement on proposed restrictions;

4. not postponing decisions awaiting perfect information but using the best available scientific information and the precautionary principle;

5. gaining the support of affected communities and involving them in the decision making process;

6. providing adequate funding both to the management authority and to supporting agencies in accordance with formal agreements.

Source: Peter McGinnity, Great Barrier Reef Marine Park Authority, Townsville, Australia.

E-Mail Contact: Peter.McGinnity@env.qld.gov.au

Editor's Note: This case updates the material published in the first edition of Marine and Coastal Protected Areas.

11. Saint Lucia: Evolution of an NGO-Managed Marine Protected Area

Introduction

In the surroundings of the small town of Soufriere in Saint Lucia, resource use conflicts between tourist divers, yachters, hoteliers, fishermen and other local people were common. The reasons for the conflicts included the following: the visiting divers cut holes in the fishermen's traps in an attempt to protect coral reef fish, yachtsmen anchored in sandy bays making the traditional fishing of coastal pelagics difficult, and the access to the beaches and the sea had become restricted with the development of the tourism industry. There were also fears that illegal spearfishing and pot fishing on the reef would continue keeping the reef fish populations at a low level, and that careless diving and boat anchoring would cause physical damage on the reef .

The major conflicts were solved through a public consultation process, which in 1994 led to the establishment of the Soufriere Marine Management Area (SMMA), a zoned Eastern Caribbean MPA. The benefits to the major user groups have included improved definition of user rights through zoning, developments in the protection of the coral reef habitat and an increase in the reef fish populations.

The SMMA is a success story in community participation, conflict resolution, user financing and integrated coastal management, in spite of the fact that five years after its establishment it is going through reorganization.

Resource uses before the SMMA

In addition to agriculture, fisheries have been the traditional source of income in the region of Soufriere in the southwestern part of St. Lucia. In fisheries, the coastal pelagics have been a major part of the catch. These inshore pelagics have been captured mostly in sandy bays with beach seine nets. The second important gear type has been the "fillet net", which is a gill net. In the coral reef areas, fish have been captured also with fish traps, which were owned by a quarter of the Soufriere fishermen in 1994. That year there were in total 150 fishermen in Soufriere and they had 78 boats.

During the growth of tourism in the eastern Caribbean in the 1980s and 1990s, increasing numbers of visitors came to dive in Soufriere. Much of the interest had its origin in the species and structural diversity of the coral reefs. When the SMMA was being created, 4,500 scuba dives per month were being made on the Soufriere reefs.

Many of the visitors stayed at the three major hotels of Soufriere, one of them being a resort specializing in scuba diving. The other tourists came to Soufriere for half-day visits from the other hotels on the island or from cruise ships. The visitors attracted to Soufriere included yachters, who were cruising in the West Indies. The yachtsmen preferred to anchor in the same sandy bays, which were used for the fishing of the pelagics.

Initial management attempts

The fact that the coastal area of Soufriere was being used intensively and the resources needed to be conserved efficiently were realized by several interests. Consequently, numerous attempts to solve the problems with conflicting resource uses were initiated during a period covering more than ten years before the establishment of the SMMA. The actors involved the Fisheries Unit (later Fisheries Department) of the Ministry of Agriculture, the Soufriere Regional Development Foundation (SRDF), the Soufriere Fishermen s Cooperative, the dive operators and the yacht charter enterprises. Usually the meetings held resulted only in temporary solutions but were unable to resolve the resource ownership and management problems in the long term.

One major example of concrete attempts was the declaration of most of the Soufriere reefs as Marine Reserves in 1986. However, this was not based on a conflict resolution process. No efficient means of enforcement was provided either. Consequently, the formal closure of the majority of the trap fishing grounds on the reefs and the creation of three fishing priority areas in the sandy bays did not win the respect of the users.

The new conflict resolution approach

As the many attempts to solve the coastal resource use conflicts in Soufriere had failed, a new attempt was initiated in 1992. The forces behind this attempt were the SRDF, the Department of Fisheries and the Caribbean Natural Resources Institute (CANARI). The goal was an agreement, which would let the coastal activities co-exist in harmony. The interest groups were assisted by professionals in a negotiation, conflict resolution and participatory planning exercise, so they could feel they had an equal footing in the process leading to a compromise. Also several government agencies were involved. Development cooperation funding from U.S.A. and French governments facilitated the implementation.

Key elements in the process were broad-based consultations together with meetings with a more targeted focus. Interest groups were asked to be represented by teams of three to six persons. Thus the groups became negotiating teams, which could be divided, to allow representation of the team in several specialized working groups simultaneously. The work started from a clear table, i.e., the existing agreements (such as those covering the marine reserves) were ignored.

From mapping to zoning

During the first consultation the participants were taken out on board vessels to map all the uses of the coastal area. As a result of the on-board exercise, a coastal resources and uses map could be drawn, with the areas of conflict and areas of concern marked on it.

After this, several working groups dealt with the issues brought up during the first stage of the process. The groups discussed the needs of the fishing, diving and yachting communities, the public access to beaches, the control of land-based pollution and the establishment of effective marine protected areas. The conclusions were then subject to discussion at another broad-based meeting, which agreed on the recommendations needed. At a third larger meeting these were presented in a written form by a committee representing the participants. The results were the basis for a Draft Agreement on the use of the Soufriere coastal area while the negotiation on some specific issues still continued.

FIGURE III-9.

Zoning plan for the Soufriere Marine Management Area.

Finally, a Preliminary Agreement on the Use and Management of Marine and Coastal Resources of the Soufriere Region was reached and could be presented to the Cabinet of Ministers for Approval. The Agreement covered 11 km of coastline and was a zoning agreement with specific rules for each zone (Figure III-9). The area was subdivided into multipurpose use areas (fishing, snorkeling and diving permitted), marine reserve areas (no fishing but snorkeling and scuba diving permitted—scuba divers would need to purchase a ticket), recreational areas (beaches reserved for public enjoyment), yacht mooring areas (mooring permitted at buoys against payment of user fee) and fishing priority areas (only fishing by licensed local fishermen permitted). When this Agreement on the Soufriere Marine Management Area (SMMA) was approved by the Cabinet in March 1994, its implementation could begin.

The start of the SMMA

One of the first stages in the implementation was a meeting of technical specialists with the purpose to draft a Management Plan for the area. The final Plan was presented in December 1994. Based on this 1994 Management Plan, the operation had the following key elements in addition to those already mentioned:

– The operation is implemented as a distinct programme of the SRDF (an NGO).

– The operations are steered by a Technical Advisory Committee (TAC), which functions as broad-based board of the operation; the main channel for communications between the SMMA manager and TAC is the Executive Director of the SRDF

– The ultimate authority is the Ministry of Agriculture. Work plans and budgets are submitted to the TAC and the Minister of Agriculture for approval.

– Technical advice in the day-to-day operations is provided by a multidisciplinary Technical Working Group.

– The area has a manager, an administrative assistant and four rangers, who are in charge of the daily management, some habitat monitoring (professional support for this is provided by CANARI and the Department of Fisheries), ticket selling to yachters, maintenance of the mooring buoys and reminding visitors of the area s rules. For their work, the rangers have an eight-meter open boat.

– The SMMA staff needs to contact the police, marine police or fisheries wardens for law enforcement, as the staff does not have such powers; the government agencies retain their enforcement powers and the role of the SMMA is an advisory and reporting one, in spite of the fact that this may result in less rapid enforcement.

– The fees for diving and the use of mooring buoys are the major sources of revenue; the objective is financial self-sufficiency (for operational costs this was achieved during the second year of operation); the SMMA makes extra revenue by installing mooring buoys outside its own area; in the SMMA the buoys are a major reef conservation tool.

– A comprehensive public education programme is part of the operation.

Problems with the SMMA

In spite of the attempts to create an MPA based on public consultation and conflict resolution, two to three years after the start of the SMMA operation, new conflicts began to emerge. The stakeholders were no longer satisfied with the management agreement and its implementation. Lack of respect of the regulations increased and there was a lack of clarity as to the roles of key organizations. Nevertheless, all involved seemed to agree that there were fundamental problems which needed to be solved.

The result was an institutional review of the SMMA in 1997 and 1998. It brought to light that the initial public consultations had failed to develop such a consensus regarding the mission and objectives of the SMMA as had been commonly believed. What had originally been reached had only been a consensus on the zoning. In this situation the stakeholders and their organizations were trying to lead the SMMA in different directions.

Other problems were found to be that the original agreement on the SMMA was not binding and that Cabinet Conclusions on the SMMA, together with the Fisheries Act, did not provide an adequate legal basis for the operation. There was no formal agreement on the sharing of responsibilities between the actors involved either—the weakest ones suffered from this. The Technical Advisory Committee had become too large and its functions too disperse for efficient leadership. Furthermore, established structures for review and revision were lacking. In the evaluation of the SMMA operation it was also concluded that the management plan was not being used effectively as a management tool.

Guidelines for the new SMMA

Meetings and consultations to solve the problems resulted in guidelines for restructuring the SMMA in 1999. It has been understood that the new management regime would need to be based on a clear mission, the management structure would need to be transparent, and that the operation would need to be politically, institutionally and financially autonomous. A strong legal basis would be needed and responsibilities of those involved would need to be clearly defined. Overall, the SMMA objectives are expected to reflect orientation towards development and promotion.

In detail, the foreseen elements of the new SMMA include the following:

–   The existing legal basis for the operation will be the Fisheries Act. Under the Act, the SMMA will be a Local Fisheries Management Area. Management and enforcement will be locally based. However, government agencies retain their statutory authority while operating within the SMMA.

–   The borders of the coastal area being managed by the SMMA remain unchanged. In the sea the SMMA will be in charge of the area which reaches from the shoreline to the depth of 75 meters.

–   The existing zoning and related regulations will be kept in force.

–   The foundation for the management will be a new agreement, which clearly defines the mission, objectives, regulations, zones and institutional arrangements of the SMMA.

–   The operational responsibility for the SMMA will be given to a new organization, i.e., the Soufriere Marine Management Association, a non-profit company. The Association will comprise all the management institutions which have management responsibilities in the area. Members will include five community and non-governmental organizations, five government agencies and one to two representatives of the District Representative and Cabinet of Ministers. Legally the new organization will become a Local Fisheries Management Authority. The SMMA is no longer under the Soufriere Regional Development Foundation.

– Instead of the TAC, the new management regime will include a broad-based advisory body called the Stakeholder Committee. On-going stakeholder and inter-institutional consultation will be a priority.

– The SMMA will be guided by the following mission statement: The mission of the SMMA is to contribute to national and local development, particularly in the fisheries and tourism sectors, through management of the Soufriere coastal zone, based on the principles of sustainable use, cooperation among resource users, institutional collaboration, active and enlightened participation, and equitable sharing of benefits and responsibilities among stakeholders.

– Good information flows based on a communication plan will be a key element in the operations.

Features of the SMMA in 1999

By September 1999, the SMMA was self-financing (covering all the operational costs). It was being used annually by approximately 6,300 scuba divers (most of them making several dives on the reefs during their visit) and 3,600 yachts. The biomass of some fish species had tripled. Also outside the non-fishing zones the fish biomass seemed to have increased—fishermen said their catches in these zones had increased. Mooring buoys were benefiting the conservation of the coral communities. The threats to the reef habitat had recently included sediment runoff and coral bleaching,

The user fees for divers being applied in August 1999 were the following:

Annual Marine Reserve Dive Fee: US$ 12

Daily Marine Reserve Dive Fee: US$ 4

The fees for using the yacht mooring buoys (Coral Conservation Fees) are as follows:

Length of vessel	Up to 2 days stay	2 days to 1 week stay
Up to 35 feet	US$ 10	US$ 15
35 to 65 feet	US$ 15	US$ 20
More than 65 feet	US$ 20	US$ 25

Lessons Learned

Key factors behind the successful establishment and continuing existence of the SMMA are:

1. There was a local awareness of the importance of the venture when the development work began. The roots for the development had come into existence before any foreign support and the need to do something about the resource use conflicts had been understood by the Soufriere community. Some of these people were local key individuals, with good contacts. Their strong personal commitment towards the success of the venture was decisive.

2. During the final preparatory stages of the SMMA, before 1994, the three agencies which got together (the Department of Fisheries, the SRDF and CANARI) had the right mix of skills in both the technical issues and those characterizing a developing society. They understood what was necessary for coral reef conservation, successful marine park operation, sustainability of tourism revenues, the future of local fisheries and, in general, for people at the subsistence level. Also seeing the local tourism business as a development partner to the government institutions was important for the success.

3. In the conflict resolution process the technically less competent and less powerful parties received assistance. Thus, it has been easier to them to respect the agreements reached than it would have been if they had not been able to get technical support. The assistance includes facilitation of access to offshore fishing grounds to the fishermen, who may fish on the reef less than in the past. Loans which allow the purchase of suitable vessels, outboard engines and deep-water fishing gear are available. When means of livelihood are taken away from a person, a good rule is to offer compensation. This rule is being followed by SMMA.

4. The pragmatic, human-centered approach in the work has contributed to success. If a complete biological resource inventory had been done first, the momentum for the MPA development could have been lost. Direct application of scientific justification as a basis for zoning might not have been realistic in the public consultations, in which zoning was mostly a way to settle the existing resource use conflicts. Related to this, it was stressed by the lead agencies that there was a need to respect the existing uses. When there was need for intervention, the aim was to interfere as little as possible. Also in this way the setting up of the SMMA was development with a human face. Balancing the ecological values with the human needs has been left as a task for the future. Perhaps luckily, the ecologically most diverse coral communities were also the most popular diving sites and many of them were included in the marine reserve zones during the original zoning.

5. The SMMA programme was designed as a self-funding operation. (reaching this target during its second year of operation.) This could be presented to the

government as a no-cost operation (Figure III-10). Because the benefits from the protection were understood by the decision-makers, they could even see the possibilities for additional income from the protection. In 1999, the Government is actually funding the infrastructure of another similar MPA operation, encouraged by the positive SMMA experiences.

FIGURE III-10.

Ranger collects mooring fee at Soufriere MPA.

6. The government let an independent entity (initially an NGO) administer the management. As an independent operator needs revenues from the operation, it is dependent on the quality of the operation to keep the paying customers satisfied. Thus the SMMA has had an incentive to do the management well and keep the marine resources in a good condition. Related to this, the government agreed that the income from the operation would be deposited on a separate bank account and could be channeled back to the operation directly. Thus, those in charge of the SMMA can count on managing the funds they have received and are also able to plan the future financially.

7. As foreign development financing helped start the operation, there was less financial pressure to cover all the costs when the programme was still at its initial stages and technical problems with buoys, signs and boats required attention. In other similar MPA situations a core deposit to a management fund by the financing agency could provide financial stability at the beginning of a programme.

8. The importance of an educational and friendly approach was stressed in the enforcement at the beginning. This helped the marine park operation get a good start.

9. As the geographic area is limited in scope, population and activities, it has been fairly easy for those involved to understand the problems, opportunities and compromises, because most of the people are familiar with the whole area and personally know many of the other actors. Although there have been communication problems in the programme, communication in a small-scale operation is more simple than in a bigger one. "Small is beautiful" has been true in this case, which may serve as an example of integrated coastal management at an easily manageable scale.

10. Although established structures for review and revision were originally lacking, the SMMA management has managed to be adaptive. A current restructuring of the SMMA shows that in spite of the problems, feedback has been successfully channeled back to the operation. Without this the programme could have collapsed during the years 1996 and 1997.

References

George, Sarah (1994): Coastal Conflict Resolution: A Case Study of Soufriere, Saint Lucia. A report provided by Sarah George, Department of Fisheries, Castries, St. Lucia. 10 pp. and two appendices.

Renard, Yves (1994): Soufriere Marine Management Area. Soufriere Regional Development Foundation. 25 pp.

Renard, Yves (1998): The New SMMA. A report provided by the SMMA. Soufriere, St.Lucia. 2 pp.

SMMA (1998): Conflict Resolution and Participatory Planning: The Case of Soufriere Marine Management Area. A report provided by the Soufriere Marine Management Area, Soufriere, St.Lucia. 16 pp.

Soufriere Regional Development Foundation (1994): Agreement on the Use and Management of Marine and Coastal Resources in the Soufriere Region, St.Lucia. Soufriere, St.Lucia. 25 pp.

Soufriere Regional Development Foundation (1994): Management Plan for the Soufriere Marine Management Area. Soufriere, St.Lucia. 9 pp. and eight appendices.

Soufriere Regional Development Foundation (1995): Soufriere Marine Management Area. A brochure of the SMMA. Soufriere, St. Lucia.

Wulf, K. (1999): Personal communication by Mr. Kai Wulf, the Manager of the SMMA.

Source: Erkki Siirila, WWF Technical Advisor in the USAID-financed Environment and Coastal Resources (ENCORE) Project in St. Lucia in 1994-1996.

E-Mail Contact: erkki.siirila@vyh.fi

12. Montego Bay, Jamaica: A Marine Park Under NGO Management

Environmental challenges

Montego Bay is one of the Caribbean's leading tourist centers (Taylor, 1993) and, largely as a result of this, has one of the most threatened near-shore coral reef ecosystems in the region (Hughes, 1994; Jameson *et al.*, 1995; Jameson and Williams, 1999). Montego Bay Marine Park (the Park) is a mosaic of marine communities that includes seagrass beds, mangrove islands, beaches, and had some of Jamaica's best coral reefs. The land is joined to the ocean through rivers, wetlands, and coastal watersheds. Jamaicans have benefited in the past from this ecosystem through the provision of fishes, conch and lobster. Montego Bay can be recalled as a scenic coastline with beautiful beaches, near-shore reefs, freshwater wetlands, and mangrove islands. Through tourism, the Park is the focal point of the economic and social health of Montego Bay and its environs.

In Montego Bay, significant changes in land use and hydrology have been occurring for the past 500 years. Several events in the coastal ecosystem most likely had the largest impacts on marine communities:

- The development of the Freeport and Seawind Island resort area by the filling in of mangrove forests and islands in 1967 and the reclamation of the entire waterfront area in the mid-1970s;

- The change in drainage patterns and nutrient loading of coastal rivers and estuaries associated with a growing human population and inadequate infrastructure;

- The bulkheading of coastlines, loss of coastal vegetation, and changes in the quality of storm-water runoff; and,

- Natural impacts such as Hurricane Allen in 1980, Hurricane Gilbert in 1988 and the sea urchin (*Diadema antillarum*) die-off in 1983-84.

Two watersheds drain into the Park—Great River and Montego River (Figure III-11). These carry the inland pollutants to the Park waters. Coastal mangroves, other wetland areas, and seagrass beds that provide breeding, feeding and nursery grounds

FIGURE III-11.

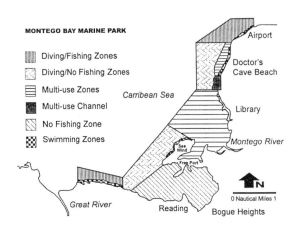

MONTEGO BAY MARINE PARK

- Diving/Fishing Zones
- Diving/No Fishing Zones
- Multi-use Zones
- Multi-use Channel
- No Fishing Zone
- Swimming Zones

Carribean Sea

Airport
Doctor's
Cave Beach
Library
Montego River
Sea Wind
Free Port
Great River
Reading
Bogue Heights

0 Nautical Miles 1

N

Proposed zoning plan for the Montego Bay Marine Park.

for fish and shrimp, are being destroyed. Harbors and near-shore water bodies have become polluted from raw sewage discharges into the Montego River (approximately 4.0 million gallons per day over the last 10 years from the hitherto dysfunctional sewage treatment plant). This water pollution (nutrient enrichment), combined with house-hold waste, associated leaching, and sedimentation, has been especially devastating to the near-shore coral reef ecosystem (Berger, 1997; Hitchman, 1997). Oil pollution and runoff of agricultural fertilizers and pesticides continually add to the problems. Once luxuriant near-shore coral reefs are now smothered by macrophytic algae and struggling for survival (Sullivan and Chiappone, 1994). Impacts from wind blown dust and illegal sand removal are causing loss of aesthetic value and failure in the rehabilitation of coastal areas.

The Montego Bay Marine Park Trust (MBMPT), charged with conserving this valuable national resource, is now faced with a long-term and expensive restoration project.

New NGO management

On September 20, 1996 a bold experiment was undertaken when the Jamaican Natural Resources Conservation Authority (NRCA) delegated management for the Park to the MBMPT (a Non-Governmental Organization or NGO) under an innovative co-management policy adopted for Jamaica's National Parks and Protected Area System (Jameson and Williams, 1999). The MBMPT embarked on an accelerated management programme for increased effectiveness. The Park headquarters was moved to Pier 1 for easy boat and operational access and start-up funds from USAID were used to purchase new enforcement boats and office equipment, install mooring buoys and develop fund raising material. The park is presently staffed by a Park Director, Chief Ranger, Science Officer, Community Relations Officer, Administrative Assistant, Receptionist and four Rangers.

A Five Year Management Plan for the expansion of the ongoing Science, Public Education and Enforcement Programmes and a business plan which outlined costs for equipment and personnel requirements were prepared. This nation-wide experiment in public-private management of national marine Parks is starting to show signs of fruit in Montego Bay (Huber and Jameson, 1999a). However, since NGO management, government funding by the NRCA for the Park has been reduced by 50% over each of the last 3 years (1997/US$65K, 1998/US$36K, 1999/US$11K). This is putting pressure on the Park to focus its limited resources on fund-raising at the expense of other Park programmes. In 1998 other sources of income included $US180K from grants and the National Parks Trust Fund (primarily for staff salaries), $US184K from USAID (primarily for hardware and consultants, only $US15K for salaries), $US21K from donations and gift shop sales, and $US21K from in-kind contributions. The collection of voluntary user fees (i.e., not government imposed or regulated) from park commercial operators will be the next phase of the revenue generation programme.

Local needs for management

Local needs for management are identified and addressed through ReefFix (Jameson and Williams, 1999), a specially designed watershed management and coral reef restoration programme designed to implement the International Coral Reef Initiative (ICRI) Framework for Action in the Tropical Americas (Woodley, 1995). ReefFix is also the implementation phase of the COral reef COasts in MOntego Bay (COCOMO) integrated coastal zone management decision support modeling programme (Huber and Jameson, 1999b). Improving water quality is the top management priority for the Park and COCOMO shows that a distant sewage outfall is the least-cost solution (Gustavson, 1999).

Unfortunately, the new Montego Bay sewage treatment plant, that will soon go on-line, will discharge nutrient rich secondary treated effluent into the Park. Park leadership is working to convince government officials of the need for an outfall beyond the reef for this effluent or to cycle it through artificial wetlands for nutrient removal before discharging it into the Park. Restoring fish and sea urchin populations are also important objectives. To accomplish this a new Park zoning plan has been designed (see Figure III-11) and alternative income programmes for fishermen as well as fish restoration programmes have been created and are awaiting funding. Other ongoing and upcoming Park "soft interventions" to address local needs for management, as well as interventions involving public-private partnerships to prevent and manage water pollution are outlined in Jameson and Williams (1999) and Huber and Jameson (1999a) respectively.

Caught in the Poverty Cycle

Implementing the necessary management measures to ensure a healthy coral reef ecosystem will not be quick or easy. In about five years, 60% of the population in Jamaica will reside in urban areas, such as Montego Bay, and a third will be located in informal settlements not served by adequate household waste disposal. Only 25% of the country's households are connected to sewer systems, and even where such connections exist, wastewater treatment is inadequate. The lack of a comprehensive waste management policy and clear lines of government responsibility delay implementation of effective waste management (Huber and Jameson, 1999a).

Taking all factors together, tourism is the largest economic engine in Jamaica today. In 1992, Jamaica received US$1,009M in foreign exchange earnings (Johnson, 1998). Government direct revenues from tourism for 1992 were US$89.87M against expenditures of US$58.57M. Tourism depends on the quality of the natural environment and, at the same time, can support its protection. However, in Montego Bay, tourism does impact itself, as well as local residents and water quality (Taylor, 1993).

While Montego Bay has the potential to create vast wealth and has had a measurable degree of success to date, little of this wealth has filtered down to the residents. All-inclusive hotels generate the largest amount of revenue but their impact on the economy is smaller per dollar of revenue than other accommodation subsectors (OAS, 1994). For 1997 in Jamaica, Johnson (1998) estimates that the all-inclusive hotels attracted about 40% of all stopover visitors and captured about 60% of the total accommodation revenues. Unfortunately, only about 23% of this revenue stays in Jamaica (Johnson, 1998). The trend towards the all-inclusive concept is increasing. Over recent years, this has led to poor earnings by local restaurants, sidewalk vendors, and shops. The non-all-inclusive accommodations import less and employ more people per dollar of revenue than the all-inclusives (OAS, 1994). For the entire tourism industry in 1997, the percentage of revenue remaining in Jamaica is about 43% (Johnson, 1998).

The hotel industry should be a sector where linkages between economic development and environmental protection can enhance the wellbeing of the local community and maintain options for present and future generations. Unfortunately this is not the case, and living conditions in Montego Bay are eroding. Over one-third of Jamaicans live below the poverty line and many survive on remittances from 4.8 million Jamaicans living abroad. People flock to the tourist centers for jobs. However, upon arrival, they find there is no affordable housing provided at these locations and therefore, informal settlements are expanding. Visitor harassment is increasing as more people move from the countryside to tourism centers without jobs. The adult and juvenile crime rate is high and illegal spearfishing (mainly for subsistence) has helped to remove all breeding size fish from snorkel depth waters in the Park.

Funding from the Government of Jamaica is totally inadequate to restore marine life. Gustavson (1998) estimates that the Marine Park is worth US$489M per annum to the economy (US$420M for tourism, US$4.75M for fisheries, and US$65M for waterfront land storm protection) but government only contributed US$11K in 1999 to the Marine Park budget. Government funds are scarce when 56% of GNP goes to pay off IMF and other foreign debts incurred as a result of the 1973 OPEC crisis. Therefore, unless the tourism sector becomes more proactive and puts money into the environment, the Montego Bay Marine Park Trust will have to go overseas or directly to the 1.2 million annual visitors for help. Population growth, without providing adequate housing and water, waste management, roads, schools and other services is resulting in a vicious cycle of poverty related environmental degradation. It is likely that human impacts will continue to prolong the recovery period of coral reef communities.

Recently, the economic environment has worsened. Inflation is down and interest rates are falling but bankruptcies are up, so is emigration. Banks are repossessing small hotels and other businesses. Two of the five independent dive shops closed recently.

Breaking the cycle

Early park management was by central government and the style was classical based on: science knows best, science informs regulations, regulations will be imposed, education will teach the children. But in a society with low education, high unemployment and little discipline, the result has been: low awareness, low compliance, public ignorance, apathy, criticism and some well informed students. The Marine Park was seen as a discrete scientific and/or regulatory body that people did not understand and did not pay much attention to except to think that the marine park would stop fishing and clean up everybody else's waste. Staff were becoming demoralized and defensive. In terms of economics, what rent was being captured was going to the private sector or the public purse and while everyone claimed to be supportive, the support was moral rather than financial. The park depended on government for funds but the environment was always low on the list of national priorities which had more pressing needs such as education, poverty, unemployment, and child welfare.

The Trust had been delegated management responsibility just over a year before this situation, so the timing of a rapid socioeconomic assessment of primary user groups (Bunce and Gustavson, 1998) was most helpful in informing a new management plan, guiding policy and shifting management style. We knew there were problems but this assessment, although "rapid" and subject to debate and further validation, provided useful feedback from users. What we learned from this study fell into two main categories; how the user groups felt about the park and the economic value of the park to them.

Awareness amongst some user groups was lower than we thought and reflected need for much more information, not just in the formal school system but to user groups and the general public. Opinions varied along a spectrum ranging from unaware to apathetic to critical to confrontational.

The fishermen were defensive towards park enforcement personnel. We responded by becoming less authoritarian, listening more to their problems and concerns about being singled out as the main problem when land-based pollutants are not being addressed. Park management is now offering practical assistance in addressing their particular issues and needs and assisting them with advocacy.

Watersports operators were supportive of park objectives but critical of enforcement efforts and wanted to become more involved in monitoring and also wanted mooring buoys installed.

Tourism players were generally supportive but critical of enforcement efforts to date. They also wanted more information for staff and guests who were largely ignorant of park regulations.

Five guiding principles emerged which were implemented (Jameson and Williams, 1999).

1. Increasing user awareness

2. Promotion of conservation benefits

3. Increasing user involvement

4. Promotion of the "community resource" concept, and

5. Improving intersectoral coordination

The data from the economic assessment (Gustavson, 1998) gave management a good picture of the financial value of the park to primary user groups which was useful in designing implementation of a user fee system to be promulgated by government. The impressive figures added drama to public presentations in showing the importance of the park. These figures were also useful to justify budget requirements to government which made an impression, even though national budget constraints prohibited adequate assistance. The data also suggested areas with potential for generating revenue through the other user groups as opposed to fees on direct use, such as hotels, beach fees and mooring buoy fees.

Park management attitude adjustment

Park management realized that a major attitude adjustment was necessary. If problems are manmade, solutions must be too. If solutions require change in behavior, then the motivations that govern behavior must be understood. Behavior is basically driven by the two opposing forces of reward and punishment. Traditionally, punishment has been used with less and less success. It's time to try incentives. Maslow (1954, 1968) defined a series of universal needs/incentives that drive the human spirit in an ascending hierarchy but you have to start at the bottom and work up. So while universal, people (whether as individuals or in groups as nations) will be at different stages depending on their education and economic situation. Therefore, it is necessary to observe, assess and listen to what makes user groups tick before making decisions, and also consider the conflicting perceptions and needs of different groups, so advocacy and negotiation between groups becomes important to success. The attitude adjustment had to start on the part of management itself.

Management style is now based on a multi-disciplinary team approach where science recommends management interventions and monitors results; regulations must be justifiable and promoted to all concerned to achieve compliance rather than enforcement; education goes on the road and takes the message to the primary user groups, community at large and the general public. Regular interaction with user groups was strengthened on issues such as the system of permits to collect data to inform carrying capacity and collect fees. Outreach efforts show the Marine Park as a repository of useful information for the community; it is a conduit for information from abroad, from central government and local government agencies and it provides feedback from the community level to those agencies.

We must promote the importance of a healthy Park using all available tools such as the internet, mass media and community associations to improve public awareness and change behavior. In terms of economics, we can now demonstrate that the marine environment supports the economy with figures to prove it. We can show the Park as of primary importance to the economic health and welfare of the entire community and change the perception that park management is a hindrance to development and oppressive to fishers.

Now we can begin the real work to involve all sectors in understanding, taking ownership responsibility and moving away from the tragedy of the commons towards equitable use of resources. Only then will we have sustainable resource management and start to attack the cycle of poverty.

Conclusion: We're all in the same boat

The local communities are the principal force behind the need for reef conservation, standing to benefit considerably by protection, but also being the principal cause of reef loss. Notwithstanding these threats, the natural areas in Montego Bay remain in sufficient condition that, if properly managed and rehabilitated, they will provide substantial opportunities for economic growth, poverty alleviation, and the maintenance of globally important biodiversity.

However, given the economic tradeoffs and local awareness of environmental issues, coral reef ecosystem preservation and associated water quality is presently seen as a luxury. Until public relations and education efforts take root and *informed government policies and programmes* dealing with pollution and poverty issues are enacted, coral reef managers are caught in a downward spiral of poverty that could defeat them. In any case, resource managers must demonstrate short-term economic benefits from conservation. Long-term payoffs mean nothing in an economy where subsistence is of primary concern.

References

Berger, L. 1997. Montego Bay environmental monitoring programme. USAID, Kingston, Jamaica.

Bunce. L.L. and KR Gustavson. 1998. Coral Reef Valuation: Rapid socioeconomic assessment of fishing, watersports, and hotel operations in the Montego Bay Marine Park, Jamaica and an analysis of reef management implications. World Bank Research Committee Project #RPO 681-05 report, LAC Unit, World Bank, Washington DC, 83 pp.

Gustavson, K.R. 1998. Values associated with the local use of the Montego Bay Marine Park, Marine system valuation: An application to coral reefs in the developing tropics. World Bank Research Committee Project #RPO 681-05, Washington, DC.

Gustavson, K.R.(ed). 1999. Decision Support Modelling for the Integrated Coastal Zone Management of Coral Reefs in the Developing Tropics. Washington, DC: The World Bank..

Hitchman, N.D.S. 1997. Eutrophication: The death angel covering coral reefs in Montego Bay, Jamaica. B.A. Honors Thesis, Environmental Science and Public Policy, Harvard-Radcliffe Colleges, Cambridge, MA

Huber, R. M. and S.C. Jameson. 1999a. Montego Bay, Jamaica: A case study in public-private partnerships for pollution prevention and management of a valuable coral reef ecosystem. Tropical Coasts 5(6) and 6(1):22-27, Manila, Philippines.

Huber R. M. and S.C. Jameson 1999b. Integrated coastal zone management in the Tropical Americas and the role of decision support models. In: Gustavson, K.R. (ed.) Decision support modelling for the integrated coastal zone of coral reefs in the developing tropics. TheWorld Bank, Washington, DC.

Hughes, T.P. 1994. Catastrophes, phase-shifts, and large-scale degradation of a Caribbean coral reef. Science 265:1547-1551.

Jameson, S.C., McManus, J.W. and M.D. Spalding. 1995. State of the Reefs: Regional and Global Perspectives. International Coral Reef Initiative, US Dept of State, Washington, D.C.

Jameson, S.C. and J.H. Williams. 1999. Local needs and interventions for management of coral reefs in the developing Tropical Americas—the Montego Bay Marine Park Case Study. In: Gustavson, K.R. (ed.). Decision Support Modelling for the Integrated Coastal Zone Management of Coral Reefs in the Developing Tropics. The World Bank, Washington, D.C.

Johnson, J. 1998. Tourism in Jamaica: An economic analysis of 1997. Prepared for the Jamaica Tourist Board, Pacific Analysis Inc., Victoria, BC, Canada.

Maslow, A.H. 1954. Motivation and Personality. 2d ed., Harper & Row, New York.

Maslow, A.H. 1968. Toward A Psychology of Being. D. Van Nostrand, New York.

OAS. 1994. Economic analysis of tourism in Jamaica. Tech Rept. of the OAS National Programme of Technical Cooperation with the Jamaica Tourist Board and the Ministry of Industry, Tourism and Commerce, Department of Regional Development and Environment Executive Secretariat, Organization of American States, Washington, D.C.

Sullivan, K.M. and M. Chiappone. 1994. Rapid ecological assessment of the Montego Bay Marine Park. The Nature Conservancy Arlington, VA, 86 pp.

Taylor, F.F. 1993. To hell with paradise: A history of the Jamaican tourist industry. University of Pittsburgh Press, Pittsburgh, PA.

Woodley JD (1995) Tropical Americas regional report on the issues and activities associate with coral reefs and associated ecosystems. International Coral Reef Initiative Regional Report, Centre for Marine Sciences, Univ. of West Indies, Kingston, Jamaica, 64 pp.

Sources: Stephen C. Jameson, Coral Seas Inc—Integrated Coastal Zone Management, 4254 Hungry Run Road, The Plains, VA 20198-1715 and Jill H. Williams, Executive Director, Montego Bay Marine Park Trust, Pier 1, Howard Cooke Blvd., Montego Bay, Jamaica.

E-Mail Contact: sjameson@coralseas.com and jill@n5.com.jm

13. Ngeruangel Atoll in Palau, Micronesia: Community Management

Marine protected areas in Palau

The Republic of Palau in western Micronesia has a long history of marine protected areas. The Ngerukewid Islands Wildlife Preserve, established under the US-administered Trust Territory government in 1956, is one of the oldest formal marine protected areas in the region. The nation of Palau, however, has had a somewhat tortuous history of administration during the last century, having put in place, after a succession of colonial governments, its constitutional government only in 1981. Until 1994 Palau was part of the UN-mandated and US-administrated Trust Territory of the Pacific Islands, created at the close of World War II; US control was mostly severed in 1994 when Palau became an independent nation in "free association" with the US.

Palau's policies and laws with regard to the use and conservation of marine resources are accordingly very young and undergoing rapid evolution. Until 1994, for example, the management of marine resources, including management of its marine protected areas, was primarily undertaken by the national government. But in the last five years a dramatic upsurge in the exercise of authority at the community level has occurred, by both the local state governments and by traditional authorities (see Graham and Idechong, 1998). Since 1994, five new marine protected areas and one terrestrial area have been established, all at the community level, and most with only minimal support from the national government. One of these was Ngeruangel Reserve, the focus of this case study.

The main Palau archipelago is quite varied geologically and ecologically. It includes a large, weathered volcanic island with developed fringing reefs and estuaries, a large lagoon to the south mostly enclosed by barrier reefs and containing hundreds of uplifted limestone islands world-renowned as the "Rock Islands," and two larger uplifted limestone islands to the south. The country also includes a scattered group of six low limestone islands several hundred miles to the southwest of the main archipelago. Ngeruangel is an uninhabited atoll of about 17 km² at the extreme northern end of the Palau archipelago (Figure III-12). It is part of Kayangel State, which includes the inhabited atoll of Kayangel and portions of a complex of reefs to the south. Kayangel has a resident community of about 180 people and is one of Palau's 16 states. With the exception of Koror, Palau's urban center, the states have small populations, typically only a few hundred people each, and a high degree and long history of social cohesiveness. In Palau, "states" and "communities" are essentially synonymous.

FIGURE III-12.

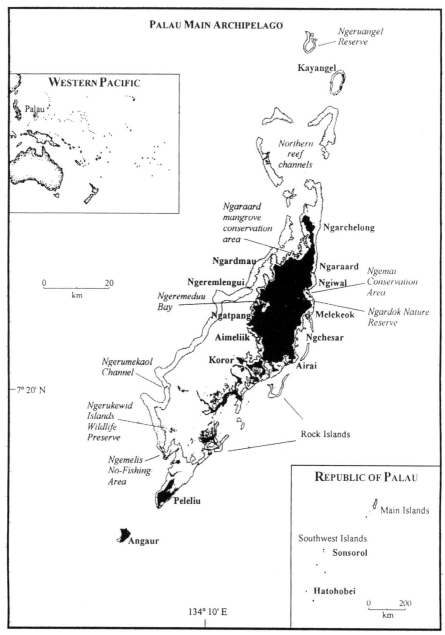

The island nation of Palau, its 16 states (in bold), and its protected areas (in italics). Ngeruangel is in the extreme north.

Establishment of Ngeruangel Reserve

In 1996 the chiefly leadership of Kayangel exercised its age-old tradition of declaring *bul* (taboo or closure) over the entirety of Ngeruangel atoll. The *bul* on Ngeruangel was one of the boldest assertions of traditional authority in many years, and certainly so with regard to marine resources. (The traditional leaders of Palau never stopped exercising their authority, even though during Palau's several colonial administrations, such power had diminished greatly.)

The reasons for the *bul* were several. First, the community had become alarmed about the depletion of the resources of the area, particularly its reef fish, which were important for both subsistence and commercial purposes. A second, and perhaps more important, reason for the closure was that the community perceived it was losing control of the atoll and its resources to fishermen from other parts of Palau, particularly from the urban center of Koror. The remoteness of Ngeruangel and Palau's other northern reefs resulted in fish resources that were abundant relative to those of most of the main Palau archipelago. These areas became increasingly attractive as fishing grounds to fishermen throughout the archipelago, particularly to commercial and recreational fishermen with fast and large boats, of which Palau saw a dramatic increase during the 1980s and 1990s as its economy grew. Ngeruangel is also attractive to sea turtle and seabird hunters. It has substantial seagrass feeding grounds and its rubble-and-sand islet provides one of Palau's most important nesting sites for the green sea turtle (*Chelonia mydas*), as well as for several species of seabirds. A third control-related concern for Kayangel's chiefs was that traditionally, fishing at Ngeruangel was done by communal groups. But with fishermen becoming increasingly independent, more fishing was being conducted individually and not under the control of the chiefs.

The degree of compliance with the *bul* was unclear. Kayangel residents probably respected the *bul*, but outside fishermen would be less compliant and also more difficult to apprehend. Moreover, they may have been politically difficult to censure, given the limited and localized authority of traditional leaders. In any case, the Kayangel chiefs requested that the local state government reinforce their *bul* with a state law, and the state did so in December, 1996. Under the law, Ngeruangel was closed to entry for three years, until December 1999, when use of the reserve would be controlled by a management plan, currently in preparation.

Partnerships

At the same time that concerns regarding Ngeruangel were growing in the Kayangel community, the national government, in partnership with the international non-governmental organization, The Nature Conservancy (TNC), was undertaking a project aimed at developing a tourist-based inshore sportfishing industry in Palau. The project was centered at Palau's northern reefs, where reef fish were most abundant. The aims of the project were to: 1) spread some of the benefits from Palau's growing tourism industry to some of its outlying communities, such as Kayangel, and 2) provide an alternative occupation as fishing guides, to local commercial fishermen, with the idea that less fish would be extracted from the reef, lessening the threats associated with overfishing (Division of Marine Resources, 1996).

The community of Kayangel became involved in the sportfishing project. The prospect of developing sportfishing in Kayangel's waters, and the recognized need to both control the activity and to ensure the continued provision of productive fishing grounds, meshed with community concerns over Ngeruangel. It provided some of the impetus needed for the chiefs to declare the *bul* and it provided an opportunity for the community to address a range of ongoing concerns.

With the sportfishing project now under the lead of the Palau Conservation Society (PCS), Ngeruangel became the focus and sportfishing became one of the underlying factors in the development of the management plan for Ngeruangel. The plan is being prepared by the state with assistance from TNC and PCS and will be implemented at the end of 1999. It will likely keep the atoll off-limits to fishing except catch-and-release sportfishing, harvesting of trochus, and probably some level of fishing for limited purposes, such as specified community events.

Effectiveness of the reserve

After almost three years of closure, it is difficult to know how well Ngeruangel has met the community's objectives of seeing the recovery of depleted fishes and the exclusion of outside fishermen. So far, the perception in the community is very favorable. There also appears to be more agreement within the community now, compared to three years ago, that the closure and reserve are good ideas and beneficial to Kayangel.

Kayangel conservation officers and local leaders are confident that while they have not completely stopped incursions into the reserve, knowledge of the reserve and its restrictions is almost universal throughout Palau and they have reduced fishing effort there substantially.

Systematic, but limited, underwater fish surveys conducted during each of the last three years have not revealed any significant changes in the fish populations. Local fishermen, after performing timed swims in coordination with the systematic surveys, perceived slight but not dramatic increases in the numbers and sizes of some of their preferred species, as well as changes in the behavior of the fish, with the fish becoming much less wary of swimmers. Data from catch-and-release spin-casting trials on the reef revealed an increase in catch rates over a period of three years. But as with the results of the underwater surveys, the limited number of catch data, combined with the many temporal and other factors that affect the location and behavior of fishes, have made it difficult to identify changes in fish abundance or sizes with any confidence.

The objectives of the reserve and monitoring programme have also been confounded by the coral bleaching event of late 1998. The reefs of Ngeruangel were hit very hard, with most areas of the atoll losing more than 50 percent of their hard corals. While there are no obvious impacts of the coral loss on local fish populations, impacts may come in the future as the coral structure breaks down and the composition of the benthos changes.

In spite of the lack of conclusive evidence of any rebound in fish populations in the reserve so far, it is clear that the community, in general, perceives the reserve as being successful with regard to fish stocks. In addition, they have commented favorably on the apparent increase in seabird nesting (seabird nesting has not been part of the monitoring programme). Part of that perception may rest in the belief that the benefits are yet to come, be they from tourism revenues or increased trochus yields. Those perceptions may or may not be realistic. But clearly, part of the perception of success has to do with the fact that the community has regained control over an area and resource that is important to them for a variety of reasons. Apart from any net benefits or costs stemming from the creation and management of the reserve, it has certainly catalyzed a sense of broader resource stewardship within the community. The reserve, although limited to only one atoll, has served to better enclose (in the economic sense) all the marine resources of Kayangel. The benefits of that are likely to be considerable.

The experience of Ngeruangel has also revealed several important constraints and challenges to effective management of the inshore marine resources of Palau. First, because most marine protected areas are being established by local communities, in response to local needs, with little national support or coordination, they are resulting in an *ad hoc* system of protected areas that may not take into account the ecology of the archipelago as well as it might. Working on such small scales, it is difficult to design protected areas to take best advantage of water currents in terms of pollution, sedimentation, and sources and sinks of pelagic larvae. As these initiatives are purely community-driven, there may be relatively little incentive to protect areas that offer valuable ecological benefits for wider areas, such as fish nursery areas and spawning aggregation sites (see Johannes, Case No. 18, this volume). Second, these local-level conservation initiatives suffer from poor economies of scale. Unless a reasonable degree of inter-state cooperation and national support can be achieved, each and every state will have to support the whole of the institutions, personnel, and operations necessary to manage their natural resources. Such a management regime is unlikely to be cost-effective, especially in areas like Ngeruangel where the potential for revenues from tourism and other activities is relatively small.

The recent upsurge in community-driven marine conservation initiatives in Palau attests to there being adequate incentive and means for villages to take conservation action. But it also begs the need for technical, legal, and financial assistance to the communities from the national government, as well as innovative enforcement techniques and better nationwide coordination.

References

Division of Marine Resources (1996). Small-Scale Sustainable Sport Fishery Development for Palau:
Assessment, Strategy, and Consensus-Building. Division of Marine Resources, Republic of Palau.

Graham, T. and N. Idechong (1998). Reconciling customary and constitutional law: managing marine
resources in Palau, Micronesia. *Ocean & Coastal Management*, 40:143-164.

World Bank (draft in prep.) Voices from the Village: A Comparative Study of Coastal Resource
Management in the Pacific Islands. Pacific Islands Discussion Paper Series Number 9, East Asia
and Pacific Region, Papua New Guinea and Pacific Islands Country Management Unit, World
Bank, Washington D.C.

Source: Tom R. Graham and Noah T. Idechong, Palau Conservation Society, P.O. Box
1811, Koror, PW 96940, Palau, and Andrew J. Smith, Coastal & Marine Programme,
Asia-Pacific Region, The Nature Conservancy, P.O. Box 1738,Koror, PW 96940, Palau.

E-Mail Contacts: pcs@palaunet.com and asmith_tnc@csi.com

14. Ras Mohammed National Park, Egypt: A Comprehensive Approach

The coral reefs of the Southern coast of Sinai in Egypt are recognized as one of the most popular and spectacular areas for SCUBA diving. In 1983, the peninsula of Ras Mohammed (both the land and the surrounding coral reefs) at the southern tip of Sinai was recognized by the Egyptian Government as a Marine Protected Area (MPA). A few years later, the rapidly encroaching tourism led the Egyptian government to request a study in order to determine the feasibility of, and the technical assistance for, the development of an upgraded National Park.

Establishment

The recommendations of the feasibility study led to the upgrading of the Marine Protected Area to a National Park (NP; IUCN Category II), thereby adding a terrestrial component to the protected area, increasing its area from 97 km^2 to 233 km^2, the establishment of a coastal zone management plan and a monitoring programme to evaluate and modify management measures (Pearson, 1988). Subsequently, technical assistance from the European Union (EU) led to the establishment of an initial development phase which provided essential equipment, recruited and trained local staff and introduced a basic monitoring programme. One of the objectives of the management in place at Ras Mohammed was to show that all development in the area was resource dependent and that the degradation of coral reefs and other marine ecosystems would limit the area's economic potential.

In 1992, access was limited and no development allowed within the designated Park boundaries. The Nabq and Ras Abu Galum Multiple Use Managed Areas, in which traditional grazing and fishing by Bedouins is permitted but no development allowed, consists of 1951 km^2 of marine and terrestrial habitats. More recently (1998), the Protected Areas Network has been further extended to include both the central mountainous area of southern Sinai (St Katherine Protectorate), the Taba Natural Monument and the remaining coastal waters of the Gulf of Aqaba as far as the border at Taba. The Southern Sinai Protectorates Network, as the protected areas system is now referred to, presently consists of 9,736 km^2 of linked marine and terrestrial habitats, covering 43 percent of the 260 km of Egypt's littoral zone on the Gulf of Aqaba

(Figure III-13), has its offices in Sharm El Sheikh and is administered by the
Protectorates Division of the Egyptian Environmental Affairs Agency (EEAA).

FIGURE III-13.

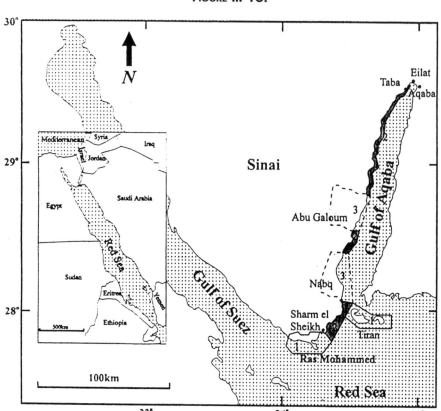

The Sinai Peninsula and its protected areas. The first areas to be given protection were (1) the Ras Mohammed
peninsula and the reefs and islands of the Tiran Straits, subsequently (2) coastal waters north from Sharm el Sheikh
up to extreme high water were included within the National Park. Later (3) two further terrestrial areas were
protected from development, at Nabq and at Abu Galum. Most recently (1996), the coastal waters north to Taba
have also been accorded National Park status.

Tourism Development

The period since the establishment of the Park has seen a remarkable growth in coastal
and reef-related tourism to the area. Whereas in 1988 there were 5 international hotels
using 5 dive centers serviced by 23 dive boats to cater for ca. 20,000 visitors, the numbers
of visitors and facilities in 1998 included >40 international hotels, 32 dive centers,
240 dive boats, 690,337 visitors (1996) and 16,564 beds (data from National Parks of
Egypt, Governorate of South Sinai and Ormond et al., 1997). To put these figures into
perspective, for example, with approximately 20% of visitors carrying out an estimated
1.5 million dives per year, the area has become one of the most dived tourist resorts
in the world (Medio et al., 1997).

Achievements: Management, Scientific Investigations and Partnerships

Management objectives favoring the development of the Southern Sinai Protectorates have been directed to respond to, and mitigate, the consequences of rapid development of a tourism-based economy in the Southern Sinai. Although such coastal development has been typically expected to have both direct and indirect effects on the health of marine resources, particularly coral reefs, due to increased sediment load arising from nearby dredging and coastal engineering and eutrophication from discharge of untreated sewage, in the Southern Sinai Protectorates many of these threats have been largely controlled by the thorough application of existing legislation (Medio, 1995; Pearson and Shehata, 1998). These controls have lead to the following results:

- infilling and the discharge of any effluents at sea have been prohibited and their implementation successfully enforced since initial protection status in 1983; this has resulted in the successful conservation of the area's marine and coastal resources, especially its coral reefs (Pearson and Shehata, 1998);

- cross-reef walkways and floating pontoons have been introduced to reduce damage from swimmers and divers crossing the fringing reef (Ormond *et al.*, 1997);

- a monitoring programme was initiated early on to assess the effectiveness of management measures in place (Medio, 1996);

- public awareness and diver training programmes have proved effective in limiting damage to reefs (Medio *et al.*, 1997);

- mandatory EIAs for all developments have been successfully enforced (Pearson and Shehata, 1998);

- continuous assessment and management of commercial and artisanal fisheries has been introduced (Pearson and Shehata, 1998);

- continuous and on-going scientific investigations with the assistance of the Great Barrier Reef Marine Park Authority and numerous European universities have provided rigorous data on key ecological issues including natural and man-made rates of damage to corals, apparent rates of coral recruitment, and reef community structure providing useful information for the management in place (Medio, 1996; Pearson and Shehata, 1998);

- training programmes for selected staff have involved qualified experts contracted by donor assisted projects (just 6 years after overseas training started, a school for rangers and managers is scheduled to open before the end of 1999, with scheduled sessions with Jordan, Yemen, Saudi Arabia, Djibouti and Oman);

- effective implementation of appropriate environmental standards, both at design and construction stages, and during operation, have been introduced and effectively implemented and enforced in order to prevent reef degradation (Ormond *et al.*, 1997).

Replicability

The Southern Sinai Protectorates have now become a benchmark for protected areas in the region and are now the focus of attention from neighbouring countries. The multiple use managed protected areas have proven to be an effective tool for coherent and consistent management of a coastal zone on the basis of protected area legislation.

The Ras Mohammed example is being used as a model for the sustainable management of coastal and marine resources by several neighbouring countries as exemplified by joint training exercises and internationally funded projects (e.g., the Global Environment Facility—GEF) involving several Red Sea countries including, amongst others, Jordan, Yemen, Saudi Arabia, Djibouti and Eritrea.

Further, there are now plans for the declaration of an International Red Sea Marine Park covering 850 kms of coastline from Hurghada on mainland Egypt to Sudan in the south, linked to Ras Mohammed and Taba in the north.

Conclusions and Lessons Learned

The success of the Ras Mohammed Sector is due in part to sound and unwavering government policies and legislation, increased awareness and full participation of the private sector and their determination to preserve the natural resources, on which they depend, along with adequate funding (the project is now in its 10th year of funding from the EU and Government of Egypt) (Pearson and Shehata, 1998; Medio et al., in press). In addition, the collaborative and community based management policies implemented throughout the 10 year project have shown that involving as many elements of the community as possible leads to a more widespread appreciation of the resource. Hence, having recognized the link between reef conservation and economic development, the management plan in place within the Sector has demonstrated how:

- resource-based tourism is limited by the health of the resource itself and its degradation would inevitably lead to decreased economic potential and rapid depreciation of existing investments.

- a resource management policy, coupled with strict protection measures, does not imply, and has not acted as, a deterrent to development activities.

- protected areas can be a well-managed common property resource which benefits both tourists, the general public and private investors.

- the high profile afforded by the protection of the resource and its consequent high economic potential is maintained by the protection measures established by the EEAA.

One last hurdle facing the management at Ras Mohammed concerns the fact that operational and management costs of protection in the protected area network are high. The present funding arrangement will, as in any successful project, have to be modified in the near future. The acceptance that all parties benefit from the protection measures established by the EEAA may result in the achievement of economic self-sufficiency through a fee structure to be levied on all users. The recognition that all users benefit from the protection of the resource should lead to the establishment of a mechanism by which the protected area achieves financial stability and ceases to rely on government or donor funding. The management at Ras Mohammed is currently planning to achieve this by opting for a daily charge which should fully cover management, operational and future development costs (Pearson, 1995).

References:

Medio, D. 1995. Sustainable tourism development in the Ras Mohammed National Park, Egypt. In: Swanson TM, Ugalde CF, Luxmoore RA (Eds.) Survey of wildlife management regimes for sustainable utilization. World Conservation Monitoring Center, Cambridge, UK pp. 147-185.

Medio, D. 1996. An investigation into the significance and control of damage by visitors to coral reefs in the Ras Mohammed national Park, Egyptian Red Sea, University of York, England, Ph.D. Thesis, 332 pp.

Medio, D., M.P. Pearson, R.F.G. Omron. 1997. Effect of briefings on rates of damage to corals by SCUBA divers. Biol. Conserv. 1:91-95.

Medio. D., C.R.C. Sheppard, and J. Gascoigne. In press. The Red Sea. In: Coral reefs of the Western Indian Ocean: their status and conservation. C.R.C. Sheppard and T. McClanahan (Eds). pp 231-255, Oxford University Press.

R. F. G. Ormond, O. Hassan, D. Medio, M.P. Pearson and M. Selem. 1997. Effectiveness of coral protection programmes in the Ras Mohammed National Park, Egyptian Red Sea. Proc. 8th Int Coral Reef Symp 2:1931-1936.

Pearson, M. P. 1988. 'Progress report for the Ras Mohammed National Park'. Egyptian Environmental Affairs Agency, Cairo, Egypt.

Pearson, M. P. 1995. Sustainable financing of protected areas in Southern Sinai. In: A. J. Hooten and M.E. Hatziolos (Eds.) Proc. Sustainable financing mechanisms for coral reef conservation. Environmentally Sustainable Development Proceedings Series (9), The World Bank, pp. 91-95.

Pearson, M.P. and A. I. Shehata. 1998. Protectorates management for conservation and development in the Arab Republic of Egypt. Parks (IUCN), pp. 29-35.

Source: David Medio, UNEP/GEF, Nairobi, Kenya.

15. Oman and Saudi Arabia: Different Approaches

The approach and selection procedure for MPAs is described for two nations of the Arabian Peninsula: the Sultanate of Oman and the Kingdom of Saudi Arabia. The approach and selection procedure for the two countries is fairly well documented, and may be of value as a prototype for the selection of marine and coastal protected areas elsewhere in the region.

Sultanate of Oman

In 1986, IUCN completed a study to define a system of protected areas for the Sultanate (IUCN, 1986b). This was the first attempt to formulate a coordinated national nature conservation programme, including the definition of conservation policy, legislation, staffing and administrative needs, and the identification of a number of potential conservation areas. There were 63 proposed protected areas that included a coastal component. Of these, five already had protected status.

A second IUCN project carefully studied each proposed protected area in the coastal sector for which a coastal zone management plan was being prepared. Where necessary, revision to the proposals and zoning details were recommended in the coastal zone management plans (IUCN, 1986a, 1988, 1989, 1990). In addition, management plans were prepared for three of the decreed protected areas (Salm, 1986, 1989).

The Sultanate's five MPAs covered a range of environments, species, objectives and management issues. The Daymaniyat Islands form a remote group of small islands that had minimal conflicts and management issues. They are of global importance for the highly endangered hawksbill turtle population that nests there, have well developed coral reefs, thousands of nesting seabirds, and nesting ospreys and sooty falcons (Salm, 1986).

The Q'urm mangroves lie in the heart of the prime residential area, and the adjacent seashore is heavily used for recreational activities. Considerable care had been taken to avoid endangering the mangrove environment during the course of urban development, particularly of the highway situated immediately inland of the estuary. Khawr Salalah is an important estuary for migrant waterfowl and waders. It too is hemmed in by development, but is fenced and guarded against intrusion.

Ra's al Hadd and Ra's al Junayz have beaches with one of the largest populations of nesting green turtles in the Indian Ocean. These mainland sites were intensively used for both recreation and fisheries. The area was closed to campers in the early 1990s because of excessive disturbance of nesting turtles. This was an area of maximum conflict between conservation objectives and escalating use. A conservation management plan for the two protected areas was formulated (Salm, 1989), and implemented.

Each of the five sites had its intrinsic values and would score high on a combined list of ecological, social, regional and economic criteria. However, *urgency* was the one criterion that determined their priority for designation as protected areas. Each site was under severe threat from development and related activities.

The government's commitment to Coastal Zone Management resulted in a significant contribution to conservation of coastal and marine environments. Coastal Zone Management is a multi-pronged approach which, through a combination of policy, law, protected areas, and issue-specific actions manages the entire coastal zone as a vast "multiple use reserve" (Salm, 1988).

Kingdom of Saudi Arabia

As part of its long term planning, Saudi Arabia's Meteorology and Environmental Protection Administration (MEPA) commissioned an appraisal of natural resources and management requirements for both the Arabian Gulf and Red Sea coasts (Ormond *et al.*, 1984a, b, c; IUCN 1987a, b, c; Price *et al.*, 1987). The studies, in conjunction with earlier initiatives of MEPA, the Environmental Protection Coordination Committee (EPCCOM) and IUCN, identified a total of 11 environmentally sensitive areas (ESAs) plus seven recreational areas in the Gulf. A further 46 ESAs (that included some recreation areas) were identified in the Red Sea. ESAs are areas that merit special protection and management, and are nearly synonymous with "critical habitats" (see Al Gain *et al.*, 1987 and Clark, 1985). These represented potential sites for a system of protected areas (known locally as marine protectorates).

ESAs in the Red Sea were identified primarily on the basis of the unique and valuable resources, or important ecological processes concentrated in them. On the Saudi Arabian Gulf coast, where coastal development was much greater, the selection procedure for ESAs was taken a step further. Information on the location of key natural resources was compared with the location of coastal and marine uses and activities. This identified the main areas of resource use conflict, and hence where site specific management measures were needed most urgently. Other factors were also taken into account (IUCN, 1987a).

This proposed protected area system was more conceptual than specific. Further analysis of the main socioeconomic issues is needed, together with more precise formulation of management objectives. These ESAs then will need to be built into the framework of an overall national Coastal Zone Management programme. Until this happens, it has been recommended that the ESAs receive temporary protected status. The 57 ESAs also need to be studied to determine how they might be combined into larger areas to facilitate management.

References

Al Gain, A., J. Clark, and T. Chiffings. 1987. A coastal management programme for the Saudi Arabian Red Sea coast. *Coastal Zone '87. Proceedings of the Fifth Symposium on Coastal Zone Management.* Amer. Soc. Civ. Eng., New York: 1673-1680.

Clark, J.R. 1985. Recommendations for a Combined Coastal Management and Protected Areas Programme for the Saudi Arabia Red Sea Coast. Summary Report submitted to IUCN by the National Park Service (USA).

IUCN. 1986a. *Oman coastal zone management plan: Greater capital area.* IUCN, Gland, Switzerland: 78 pp.

IUCN. 1986b. *Proposals for a system of nature conservation areas.* IUCN, Gland, Switzerland: 469 pp.

IUCN. 1987a. *Saudi Arabia: An assessment of biotopes and management requirements for the Arabian Gulf.* IUCN, Gland, Switzerland: 250 pp.

IUCN. 1987b. *Saudi Arabia: An assessment of coastal zone management requirements for the Red Sea.* IUCN, Gland, Switzerland: 106 pp.

IUCN. 1987c. *Saudi Arabia: An assessment of national coastal zone management requirements.* MEPA/IUCN report, Gland, Switzerland: 41 pp.

IUCN. 1988. *Oman coastal zone management plan: Quriyat to Ra's al Hadd.* IUCN, Gland, Switzerland: 57 pp.

IUCN. 1989. *Oman coastal zone management plan: Dhofar, Vol. 1. Action Plan.* IUCN, Gland, Switzerland: 37 pp.

IUCN. 1990. *Oman coastal zone management plan: Musandam.* IUCN, Gland, Switzerland: 70 pp.

Ormond, R.F.G., A.R. Dawson Shepherd, A.R.G. Price, and R.J. Pitts. 1984a. *Report on the distribution of habitats and species in the Saudi Arabian Red Sea (Parts 1 & 2).* IUCN, Gland, Switzerland: 247 pp.

Ormond, R.F.G., A.R. Dawson Shepherd, A.R.G. Price, and R.J. Pitts. 1984b. *Distribution of habitats and species along the southern Red Sea coast of Saudi Arabia.* IUCN, Gland, Switzerland.

Ormond, R.F.G., A.R. Dawson Shepherd, A.R.G. Price, and R.J. Pitts. 1984c. *Management of Red Sea coastal resources: Recommendations for protected areas.* IUCN, Gland, Switzerland: 113 pp.

Price, A.R.G., T.W. Chiffings, T.J. Atkinson, and T.J. Wrathall. 1987. Appraisal of resources in the Saudi Arabian Gulf. *Coastal Zone '87. Proceedings of the Fifth Symposium on Coastal Zone Management.* Amer. Soc. Civ. Eng., New York: 1031-1045.

Salm, R.V. 1986. *The proposed Daymaniyat Islands National Nature Reserve management plan.* IUCN Coastal Zone Management Project, Oman: 45 pp.

Salm, R.V. 1988. *Coral reef management planning: Indonesia and Oman.* Paper presented at the Workshop on Innovative Ways of Planning and Managing the Great Barrier Reef Marine Park, 20-22 July 1988, Townsville: 6 pp.

Salm, R.V. 1989. *A proposed management plan for the turtle nesting beaches in the Ra's al Hadd National Scenic Reserve and Ra's al Junayz National Nature Reserve.* IUCN Coastal Zone Management Project. CZMP3:I11: 49 pp.

Source: Rodney V. Salm, The Nature Conservancy, Hawaii, USA.

E-Mail Contact: rsalm@tnc.org

16. Celestun Estuary, Mexico. Training of Nature Guides

Less than ten years ago, Ramiro Lara Castillo was a fisherman at Celestun, a small coastal town with a more than 20 kilometers long estuary located on the northern Gulf Coast of the Yucatan Peninsula, Mexico. He was one of the hundreds of fishermen depending on an unreliable and diminishing resource. Today, he is one of several Nature Guides who take local and international visitors in their own motor boats to see one of the world's most accessible flocks of pink American Flamingos (*Phoenicopterus ruber ruber*), along with many other resident and migrant birds that can be found in the estuary, within the Celestun Biosphere Reserve.

In 1979, the Mexican Federal Government declared 59,130 hectares of pristine coastal ecosystems at Celestun a wildlife refuge, comprising the estuary and its surrounding mangroves, seasonally flooded low tropical forests, savannas, mangrove hummocks (locally called *petenes*) and coastal dunes.

The Celestun estuary is well known as an important flamingo feeding area (Figure III-14), with one of the species' main breeding grounds located at the "Ria Lagartos" estuary, more than 300 kilometers northeast of Celestun, in the central northern coast of the Yucatan Peninsula. Both areas were declared Wildlife Refuges in the same year with the specific objective of protecting the flamingo's principal feeding and nesting habitats in the Yucatecan coastal wetlands.

The government's early conservation policies resulted in the creation of wildlife refuges designed to protect particular species, with little thought paid to the whole system of interactions between people and nature. However, the pace of change was rapid in the mid-1980's as a new generation of conservationists spearheaded the creation of Mexico's first ever Ministry of Ecology: Urban Development and Ecology Secretariat (SEDUE, according to the Spanish acronym). Approximately ten years after the creation of the Celestun Wildlife Refuge, SEDUE launched a Natural Protected Areas System, and the concept of Biosphere Reserves started to have an important role in the proposal of natural protected areas.

FIGURE III-14.

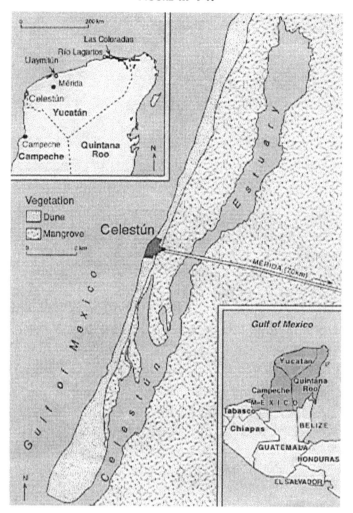

The Celestun MPA protects a rich estuary on the west coast of Yucatan.

After several attempts to change the Celestun Wildlife Refuge status, it recently became a Biosphere Reserve, meaning that Celestun is now recognized not only for the biological value of its American Flamingo populations, but for the diversity of natural resources that can be used by human communities living in the area, with emphasis on sustainable use and conservation.

This process summarized here in a few paragraphs cannot do justice to the efforts of Municipal, State and Federal government offices, research centers, local non-governmental organizations (NGOs), and community members working for the sustainable and diversified management of a protected coastal area. The former SEDUE has evolved and become the Mexican Secretariat for Environment, Natural Resources and Fisheries (SEMARNAP, according to the Spanish acronym). One of SEMARNAP's policies is to work closely with NGOs for the establishment of natural protected area management plans.

A management plan for the Celestun Biosphere Reserve is currently being drawn up at the Pronatura Peninsula de Yucatan offices in Merida. PPY is a local NGO and one of the first conservation organizations in the country. Designed together with the Federal Government, the goal of Celestun's management plan is to provide a variety of productive strategies which range from legalizing traditional subsistence shrimp fisheries based on scientific data about shrimp populations, to promoting nature-based tourism with the training of local guides.

It appears that Celestun has every opportunity to capitalize on the good fortune of having an abundance of natural resources capable of supporting local development. The challenge is to diversify the range of productive activities so that this rich, biodiverse environment can sustain local communities without allowing such human use to threaten the resource base.

Birds and aquatic life in the Celestun estuary, bordered by wide belts of healthy mangrove forest, together with the white sandy beaches of tranquil seas across the coastal dunes, are among the major attractions for visitors from all over the world. Capitalizing on this situation, Ramiro Lara Castillo is one of the ten local boat operators who have been trained as Nature Guides by the RARE Center for Tropical Conservation.

The RARE Center is a North American organization devoted to developing options for community-based and nature-oriented tourism. "Ecotourism" is an option considered within the management plan of the Celestun Biosphere Reserve, and in 1997, the RARE Center, together with local NGOs, initiated their Nature Guide Training Programme on the Yucatan Peninsula, and trained the first nature guides from Celestun.

During the course, the guides learned the natural history of their region, nature interpretation, learned how to use field guides and binoculars, and other skills such as group management and clear communication (Figure III-15). Since English has been identified as the language most foreign visitors use, the guides learned to speak English at a very acceptable level to communicate with foreign visitors.

Since the course, some of the Nature Guides have participated in various workshops, organized locally to promote community participation in coastal management strategies. PPY has a follow-up programme to work with the Nature Guides in several tourism management strategies, such

FIGURE III-15.

Photo by John Clark.

Guides at the Celestun Wildlife Refuge MPA receive special training.

as local training for more guides and regulation of boat traffic in the estuary to prevent disturbance of flamingo flocks.

There is an organization of boat operators led by one of the RARE Nature Guide graduates (as they ask to be called, not without a certain trace of pride). The Federacion de Lancheros (boat operators) from Celestun has been playing a very important role both in promoting tourism development and keeping strict rules to navigate along the estuary in order to prevent flamingo flocks from being disturbed.

Of course it's not always clear sailing, but it is certainly a new way of looking for opportunities for nature based tourism at Celestun. Even local investors are interested in supporting the training of more Nature Guides. Interviews with visitors show their preferences for locally managed tourism, and evaluation surveys about Nature Guides tour experiences clearly demonstrate that a good guide with nature interpretation skills makes a big difference in terms of both learning about and enjoying the unique natural surroundings of the reserve.

When Ramiro became a boat operator, he was hardly able to tell a Brown Pelican from a Great Blue Heron. Now, after intensive training as a Nature Guide, he knows around 60% of the bird species that can be found in the estuary, and even more importantly, is very aware of the fact that his behavior in the motor boat can seriously disturb flamingo flocks and submerged vegetation patches that hold their main food items, causing birds to temporally abandon the area, with a consequent risk to his new job.

Some of the Celestun Nature Guides are sharing with their fellow boat operators information about flamingo behavior and ecology, the names of the most common aquatic birds (in Spanish and English), and the adaptations of mangrove species to estuarine ecosystems. One of them has started a new and locally-based tourism enterprise to promote nature tours within the Celestun Biosphere Reserve.

Of course, there are numerous obstacles still to be overcome, but certainly there is an effort being made at Celestun to promote the sustainable development of a new economic activity providing income to a substantial sector of the community. Local Nature Guides training is an option for promoting conservation and at the same time providing economic benefits to local populations and educational opportunities to outside visitors.

But there is still an important aspect to be considered. Training itself will have little value unless there is a programme that integrates the work of the course graduates with the management plans for each particular site.

That is precisely one of the lessons learned from this experience: training could be an important component of any attempt to develop community based tourism on coastal areas. The other very important part should be an integrated management plan that provides trainees with the means for applying their new knowledge.

There is a waiting list of Celestun boat operators to be trained as Nature Guides, and the Celestun Biosphere Reserve is now considering both training and trainee programmes to integrate a management strategy for developing nature based tourism. That could certainly bring benefits for the community and for the conservation of the wide variety of ecosystems and species across this vast coastal landscape.

Source: Eduardo C. Galicia, University of Quintana Roo, Mexico.

E-Mail Contact: egalicia@coreo.uqroo.mx

17. Turtle Islands National Park, Sabah, Malaysia: Regional Perspective

In formulating conservation policy for Sabah, Malaysia, off the north coast of Borneo, it was decided to concentrate turtle conservation efforts on the three most important nesting islands (Pulau Selingaan, Pulau Bakkungan Kechil, and Pulau Gulisaan), since it was considered impossible to protect every rookery in the state. These three islands lie off the southeast coast of Sabah near the Philippines and Indonesia. De Silva (1984) describes some of the problems encountered and procedures followed in establishing a protected area for turtles in the Sabah turtle islands, as reviewed below.

As a first step in managing the turtle stock, March was declared a closed season for the collection of turtle eggs. The prevailing northeast monsoon made travel of rangers to the islands difficult and enforcement of the closure ineffective. Consequently, involvement of the islanders was sought to win their cooperation and create new jobs to ease the labour problems. The venture proved unsuccessful.

Despite opposition from islanders, turtle hatcheries were established on all three islands. Eggs were purchased from the islanders with great difficulty and at inflated prices. Islanders antagonistic toward interference with their long-established industry tampered with or stole egg clutches, resulting in the loss of several hundreds of clutches. Rangers attracted further resentment because they observed and curbed other illicit activities.

In addition to the serious depredation of turtle eggs, sand and coral mining for mainland construction projects threatened the nesting habitat. Any clutches that escaped harvest were inevitably dug up in this way. The islanders refused to believe that their activities could eliminate the turtle stocks.

An additional problem arose offshore. Trawler fishing greatly increased close to the islands and a check revealed that adults and hatchling turtles were being caught in the nets. Fortunately the state fisheries department cooperated by banning trawling within one mile of the islands and the trawler fishermen generally honored the ban.

The government eventually had to buy the three islands to enable sufficient control of the egg collection. The islands were declared game and bird sanctuaries, which resulted in far better control of the nesting beaches. Occasional thefts continued, chiefly at night. Coral mining and fishing with explosives continued on reefs near the islands. In addition, brightly lit fishing vessels, anchoring off the islands to clean and pack their catch, frightened off turtles approaching the beaches to lay their eggs. Furthermore, the discarded fish, offal and edible refuse dumped overboard attracted sharks and predatory fishes that ate hatchling turtles entering the sea. Surviving hatchlings were disoriented by the bright lights and converged around the trawlers where they were easy prey to lurking predators. The bilge and toilet discharges and jettisoned garbage contaminated the coral reefs and island beaches.

It became apparent that protecting nesting beaches alone was insufficient to safeguard the turtle stock. For this reason, the 1,740-ha Turtle Islands National Park was established to protect the three islands and their intervening coral reefs. Turtles tagged on nesting beaches in Sabah have been found nesting in Indonesia, and they presumably also nest on the nearer Philippine Islands. It appears that the three nations share a common turtle population. Indonesia and the Philippines do not yet match Sabah's efforts at turtle conservation. In fact, Philippine fishing trawlers actively hunt turtles in the Sulu Sea, even close to the national park.

It is clear that Sabah's efforts to conserve green turtle stocks will amount to little without the cooperation of both Indonesia and the Philippines. A multinational reserve, including the major nesting beaches and feeding grounds in each nation, would give better protection to the turtle population and would facilitate jurisdiction over all parts of the reserve.

As a happy postscript, turtle nesting has increased on these islands, which are now considered to be a model of hawksbill turtle recovery.

Source: Adapted from DeSilva, G.S. 1984. Protected areas and turtle eggs in Sabah, East Malaysia. *In:* J.A. McNeely and K.R. Miller (eds.) *National parks, conservation and development: The role of protected areas in sustaining society.* Washington, D.C., Smithsonian Institution Press. Updated by Rodney V. Salm (1999).

E-Mail Contact: rsalm@tnc.org

18. Palau: Protection of Reef Fish Spawning Aggregations

Many different species of coral reef food fish aggregate at specific locations each year in order to spawn. Groupers are best known for this habit because they tend to stay at such sites for 1—2 weeks per lunar month during the spawning season. But snappers, jacks, emperors and surgeonfish are among the food fishes that also use such sites.

The spawning aggregations of these fishes are less well studied than those of groupers because they are less conspicuous. The fish tend to aggregate for fewer days per spawning period and sometimes come to the aggregation site for only a short period near dusk. Nevertheless, fishers often know the locations and seasonal and lunar timing of these aggregations, making them, like those of groupers, especially vulnerable to overfishing.

In the case of groupers, spawning aggregations have been completely obliterated by overfishing at a number of locations in both the Atlantic and the Pacific (reviewed by Johannes, et al 1999). In recent years, moreover, fishers in the billion dollar live reef food fish industry, centered in the Southeast Asia and spreading into the Pacific and Indian Ocean islands, have taken to targeting spawning aggregations. Some of their operations focus exclusively on these aggregations, and some use cyanide to stun the fish.

A growing number of reports reveal that this industry is depleting grouper spawning aggregations and the stocks they represent at unprecedented rates. Typically it takes only three to four years for live reef fish operations to deplete an area to the point where it is no longer economical to fish for groupers there (Johannes and Riepen, 1995; Erdmann and Pet, 1999; Bentley, in press). Where cyanide is used, the collateral destruction of other fish and invertebrates, including corals, is substantial.

Even where this trade does not operate, fishing pressure is heavy and increasing in many areas due to the demands of growing populations and expanding export markets. Coastal waters in much of Asia, for example, are severely overfished.

Under such circumstances, the fact that reef fish spawning aggregations have been ignored by most fisheries managers in the Indo-Pacific is almost as incomprehensible as it is unfortunate. Most Caribbean countries, which do not have the problem of the live reef food fish trade to contend with, nevertheless employ a host of measures to protect their reef fish spawning aggregations (reviewed by Johannes *et al.*, 1999).

Proponents of MPAs routinely assert that their most important function is to protect spawning stock biomass and improve recruitment to fished areas by means of larval dispersal. Yet, with rare exceptions, the locations of important spawning aggregation sites seem almost never taken into account by MPA planners in the tropical Indo-Pacific. Even Australia, with the biggest coral reef in the world, is only now beginning to consider the need for protecting spawning aggregations.

The tiny country of Palau in Micronesia is twenty years ahead of the rest of the Indo-Pacific in giving legal protection to a spawning aggregation site. Palauans, like many other Pacific islanders, had a variety of traditional marine resource management practices, including the protection of spawning aggregations through placing taboos on them. But traditional authority has weakened in the past half century so that government regulation was sought by Palauan fishermen to help fill the vacuum.

Accordingly, in 1976 a law was passed to prohibit fishing from April through July in Ngerumekaol Channel, Palau's best known spawning aggregation site. Fishermen volunteered that this was the peak season for spawning aggregations of three species of groupers; for about ten days prior to the new moon they aggregate there by the thousands in order to spawn. Recent research has shown, moreover, that more than 50 other species of reef fish spawn there, including snappers and unicorn fish. The last of these is the single most important fish in the commercial reef catch (Johannes *et al.*, 1999). Some of the smaller species that spawn there also spawn in many other locations. But the larger species migrate there specifically to spawn.

Shortcomings of the 1976 protection scheme for Ngerumekaol have emerged. Efforts to educate Palauans to the law concerning Ngerumekaol were inadequate, as were enforcement efforts. In addition, the fishing ban was limited to Ngerumekaol Channel. Spawning aggregations tended to extend beyond the channel where they could be exploited with impunity. Second, poaching was carried out, even in daylight. Poachers could simply pull up their anchors when they saw a suspicious boat (i.e., one possibly bearing fisheries law enforcement personnel) approaching. By the time the boat arrived the poachers' boat would have drifted well out of the channel.

The degree of protection that the Ngerumekaol spawning aggregation was given, although insufficient, probably prevented it from disappearing altogether. Some grouper spawning aggregations have already disappeared in Palau, and the Ngerumekaol spawning aggregation site is an easy half hour boat ride from Koror where the bulk of Palau's human population resides.

In recognition of the need for improved management, Palauan authorities have recently introduced legislation to redefine the Ngerumekaol Protected Area so as to include not only the channel, but also a well-marked and substantial buffer zone around it. Routine monitoring of the grouper aggregations has been introduced, coupled with much improved surveillance. Efforts are also being made to acquaint Palauans with the law and with the need for it.

A year-round closure to fishing is also being considered, because recent research has shown that spawning is not limited to the four months of the original closure. Consideration is also being given to limiting access to the channel by recreational divers since they may disturb certain aggregating species.

While Palau is still feeling its way towards optimum protection for this important reef fish spawning aggregation site, it is nevertheless well ahead of the rest of the Indo-Pacific in this regard and provides an example from which other countries can learn. (The small Micronesian state of Pohnpei has recently moved to protect its grouper spawning aggregations, apparently the only other state in the Indo-Pacific to do so).

Nowhere throughout all of tropical Asia do important multi-species reef fish spawning aggregation sites appear to be protected. If one were to judge by the scientific literature, marine biologists doing research in the countries of Southeast Asia are rarely even aware of their existence—in striking contrast to the fishermen that harvest live fish.

Why have the locations of important spawning aggregation sites almost never been taken into consideration when delineating MPAs in the Indo-Pacific, and why have other measures, such as closed seasons not been taken to protect them? Some fisheries managers say that they do not have adequate data to prove that the spawners are threatened.

There are two responses to this:

1. Waiting for adequate data will, in many cases, mean waiting forever; there are vast areas of tropical nearshore waters where obtaining such data is impractical or too expensive, and will remain so indefinitely (Johannes, 1998)

2. Where data *have* been collected, grouper (and snapper) suffer most; typically they are the first reef fish stocks to collapse in response to increasing fishing pressure.

Under the circumstances, precautionary protection of reef fish spawning aggregations, via MPAs or other approaches, is not merely appropriate; it is vital.

References

Bentley, N. (in press) The exploitation and trade of live reef fish in South East Asia. A report for TRAFFIC South East Asia.

Erdmann, M.V. and J.S. Pet. 1999. Krismon & DFP: some observations on the effects of the Asian financial crisis on destructive fishing practices in Indonesia. SPC Live Reef Fish Information Bulletin 5: 22-26.

Johannes, R. E. 1998. The case for data-less marine resource management: examples from tropical nearshore fisheries. Trends in Ecology and Evolution 13: 243-246.

Johannes, R. E. and M. Riepen. 1995. Environmental, economic and social implications of the live reef fish trade in Asia and the Western Pacific. Report to The Nature Conservancy and the Forum Fisheries Agency. 83 pp.

Johannes, R.E., L. Squire, T. Graham, Y. Sadovy, and H. Renguul (1999) Spawning Aggregations of Groupers (Serranidae) in Palau. The Nature Conservancy Marine Conservation Research Series Publication #l. 144pp.

Source: R.E. Johannes, R.E. Johannes Pty. Ltd., Bonnet Hill, Tasmania, Australia.

E-Mail Contact: bobjoh@netspace.net.au

19. Bunaken Islands, Indonesia:
Criteria for Zoning

Although they can be useful, criteria often simply show what is intuitively obvious. Often their greatest benefit is that they allow us to justify what we already know and to build up a case for proposed zoning plans. Rigorous application and quantification of criteria generally does not apply in sparsely populated areas. However, this is important near urban centers and fishing communities where existing uses will be displaced or modified to suit new objectives.

An area of sea and reefs surrounding Bunaken and its five neighbouring islands was declared a marine park by decree of the provincial governor in 1980. The site was later proposed as a National Park (see Case History 1).

Here, tourism is of paramount importance. Conservation of reef biota is also important, but is a secondary objective. In this case local policy decreed that conflicting interests of local islanders should be secondary to the design of the marine park. Thus the principal management objective (conservation of important areas for tourism) was derived directly from the policy of the governor's office. The approach used is explained below.

Procedure

1. Determine the principal and secondary objectives of the protected area (in this case, tourism was defined as the main objective and conservation as the second objective).

2. List the activities that require separation into different zones.

3. Define criteria to evaluate different parts of the protected area for various activities.

4. Survey the area in detail to measure scores for each criterion at different sites (reefs, islands, mangroves, and/or bays, depending on the nature of the site).

5. Sum up the scores of all criteria at each site.

6. Map the area, indicating the locations of areas with higher, medium, and lower values for each activity of interest. Areas with higher values (i.e., higher criteria scores) can be given a darker colour and those with lower values shown by a lighter tone.

7. Select zones on the basis of colour (activity value) and define permissible activities for each.

Applying Criteria

The simple criteria in Tables III-1 and 2 were defined to help determine which of the five reefs were best suited to different pursuits, and to identify zones for the segregation of incompatible activities. The reefs were surveyed to provide quantitative estimates for each of these criteria.

The reefs were surveyed and all parameters defined for each criterion were measured. This enabled each criterion to be assigned scores that, when summed up, gave a total value for each reef. However, each reef was surveyed in its entirety in a general way, as well as in detail at specific sites. It was clear from the criteria score that the value for conservation or tourism varied within as well as among reefs. Thus, just as they enabled evaluation for different activities among reefs, criteria helped identify specific parts of reefs of higher or lower value for each activity.

The tourism and conservation values calculated by applying the criteria in Tables III-1 and III-2 were used to identify the management objective for each reef and to provide a quasi-quantitative justification to the authorities for this selection. Areas with clearly greater values for tourism will be managed to promote underwater activities (Bunaken and Manado Tua). Areas with greatest value for conservation will be managed to protect coral reef communities (Nain). The remaining two reefs combine conservation with a low level of tourism (one diving site at each).

Table III-1. Tourism Value of Reefs of the Bunaken Islands Marine Park					
Criterion	**Nain**	**Bunaken**	**Mantehage**	**Siladen**	**Manado Tua**
Aesthetics	1	2	0	1	1
Safety	2	1	2	1	2
Accessibility	0	2	1	1	2
Fishing activity	0	0	1	1	0
Total	3	5	4	4	5
Tourism value	43	71	57	57	71

Note: "Aesthetics" implies a high percentage cover of living coral, large intact coral colonies, varied reef profile (dropoffs, caves, crevices), and clear water (0 = low, 1 = medium, and 2 = high aesthetic appeal). "Safety" implies little or no wave action, no strong currents, and no chance of entanglement by nets or of proximity to explosives fishing (0 = low, 1 = medium, and 2 = high safety factor). "Accessibility" is measured as the distance from the mainland hotels and the ease of entry for divers from a boat (0 = low, 1 = medium, and 2 = high accessibility score). "Level of fishing activity" is an estimate based on the distance from villages and the number of fishermen in villages fishing the area (0 = high and 1 = low level of fishing activity). "Tourism value" calculated as a percentage of the maximum potential score (= 7).

Table III-2. Conservation Value of Reefs of the Bunaken Islands Marine Park

Criterion	Nain	Bunalken	Mantehage	Siladen	Manado Tua
Habitat variety	5	3	3	2	2
Unique coral habitat	1	0	1	0	1
Coral cover	1	2	1	2	1
Diversity	2	2	1	1	1
Intactness	1	0	1	1	0
Total	10	7	7	6	5
Conservation value	83	58	58	50	42

Note: "Habitat variety" is the sum of each of the following habitats present: barrier reef, fringing reef, lagoonal reef, mangroves, sea grass beds (0 = absent and 1 = present). "Unique coral habitat" indicates the presence of a coral habitat not found elsewhere among the islands: Nain has fragile lagoonal coral colonies; Mantehage has coral assemblages in mangrove creeks; Manado Tua has unusual confluent mounds of *Euphyllia* (Euphyllia) and E. (*Fimbriaphyllia*) *ancora* covering about 0.25 ha (0 = absent and 1 = present). "Coral cover" is the estimated percentage of the substrate covered by living corals (0 = less than 60%, 1 = 60-85%, and 2 = more than 85%). "Diversity" is the total number of coral genera recorded from the surface to a depth of 20 m (0 = fewer than 30, 1 = 30-40, and 2 = more than 40). "Intactness" is an estimate of the percentage of coral colonies that are broken between depths of about 2 m and 5 m (0 = more than 15% and 1 = 0-15% damaged coral). "Conservation value" calculated as the percentage of the maximum potential score (= 13).

Zones were defined around the specific areas of each reef that were most valuable for each pursuit. All Snorkeling/Diving Areas were defined in a radius of 100 m from a central mooring. The moorings were to be located in larger Conservation Zones that safeguard surrounding communities should it prove necessary to move moorings. Conservation zones were kept far from fishing villages where possible, and to larger than 300 ha (see Section II-1 on coral reefs). Remaining reef areas were established as Reef Fishery Zones for the exclusive use of island residents. The remaining area would form the Deep-Sea Fishery Zone.

Source: This case is adapted from that prepared for the first edition of Marine and Coastal Protected Areas by Rodney V. Salm.

E-Mail Contact: rsalm@tnc.org

Editor's Note: See also Case History No. 1, "Participatory Management: Bunaken National Park, Indonesia, which brings the Bunaken situation up to the present (1999).

20. Sea Turtle Conservation Programmes: Factors Determining Success or Failure

This case discusses three sea turtle conservation programmes, one MPA deemed a failure, and two which have been successful in reversing population decline. The protective measures implemented by each programme are described along with the historical events that led to problems. These are evaluated in an effort to discern what factors determine success or failure of such programmes. The case studies involve: the leatherback (Dermochelys coriacea) rookery at Rantau Abang, Malaysia; the hawksbill (Eretmochelys imbricata) rookery at Cousin Island, Seychelles; and the populations of green turtles (Chelonia mydas) and hawksbills in the Chagos archipelago, British Indian Ocean Territory (BIOT).

The Leatherback Turtles of Malaysia

In 1956, leatherback turtles laid more than 10,000 egg clutches along the east coast of Peninsular Malaysia (Hendrickson & Alfred, 1961) making the Rantau Abang leatherback population one of the most important in the world (Wyatt-Smith, 1960). Unfortunately, virtually all the eggs have been harvested for human consumption. In 1961, a hatchery was established and during the next 26 years an average of 33,000 eggs were incubated annually. But, this represented only 4% of the estimated annual egg production of 1956, and hatching success was low, averaging only 50% (Fisheries Department Statistics; Mortimer, 1989).

Since 1956, the nesting population has declined catastrophically (Figure III-16) as documented by a tagging programme conducted in 1967-76 by the Fisheries Department of Terengganu (Chua, 1988), surveys of egg collectors in 1978 (Siow & Moll, 1982) and 1979-84 (Siti & de Silva, 1985), and by systematic compilation of nesting statistics since 1984 (Fisheries Department of Terengganu). Malaysian conservationists, scientists, and fisheries personnel put pressure on the authorities to implement protective measures (Chan, 1993).

FIGURE III-16.

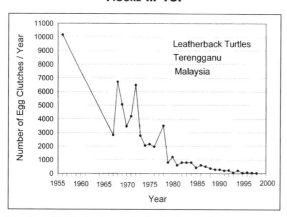

Number of leatherback egg clutches laid annually in Terengganu, Malaysia between 1956 and 1998.

In 1988 the State Government of Terengganu established the Rantau Abang Turtle Sanctuary along 14 km of prime leatherback nesting beach, and adopted regulations to control the activities of tourists within the sanctuary and to curb further development within its borders. It also banned the commercial sale and consumption of leatherback eggs in Terengganu, thus requiring 100% of leatherback egg harvest to be sold to the Department of Fisheries for incubation in hatcheries.

Studies by Chan *et al.* (1988) and the Department of Fisheries (Jabatan Perikanan Terengganu, 1989) highlighted threats posed by large-mesh gill nets, and led (in 1990) to a national ban on the use of driftnets with mesh sizes exceeding 25.4 cm. A radio-telemetry study (Chan *et al.*, 1991) identified the offshore zone where internesting activity was most concentrated, and led to establishment of the Rantau Abang Fisheries Prohibited Area (in 1991) as an offshore sanctuary (extending 10 km seaward, along 30 km of shoreline) to protect gravid leatherback turtles during the nesting season.

Unfortunately, the leatherback population continued to decline, and nesting became more diffuse after 1987 (Figure 2), with 32-71% occurring outside the

FIGURE III-17.

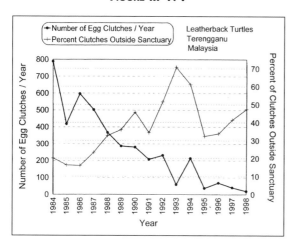

boundaries of the Turtle Sanctuary, compared to 16-23% during 1984-87 (Figure III-17). Whether the turtles were driven out of the Sanctuary by disturbances from uncontrolled and unsupervised crowds of tourists (Chan & Liew, 1996), or by a decline in nesting site fidelity associated with a reduction in population size below some critical threshold, the effect was to undermine whatever protection the offshore sanctuary may have afforded the inter-nesting females. In 1998, only 19 egg clutches were laid in Terengganu, 47% of them outside the Sanctuary (Department of Fisheries Statistics).

Relationship between the number of leatherback egg clutches laid annually in Terengganu and the percentage of those nestings that occurred outside the boundaries of the Rantau Abang Turtle Sanctuary during 1984-98.

The provisions of the Rantau Abang Sanctuary and Fisheries Prohibited Area might have been adequate to protect the nesting population had they been implemented 20 (or perhaps even ten) years earlier. Unfortunately, by the time the authorities took action in 1988, the population was already on the verge of extinction (Mortimer, 1991, 1995). Eggs had been harvested intensely for at least four decades--since well before 1951 (Chan & Liew, 1996).

The decline of the Malaysian leatherback population was also exacerbated by mortality from fishing gear in both international and Malaysian waters. Chan & Liew (1996) identified two periods of especially sharp declines in the nesting population: one, from 1972-74, which correlated with rapid development in the fishing industry in Terengganu; and the other, from 1978-80, which coincided directly with the introduction of the Japanese high seas squid driftnet fishery of the North Pacific. In Malaysian waters, mortality is caused by trawling nets, drift nets, and gill nets (Chan *et al.*, 1988). Entanglement in the float lines of sunken fish traps set in near shore water was involved in the mortality of at least 5-10% of the females that nested during the 1989-91 nesting seasons (Mortimer, 1989, pers. observ.). Spotila *et al.* (1996) implicated accidental capture of adults and juveniles in fishing gear as a major factor in the worldwide decline of leatherback populations.

The Hawksbill Turtles of Cousin Island, Seychelles

In 1968, the designation of two nature reserves in the colony of Seychelles, at Cousin Island and Aldabra Atoll, constituted the first protection afforded nesting hawksbills in Seychelles. Although legislation adopted in 1979 by the Republic of Seychelles prohibited turtle harvest at an additional four sites, enforcement was problematic (Mortimer, 1984). During the period from the 1960's through the early 1990's, the Japanese paid such high prices for raw turtle shell that most hawksbills attempting to breed in Seychelles were slaughtered, often before they laid eggs (Mortimer, 1984).

At Cousin Island, however,—a nature reserve administered by BirdLife International (formerly ICBP) and now BirdLife Seychelles—nesting hawksbills have been well protected since 1970 (see Case 6 in Part III). This is due to a combination of factors, including dedicated staff and a relatively easily patrolled coastline. Unauthorized vessels have been restricted within one km of the high tide line, thus facilitating protection of mating pairs and gravid females in offshore waters. During the past 27 years, apparently in response to this protection, nesting activity has more than tripled at Cousin (Figure III-18), increasing from some 30 females per year to 70-130 (Mortimer & Bresson, 1994). Nevertheless, there was concern as to whether this relatively small population (which in the early 1980s represented only 5% of the total hawksbill population of Seychelles (Mortimer, 1984) could maintain itself over time, should other hawksbill rookeries in the country be exterminated (Mortimer & Bresson, 1994).

FIGURE III-18.

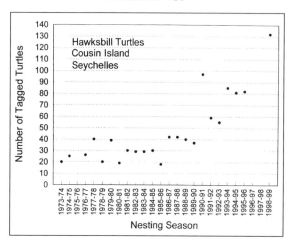

Number of individual female hawksbills nesting per season at Cousin Island, Seychelles between 1973-74 and 1998-99 (excluding the 1975-76, 1996-97, and 1997-98 seasons for which data are not reliable.)

Fortunately, in the 1990s, the situation elsewhere in Seychelles improved dramatically. Beginning in 1992, the management of nearby Cousin Island began actively protecting its hawksbills, and the Government of Seychelles took extraordinary action on behalf of the hawksbill. In 1993-94, it implemented an artisan compensation and re-training programme that eliminated domestic trade in hawksbill shell. In 1994, it provided complete legal protection for all sea turtles, and in 1998, publicly burned its stockpile of raw hawksbill shell during the Miss World Pageant (Mortimer, 1999).

Before 1970, most of the hawksbills that came to nest at Cousin Island were killed during their first breeding season. If protected, however, female hawksbills have the potential to lay 25 to 50 egg clutches over a 20 year period (Mortimer & Bresson, 1999). Thus, the increase in nesting activity reported during the past two decades probably results from an increase in average reproductive output per turtle. Because individual hawksbills can take decades to mature (Limpus, 1992), it may yet be too early to expect to see a large number of new females in the population. Nevertheless, the increased reproductive output is expected to eventually yield a true population increase.

The increase in nesting activity at Cousin Island suggests that now rates of adult mortality at the foraging grounds are probably relatively low, thus enabling hawksbill turtles that escape slaughter at the nesting beach to survive to breed again in a subsequent nesting season. This is corroborated by catch statistics and satellite tracking data. During 1979-86 when it was legal to kill adult hawksbills in Seychelles, catch statistics included few captures of adults outside the nesting season (Mortimer, 1984, unpubl. data). Nor have any tagged females been recovered outside the country. Satellite transmitters, attached to five post-nesting hawksbill turtles at Cousin Island in 1998, showed the adult foraging habitats to be located within the boundaries of the Seychelles Bank (Mortimer & Balazs, in press) in habitats that apparently lack significant agents of turtle mortality.

Hawksbills and Green Turtles in the Chagos Archipelago

The first permanent settlement of the islands of the Chagos Archipelago occurred in the late 1780s when coconut plantations were established on Diego Garcia atoll. During the 1800s coconuts were intensely planted and harvested on all atolls in the group (Stoddart, 1971). The workers greatly relished green turtle meat and eggs and historical documents indicate that exploitation of hawksbill shell occurred throughout the period of human settlement. Export statistics are available only for the present century, but show a decline in the numbers of hawksbills captured between 1904 and 1929 (Frazier, 1977). Historical documents also indicate that the abundance of both green turtles and hawksbills was much greater during the early years of settlement (Mortimer & Day, 1999).

The turtles got some relief from exploitation in the mid-1900s when rising costs of transportation and labour resulted in many islands being abandoned. Although regulations were enacted in 1968 to prohibit the take of green turtles, interviews with island residents in 1970 indicated a continuing harvest (Frazier, 1977). The harvest was effectively terminated during 1970 and 1971, however, when the last island residents were evacuated to Mauritius in preparation for an Anglo-American military base which was constructed and has been active ever since (Stoddart, 1971).

Today, the only permanent human habitation on Chagos is the military base at Diego Garcia (British Indian Ocean Territory—BIOT) which occupies less than 25% of the land area of the atoll. The movements of base personnel are restricted and all wildlife is strictly protected (creating a *de facto* MPA). Ongoing habitat damage associated with the base appears to be minor. Currently, the greatest threat to Chagos turtles may be *illegal* harvest by commercial fishing vessels or private yachts (Mortimer & Day, 1999).

Overall, the protection afforded the Chagos turtles by the BIOT administration appears to have been effective. In 1970, Frazier (1977) estimated the nesting population to number some 300 females of each species. Data collected by Mortimer (Mortimer & Day, 1999) during a six week survey of the archipelago in 1996 indicate that twice as many turtles now nest annually, including some 400-800 green turtles and 300-700 hawksbills.

A significant population of immature hawksbills forages in the lagoon at Diego Garcia and is also well protected by BIOT (Mortimer & Day, 1999). Analysis of patterns of mitochondrial DNA variation could not differentiate populations of juvenile hawksbills foraging at Diego Garcia from those foraging in the Seychelles (Mortimer & Broderick, 1999). This suggests that the juvenile foraging populations of both countries comprise individuals originating from rookeries either in Seychelles, Chagos, or possibly the Arabian Peninsula or other unsampled localities in the region. Thus, the protection provided the turtle populations in Chagos is of regional importance to sea turtle conservation.

Conclusions

Turtles are particularly vulnerable during reproduction, and historically, over-exploitation of eggs and breeding adults has probably been the most important factor in the demise of sea turtle populations. Thus, protection at the nesting beach may be the most critical component of any sea turtle conservation programme. But, marine turtles have complicated life cycles. As a turtle passes from one life history stage to another (egg, hatchling, juvenile, subadult and adult) it utilizes a series of habitat types which may be separated from each other by hundreds or thousands of kilometers (Musick & Limpus, 1997). Extinction is avoided when a turtle population maintains adequate rates of survival at all stages in the life cycle. To achieve this end, regional cooperation is essential. The involved states need to endorse and support international agreements and programmes that provide for coordinated species protection and MPA habitat conservation measures.

Literature Cited

Chan, E.H. 1993. The conservation-related biology and ecology of the leatherback turtle, *Dermochelys coriacea*, in Rantau Abang, Terengganu, Malaysia. Unpublished doctoral dissertation submitted to Kagoshima University. 150 pp.

Chan, E.H. and Liew, H.C. 1996. Decline of the leatherback population in Terengganu, Malaysia, 1956-1995. Chelonian Conservation and Biology 2(2):196-203.

Chan, E.H., Liew, H.C. and Mazlan, A.G. 1988. The incidental capture of sea turtles in fishing gear in Terengganu, Malaysia. Biol. Conserv. 43:1-7.

Chan, E.H., Eckert, S.A., Liew, H.C., and Eckert, K.L. 1991. Locating the internesting habitats of leatherback turtles *(Dermochelys coriacea)* in Malaysian waters using radiotelemetry. In: Uchiyama, A. And Amlaner, C.J. (Eds.). Biotelemetry XI: Proc. Eleventh International Symposium Biotelemetry, Yokohama, Japan, pp. 133-138.

Chua, T.H. 1988. Nesting population and frequency of visits in *Dermochelys coriacea* in Malaysia. Journal of Herpetology 22(2): 192-207.

Frazier, J. 1977. Marine turtles in the western Indian Ocean: British Indian Ocean Territory, Comores. Typescript. ii+33, vi+114 pp.

Hendrickson, J.R. and Alfred, E.R. 1961. Nesting populations of sea turtles on the east coast of Malaya. Bull. Raffles Mus. 26:190-196.

Jabatan Perikanan Terengganu. 1989. Kajian risikan kesan pukat penyu keatas penyu di negeri Terengganu. Kertas Bil. 3/89, Mesyuarat Majlis Penasihat Santuari Penyu, 20 Feb.1989, Kerajaan Negeri Terengganu.

Limpus, C.J. 1992. The hawksbill turtle, *Eretmochelys imbricata*, in Queensland: population structure within a southern Great Barrier Reef feeding ground. Aust. Wildl. Res. 19:489-506.

Mortimer, J.A. 1984. Marine Turtles in the Republic of Seychelles: Status and Management. Publication of the IUCN Conservation Library: Gland, Switzerland. 80 pp.+ 4pl.

Mortimer, J.A. 1989. Threats to the Survival of Terengganu's Sea Turtles and a Review of Management Options. Report to the Turtles Sanctuary Advisory Council of Terengganu and WWF/Malaysia, July 1989. 21 pp.

Mortimer, J.A. 1991. Marine turtle conservation in Malaysia. Pp. 21-24, in Richardson, T.H., Richardson, J.I., Donnelly, M. (Compilers). Proceedings of the 10th Annual Workshop on Sea Turtle Research and Conservation. NOAA Tech. Memo. NMFS-SEFC-278.

Mortimer, J.A. 1995. Teaching Critical Concepts for the Conservation of Sea Turtles. Marine Turtle Newslet. 71:1-4.

Mortimer, J.A. 1999. World's first turtle shell stockpile to go up in flames as Miss World 1998 contestants look on. Chelonian Conservation and Biology 3(2): 376-377.

Mortimer, J.A. and Balazs, G. in press. Post-nesting migrations of hawksbill turtles in Seychelles and implications for conservation. Proceedings of the 19th Annual Sea Turtle Symposium. South Padre Island, Texas.

Mortimer, J.A. and Bresson, R. 1999. Temporal distribution and periodicity in hawksbill turtles *(Eretmochelys imbricata)* nesting at Cousin Island, Republic of Seychelles, 1971-1997. Chelonian Conservation and Biology 3(2): 318-325.

Mortimer, J.A. and Bresson, R. 1994. The hawksbill nesting population at Cousin Island, Republic of Seychelles: 1971-72 to 1991-92. Pp. 115-118, in Schroeder, B.A. and Witherington, B.E. (compilers). Proceedings of the 13th Annual Symposium on Sea Turtle Biology and Conservation. NOAA Tech. Memo. NMFS-SEFSC-341.

Mortimer, J.A. and Broderick, D. 1999. Population genetic structure and developmental migrations of sea turtles in the Chagos Archipelago and adjacent regions inferred from mtDNA sequence variation. Pp. 185-194, in Sheppard, CRC and Seaward, MRD (eds). The Chagos Archipelago. Linnean Society London. Occasional Publications.

Mortimer, J.A. and Day, M. 1999. Sea turtle populations and habitats in the Chagos Archipelago. Pp. 159-172, in Sheppard, CRC and Seaward, MRD (eds). The Chagos Archipelago. Linnean Society London. Occasional Publications.

Musick, J.A. and Limpus, C.J. 1997. Habitat utilization and migration in juvenile sea turtles.

Pp. 137-163, in Lutz, P.L. and Musick, J.A. (Eds.). The Biology of Sea Turtles. CRC Press, New York.

Siow, K.T. and Moll, E.O. 1982. Status and conservation of estuarine and sea turtles in West Malaysian waters. In: Bjorndal, K.A. (Ed.). Biology and Conservation of Sea Turtles. Smithsonian Institution Press, Washington, D.C., pp. 339-348.

Siti, K.D. and de Silva, M.W.R.N. 1985. Survey of turtle nesting sites in the Chukai-Rantau Abang coastline in Terengganu. Report submitted to ESSO Production Malaysia Inc., Universiti Pertanian Malaysia.

Spotila, J.R., Dunham, A.E., Leslie, A.J., Steyerwark, A.C., Plotkin, P.T. and Paladino, F.V. 1996. Worldwide population decline of Dermochelys coriacea: are leatherback turtles going extinct? Chelonian Conservation and Biology 2(2):209-222.

Stoddart, D.R. 1971. Settlement and development of Diego Garcia. In: Stoddart, D.R., Taylor, J.D. (Eds). Geography and Ecology of Diego Garcia Atoll, Chagos Archipelago. Atoll Research Bulletin 149:209-217.

Wyatt-Smith, J. 1960. The conservation of the leathery turtle, *Dermochelys coriacea.* Malayan Nature Journal 14: 194-199.

Source: Dr. Jeanne A. Mortimer, University of Florida, Gainesville, FL.

E-Mail Contact: jmort@nersp.nerdc.ufl.edu

21. Trinidad: Dilemma of the Scarlet Ibis in the Caroni Swamp Wildlife Sanctuary

Introduction

Caroni Swamp in western Trinidad covers an area of 5611 ha and contains the largest expanse of mangroves in Trinidad. A wildlife sanctuary of 135 ha was established there in 1953 to give protection to the resident population of Scarlet Ibis, which numbered nearly 10,000 birds at that time. The Ibis was of great cultural and economic importance, having been adopted as a national bird and forming the focus of a fast developing tourist business (Figure III-19). The sanctuary was extended in the following years to a total of 199 ha, as the original area did not contain enough of the bird's feeding and nesting habitat (Bacon & ffrench, 1972).

Without a doubt, Caroni Swamp has achieved a great measure of success as it is well known locally and internationally as a prime ecotourism destination. However, its future will be jeopardized if breeding failure by the Scarlet Ibis leads to the loss of its key attraction.

FIGURE III-19.

Photo by John Clark.

Guiding tourists to the Caroni Wildlife Sanctuary in Trinidad is a profitable business.

Protection of the sanctuary was provided by the Forestry Division of the Ministry of Agriculture, through specially assigned game wardens. However, the limited facilities of Forestry, and the later established Wildlife Section, proved inadequate against continuing illegal hunting and other forms of disturbance, even during the nesting season. Protection of the small sanctuary area was rendered difficult because of virtually uncontrolled resource use throughout the remainder of the swamp. Hunting and disturbance of the Scarlet Ibis was reduced, but numbers declined slightly even while the numbers of visitors began to increase.

In June 1987, Government moved to provide more effective protection by declaring a major part of Caroni Swamp a Protected Area and to seek restricted access and resource exploitation activity within the whole area. The number of Scarlet Ibis remained fairly constant, but nesting activity had rapidly declined and virtually ceased by the late 1980's. It appeared that the management system designed for this coastal MPAwas proving ineffective.

This study examines some of the factors that may have contributed to the decline in ibis nesting and the ecological status of its mangrove habitat, in relation to the management strategy used. The lessons learned have general application to other tropical coastal protected areas.

Problems in Protected Area Management

The management system introduced in Caroni was a traditional 'top-down' approach, using a government agency to enforce protective legislation. However, the low level of national commitment to habitat and wildlife conservation during the 1980's and early 1990's resulted in inadequate provision for manpower and equipment for effective policing. Shortages of wardens, vehicles, boats and finance at the Wildlife Section led to poor enforcement, despite a high level of commitment by the staff. Further to this, the regulatory agency experienced a lack of cooperation from resource users on two fronts. Firstly, establishment of the sanctuary and the later expansion of the protected area alienated fishermen, oyster collectors and hunters; many of whom had a long history of access and resource use in the Caroni Swamp. Secondly, there was a regrettable failure to involve the tour boat operators in conservation decision-making. This resulted in an inequitable situation in which large sums of money were being made by some tour operators, while Government had to foot the bill for management of the swamp resources on which their livelihood depended.

Secondly, when a period of further research was initiated by the University of the West Indies in 1993, it became apparent that a number of ecological changes had occurred in Caroni Swamp. These included a marked increase in ambient salinity, considerable spread of mangrove vegetation resulting in occlusion of several of the swamp channels and areas of open lagoon, and a general decline in plant and animal diversity. The managers appeared to be unaware of these changes, and made no adjustment to customary management practices (although a number of regular visitors commented on the deterioration in the tourism experience).

Lessons Learned

An initial mistake appears to have been providing protection only to one component of the ibis habitat range. Mangrove forest and tidal mudflats were effectively protected, but the associated freshwater habitat was not—meanwhile this was being reclaimed and depleted. The sizeable area of mangrove swamp which was protected provided adequate feeding, roosting and nesting habitat for adult birds but it was not appreciated that Scarlet Ibis have a further habitat requirement and that is for freshwater prey to feed the nestlings during the breeding season (Bildstein, 1990). All habitat requirements must be fully understood before the required protected area for a target species can be designated.

The loss of freshwater marshes on the eastern, landward, side of Caroni had important implications for target species management. In addition, marsh loss had reduced the wetland's floral and avifaunal diversity considerably; while the corresponding reduction in habitat diversity had reduced the variety in the tourist experience.

Marsh loss had resulted from catchment river modifications, including reservoir construction, embanking of feeder rivers and diversion of wet season flooding (Gerald, 1986). None of this had been factored into the ecological requirements for freshwater in Caroni Swamp. The most important lesson learned here was the rather obvious one, that an MPA cannot be managed in isolation from its landscape unit—in this case the Caroni river basin. It had proven impossible to maintain the ecological character of the site, when external forcing functions had not been controlled or come under the influence of the park managers.

A second problem was that caused by attempting to manage the system as if the ecological character determined in the 1960's (Bacon, 1970) was static. There appears to have been no understanding, and no research to gain such understanding, of the natural processes of change in a coastal wetland system. Management objectives and practices remained focused on species protection, while the habitat was changing drastically as a result of hydrologic diversion, channel silting and mangrove succession and spreading. Considering the current scenario of sea level rise, considerable ecological change can be expected in the future so coastal protected area management must be responsive to likely changes. Short-term change in mangrove systems is poorly documented or understood—there are few case studies available for the Caribbean Region. However, it is clear that any management system for MPAs must be resilient to ecological change.

A third problem is related to the lack of controls over resource users and the accompanying lack of cooperation by these stakeholders. The objectives of MPA management in Caroni Swamp were species focused and gave little attention to traditionally dependent human communities. The inadequate provision by the regulatory agencies for wardens, policing and control, coupled with resource user indiscipline and the widespread dislike of government controls led to an unpleasant conflict situation that hampered effective management.

Management failure was closely related to the absence of planning for stakeholder involvement, particularly when it was obvious that the regulatory authorities were unable to mount an effective conservation programme. The focus on a bird species, rather than the benefits that conservation of the entire swamp could bring to local communities hindered the Wildlife Section's work. A much-needed area of research and the production of management guidelines relates to demonstrating how resource use and economic gain can be maximized, while protecting important ecological values.

Source: Peter R. Bacon, Department of Life Sciences, University of the West Indies, Trinidad

E-mail contact: pbacon99@hotmail.com

References

Bacon, P.R. 1970. The Ecology of Caroni Swamp, Trinidad. Central Statistical Office, Port of Spain, Trinidad; 68 pages.

Bacon, P.R. & ffrench, R.P. 1972. The Wildlife Sanctuaries of Trinidad and Tobago. Wildlife Conservation Committee, Ministry of Agriculture, Lands & Fisheries,

Bildstein, K.L. 1990. Status, conservation and management of the Scarlet Ibis, Eudocimus ruber, in the Caroni Swamp, Trinidad. Biological Conservation, 54; 61-78.

Gerald, L. 1986. The changing Caroni Swamp 1922—1985. Naturalist (Trinidad & Tobago); 14-17.

22. Roatan, Honduras: Protected Area Under Management of Business Community

Background

Honduras, is the site of a spectacular and biologically diverse coral reef ecosystem, attracting divers from all over the world.[1] This case describes the development of a management plan for the Sandy Bay-West End Marine Reserve, which is under the management of a local NGO, the Bay Islands Conservation Association (BICA). Two management plans have been developed for the Reserve. The first is the "Plan for the Management and Development for the Sandy Bay-West End Marine Reserve", which was commissioned in 1997 by a Sandy Bay resort owner as a result of development permit conditions required by the Secretary of the Environment. The second, a draft released for review in July 1999, is the "Management Plan and Operational Plan for the Sandy Bay-West End Marine Reserve" (MPOP) prepared by the Wildlife Conservation Society (WCS).[2]

In 1996, BICA was entrusted by the Government of Honduras through the *Administración Forestal del Estado-Corporación Hondureña de Desarrollo Forestal—*Forestry Administration of the State-Honduran Corporation of Forestry Development (AFE-COHDEFOR)—to manage the Reserve.[3] BICA's Board of Directors administers the Reserve.[4] The *Asociación de Hoteleros de Roatán*, an organization of hotel and resort owners on the northwest portion of the Island, provides financial support to BICA for protection of the reefs in the Reserve.

In 1994, the Inter-American Development Bank approved a $US 27 million loan to prepare the *Programmea de Ordenamiento Ambiental de las Islas de la Bahía—*Programme for the Environmental Management of the Bay Islands (PROAMIB). The goals are to protect and manage the marine resources by legally establishing a system of marine parks and provide for sustainable utilization of the resources in conjunction with maintaining the health and vigor of the coastal and marine ecosystems.

Problem

BICA has done a commendable job of initiating environmental education programmes, coordinating beach cleanups and providing input in the environmental review process for coastal development permits. However, most of the poor and middle-income islanders feel estranged from BICA's goals and objectives. BICA has not made the effort to address the socio-economic concerns of the Bay Islanders regarding the allocation and use of coastal and marine resources (Stonich, 1998). The fact that the families of the two highest officers of BICA are major stakeholders in Roatán's tourism industry adds to the skepticism of the local people about the motives of the organization. Additionally, financing of the Reserve by the *Hoteleros de Roatán* is an immediate conflict of interest, allowing one stakeholder group to dominate through financial patronage, and thereby, their interests to prevail.

The perception of the poor who depend upon the resources from the Reserve, is that they are being asked to restrict environmentally damaging activities (e.g., harvesting of conch, fish and lobster) while the illegal activities of the wealthy and powerful continue unchallenged (e.g., dredging, construction in the mangroves) (Alevizon, 1994). Penalties such as fines for alleged violations within the Reserve appear to be imposed on a selective basis.[5] There is an apparent reluctance to take action against certain violators. Work has continued on large and highly visible environmentally destructive projects (e.g., marina construction and hotels) while small projects with minor violations (e.g., extension of docks) have been given cease and desist orders (Forest, 1998). For the disenfranchised groups that engage in these practices, and break the law in order to provide for their families, alternative livelihoods must be provided.

The numerous delays of the IDB-PROAMIB project have frustrated many of the residents on Roatán. The Islanders, regardless of their socio-economic status, have indicated that they were tired of studies and consultants coming and going (Forest, 1998). The false expectations of the IDB/PROAMIB, the long history of animosity, and the delays, distrust and poor communications between the stakeholders, have adversely effected the current efforts of the WCS-USAID to fully involve the stakeholders in the planning process.[6]

In a survey conducted by WCS in preparing the MPOP, 43 individuals were asked to comment on the following three aspects: 1) permitted activities within specific zones; 2) the locations and sizes of the zones; and 3) the concept of user fees as a financing strategy for operation and maintenance. However, the survey field notes also recorded comments not specific to the three management issues in the plan. More than 50 percent expressed concern about ineffective enforcement and the need for stronger and more equitable enforcement within the Reserve. Specific concerns include:

- Ineffective patrolling in the Reserve, ("Poachers wait for the reserve boat to go by, then they pull out... no night patrols");

- Inability of guards to communicate in English with tourist—particularly divers and snorkelers;

- Selective use of arrests, ("They let off their own people but arrest Islanders");

- Reluctance of the guards to perform their jobs in a professional manner, ("I see the guards sitting around under the trees with [their] radio turned off... they hang around the dock for hours...");

- Disagreement over hired staff from outside the community, ("Reserve guards should be hired from people who live and work around this end of the island and know the water conditions").

Thirty-three percent of the respondents expressed concerns over the conflicts between BICA and the communities:

- The lack of unity between BICA, the user groups and the marine reserve staff, ("Neither locals or business people are motivated to work together on the situation or attend community meetings");

- Lack of community respect of BICA, ("BICA doesn't represent the community anymore");

- Inadequate surveillance, ("Do they [guards] exist? Do they have boats? What do they do?");

- Unilateral decision-making, ("...one person makes all the decisions without answering to anyone").

Solutions

The survey responses indicates that the problems are clearly far more complicated than simply determining zoning or boundary limits, or the means or amount of fee collection. It is apparent from the WCS survey that BICA must begin to make fundamental changes in its governance style and arrangements. In order for BICA to be accountable for management decisions, it is necessary that: 1) the decision-making process be transparent; 2) the resource users are equitably represented on the Board of Directors and allowed to freely participate in decision-making; and 3) there is a provision for an independent process of management decisions.

A number of recommendations were suggested by individuals who own business or reside in the communities adjacent to the Marine Reserve:

- Increase coordination between AFE-COHDEFOR, BICA and the municipality;

- Consider appointing representatives outside of the diving community (e.g., fishermen and taxi boat operators) to serve on BICA's Marine Reserve Board; and

- Elect a Board of Directors, who are familiar with the dynamics of the reef, are knowledgeable about the resources, and will be actively involved in the management process.

Lessons Learned

An important lesson to be learned from the Bay Islands experience is that constituency building and accountability of decisions are crucial and dual steps in the planning and acceptance of a management programme for marine protected areas. It is critical to involve the stakeholders and interest groups in all aspects of planning and management of a marine protected area—not only within the Reserve—but all lands and waters outside the core area, the use of which can affect its environmental qualities. In the Sandy Bay-West End Marine Reserve, preemption of authority, unilateral decision-making, lack of community participation, and selective allocation and access to resources, have contributed to the political imbalance and polarization of the Bay Islanders. This has resulted in decisions that have generated adverse environmental, political and socioeconomic impacts of a greater magnitude than would have occurred with an open process (Forest, 1995, 1998).

Reorganization of management should strongly consider allowing the Board of Directors to have autonomy in order to direct the day-to day management of the Reserve. The role of BICA as the designated entity by the Honduran government should be that of overall long-term administration and coordination with the Roatán municipality, the *Departamento de las Islas de la Bahía*, and AFE-COHDEFOR, as well as other national institutions. Also needed is commitment at the national level to be accountable for management decisions.

A second lesson learned, is that even the best intentions and extensive efforts to provide a open process of planning and decision-making, can be adversely affected by a long history of mistrust of a management entity based on years of poor communication, ineffective leadership and unilateral decision-making. It will take several years of concerted efforts to reverse the situation, and for the local community members to begin to trust and to eventually participate in the planning process. On Roatán, if consensus building had been incorporated, the intense conflicts among the resource users could have been avoided. Actions or perceptions of favoritism and inequity could also have been avoided. Management initiatives must reach a consensus, otherwise, regulations will be viewed as punitive, burdensome, unreasonable, and inequitable.

In all likelihood, the MPOP will eventually be implemented. However, until the negative perceptions and attitudes surrounding BICA and its management approaches are resolved and the community feels that management is equitable and responsive to their needs, the following scenarios can be expected:

- Continued lack of respect for the management plan and the management entity;

- Escalating conflicts among all the stakeholders;

- Further degradation of the marine and coastal resources; and

- A decline in the quality of life for Bay Islanders who depend upon the resources of the reserve.

An open and highly participatory process promotes the sharing of values and responsibilities to arrive at a common vision that will enable the community to assert their right to use and manage their resources for benefits they can derive from wise utilization of their coastal resources.

Current Status of the Management Plan and Operational Plan

WCS is continuing to work with the Sandy Bay and West End communities in modifying the Reserve management plan to re-establish links between the benefits of the reserve and the community, and to reestablish cooperation between BICA and the communities. A second draft of the plan is in preparation.

Conclusion

Resolving the problems of managing the Sandy Bay-West End Marine Reserve is a challenging and long-term task. Considering the mistrust of the management entity and inadequate leadership that began long before the WCS-USAID (or the IDB-PROAMIB) planning process was underway, it will take several years for BICA to regain the trust of local residents. The intent of the WCS-led team is to encourage and provide the means by which the less powerful stakeholders can demand accountability for management decisions, can collectively contribute to the planning efforts and create a context that allows for ventilation of issues. Additionally, the WCS team's efforts to facilitate a highly participatory planning process can be the opportunity for all stakeholders to send a clear message of the intent to take action and responsibility to manage the resources in a cooperative/consensus-based manner that contributes long-term social and economic benefits to the community members.

Notes

1. For extensive history, context and background on the Bay Islands, refer to, "Assessment of Coastal . Regulations and Implementation: Case Study of Roatán, Bay Islands, Honduras". In Coastal Management, 1998, 26:125-188.

2. This is a project, financed by the United States Agency for International Development, the Honduran Environmental and Development Foundation (*Fundación VIDA*) through the Government of Honduras and the Wildlife Conservation Society (1999).

3. BICA was established in 1990 at the initiative of a group of Island residents concerned with environmental conservation of the Islands. In 1991 BICA received a request to direct and manage the Reserve.

4. According to the by-laws, the Board is elected annually by its members.

5. The most common penalty is the imposition of fines. Under *Acuerdo Dos* (Agreement No. 2) the maximum fine is approximately $US 50 which by middle and high-income individuals is simply considered the cost of doing business. In contrast, *Acuerdo* 99-93, imposes fines between $US 100-10,000 and/or successively accumulate if work on the project does not cease.

6. From e-mail communications (September 1999) with Jim Barborak and Cathryn Wild, consultants with WCS.

Acknowledgments

The author thanks Jim Barborak and Cathryn Wild of WCS for providing the draft management plan for review and additional information regarding the team's extended efforts on Roatán. The author also acknowledges the following colleagues for their extensive reviews: Bill Alevizon, Patrick Christie, Rafael Calderón, lic., Ian Dutton, Marea Hatziolos, Larry Hildebrand, Michele Lemay, Bernard Nietschmann, Leonard Nurse, Jens Sorensen, Daniel Suman and Alan White. Their comments have been most valuable in improving the contents of this case study. An earlier version of this study was sent to the Bay Islands for comments (BICA, Dr. Cordero-Executive Director of the Comisión para Desarrollo de las Islas de la Bahía, Julio Galindo Sr., and NAPIBLA.)

Nelia Badilla Forest
501 McCone Hall, Department of Geography
University of California—Berkeley
Berkeley, CA 94720
nforest@igc.org
nelia@socrates.berkeley.edu

References

Alevizon, W. S. An Ecological Assessment of Marine Reserves in the Bay Islands of Honduras. Tropical Research and Development, Gainesville, Florida.

Forest, N. B. 1995. Coastal Regulations and Implementation: Case Study of Roatán, Islas de la Bahía, Honduras, Central America. Masters Thesis. University of California—Berkeley.

Forest, N. B. 1998. "Assessment of Coastal Regulations and Implementation: Case Study of Roatán, Bay Island Honduras". Coastal Management Journal, 26:125-155.

Stonich, S. C. 1998. "Political Ecology of Tourism". Annals of Tourism Research, Vol. 25, No. 1.

Wildlife Conservation Society. 1999. *Plan de Manejo y Plan Operativeo de la Reserva Marina Sandy Bay-West End*. USAID/Honduras y Funcacíon VIDA.

23. Bonaire and Saba: Cost Recovery through User Fees

Bonaire and Saba are typical of small Caribbean island communities which are both struggling to become economically self sufficient and challenged by the dual tasks of managing their tourism industry and the natural environment on which this is based. Both have chosen to manage their marine resources by establishing Marine Parks and both have successfully opted to charge user fees to visiting divers in order to pay for their management.

For the Bonaire Marine Park the path to financial independence has been a rocky one. The Park was first established in 1979 with grant funding from World Wildlife Fund, Holland. The first three years of the project went well with the establishment of a system of permanent moorings, provision of interpretive materials and the drafting of comprehensive legislation to protect the Park. However, when the grant funding dried up, Bonaire learned its first lesson in marine resource protection: *no money, no park*. The Marine Park had joined the ranks of the so called "paper parks" which exist in theory, but have no active management.

It was nearly eight years before there was sufficient concern on the island to attempt to breathe new life into the Bonaire Marine Park. This was driven in part by the tremendous success of the dive tourism industry in attracting divers to Bonaire and its increasing economic importance to the island. The number of dive operators on Bonaire had tripled in the intervening period and the number of arriving divers had increased fourfold to around 20,000 per annum.

This time, in order to secure grant funding beyond the first year, Bonaire had to demonstrate that it was prepared find a means for the Marine Park to become self-financing. With this imperative in mind a number of different funding options were considered including an "eco-tax" similar to the ubiquitous airport departure tax, franchises for local dive operators and user fees.

The decision to introduce Marine Park admission fees for SCUBA divers was a logical one, "tourists come to Bonaire to dive, divers benefit most directly from a well managed and maintained Marine Park." Additionally the island could guarantee that the admission fees would only be used for the upkeep and maintenance of the Marine Park. It was also easy to ensure compliance since divers are dependent on a constant supply of compressed air.

Not everyone agreed with this logic. Bonaire's dive industry in particular, backed by U.S dive industry professionals were at best skeptical about "targeting" divers in this way. It was widely held that divers, given a choice and knowing that they would have to pay a "park fee"on Bonaire, would opt to visit other destinations. A previous attempt to introduce diver admission fees had been thwarted by the editor of a major US dive magazine who had threatened to cease covering and advertising Bonaire as a diver destination if the island went ahead.

This time Bonaire's government stood firm and a $10.00 per annum diver admission fee was introduced on the 1st January 1992. The level of the fee was simply determined by calculating how much it would cost to run the Marine Park annually and dividing this by the number of visiting divers. By July of the same year, the Marine Park was self-financing with regard to its operational costs and salaries. The current annual budget of the Marine Park lies between $300,000 and $475,000 of which over 60% is contributed by dive admission fees.

On Saba the situation was somewhat different. After learning lessons from Bonaire and Curacao on the challenges of securing continuing funding, when the Saba Marine Park was established in 1987, it was a condition of the grant money that the island institute a visitor fee programme for revenue generation. This ensured that there would be an ongoing funding mechanism for the continuing management of the Marine Park. As with Bonaire, it was a mechanism which made sense: the Park was—in part— established to promote the island's dive tourism and diversify the island economy and visiting divers would be financially supporting its operation. And it worked. With only three shore-based dive operators and effectively no shore diving, visitor fees were collected on a 'per dive' basis through the dive operations themselves.

How did the divers themselves react? The admission fees have enjoyed unilateral support from visiting divers both on Bonaire and Saba who were happy to contribute towards the upkeep and maintenance of "their" Marine Park. Furthermore the existence of well-managed and maintained Parks have become strong positive marketing tools for the islands themselves. Since on Bonaire divers are required to "pay and display" by attaching a plastic tag to their dive gear, the system is self policing with peer pressure ensuring better than 95% compliance with the fee. The plastic tags have meanwhile become collectors' items.

Additionally divers not only support the Marine Park financially, they are also some of its strongest advocates. Having paid, they have a vested interest in discovering what their money is being used for. They become more receptive to conservation messages and seem to show a greater willingness to learn about the marine environment as well as visitation rules and safe diving practices. Divers also make a significant contribution towards the policing of the Park. Since they are paying for its upkeep, many develop a strong interest in ensuring that prohibited practices are really being banned.

The final question of course has to be are sufficient funds being generated from diver admission fees to adequately manage the Marine Parks?

On Saba the answer was clearly no and they have moved to correct this. Saba Marine Park generates approximately 70% of its total income from diver admission fees. The other 30% is generated through the sales of souvenirs (20%), yacht fees (5%) and donations (5%). Grant money is not included and normally is applied to non-personnel and time-limited investments, i.e., hardware, repairs and replacement of equipment, research, etc. The Marine Park has increased its admission fee three times over the past eight years from $1.00 per dive in 1992 to $3.00 per dive by 1998. However, the last fee increase was not uniformly well-received by the dive operators, even though it still constitutes less than 10% of the total cost per dive. Yet the Marine Park is still understaffed—with just three full-time employees—and an ever-increasing workload. Since divers do an average of 4.5 dives/diver, the actual income generated per diver is comparable to Bonaire; however, visitation levels are much lower (just over 5,000 in 1997, compared to over 27,000 on Bonaire).

Bonaire's situation is even more precarious. It too is understaffed and struggling to stay afloat. Despite evidence from surveys conducted in 1993 that divers are prepared to pay up to $25.00 per annum in admission fees to the Marine Park, resistance from the dive industry has meant that the fee has remained at the 1991 level. It has not been possible to apply a flat rate across the board fee to all Marine Park users as this does not meet with the approval of the Park's management body.

Therefore the Marine Parks have simply had to become more creative in terms of their funding strategies. The sale of souvenirs, particularly T-shirts, accounts for approximately one third of Saba Marine Park's total income. A shop and office conveniently located at the yacht check in point certainly help in this regard. User fees are charged for use of public moorings and this too accounts for a significant part of the Park's income along with a "friends" group and income from their recompression facility.

On Bonaire, grant funding accounts for much of the short fall in income. Although this is not a dependable source of income and can rarely be used to cover salaries or running cost, it can be a good source of project funding and is useful for replacing or acquiring capital equipment such as boats, vehicles, computers and the like. Special relationships have been established with a number of different groups and individuals who sponsor various Marine Park programmes, such as its kids snorkel programme, marine activities in schools and mooring programme. Other user fees are also being charged for use of overnight public moorings, for private moorings and there are now plans to charge annual fees to owners of private piers.

Both Saba Marine Park and Bonaire Marine Park have petitioned the Antilles Central Government to assist in exploring the possibility of setting up a "Trust Fund for Nature," the interest from which would be used to support all of the land and marine parks within the Netherlands Antilles.

In conclusion it is clear that, whilst they are not the whole answer, user fees are an excellent source of on-going funding for Marine Parks which are tourism dependent. They involve the dive industry and diving community making it easier to put across conservation messages. They can help to generate a custodial feeling towards the resource, which not only enhances conservation but also may help with enforcement of legal protection for the Park. User fees are an option that is being chosen more and more to ensure the continuation of Marine Parks that really do the job!

Source: Kalli de Meyer, Manager, Bonaire Marine Park.

E-Mail Contact: marinepark@bmp.org

24. Tanga, Tanzania: Collaborative Fisheries and Coral Reef Management

Introduction

Over the last decade there have been major changes in the way MPAs are created and managed. This has been driven by an increasing recognition that for management to be sustainable it has to have the support of communities impacted by MPAs. The development of collaborative management systems as opposed to the more traditional public sector (e.g., government) management regimes has been a direct response to the need for more community support. This in turn has led to the development of participatory approaches to involve all stakeholders from the public and private sectors (including local communities) in the creation and development of MPAs. This case describes the processes used during the creation and management of a series of small MPAs in Tanga Region, Tanzania along with; key lessons learned and how a similar initiative could be conceived in light of those lessons. The Programme was supported by Irish AID and IUCN.

Background

The Tanga Coastal Zone Conservation and Development Programme was initiated in July 1994 with the overall goal of achieving sustainable development and use of coastal resources in the Tanga Region. Tanga Region is the northern coastal administrative region of Tanzania and extends 180 km. south from the Kenya-Tanzania border. The coast is characterized by 96 fringing and patch coral reefs, seven medium sized mangrove forests, numerous seagrass beds, and several estuaries and bays. Administratively, the region is sub-divided into three coastal administrative Districts, Muheza, Pangani and Tanga. The population of approximately 379,000 live in two towns (Tanga, 223,000; Pangani, 6,000) and 42 coastal villages (150,000). The economy of most coastal households depends on a combination of activities that in the rural areas invariably involve fishing and farming. Many of the issues that the Tanga Programme was designed to address also face many other coastal communities and governments throughout the developing tropical world. These included declining fish catches; deteriorating status of coral reefs and mangroves; poor governance with low levels of accountability and lack of transparency in decision making, co-ordination of sectoral management, and participation of key stakeholders.

The Initial Process

Key principles adopted by the Tanga Programme during the initial implementation of activities were: work through those institutions which currently held the mandate for management of coastal resources (government agencies); identify and involve all stakeholders from the outset; and start small and keep it simple. The Programme adopted a project cycle of listening, piloting, demonstrating and mainstreaming (Picotto and Weaving, 1994) which was better suited to the above principles than the more traditional, planning, implementation, monitor and review model.

Following these principles, the Programme trained government staff for a facilitating rather than their previously directive role in development of management. These staff members and villagers undertook participatory resource and socioeconomic surveys. The surveys also included stakeholder identification, investigation of indigenous management and knowledge as well as preliminary issue and solution identification. Information from these surveys was used by the District Governments to select "pilot villages" (one per administrative district). In village meetings facilitated by government staff, villagers of the selected pilot villages used the survey information to identify, analyze and agree about issues and suggest solutions for the issues they had identified. The meetings agreed on the need for a plan to implement the agreed solutions, the area in which management actions would be implemented, the principles of management to be applied, and the timeline of the plan. Agreed solutions became result areas in a plan whose overall objective directly addressed the agreed issue.

Villagers then formed committees representative of interest groups within the village to define actions, who would undertake them and when. Committees also defined how rules would be enforced, what the penalties for non-compliance would be, what training was necessary for identified implementers, objectively verifiable indicators for the objective and results and a monitoring programme to assess them. The reefs to be closed were chosen using criteria villagers and government staff identified. These included reef condition, ease of monitoring, current patterns and accessibility to older members of the community. Committee members presented the completed plan to all villagers and to other villages sharing the fisheries resources and to the relevant local and central government agencies. All these bodies confirmed their support for the plan by signing written agreements.

The outputs of this process were plans that adopted an adaptive management strategy. This type of management strategy attempts to address the priority issues, monitors and evaluates the actions taken, and adapts future measures to meet the outcome of the evaluation. The objectives and results of the plans directly addressed the issue and its principal causes respectively. Another key aspect of the plans was that villagers took the responsibility of being the main implementers (including the monitoring programme) with government playing a supportive, not principal role.

Each of the plans had a life of one year. At the end of that period all stakeholders would review the plans, including the partner villages who shared the resources. The objectives of the review process were to assess progress and effectiveness of actions in obtaining results. Members of the village monitoring teams presented data on catch per gear, density of important fish species and status indicators of reef health on both closed and fished reefs to stakeholders in partner villagers. Using this information and their own perceptions and needs, the meetings decided whether the objectives and results required modification, omission or that they should stand as originally formulated. This process was repeated in the original pilot village. Representatives of the partner villages presented the views of their villages. If there was disagreement on an issue, a vote of all stakeholders was taken to decide the issue.

Implementation

Implementation of these plans over two years enhanced both fish catches by approximately 10% and conservation of the area by facilitating the closure of three reefs and effective enforcement of laws, rules and regulations. The initial key to the success of the plans was the control of dynamite fishing where government efforts had not been successful in 30 years. Collaboration between villagers and government has led to the cessation of this fishing technique in established management areas. This success had its difficulties as initial efforts with marine police and villagers without external assistance were unsuccessful. It was only when Navy personnel supported villagers that consistent control of dynamite fishing was realized. This success has not only led to the cessation of a fishing technique that destroyed 10 reefs and damaged numerous others, but has also helped government realize that villagers are capable, with the right assistance, to play a significant role in marine resource management.

Effective awareness and enforcement of laws, rules and regulations were also important in ensuring initial compliance with other management measures including reef closures. Although it was villagers that identified the need for reef closures as means to replenish stocks, not all agreed with the closures. Despite an initial attempt at voluntary compliance there were some individuals who were not deterred until sterner measures such as fines were implemented. Reef closures were by far the most controversial measure of the plans. Although the monitoring programme clearly showed that they were successful in replenishing stocks on those reefs, villagers trained in fish counting techniques had recorded this and others had been taken to see for themselves, there was still pressure from some groups to open the reefs. Over the two years of implementation, pressure has grown amongst some vociferous groups to reopen the reefs despite the rise in catches and stocks on those reefs.

During the same period, differences (the user committees on one side and the village government on the other) over collection and use of revenues led to the committees being brought under the control of the village government. In Tanzania, each village has a government, representatives of which are affiliated to political parties. Political pressure brought by elections resulted in the village government of the original pilot village to declare the reefs open. This decision was taken unilaterally with one day's notice and so contravened verbal agreements made with the other villages and the District administration. This lack of adherence to agreed procedures has led to the loss of an important component of the plans and it will be of interest to see what measure(s) will be taken by the other partners in light of this decision.

Key Lessons Learned

-   The participatory approach was successful in gaining initial agreement between government and users as to what should happen and who should do it. There have been and still are problems between parties regarding the pace of implementation and who should take ultimate responsibility for shared actions.

-   The process was also successful as a means to initially shift responsibility for management actions from government to the community. However, it did not prevent the government institutions when politically motivated to take back decision-making power despite successes in implementation. More legally binding agreements may provide better adherence to agreed procedures.

-   The plans produced by the process were simple, direct and easily understood by all parties. This has made monitoring and evaluation simple and direct but the plans alone did not adequately ensure that management institutions had to follow procedures.

-   Destructive fishing was controlled by a collaborative effort between government and communities. Both had failed to control the problem when acting individually.

-   Villagers can collect reliable monitoring data and feed it back to their communities. The problem lies in that some groups refuse to believe findings even from information collected by members of their own group if they see it being against their self interest. Despite this, many other groups have accepted the village monitors as being their own experts and seek their opinions on issues brought up during management discussions. There is an increasing need for government to recognize the skills of these village level teams to ensure sustainability of management.

Summary

Development of collaborative management in Tanga has produced environmental benefits in terms of improved reef status and reef fish stocks as well as improved catches for legal fishing techniques. The procedure for formulating these plans increased awareness of how communities can deal with their own issues and monitor their success. However, sustainability of this type of management is dependent on different levels of government recognizing the ability of villagers and ensuring adherence to agreed procedures for management actions. A further challenge to this type of management will be the long term financing strategy that must ensure that the collaborating parties each receive the funds they require to effectively implement, monitor and agree ongoing and future management actions. This aspect of management has not been adequately addressed by the Tanga programme to date but will be an important component of future work.

References

Piccotto, R and Weaving, R. 1994. A New Project Cycle for the World Bank? Finance and Development. World Bank. December 1994.

Source: J.C. Horrill, Technical Advisor, Tanga Coastal Zone Conservation and Development Programme, IUCN.

E-Mail Contact: chorrill@raha.com

25. Tanga, Tanzania: Involvement of Women in Village Committees

The Tanga Coastal Zone Conservation and Development Programme has been addressing coastal resources management in Tanga Region, Tanzania, since July 1994. Issues being addressed are overfishing, destructive means of fishing, destruction of mangroves, coastal erosion, and poor agricultural production due to vermin and poor government enforcement. How women became significantly involved in the process is the subject of this case, particularly as regards village management plans and creation of reserves for coral reefs and mangroves.

The programme took a collaborative approach between government agencies and local resource users. Following participatory resource appraisals and a large regional workshop for all stakeholders, a set of specific results and activities were agreed. Government officers received training to facilitate a participatory process in the villages of analysis of issues, action planning, and implementing and monitoring activities in some pilot villages.

The villagers formed committees to take actions to deal with their priority issues according to three-month action plans developed by themselves. Village initiatives resulted in reduced levels of dynamite fishing and mangrove cutting, improved enforcement of regulations and by-laws, and increased fish catches. Under the programme the formulation of fisheries and mangrove management plans/agreements were initiated. Because fisheries and mangrove areas are usually shared with other villages this evolved into management plans for fisheries management areas, first with limited participation of other villages, then with equal participation of other villages (see also Case No. 24).

How Women Were Involved

Right from the start the programme took an interest in involving women in all steps of the process: in setting priorities, analysis of issues, and planning, implementation and monitoring of activities. A series of specific actions were taken in the different steps of the process used by the programme (Box III-4), including the following:

Box III-4. Women involvement in Kigombe village

In Kigombe village women were initially not attending village meetings. These were the meetings for analyzing their priority issues (fish scarcity and vermin).

Special meetings were held then with the women to analyze consequences and causes of them not attending these meetings. The women recognized that by not attending the meetings they would not be informed of what was going on and they would not be able to benefit from Programme activities. They listed a number of causes why they were not attending the meetings. The main reason was that the men wouldn't listen to them anyway so they did not want to waste their (own) valuable time. The second reason was that the meetings were on times that were not suitable for them. They also complained that they were not properly informed about the meetings.

Then a meeting was held with women and men about the subject. The men recognized that if women would not attend the meetings they would fall behind and that the men would not benefit from the ideas, experiences, suggestions and help they could get from the women. Asked about the causes they said that it was a matter of customs and tradition. Obviously men and women had different perceptions of the issue. The women did not react to the statements of the men initially but when asked to present the conclusions of the previous meeting they did. We then discussed the differences in conclusions (especially the causes of the absence of women in meetings).

The women decided then that they would attend the meetings and men promised that they would listen to the women. They also decided that meetings would be held on another time and they agreed on how the meetings should be announced.

After this women indeed attended these and other general meetings. They were present in meetings analyzing the priority issues and solutions, they took seats in the village management committees that are planning, overseeing and monitoring implementation of activities, and participated in the formulation of a fisheries management agreement. However, participation stayed lower than in the other pilot villages.

One year later (November 1996) participation of women was assessed in three villages. In Kigombe 10 of the 42 committee members (24%) were female, in Mwambani 14 of 29 (48%), and in Kipumbwi 13 of 28 (46%). Some women were again complaining about meetings coinciding with farm work or other commitments and that meetings were not properly announced. Findings were discussed with the committee members and measures taken to improve women participation. At present 21 of 48 committee members (44%) in Kigombe are female.

Early 1997 some women in Kigombe formed their own group to establish a woodlot, and to start seaweed farming and handcraft activities. They established a woodlot, but had problems with land tenure ship. After they had prepared the land and planted the seedlings, other people claimed the land was theirs. Because the women had no written permission from the village government to use the land it took more than half a year before the dispute was settled and the women got permission to stay on their piece of land.

1. *Involving women in assessment and extension teams.*

2. *Using participatory approaches throughout.*

3. *Using special techniques to stimulate women participation and dialogue and cooperation between the sexes in all steps of the process.*

4. *Collecting and monitoring of gender disaggregated data.*

5. *Conducting special meetings or actions when participation of women is low or absent:* In cases where women did not participate well in meetings special meetings were conducted, first with women alone and finally with men to discuss women's participation. This resulted in a better understanding of men and women of the importance of women's participation, as well as a better participation of women in meetings afterwards.

6. *Insisting on equal representation in activities like training courses, study tours, workshops,* etc. This was instrumental in building women's self-confidence.

7. *Insisting on a fair (not necessarily equal) representation in village meetings and village committees.*

8. *Assessing gender equity in addressing priority issues, allocation of funds and materials, and other benefits on a yearly basis.*

As a result of these steps, progress was made in raising awareness and support among women and men of the importance of the participation of both sexes; and in achieving more equitable representation of women and men in committees and decision making, in training and in study tours. Women's confidence has increased through their successful participation and some are even actively participating in typical 'male' activities like village patrols. In general women's and men's issues are equally addressed. Although some activities are male dominated and others are female dominated, there is mutual understanding and support.

Lessons Learned

- A combination of different measures (see above) can effectively contribute to improved women participation and gender equity in coastal zone management.

- Working in a Moslem environment—where customs and traditions are often seen as an obstacle to gender equity—cannot be an excuse to not bother with improving women's participation. Programme experience shows that ways can be found to improve women participation without violating customs and traditions.

- It is important that both men and women see the necessity and the advantages of women participation in all steps of the process, and of dialogue and cooperation between the sexes.

Source: Trudi van Ingen, Chief Technical Advisor, Tanga Coastal Zone Conservation and Development Programme, IUCN.

E-Mail Contact: tangacoast@raha.com

PART IV

References

Agardy, T.S. *Marine Protected Areas and Ocean Conservation*, Environmental Intelligence Unit, R.G. Landes Company, Austin, 1997

Alcala, A.C. & E.D. Gomez. 1987. Dynamiting coral reefs for fish: a resource-destructive fishing method. Pp. 51-60 in Salvat, B. (ed). *Op. Cit.*

Alcala, A. C. 1982. Standing stock and growth of four species of molluscs (Tridacnidae) in Sumilon Island, Central Visayas, Philippines. Proceedings of the 4th International Coral Reef Symposium, Manila. Quezon City, Philippines: Marine Sciences Center, University of the Philippines.

Baccar, H. 1982. The role of Ichkeul National Park in conserving genetic resources. Paper presented at 3rd World Congress on National Parks, Coastal and Marine Workshop, Bali, Indonesia.

Banner, A. H. 1974. Kaneohe Bay: Urban pollution and a coral reef ecosystem. Pp. 685-702 in: Proceedings of the 2nd International Coral Reef Symposium. Brisbane, Australia: Great Barrier Reef Committee.

Barber, C., and Pratt, V., 1998, 'Poison and profits: cyanide fishing in the Indo-Pacific', *Environment* 40(8)

Beaumont, J. 1997. Community participation in the establishment and management of marine protected areas: a review of international experience. *Marine Reserves Task Group*. p. 53-62.

Berg, C. J. (ed.). 1981. Proceedings of the Queen Conch fisheries and mariculture meeting. Wallace Groves Aquaculture Foundation.

Birkeland, C. 1997. *Life and death of coral reefs*. Chapman & Hall, N.Y.

Bjorndal, K.A. (ed.). 1995. *Biology and Conservation of Sea Turtles*. Revised Edition. Smithsonian Institution Press, Washington and London: 615 pp.

Boelart-Suominen, S., and C. Cullinan. 1994. *Legal and Institutional Aspects of Integrated Coastal Area Management in National Legislation*. United Nations, Development Law Service, Rome. 118 p.

Borrini-Feyerabend, G. (ed.). 1997a. *Beyond Fences: Seeking Social Sustainability in Conservation. Volume 1: A Process Companion*. IUCN, Gland, Switzerland: 129 pp.

Borrini-Feyerabend, G. (ed.). 1997b. *Beyond Fences: Seeking Social Sustainability in Conservation. Volume 2: A resource Book*. IUCN, Gland, Switzerland: 283 pp.

Bouchet, P. 1979. Coquillages de collection et protection des recifs. Centre de Noumea, New Caledonia: ORSTOM.

Bourne, W. R. P. 1981. Rats as avian predators. Atoll Res. Bull. 255:69-72.

Brainerd, T.R. 1994. Socioeconomic research on fisheries and aquaculture in Africa. *In* Charles, A.T., T.R. Brainerd, A. Bermudez M., H.M. Montalvo & R.S. Pomeroy (eds). *Fisheries Socioeconomics in the Developing World: Regional Assessments and an Annotated Bibliography*. IDRC, Ottawa: pp. 12-37.

Brown, B.E. 1987. Heavy metals pollution on coral reefs. *In* Salvat, B. (ed). *Human Impacts on Coral Reefs: Facts and Recommendations*. Antenne Museum E.P-.H.E., French Polynesia: Pp. 119-134.

Brown, B.E. (ed). 1990. Coral bleaching. *Coral Reefs* 8: 153-232.

Bryant, D., L. Burke, J. McManus and M. Spalding. 1998. *Reefs at Risk. A Map-Based Indicator of Threats to the World's Coral Reefs*. World Resources Institute, Washington, D.C., USA: 56 pp.

Butler, M.J.A., C. LeBlanc, J.A. Belbin, and J.L. MacNeill. 1987. *Marine Resource Mapping: An Introductory Manual*, United Nations, FAO, Fisheries Tech. Paper No. 274. 256 p.

Carpenter, R. (ed.). 1983. Natural systems for development. New York: Macmillan Publishing Co. 485 pp.

Central Intelligence Agency. 1976. Indian Ocean atlas. Washington, D.C.: Central Intelligence Agency.

Cesar, H. 1996. *The economic value of Indonesian coral reefs*. The World Bank, Washington, D.C.: 9 pp.

Cesar, H., C.G. Lundin, S. Bettencourt & J. Dixon. 1997. Indonesian coral reefs—An economic analysis of a precious but threatened resource. *Ambio*, 26(6): 345-350.

Charlier, R.H. and D.DeCroo. 1991. *Coastal Erosion. Response and Management*. Haecon N.V. (Ghent, Belgium), IWK 133/91.04462.

Christie, P. & A.T. White. 1994. Community-based coral reef management in San Salvador Island, the Philippines. *Society and Natural Resources* 7:104-118.

Chua, T.E. and Scura, L.F. 1992. *Integrative Framework and Methods for Coastal Area Management*. ICLARM, Manila. 169 pp.

Ciereszko, L. S., and T. K. B. Karns. 1973. Comparative biochemistry of coral reef coelenterates. Pp. 183-203 in 0. A. Jones and R. Endean (eds.), Biology and geology of coral reefs, vol. 2, Biology 1. New York, San Francisco, London: Academic Press. 480 pp.

Clark, J. 1974. Coastal ecosystems: Ecological considerations for the management of the coastal zone. Washington, D.C.: The Conservation Foundation. 178 pp.

Clark, J. R. 1977. Coastal ecosystem management: A technical manual for the conservation of coastal zone resources. New York, London, Sydney, Toronto: John Wiley & Sons. 928 pp.

Clark, J., J. S. Banta, and J. A. Zinn. 1980. Coastal environmental management: Guidelines for conservation of resources and protection against storm hazards. Washington, D.C.: U. S. Government Printing Office. 161 pp.

Clark, J. R., and S. McCreary. 1983. Community flood hazard management for the coastal barriers of Apalachicola Bay, Florida. Pp. 213-225 in: Preventing coastal flood disasters. Madison, Wisc.: Association of State Floodplain Managers.

Clark, J.R, A. Al Gain, and T. Chiffings. 1987. A coastal managment programme for Saudi Arabian Red Sea coast. *Coastal Zone '87* , Vol.II, American Society of Civil Engineers, New York. pp 1673-1681.

Clark, J. R. 1988. *Rehabilitation of coral reef habitats*. Rept. of a Science Workshop held at St. John, USVI, December, 1987 (unpub), University of Miami/RSMAS and U.S. National Park Service. 16 p.

Clark, J. R., B. Causey, and J. A. Bohnsack. 1989. Benefits from coral reef protection: Looe Key Reef, Florida. In: *Coastal Zone '89*, Vol. 4. American Society of Civil Engineers, New York. Pp. 3076-3086.

Clark, J. 1991a. *The status of Integrated Coastal Zone Management: A Global Assessment*, U.of Miami/RSMAS. 118 pp.

Clark, J. (Ed.) 1991b. *Carrying Capacity. A Status Report on Marine and Coastal Parks and Protected Areas*. Third Intl. Seminar on Coastal Reserves. US NPS/OIA and RSMAS/Univ of Miami. 73 p.

Clark, J. 1996. *Coastal Zone Management Handbook*. CRC/Lewis Publ., Boca Raton, Florida (USA). 694 p.

Clark, J. 1998. *Coastal Seas: The Conservation Challenge*. Blackwell Science, Oxford. 134 p.

Classen D.B. van R. 1989. Map Analysis Techniques. In: *How to Assess Environmental Impacts on Tropical Islands and Coastal Areas*. East/West Center, Honolulu. pp. 105-108.

Collete, B. B., and F. H. Talbot. 1972. Activity of coral reef fishes with emphasis on nocturnal-diurnal changeover. Bull. Nat. Hist. Mus. Los Angeles County 14.

Connell, J. H. 1978. Diversity in tropical rain forests and coral reefs. Science 199:1302- 1310.

C.O.E. 1984. *Shore Protection Manual*. Vols 1-3. Coastal Engineering Research Center. U.S. Army Corps of Engineers, Washington, D.C.

Cooper, J.A.G., T.D. Harrison & A.E.L. Ramm. 1995. The role of estuaries in large marine ecosystems: examples form the Natal coast, South Africa. *In* Okemwa, E., M.J. Ntiba & K. Sherman (eds). *Status and future of Large Marine Ecosystems of the Indian Ocean: A Report of the International Symposium and Workshop*. A Marine Conservation and Development Report. IUCN, Gland, Switzerland: Pp. 92-100.

Craik, W., 1994, 'The economics of managing fisheries and tourism in the Great Barrier Reef Marine Park', in Munasinghe, M. and McNeely, J., (eds) *Protected Area Economics and Policy: Linking Conservation and Sustainable Development*, IUCN and the World Bank, Washington D.C.

Davey, A.G. 1998. *National System Planning for Protected Areas*. IUCN, Gland, Switzerland and Cambridge, UK: 71 pp.

Davis-Case, D. 1989. *Community Forestry: Participatory Assessment, Monitoring and Evaluation.* Community Forestry Note 2. FAO, Rome: 150 pp.

Davis-Case, D., T. Grove & C. Apted. 1990. *The community's toolbox: The idea, methods and tools for participatory assessment, monitoring and evaluation in community forestry.* Community Forestry Field manual 2. FAO, Rome: 146 pp.

Davis, G. E. 1977. Anchor damage to a coral reef on the east coast of Florida. Biol. Conserv. 11:29-34.

De Fontaubert, A.C. 1994. *The United Nations Global Conference on the Sustainable Development of Small Island Developing States,* 24 Ocean and Coastal Management. 208-11.

De Fontaubert, A.C. 1996. *The United Nations Conference on Straddling Fish Stocks and Highly Migratory Fish Stocks: Another Step in the Implementation of the Law of the Sea Convention.* Ocean Yearbook 12. University of Chicago Press.

De Fontaubert, A.C., Downes, D.R, and Agardy, T.S. *1996. Biodiversity in the Seas: Implementing the Convention on Biological Diversity in Marine and Coastal Habitats,* IUCN-CIEL-WWF, Cambridge and Gland.

De Fontaubert, A.C. 1998. Critical analysis of the SPAW Protocol: The Dilemma of Regional Cooperation.

Department of Business Development, Port Moresby. 1977. Seashells as a business. Port Moresby, New Guinea: Department of Business Development.

Diamond, J. M. 1975. The island dilemma: Lessons of modern biogeographic studies for the design of natural reserves. Biol. Conserv. 7:129-146.

Diamond, J. M. 1976. Island biogeography and conservation: Strategy and limitations. Science 193: 1027-1029.

Diamond, J. M., and R. M. May. 1976. Island biogeography and the design of natural reserves. Pp. 163-186 in R. M. May (ed.), Theoretical ecology: Principles and applications. Philadelphia, Toronto: W. B. Saunders & Co. 317 pp.

Dixon, J.A. and P.B. Sherman. 1990. *Economics of Protected Areas. A New Look and Benefits and Costs.* Island Press, Washington, D.C. and Covelo, California: 234 pp.

Douglas, G. 1969. Draft checklist of Pacific oceanic islands. Micronesica 5(2):327-463.

DuBois, R., L. Berry, and R. Ford. 1984. Catchment land use and its implications for coastal resources conservation. In: A casebook of coastal management. Columbia, S.C.: Research Planning Institute.

Dulvy, N., Stanwell-Smith, D., Darwall, W. and Horrill, C., 1995, 'Coral mining at Mafia Island, Tanzania: a management dilemma', *Ambio* 24(6): 358-365

Dyer, C.L. & J.R. McGoodwin. 1994. Introduction. *In* Dyer, C.L. & J.R.

McGoodwin (eds). *Folk Management in the World's Fisheries: Lessons for Modern Fisheries Management.* University Press of Colorado (USA): Pp. 1-15.

Eichbaum, W. and Agardy, T. *The Role of Marine and Coastal Protected Areas in the Conservation and Sustainable Use of Biological Diversity,* 9 Oceanography 60 (1996).

Elliott, H. F. 1. 1972. Island ecosystems and conservation with particular reference to the biological significance of islands of the Indian Ocean and consequential research and conservation needs. J. Mar. Biol. Ass. India 14(2):578-608.

Emerton, L., 1997, *Seychelles Biodiversity: Economic Assessment,* IUCN Eastern Africa Regional Office, Nairobi and Republic of Seychelles Conservation and National Parks Section, Division of Environment, Ministry of Foreign Affairs, Planning and Environment, Mahé.

Emerton, L. and Asrat, A., 1998, *Eritrea Biodiversity: Economic Assessment,* IUCN Eastern Africa Regional Office, Nairobi and Department of Environment, Ministry of Land, Water and Environment, Government of the State of Eritrea

Emerton, L., 1999, *Financing the Management of Kisite Marine National Park and Mpunguti Marine National Reserve, Kenya through Partnerships with Stakeholders,* IUCN Eastern Africa Regional Office Biodiversity Economics Working Paper.

Endean, R. 1976. Destruction and recovery of coral reef communities. Pp. 215-254 in 0. A. Jones and R. Endean (eds.), Biology and geology of coral reefs, vol. 3, Biology 2. New York, San Francisco, London: Academic Press. 435 pp.

English, S., C. Wilkinson & V. Baker (eds.). 1997. *Survey manual for tropical marine resources*. Second edition. Australian Institute of Marine Science., Townsville: 390 pp.

FAO/UNEP. 1981. Conservation of genetic resources of fish: Problems and recommendations (FAO Fisheries Technical Paper 217). Report of the expert consultation on the genetic resources of fish, Rome, 9-13 June, 1980. Rome: United Nations Food and Agriculture Organisation. 43 pp.

FAO. 1994. *Mangrove forest management guidelines*. FAO Forest Paper 117. FAO, Rome: 319 pp.

Farnsworth, N.R. and R.W. Morris. 1976. Higher plants: The sleeping giant of drug developmen. *Amer.J.Pharmacol.*, 146. pp 46-52.

Fay, M.B. 1992. Maziwi Island off Pangani (Tanzania): History of its destruction and possible causes. *UNEP Regional Seas Reports and Studies No. 139*. UNEP, Nairobi, Kenya: 20 pp., 28 figs.

Freestone, D. 1992. Protection of Marine Species and Ecosystems in the Wider Caribbean—The Protocol on Specially Protected Areas and Wildlife. Marine Pollution Bulletin, Vol.22, No.12, pp. 579-581.

Gardner, J. 1982a. An overview of institutional arrangements for coastal conservation in several countries. Paper presented at 3rd World Congress on National Parks, Coastal and Marine Workshop, Bali, Indonesia.

Gardner, J. 1982b. Institutional arrangements for coastal conservation. Paper presented at 3rd World Congress on National Parks, Coastal and Marine Workshop, Bali, Indonesia.

Geoghegan, T., I. Jackson, A. Putney and Y. Renard. 1984. *Environmental Guidelines for Development in the Lesser Antilles.*, Eastern Caribbean Natural Areas Mgmt. Programme, St. Croix, U.S.A., V. I. 44 p.

Geoghegan, T., 1996, 'Revenue generation to sustain coral reef conservation', *Intercoast Network* 27: 6/10

GESAMP. 1996. *The Contribution of Science to Integrated Coastal Management*, United Nations/FAO, Repts. and Studies No. 61. 66 p.

Gilbert, A.J. & R. Janssen. 1997. The use of environmental functions to evaluate management strategies for the Pagbilao mangrove forest. *CREED Working Paper Series No. 15*. IIED, London and IVM, Vrije Universiteit, Amsterdam: 40 pp.

Goeden, G. B. 1979. Biogeographic theory as a management tool. Environ. Conserv. 6(1):27-32.

Grassle, J.F. 1991. Deep-sea benthic biodiversity. *Bioscience* 41(7): 464-469.

Grigalunas, T.A. & R. Congar (eds.). 1995. *Environmental economics for integrated coastal area management: valuation methods and policy instruments*. Regional Seas Reports and Studies No. 164. UNEP, Nairobi, Kenya: 165 pp.

Glynn, P.W. 1988. El Niño warming, coral mortality and reef framework destruction by echinoid bioerosion in the eastern Pacific. *Galaxea* 7: 129-160.

Glynn, P.W. 1990. Coral mortality and disturbances to coral reefs in the tropical eastern Pacific. *In* Glynn, P.W. (ed). *Global ecological consequences of the 1982-83 El Niño-Southern Oscillation*. Elsevier Oceanography Series, Amsterdam. pp. 55-126.

Glynn, P.W., J. Cortes, H.M. Guzman & R.H. Richmond. 1988. El Niño (1982-83) associated coral mortality and relationship to sea surface temperature deviations in the tropical eastern Pacific. *Proc. 6th Int. Coral Reef Symp., Australia, 1988* 3:237-243.

Gomez, E.D., A.C. Alcala & H.T. Yap. 1987. Other fishing methods destructive to corals. Pp. 51-60 in Salvat, B. (ed.). *Op. Cit.*

Guard, M & M. Masaiganah. 1997. Dynamite fishing in Southern Tanzania, Geographic Variation, Intensity of Use and Possible Solutions. *Mar. Poll. Bull.* 34: 758-762.

Gubbay, S. (ed.). 1995. *Marine Protected Areas: Principles and Techniques for Management*. Chapman & Hall, London: 232 pp.

Hamilton, L. S., and S. C. Snedaker (eds.). 1984. Handbook for mangrove area management. Honolulu, Hawaii: East-West Center. 123 pp.

Hatziolos, M, C.G. Lundin & A. Alm. 1994. *Africa: A Framework for Integrated Coastal Zone Management*. The World Bank, Washington, D.C.: 150 pp.

Heslinga, G. A., and A. Hillman. 1980. Hatchery culture of the commercial top shell *Trochus niloticus* in Palau, Caroline Islands. Aquaculture 22:35-43.

Hockey, P.A.R. & G.M. Branch. 1994. Conserving marine biodiversity on the African coast: implications of a terrestrial perspective. *Aquat. Conserv.* 4: 345-362.

v'ant Hof, T. 1996. Bonaire:carrying capacity limits, *In*: Clark, J.R., *Coastal Zone Management Handbook*, CRC/Lewis Publishers, New York. pp. 498-500.

Holmes, R.E. 1979. Bone regeneration within a coralline hydroxyapatite. *Implant. Plast. & Reconstr. Surg.* 63(5): 626-633.

Hooten, A.J., & M.E. Hatziolos (eds.). 1995. *Sustainable financing mechanisms for coral reef conservation: Proceedings of a workshop*. Environmentally Sustainable Development Proceedings Series No. 9. The World Bank, Washington, D.C.: 116 pp.

Horrill, J.C., T. van Ingen. 1997. *Assessment of community dependence on and management of coastal resources*. Second Meeting for Preparation of the Transboundary Diagnostic Analysis of the Western Indian Ocean Nairobi, Kenya 1-4 December 1997. UNEP, Nairobi: 15 pp.

Hudson, B.E.T. 1988. User and public information. In: *Coral Reef Management Handbook*, R.A. Kenchington and B.E.T. Hudson (Eds). UNESCO Regional Office for Science and Technology for South East Asia, Jakarta. Pp. 163-176.

ICAM, 1999, *Stakeholder Participation in the Management of Diani-Chale Marine National Reserve: a Concept for Action*, Integrated Coastal Area Management, Coast Development Authority, Mombasa

IIED. 1994. *Whose Eden? An overview of community approaches to wildlife management*. IIED, London: 124 pp.

Insull, A.D., U.C. Barg & P. Martosubroto. 1995. Coastal fisheries and aquaculture within integrated coastal area management in East Africa. *In* Linden, O. (ed). *Proceedings of the Workshop and Policy Conference on Integrated Coastal Zone Management in Eastern Africa including the Island States, Arusha, Tanzania*. Coastal Management Center (CMC) Conf. Proc. 1. Metro-Manila, Philippines. pp. 19-36.

IUCN, 1994, *Report on the First Global Forum on Environmental Funds*, IUCN—The World Conservation Union, US, Washington D.C.

IUCN. 1994. *Guidelines for Protected Area management Categories*. IUCN, Cambridge, UK and Gland, Switzerland: 261 pp.

IUCN/UNEP/WWF. 1991. *Caring for the Earth: A Strategy for Sustainable Living*. IUCN, Gland, Switzerland: 228 pp.

IUCN/WWF/UNEP. 1979. Proceedings: Workshop on Cetacean Sanctuaries, Tijuana and Guerrero Negro, B.C. Mexico. Gland, Switzerland: International Union for Conservation of Nature and Natural Resources. 51 pp.

Johannes, R.E. 1978. Traditional marine conservation methods in Oceania and their demise. *Annual Review of Ecology and Systematics* 9: 349-364

Johannes, R. E. 1975. Pollution and degradation of coral reef communities. Pp. 13-51 in E. J. Ferguson Wood and R. E. Johannes (eds.), Tropical marine pollution. Amsterdam, Oxford, New York: Elsevier Publishing Company. 192 pp.

Johannes, R.E. 1984. Marine conservation in relation to traditional life-styles of tropical artisanal fishermen. *In* Hanks, J. (ed.). *Traditional life-styles, conservation and rural development*. Commission on Ecology Papers No. 7. IUCN, Gland, Switzerland. pp. 30-35.

Kapetsky, J. M. 1981. Some considerations for the management of the coastal lagoon and estuarine fisheries (FAO Fisheries Technical Paper 218). Rome: United Nations Food and Agriculture Organisation. 47 pp.

Kearney, R. E. 1980. Some problems of developing and managing fisheries in small island states. In: The island states of the Pacific and Indian Oceans: Anatomy of development (Development Studies Monograph 23). Canberra: A.N.U. Press.

Kelleher, G. and R. Kenchington. 1992. *Guidelines for establishing marine protected areas.* A Marine Conservation and Development Report. IUCN, Gland, Switzerland.

Kelleher, G., C. Bleakley, & S.M. Wells (eds). 1995. *A Global Representative System of Marine Protected Areas.* GBRMPA, The World Bank and IUCN, Washington DC, USA.

Kelleher, G. 1996. Public participation on "the Reef". *World Conservation,* 2/96, IUCN. pp 21-23.

Kelleher, G., and T. Van 't Hof. 1982. Report on the Implementing Management Session of the Coastal and Marine Workshop, 3rd World Congress on National Parks, Bali, Indonesia.

Kenchington, R.A. and B.E.T. Hudson (Eds). 1988. *Coral Reef Management handbook.* UNESCO, Jakarta. 321 pp.

Kimball, L. Article on GPA LBS

Koslow, J.A. 1997. Seamounts and the ecology of deep-sea fisheries. *American Scientist* 85(2): 168-176.

Lausche, B. J. 1980. Guidelines for protected areas legislation (IUCN Environmental Policy and Law Paper No. 16). Gland, Switzerland: International Union for Conservation of Nature and Natural Resources.

Lewis Smith, R.I., D.W.H. Walton, P.R. Dingwall (eds.). 1994. *Developing the Antarctic protected area system.* IUCN, Gland, Switzerland and Cambridge, UK. 137 pp.

Limpus, C.J. 1995. Global Overview of the Status of Marine Turtles: A 1995 Viewpoint. In *Proceedings of the World Conference on Sea Turtle Conservation, Washington D.C. 26-30 November 1979 with Contributions on Recent Advances in Sea Turtle Biology and Conservation, 1995.* Smithsonian Institution Press, Washington, D.C.: 615 pp.

Loya, Y. & B. Rinkevich. 1987. Effects of petroleum hydrocarbons on corals. Pp. 91-102 in Salvat, B. (ed). *Op. Cit.*

Loya, Y. 1976. Recolonization of Red Sea corals affected by natural catastrophe and man-made perturbations. Ecology 57:278289.

Lucas, P. H. C. 1984. How protected areas can help meet society's evolving needs. In J. A. McNeely and K. R. Miller (eds.), National parks, conservation and development: The role of protected areas in sustaining society. Washington, D.C.: Smithsonian Institution Press.

MacArthur, R. H., and E. O. Wilson. 1963. An equilibrium theory of insular zoogeography. Evolution 17: 373-387.

Makoloweka, S. & K. Shurcliff. 1996. Silencing the dynamiters. *People & the Planet,* 6(2): 24-25.

Makoloweka, S., M. Gorman, J.C. Horrill, H. Kolombo, C. Kawau, Z. Lugazo, K. Shurcliff, G. Urono & T. van Ingen. 1997. Establishing coastal management in Tanga Region, Tanzania: an experimental approach. Pp. 50-60 in Humphrey, S. & J. Francis (eds.). *Op. Cit.*

Marine Reserves Task Group. 1997. *Towards a New Policy on Marine Protected Areas for South Africa.* SANCOR Occasional Report No. 2: 127 pp.

Marszalek, D.S. 1987. Sewage and eutrophication. Pp. 77-90 in Salvat, B. (ed). *Op. Cit.*

Matthes, H. & J.M. Kapetsky. 1988. Worldwide compendium of mangrove-associated aquatic species of economic importance. *FAO Fish. Circ.* (814): 236 pp.

May, R. M. 1975. Island biogeography and the design of wildlife preserves. Nature 254:177- 178.

McEachern, J. and E. L. Towle. 1974. Ecological guidelines for island development. Gland, Switzerland: International Union for Conservation of Nature and Natural Resources.

McGoodwin, J.R. 1990. *Crisis in the World's Fisheries: People, Problems, and Policies.* Stanford Univ Press, Stanford, California: 235 pp.

McHarg, I. 1969. *Design with Nature.* The Natural History Press, Garden City, New York. 197 pp.

McNeely, J.A. 1988. *Economics and biological diversity*. IUCN, Gland, Switzerland: 236 pp.

McNeely, J.A., K.R. Miller, W.V. Reid, R.A. Mittermeier, & T.B. Werner. 1990. *Conserving the world's biological diversity*. IUCN, Gland, Switzerland; WRI, CI, WWF-US and the World Bank, Washington, DC: 193 pp.

Mitchell, R., and H. Ducklow. 1976. The slow death of coral reefs. Nat. Hist. 85(8):106-110.

Monteforte, M. & M. Carino. 1992. Exploration and evaluation of natural stocks of pearl oysters *Pinctada mazatlanica* and *Pteris sterna* (Bivalvia: Pteriidae): La Paz Bay, South Baja California, Mexico. *Ambio* XX1(4): 314-320.

van Mulekom, L. 1999. An institutional development process in community based coastal resource management. *Ocean & Coastal Management,* 42 (5). p.439-458.

Munro, J. L., and G. A. Heslinga. 1982. Prospects for the commercial cultivation of giant clams. Paper presented at the 35th meeting of the Gulf and Caribbean Fisheries Institute, Nassau, Bahamas.

Narain, U. and Fisher, A., 1994, 'Modelling the value of biodiversity using a production function approach', in Perrings, C., Mäler, K-G, Folke, C, Jansson, B-O and Holling, C., (eds), *Biodiversity Conservation: Policy Issues and Options*, Kluwer Academic Publishers, Dordrecht

Nature Conservancy Council. 1979a. Nature conservation in the marine environment. Report of the NCC/NERC Joint Working Party on marine wildlife conservation. London: Natural Conservancy Council. 64 pp.

Naturvårdsverket. 1980. Utredning om skyddsvärda områden längs Sveriges kust. Marina reservat 1980, SNV PM 1297 (Swedish EPA), cited in Nilsson 1998 *op. cit.*

Neelakantan, K.S. 1994. *Management Plan for the Gulf of Mannar Marine Biosphere Reserve*. Forest Dept., Tamil Nadu, India. 118 pp.

Neudecker, S. 1987. Environmental effects of power plants on coral reefs and ways to minimize them. Pp. 103-118 in Salvat, B. (ed). *Op. Cit.*

Nilsson, P. 1988. *Criteria for the selection of marine protected areas. An analysis*. Swedish Environmental Protection Agency, Stockholm, Sweden: 54 pp.

Nordiska Ministerrådet. 1995. Marina reservat I Norden. Del I—Nordiska Ministerrådet, Kopenhamn, TemaNord 1995: 553—cited in Nilsson 1998 *op. cit.*

Nordlie, F. G., and D. P. Kelso. 1975. Trophic relationships in a tropical estuary. Rev. Biol. Trop. 23(1): 77-99.

Norse, E.A. (ed.). 1993. *Global marine biological diversity: A strategy for building conservation into decision making*. Island Press, Washington, D.C.: 383 pp.

Odour-Noah, E., I. Asamba, R. Ford, L. Wichhart, F. Lelo. 1992. *Implementing PRA: A handbook for facilitate participatory rural appraisal*. Programme for International Development, Clark University, Worcester, Maine, USA: 67 pp.

Odum, E. P. 1971. Fundamentals of ecology. Philadelphia: W. B. Saunders Co. 547 pp.

Ogden, J. C., and J. C. Zieman. 1977. Ecological aspects of coral reef-seagrass bed contacts in the Caribbean. Pp. 277-382 in: Proceedings of the International Coral Reef Symposium, Miami.

Ogilvie, P., and N. M. Wace. 1982. Report on the Island Session of the Coastal and Marine Workshop, 3rd World Congress on National Parks, Bali, Indonesia.

Pabla, H. S., S. Pandey, and R. Badola. 1993. *Guidelines for Ecodevelopment Planning*, UNDP/FAO Project, Wildlife Institute of India, Dehradun, India. 40 p.

Panayotou, T., 1994, 'Conservation of biodiversity and economic development: the concept of transferable development rights', *Environmental and Resource Economics* 4(1): 91-110

Parks Canada. 1983. National marine parks: drain policy. Quebec: Parks Canada, National Parks System Division.

Perrings, C., C. Folke, K.-G. Maler. 1992. The ecology and economics of biodiversity loss: The research agenda. *Ambio* 21(3): 201-211.

Pet-Soede, C., Cesar, H. and Pet J., 1999, 'An economic analysis of blast fishing on Indonesian coral reefs', *Environmental Conservation* 26(2): 83-93.

Pheng, K. S. and W. P. Kam. 1989. Geographic information systems in resource assessment and planning, *Tropical Coastal Area Management*, Vol. 4, No. 2, International Center for Living Aquatic Resources Management, Manila.

Piccotto, R. and Weaving, R. 1994. A New Project Cycle for the World Bank? Finance and Development. World Bank, Washington, D.C.

Pimm, S.L. 1984. The complexity and stability of ecosystems. *Nature*, 307(5949): 321-326.

Prescott-Allen, R., and C. Prescott-Allen. 1984. Park your genes: Protected areas as genebanks for the maintenance of wild genetic resources. In J. A. McNeely and K. R. Miller (eds.), National parks, conservation and development: The role of protected areas in sustaining society. Washington, D.C.: Smithsonian Institution Press.

Pretty, J.N., I. Guijt, J. Thompson & I. Scoones. 1995. *A trainer's guide for participatory learning and action*. IIED Participatory Methodology Series. IIED, London: 267 pp.

Price, A.R.G. 1990. Rapid assessment of coastal zone management requirements: Case study in the Arabian Gulf. *J. Ocean Shorel. Manag. 13(1990): 1-19*.

Price, A. & S. Humphrey. 1993. *Application of the Biosphere Reserve concept to coastal marine areas*. IUCN, Gland, Switzerland: 114 pp.

Pritchard, D. W. 1967. What is an estuary: physical viewpoint. Pp. 3-5 in G.H. Lauff (ed.), Estuaries (AAAS Publication No.83). Washington, D.C.: American Association for the Advancement of Science. 757 pp.

Raven, P. 1992. The nature and value of biodiversity. Pp. 1-5 in: WRI/IUCN/UNEP. *Op. cit.*

Ray, C. 1968. *Marine Parks for Tanzania*. The Conservation Foundation, Washington, DC: 47 pp.

Ray, G.C. 1988. Ecological diversity in coastal zones and oceans. Pp. 36-50 in: E.O. Wilson (ed.). *Op. cit.*

Ray, G.C. 1991. Coastal-zone biodiversity patterns. *Bioscience* 41(7): 490-498.

Ray, G. C., J. A. Dobbin, and R. V. Salm. 1978. Strategies for protecting marine mammal habitats. Oceanus 21(3):55-67. (Reprinted 1981 in Priroda 8:95-101).

Ray, G.C. & J.F. Grassle. 1991. Marine biological diversity. *Bioscience* 41(7): 453-457.

Read. T & L. Cortesi. 1995. Charting coastal resource development in Papua New Guinea: Lessons from a participatory workshop. Greenpeace: 66 pp.

Reina, A., 1998, 'Bazaruto Project: a brief overview May 1998', in Salm, R. and Tessema, Y., (eds) 1999, *Partnership for Conservation: Report of the Regional Workshop on Marine Protected Areas, Tourism and Communities*, IUCN Eastern Africa Regional Office and Kenya Wildlife Service, Nairobi

Renard, Y. 1996. Sharing the benefits of coastal conservation. *World Conservation* 2/96, Intl. Union for Conservation of Nature Gland, Switzerland. p. 21-23.

Riedmiller, S., 1998, 'The Chumbe Island Coral Park Project: a case study of private marine protected area management', in Salm, R. and Tessema, Y., (eds) 1999, *Partnership for Conservation: Report of the Regional Workshop on Marine Protected Areas, Tourism and Communities*, IUCN Eastern Africa Regional Office and Kenya Wildlife Service, Nairobi

Roberts, C.M. 1997. *Connectivity and Management of Caribbean Coral Reefs*. Science Magazine, Vol. 278, No 5342, 21 November 1997, pp. 1454-1457.

Ruddle, K. & T. Akimichi (eds). 1984. *Maritime institutions in the western Pacific*. Senri Ethnological Studies No. 17. National Museum of Ethnology, Osaka, Japan.

Ruddle, K. & R.E. Johannes (eds). 1985. *The traditional knowledge and management of coastal ecosystems in Asia and the Pacific*. UNESCO Regional Office for Science and Technology for Southeast Asia, Jakarta, Indonesia.

Ruggieri, C. D. 1976. Drugs from the sea. Science 194:491-497.

Saenger, P., E. J. Hegerl, and J. D. S. Davie (eds.). 1983. Global status of mangrove ecosystems (Commission on Ecology Paper No. 3). Gland, Switzerland: International Union for Conservation of Nature and Natural Resources.

Salm, R. V. 1976a. Marine turtle management in Seychelles and Pakistan. Environ. Conserv. 3(4): 267-268.

Salm, R. V. 1976b. The dynamics and management of the Ponta Torres coral reef, Inhaca Island—Mocambique. Mems. Inst. Invest. Cient. Mocamb. 12 (Series A):25-40.

Salm, R. V. 1978. Conservation of marine resources in Seychelles: Report on current status and future management for the Government of Seychelles. Morges, Switzerland: International Union for Conservation of Nature and Natural Resources. 41 pp.

Salm, R. V. 1980a. Alternativas para el control de las perturbaciones provocadas por el hombre en el ecosistema de la Laguna de Tacarigua. Caracas, Venezuela: Ministerio del Ambiente y de los Recursos Naturales Renovables. 27 pp.

Salm, R. V. 1980b. The genus-area relation of corals on reefs of the Chagos Archipelago, Indian Ocean. Ph.D. dissertation, The Johns Hopkins University. 125 pp.

Salm, R. V. 1981a. Coastal resources in Sri Lanka, India and Pakistan: Description, use and management. U.S. Fish and Wildlife Service, International Affairs Office. 260 pp.

Salm, R. V. 1981b. Fried rice without shrimp? Conservation Indonesia: Newsletter of the WWF Indonesia Programme 5(3, 4):4-6.

Salm, R. V. 1982. Guidelines for the establishment of coral reef reserves in Indonesia. (FO/INS/78/061 [Special Report]). Bogor, Indonesia: FAO/UNDP National Parks Development Project: 63 pp.

Salm, R. V. 1983. Coral reefs of the Western Indian Ocean: A threatened heritage. Ambio 12(6):349-353. 24~i ~ 2/

Salm, R.V. 1984. Ecological boundaries for coral reef reserves: Principles and guidelines. *Environ. Conserv.* 11(1): 7-13.

Salm, R.V. 1987. Coastal zone management planning and marine protected areas. *Parcs Parks Parques,* 12(1): 18-19.

Salm, R.V. 1993. Coral reefs of the Sultanate of Oman. *Atoll Res. Bull.,* 380: 85 pp.

Salm, R.V. 1995. Marine biodiversity of the Western Indian Ocean: status and conservation framework. *In* Linden, O. (ed.) *Proceedings of the Workshop and Policy Conference on Integrated Coastal Zone Management in Eastern Africa including the Island States, Arusha, Tanzania, 21-23 April 1993.* Coastal Management Center (CMC) Conf. Proc. 1. Manila, Philippines. pp. 101-130.

Salm, R.V. & J.A. Dobbin. 1989b. *Planning, management, and administrative processes for marine protected areas.* Keynote Paper #7, Unesco/IUCN Workshop on the Application of the Biosphere Reserve Concept in Coastal Areas, 14-20 August 1989, San Francisco.

Salm, R.V., S. Humphrey & M. Donnelly. 1996. Integrated approaches to sea turtle conservation in the western Indian Ocean. *In* Humphrey, S.L. & R.V. Salm (eds). Status of Sea Turtle Conservation in the Western Indian Ocean. Proc. Western Indian Ocean Training Workshop and Strategic Planning Session on Sea Turtles. *UNEP Regional Seas Reports and Studies,* No. 165: Pp. 19-26.

Salm, R. & A. Price. 1995. Selection of marine protected areas. Pp. 15-31 in Gubbay, S. (ed.) *Op. cit.*

Salm, R.V. 1998. Community dependence on and management of marine and coastal resources in the Western Indian Ocean: the role of non-governmental organisations. Paper prepared for UNEP Water as a contribution to the Preparation of a Transboundary Diagnostic Analysis and Strategic Action Programme for the Marine and Coastal Environment of the Western Indian Ocean. 32 pp.

Salvat, B. 1967. Importance de la faune malacologique dans les atolls Polynesiens. Cah. Pacifique 11:7-49.

Salvat, B. 1974. Degradation des ecosystemes coralliens. Courr. Nature 30:49-62.

Salvat, B.(ed). 1987a. *Human Impacts on Coral Reefs: Facts and Recommendations*. Antenne Museum E.P-.H.E., French Polynesia: 253 pp.

Salvat, B. 1987b. Dredging in coral reefs. Pp. 165-184 in Salvat, B. (ed). *Op. Cit.*

Salvat, B. 1978. Trouble in paradise part 1: Assault on coral reefs and lagoons. Parks 3(21: 1-4.

Samyal, P. 1983. Mangrove tiger land—the Sunderbans of India. Tigerpaper 10(3): 1-4.

Schumacher, E. F. 1974. Small is beautiful: A study of economics as if people mattered. London: Abacus Books.

Shah, N.J. 1995. Coastal Zone Management in the Seychelles. *Proceedings of the National Workshop on Integrated Coastal Zone Management in the Seychelles*. The World Bank, Environment Dept., and Sida/SAREC: 14-125.

Sheppard, C. R. C. 1979. Status of three rare animals on Chagos. Environ. Conserv. 6(4):310.

Sheppard, C. R. C. 1980. Coral cover, zonation and diversity on reef slopes of Chagos Atolls, and population structures of the major species. Alar. Ecol. Prog. Ser. 2:193-205.

Sheppard, C. R. C. 1981. The reef and soft substrate coral fauna of Chagos, Indian Ocean. J. Nat. Hist. 15:607-621.

Simberloff, D. S., and L. G. Abele. 1976a. Island biogeography theory and conservation practice. Science 191:285-286.

Simberloff, D. S. 1976b. Island biogeography and conservation: strategy and limitations. Science 193:1032.

Simmons, I. G. 1980. Ecological-functional approaches to agriculture in geographical contexts. Geography 65:305-316.

Sladek Nowlis, J., C.M. Roberts, A.H. Smith & E. Siirila. 1997. Human-enhanced impacts of a tropical storm on nearshore coral reefs. *Ambio* 26(8): 515-521.

Smith, C. L., and J. C. Tyler. 1972. Spare resource sharing in a coral reef fish community. Bull. Nat. Hist. Mus. Los Angeles County 14.

Snow, D.W. 1970. The eastern Indian Ocean islands—A summary of their geography, fauna and flora. Papers and proceedings, 11th Technical Meeting of IUCN (New Dehli), Vol. 17. Gland, Switzerland: International Union for Conservation of Nature and Natural Resources.

Sorensen, J.C. and S.T. McCreary. 1990. *Institutional Arrangements for Managing Coastal Resources and Environments*, Coastal Management Publication No. 1 [Rev.] NPS/USAID Series, National Park Service, Office of International Affairs, Washington, D.C. 194 pp.

Sorokin, Y. I. 1973. Microbial aspects of the productivity of coral reefs. Pp. 17-45 in 0. A. Jones and R. Endean (eds.), Biology and geology of coral reefs, vol. 2, Biology I. New York, San Francisco, London: Academic Press. 480 pp.

Soufriere Foundation. 1994. Soufriere Marine Management Area. Soufriere Regional Development Foundation, Soufriere, St. Lucia. 25 pp.

Spurgeon, J. and Aylward, B., 1992, *The Economic Value of Ecosystems: 4—Coral Reefs*, Gatekeeper Series no LEEC GK 92-03, IIED/UCL London Environmental Economics Centre, London.

Stevenson, D. K., and N. Marshall. 1974. Generalizations on the fisheries potential of coral reefs and adjacent shallow-water environments. Pp. 147-156 in: Proceedings of the 2nd International Coral Reef Symposium. Brisbane, Australia: Great Barrier Reef Committee.

Stoddart, D. R., and J. A. Steers. 1977. The nature and origin of coral reef islands. Pp. 59-105 in 0. A. Jones and R. Endean (eds.), Biology and geology of coral reefs, vol. 4, Geology 2. New York, San Francisco, London: Academic Press. 337 pp.

Tejam, C. and Ross, A., 1997, *Manual of Practice: Contingent Valuation Survey for Integrated Coastal Management Applications*, GEF/UNDP/IMO Regional Programme for the Prevention and management of Marine Pollution in the East Asian Seas, Quezon City

Terborgh, J. 1974. Faunal equilibria and the design of wildlife preserves. Pp. 369-380 in F. B. Golley and E. Medina (eds.), Tropical ecological systems. New York: Springer-Verlag.

Tilmant, J.T. 1987. Impacts of recreational activities on coral reefs. Pp. 195-214 in Salvat, B. (ed). *Op. Cit*.

Trono, R.B. 1994. The Philippine-Sabah Turtle Islands: a critical management area for sea turtles of the ASEAN. In *Proceedings of the First ASEAN Symposium-Workshop on Marine Turtle Conservation, Manila, Philippines 1993*, WWF, Manila: 167-180.

Tvedten, I. & B. Hersoug (eds). 1992. *Fishing for development: small-scale fisheries in Africa*. Nordiska Afrikainstitutet, Uppsala, Sweden: 227 pp.

UNEP/IUCN. 1988. *Coral Reefs of the World*. Volumes 1-3. UNEP Regional Seas Directories and Bibliographies, IUCN, Gland, Switzerland and Cambridge/UNEP, Nairobi, Kenya.

United Nations. 1992. Conference on Environment and Development, Agenda 21. Programme of Action for Sustainable Development, Chapter 17, para. 17.10.

Voss, G. L. 1973. Sickness and death in Florida's coral reefs. Nat. Hist. 82(7):40-47.

Wace, N. M. 1979. Oceanic Islands-World Conservation Strategy contribution. (Unpub.)

Wace, N. M. 1980. Exploitation of the advantages of remoteness and isolation in the economic development of the Pacific Islands. Pp. 87- 118 in: The island states of the Pacific and Indian Oceans: Anatomy and development (Development Studies Centre Monograph 23). Canberra: A.N.U. Press.

Wace, N. M. 1982. Protecting island habitats. Paper presented at 3rd World Congress on National Parks, Bali, Indonesia.

Wace, N. M., and M. W. Holdgate. 1976. Man and nature in the Tristan da Cunha Islands (IUCN Monograph 6). Gland, Switzerland: International Union for Conservation of Nature and Natural Resources.

Wagner, P.R. 1973. Seasonal biomass, abundance, and distribution of estuarine dependent fishes in the Caminada Bay system of Louisiana. Ph.D. dissertation, Louisiana State University, Baton Rouge.

Wallace, A. R., 1880. Island life. London: Macmillan.

WCMC. 1992. *Global Biodiversity: Status of the Earth's Living Resources*. Chapman & Hall, London. 594 pp.

Wells, S. 1998. Marine Protected Areas. WWF International. Gland, Switzerland. 56 pp.

Wells, M., K. Brandon & L. Hannah. 1992. *People and Parks: Linking protected area management with local communities*. The World Bank, Washington, D.C.: 99 pp.

Wells, S. & N. Hana. 1992. *The Greenpeace Book of Coral Reefs*. Sterling Publishing Co., Inc., New York: 160 pp.

Wells, S. & A.T. White. 1995. Involving the community. Pp. 61-84 in Gubbay, S. (ed.). *Op. Cit*.

Whitcomb, R. F., J. F. Lynch, P. A. Opler, and C. S. Robbins. 1976. Island biogeography and conservation: Strategy and limitations. Science 193:1030-1032.

White, A. 1987. Why public participation is important for marine protected areas. *CAMPNET Newsletter*. U.S. National Park Service. pp. 5-6.

White, A.T. 1988. The effect of community-managed marine reserves in the Philippines on their associated coral reef fish populations. Asian Fish. Sci. 1(2): 27-42.

White, A.T. 1989. Two community-based marine reserves: lessons for coastal management. *In* Chua T.-E. & D.Pauly (eds.). *Coastal area management in Southeast Asia: policies, management strategies and case studies*. ICLARM Conference Proceedings 19. ICLARM, Manila, Philippines: pp. 85-96.

White, A.T., L.Z. Hale, Y. Renard & L. Cortesi (eds). 1994. *Collaborative and community-based management of coral reefs: lessons from experience*. Kumarian Press: 130 pp.

Wiebe, W. J., R. E. Johannes, and K. L. Webb. 1975. Nitrogen fixation in a coral reef community. Science 188:257-259.

Wilkinson, C.R. 1992. Coral reefs of the world are facing widespread devastation: can we prevent this through sustainable management practices? *In* Richmond, R.H. (ed). *Proc. 7th International Coral Reef Symp, Guam, 22-27 June 1992.* Vol 1. pp. 11-21.

Willis, E. O. 1974. Populations and local extinction of birds on Barro Colorado Island, Panama. Ecol. Monogr. 44:153-169.

Wilson, E. O., and E. O. Willis. 1975. Applied biogeography. Pp. 522-534 in M. L. Cody and J. M. Diamond (eds.), Ecology and evolution of communities. Cambridge, Mass.: Harvard University Press.

Woodland, D. J., and J. N. A. Hooper. 1977. The effect of trampling on coral reefs. Biol. Coursers. 11: 1-4.

World Bank. 1996. *Guidelines for using social assessment to support public involvement in World Bank-GEF projects.* The World Bank, Washington, D.C.. 66 pp.

World Conservation Monitoring Center, The Biodiversity of the Seas: a regional approach, World Conservation Press, 1996

WRI/IUCN/UNEP. 1992. *Global Biodiversity Strategy.* WRI, Washington, D.C./IUCN, Gland, Switzerland/UNEP, Nairobi, Kenya. 244 pp.

Zerner, C. 1994a. Tracking *Sasi*: The transformation of a central Moluccan reef management institution in Indonesia. Pp. 19-32 in White *et al.* (eds). *Op. Cit.*

Zerner, C. 1994b. Transforming customary law and coastal management practices in the Maluku Islands, Indonesia, 1870-1992. *In* Western, D. & M. Wright (eds). *Natural Connections: Perspectives in Community-based Conservation.* Island Press, Washington, D.C. pp. 80-113.

Québec, Canada
2000